SOCIAL DEMOCRATIC PARTIES IN WESTERN EUROPE

Social Democratic Parties in Western Europe

Edited by
WILLIAM E. PATERSON
and
ALASTAIR H. THOMAS

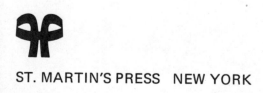

ST. MARTIN'S PRESS   NEW YORK

All rights reserved. For information, write:
St. Martin's Press, Inc., 175 Fifth Avenue, New York, N.Y. 10010
Printed in Great Britain
Library of Congress Card Number: 77-77314
ISBN: 0-312-73175-2
First published in the United States of America in 1977

CONTENTS

For William, John and Simon

CONTRIBUTORS

Byron Criddle is a Lecturer in Politics at the University of Aberdeen, Scotland.

Knut Heidar is a Research Associate at the Institute of Political Science, University of Oslo, Norway.

Ralf Helenius is acting Professor of Political Science at Svenska Handelshögskolan, Helsinki, Finland.

David Hine is Lecturer in European Politics at the University of Newcastle-upon-Tyne, England.

Val Lorwin is Emeritus Professor of History at the University of Oregon, Eugene, Oregon, USA.

Xavier Mabille is at the Centre de Recherche et d'Information Socio-Politique – Crisp, Brussels, Belgium.

James May is completing his doctorate at the University of Manchester, England and at the time of writing was a visiting Research Fellow in the Department of European Studies, Manchester Institute of Science and Technology, England.

Lewis Minkin is Lecturer in Government at The University, Manchester, England.

Andrew Orridge is a Lecturer in the Department of Political Science at the University of Birmingham, England.

William E. Paterson is Senior Lecturer in Politics at the University of Warwick, England.

Richard Scase is a Lecturer in Sociology at the University of Kent, Canterbury, England.

Patrick Seyd is Lecturer in Modern British Politics at the University of Sheffield, England.

Johanthan Story is a Professor at l'Institut Européen d'Administration des Affaires (INSEAD), Fontainebleau, France.

Melanie A. Sully is Lecturer in Modern History in the Department of Humanities, North Staffordshire Polytechnic, Stafford, England.

Alastair Thomas is Senior Lecturer in Government at Leicester Polytechnic, England.

Steven B. Wolinetz is Assistant Professor of Political Science at Memorial University, St. John's, Newfoundland, Canada.

PREFACE

The present volume grew out of a conference held at Birmingham University in December 1974, sponsored by the University Association for Contemporary European Studies and the European Educational Research Trust, on Social Democratic Parties of the European Community.

The transformation of an idea into a book has relied on the support of friends, colleagues and institutions. The editors would like to thank Joan Saddington for fast and efficient typing and Merrill Clarke, Martin Kolinsky, Patricia Mounfield, Dorothy Parkin, Jeff Richards, Janet Thomas, David Wilson and Evi Wohlgemuth for their help. Alastair Thomas would like to thank Leicester Polytechnic for leave of absence, the Institutes of Modern History and Political Studies of Copenhagen University and colleagues, friends and relations in Denmark for hospitality in March/April 1976 and, above all, his wife Janet for her encouragement, understanding and support. William Paterson is indebted to Hanna Jäde and Kurt Schmitz for their help, and the Bank of Scotland for its forbearance.

May Day, 1977

1 INTRODUCTION

Section One

A major feature of the political history of Western Europe in the last
century has been the establishment and growth of parties identified
with the complex of ideas that we now take to be essentially social
democratic. By that, we mean a belief that social and economic reform
designed to benefit the less privileged should be pursued within a
framework of democracy, liberty and the parliamentary process.
Debate about what is and what is not Social Democracy is long and
usually circuitous.[1] Basically the debate revolves around broad and
narrow definitions of Social Democracy. For many in the European
Socialist parties, both those who oppose and those who espouse Social
Democracy, it has a specific content and there would probably not be
too much disagreement on the five tenets delineated by Crosland:
political liberalism, the mixed economy, the welfare state, Keynesian
economics and a belief in equality. For others, however, Social
Democracy simply means democratic Socialism and would include all
parties of the non-communist Left. Even this criterion has become
much harder to sustain since the advent of 'Eurocommunism' and the
espousal by some of the most important European Communist parties
of parliamentary democracy. The contribution by David Hine, below,
argues that the Communist Party could be seen as the most important
force for Social Democracy in Italy today. In this study the operational
criterion will be membership of the Socialist International.

The vast majority of Social Democratic parties were established
during the period of the extension of the franchise in the last quarter
of the nineteenth century. This early Social Democracy was confined
at the level of national politics to an opposition role before 1914 and
was distinctive mainly in its articulation of anti-capitalist and
internationalist ideas. The outbreak of war in 1914 demonstrated the
fragility of its commitment to these ideas and the claims of patriotism
and national solidarity (including solidarity with the reviled Capitalists)
weighed more heavily than international solidarity with the leaders of
all the main parties after war broke out. After the collapse of 'the old
order' in 1918 Social Democrats had their first experience of
government (the Finnish Social Democratic Government of 1916-17
was the sole exception). Unfortunately for these parties the end of the

First World War had brought about not only the destruction of the autocracies, but had led, through the success of the Russian Revolution of 1917, to the establishment in almost all of the Western European countries of Communist parties committed to the realisation of Socialist goals by revolutionary means. Thus in France the SFIO,* already weakened by the assassination of Jean Jaurès in 1914, was dealt a very serious blow by the decision of a large majority at the Tours Congress in 1920 to affiliate with the Third International and set up the French Communist Party. The threat posed by these parties helped create a situation in which Social Democratic parties and politicians normally spent more of their energies in defending democracy, which they identified with existing parliamentary institutions and régimes, than in attempting to bring about the realisation of the Socialist goals to which they were still largely pledged.

At the same time the implacable hostility to Social Democracy of the Third International (the Communist International or Comintern, formed in 1919) had brought a revival of the Second International and thus opened up the division between the two forms of Socialism which was to prove of such far-reaching significance during the 1930s and 1940s. After 1919 Social Democracy generally defined itself in opposition to Communism, but in Austria the Socialists attempted to embrace both Communist and Social Democratic philosophies.

In the Second World War Social Democratic parties did not experience the same tension between international class solidarity and partiotism as they had in the First World War, since patriotism and ideology both pointed in the same direction, except in Germany and Italy; but in these two cases the nature of their Fascist régimes made it possible for Social Democrats to feel patriotic even in supporting their country's enemies.

Thus by 1945 Social Democratic parties promised to be the strongest political force in Western Europe. They formed the governing party or were an important element in coalition Governments throughout much of the area. Their long-term prospects appeared even better. Whereas conservatives and parties of the Right had largely been discredited by the war and occupation, the Socialists through their prominence in the resistance and in Britain by their participation in the wartime Government had revived some of the prestige they had lost in the 1930s. But apart from France and Italy, the challenge from the Left was relatively weak and was likely to remain so because of the

*A list of abbreviations is given at the end of this Introduction.

involvement of the Western allies, particularly the United States, in the post-war administration of much of Western Europe.

In this situation the British Labour Party assumed a key role. In sharp contrast to other periods when it had often seemed irrelevant to or remote from Continental experience, Labour's victory in 1945 was considered to be of overwhelming importance. Britain was expected to provide a lead in supporting an alternative to both Capitalism and Communism. Parallels were drawn with the exporting of the French and Russian Revolutions. These hopes were given a boost by Ernest Bevin's speech to the 1945 Labour Party Conference when he spoke about Britain leading a 'third force' for a Social Democratic Western Europe. But the British Government, completely dependent as it was on American financial aid, proved to have neither the will nor the capacity to bring about change in a Social Democratic direction elsewhere in Europe and by 1947, as the American involvement in Europe became more and more manifest, and as the wartime 'collapse of social distance' diminished with the passage of time, the pendulum swung ever more clearly against the forces of democratic socialism.

In Scandinavia the 1950s saw the continuation or establishment of what was to be a lasting period of Social Democratic rule, but elsewhere in Western Europe the decade was a bleak one for Social Democracy, and conservative or Christian Democratic parties were in the ascendant. France was a significant exception, however, with a predominantly Socialist Government in 1956-7 presided over by Guy Mollet. Indeed the SFIO participated in 21 of the 27 Governments formed between September 1944 and June 1958 and provided the prime ministers of five. But the involvement of Mollet's ministry in the Suez operation and its Algerian policy led to the virtual isolation of the SFIO among Western European Social Democratic parties.

General reasons for the difficulties experienced by the Social Democratic parties are not hard to find. The 1950s in most West European countries were years deeply influenced by the twin phenomena of continually expanding prosperity and anti-Communism. Their general impact placed the parties on the defensive both electorally and intellectually, so much so that by the end of the 1950s there were many who talked of an 'end of ideology', and some even predicted the gradual demise of Social Democracy, at least as an electoral force in Western Europe.

One of the most distinguished analysts of European politics, Otto Kirchheimer, devoted much of his considerable intellectual energies to demonstrating that some of what had been held to be the most important preconditions for the success of Social Democracy had been eroded. He wrote of a reversion to 'privatisation', of the declining numbers of the proletariat and of 'a substantial new middle class of skilled workers, the middle ranks of white-collar people and civil servants'.[2]

The very pervasiveness of evidence for these analyses encouraged their uncritical acceptance. They rested on the assumption that prosperity was going to continue to expand on a linear trend. They also exaggerated the difficulties of the Social Democrats since they failed to emphasise the asymmetric impact of the trends. Whilst the phenomena described above tended to favour the conservative electoral competitors of the Social Democratic parties, they were in general much more harmful to their Communist rivals.

The disappointing electoral performance of the Social Democrats in the 1950s eventually resulted in their making major adjustments. The parties have always had as a prominent tactical goal the winning of electoral support. In the early period the expansion of membership and its incorporation into the life of the party as movement had often been as important as that tactical goal.[3] In these parties there was traditionally a high ratio of members to voters, with the pre-war Austrian Socialists constituting the ideal type.[4] By the late 1950s this was clearly no longer the case and in most Western European Social Democratic parties the 'movement model' of a party explicitly orientated towards the industrial worker was replaced by a 'people's party model': a catch-all party which sought to attract voters not converts and operated on all strata of society. This concept was most successful in Austria and West Germany but affected all the parties to some degree. In the British Labour Party an important group around the Party leader, Hugh Gaitskell, attempted to 'modernise' the party and to drop the party's commitment to 'the common ownership of the means of production' contained in Clause 4 of its 1918 constitution, but this move failed. In a similar vein, Anthony Crosland suggested that the manual worker's 'cloth cap' image of the British Labour Party was socially inappropriate and that the Party should seek to build a new identity as a 'people's party'.

In the 1960s the fortunes of Social Democracy revived somewhat. Whilst politics may not have been so polarised as at some points in the past, class has continued to play a dominant role in structuring voting preferences in the advanced industrial societies of Western Europe. Indeed there is some force in the argument that as other cleavages, especially religion (as in the Netherlands) have become less important, class has become even more salient than in the past. This is the paradox to which Butler and Stokes drew attention: 'The intensity of the class tie may have declined at the same time as its extent became more universal.'[5] This has worked to the advantage of the Social Democratic parties.

The revived fortunes of the parties were reflected in increased participation in government. This was true even of Ireland and Portugal on the European periphery. Yet this apparent success was accompanied by much public disquiet and by increased problems of party management in almost all the West European countries, the SPD and the British Labour Party being particularly striking cases.

This apparent paradox, of increased participation in government together with increased problems of party management, can be explained in various ways. An initial explanation would relate such difficulties simply to the change from an opposition to a government role: the party leadership was now judged by its actions rather than, as in opposition, by the words or programmatic utterances which could be used to satisfy all tendencies and thus help to contain factionalism.

A second explanation would relate the new difficulties to events and processes in the international environment; in particular, the impact of détente. Acceptance (reluctantly or enthusiastically) of NATO had by the early 1960s almost become a defining characteristic of Social Democratic parties, except in the case of the PSI and the parties of neutral countries. De-Stalinisation, followed by détente, served to undermine this and set up tensions on the left wing of nearly all the Social Democratic parties. These tensions were aggravated by the delegitimation of American leadership because of the Vietnam war. In some cases these factors resulted in fission, as with the emergence of the Scandinavian Socialist People's Parties and Left Socialists. At a later period this problem was heightened by the changing stance of the European Communist parties. Ironically, just as some Social Democratic parties were rethinking their attitude to NATO it was accepted, rhetorically at least, by the Italian Communist Party.

An important factor at the intersection of the domestic and foreign environments which placed at least two of the parties — the British Labour Party and Arbeiderpartiet in Norway — under great strain, with serious tensions between the party base and the party's governmental representatives, was the question of adherence to the European Community. In both cases the referendum device played an important part. In Norway the referendum campaign generally increased tensions within the party and the Norwegian 'No' was seen as a rejection of the governmental wing of Arbeiderpartiet. By contrast, in Britain the introduction of the referendum, although it made manifest the opposition between the party and the bulk of governmental opinion, demonstrated that the governmental wing enjoyed an overwhelming measure of public support on this issue, making it possible for the Party to accept British entry. In the long established member countries of the European Community 'the European question' is not now one which generally divides the membership or significant sections of it from the Party leadership.

A third explanatory factor was the world economic recession which followed in the wake of the Yom Kippur war. The changed economic climate placed the Social Democratic parties, especially those in government, under severe strain. These strains were felt especially severely by the countries on the European economic periphery, such as Britain, Denmark, Ireland and Portugal. On the other hand it is at least arguable that the impact of the world economic recession dimmed the ardour of the Left in the Netherlands and West Germany, making these parties' problems of party management less intractable.

In two of the parties studied a further cause for strain has been the reassertion of territoriality. An old dilemma for Socialists and Social Democrats existed in the tensions between democratic/participatory ideals and economic policies which normally stress the need for centralisation. In Belgium this crisis is largely over, but it is still acute in Britain and may well pose an increasingly severe test for the unity of the Spanish socialist party.

Section Two

In the preceding pages we have attempted very generally to delineate some factors which disturbed the cohesion of the Social Democratic parties. We shall now examine some more specific influences on the shape and cohesion of the parties: in particular, their relationship to the trade unions, the role of party programmes and ideology, the changing composition of membership and the parties' electoral and alliance strategies.

The Trade Unions and the Social Democratic Parties

It is often assumed in Britain that the symbiotic attachment of the trade unions to the Labour Party is a characteristic of all West European Social Democratic parties. In fact a close organic connection pertains only in Britain, though arrangements usually exist to give trade unions access to the decision-making bodies of the various European parties.

Most parties have experimented with and rejected the Labour Party model. In this study we have three interesting examples of the interaction of trade unions and factionalism within the parties. Lewis Minkin and Patrick Seyd in their study of the Labour Party properly focus attention on the trade unions and assign a causal role to them: increasing trade union militancy led to a change of leadership in many of the major unions in the early 1970s which directly benefited the Left of the Labour Party. William Paterson takes the view in relation to the SPD that although there is no formal interconnection between the DGB and the leadership of the SPD, trade unionists have played and continue to play a role in the factional struggle inside the SPD, sustaining the Right-wing governmental leadership of the party. Steven Wolinetz assigns a negative role to the NVV in his study of the Dutch PvdA: it was their decision not to intervene that helped make the success of the New Left possible. By contrast, the Swedish labour movement has presented itself as the most important instrument for reform in society.

Party Programmes and Ideology

Traditionally party programmes have been a means both of asserting the identity of the party within the political system and of integrating the diverse tendencies within the party. This assertion of identity through a distinctive party programme has normally been held to be particularly important in a multi-party system operating under proportional electoral representation, since parties in such a system exist primarily to serve their clientele: the so called 'Parties of Mass Integration'. In the case of the Social Democratic parties this identity was normally expressed in a theoretical commitment to at least some of the tenets of Marxism. The abandonment of this and the adoption of 'the People's Party' or 'Catch-all party' model was accompanied by considerable programmatic activity, of which the most famous manifestation was the Bad Godesberg Programme of the SPD. To the extent that the 'Catch-all' party model has come under fire there has been renewed concern with party programmes, particularly marked in West Germany, the Netherlands and Denmark. It has been much more difficult for the party leadership to handle programmatic discussion than in the past since party members now expect more participatory modes of procedure. The espousal of the 'People's Party' model had placed electoral considerations at the centre of the parties' work and inevitably carried with it the view that policy should be left to the professionals –

the party leadership, advised by specialists in public opinion and market research. The new members who came into the party, sometimes ironically from these areas, stressed the old democratic and participatory values. There is a vivid contrast between the lack of opposition to the Bad Godesberg Programme and the travail surrounding the birth of the *'Orientierungsrahmen 85'* which, in the last analysis, says all things to all men. Steven Wolinetz points out that a draft of the 1977 election programme under discussion in the Dutch Labour Party elicited more than 5,000 amendments. The Danish Social Democrats set aside a four-year period for debate of the new programme to be adopted at their 1977 congress. But the attempt by the social democratic parties of the nine member countries of the European Community to arrive at a common European programme under the aegis of Sicco Mansholt is now generally considered to have failed.

The Changing Composition of Party Membership

In this study we have attempted to incorporate what is known about the sociology of party membership of the various parties. There is a discernible trend in all parties, with the possible exception of the British Labour Party,[7] for the party membership to become more middle class and for the number of working class members to fall. This process is even more marked at the level of parliamentary and governmental representation.

Frank Parkin has attributed the changing nature of social democracy to this increasingly middle class membership: 'The greater the inflow of bourgeois recruits, the less militant the party becomes, so making it even more attractive to those who favour the interpretation of equality along meritocratic and welfare lines'.[8] This process is, as Parkin points out, distinct from the embourgeoisement of working class leaders as a cause of moderation, put forward by Michels: the leaders are middle class before they assume office. In fact the relation between the class composition of the social democratic parties is a much more complex and subtle one. The social class of the members and their leaders is only one variable among many, including the nature of party competition, the type of electoral system (a particularly significant factor in the Netherlands) and the nature of the socialist tradition in the country concerned. Thus the PS, the French Socialist Party, is recognisably to the left of most social democratic parties, whilst their leadership and membership are more middle class than most. Again, Olof Palme comes from a more rarefied social background than his predecessors but is generally considered to have moved the Swedish Social Democrats further leftwards.

Sophisticated analysis is necessary of the changes in social composition of the Social Democratic parties of Western Europe which have occurred since the late 1960s. In most cases the influx has been not only middle class but also young and often active in the student movement; and where, as in Denmark, the Social Democrats have been unable to attract this social group, the vigour of their membership has suffered by comparison with other parties further to their left and they risk serious electoral decline. As both Heidar and Wolinetz show, in the chapters on Norway and the Netherlands, the concept of 'middle class' also requires close examination. No longer can it be thought of as comprising only the bourgeoisie of classical Marxist analysis, embracing as it now does the large new categories of peoples employed either by public authorities and in the 'soft professions', and whose political attitudes may differ substantially from those of the more settled members of the middle class and may, indeed, be more radical than those of most manual workers.

Electoral Strategy – Who is the Target?

Traditionally Social Democratic parties scarcely needed to ask themselves this question.[9] They were there to represent and mobilise the industrial working class. The almost universal acceptance of the primacy of electoral success in the late 1950s resulted in a move away from a narrow class appeal by the main parties. Great attention was paid to the decline in the percentage of the workforce comprising 'blue-collar' workers and the concurrent rise of the 'white-collar' percentage. At the same time the residue of 'blue-collar' workers was seen as subject to a process of embourgeoisement, an alleged tendency to accompany their acquisition of increased material goods with an aspiration towards middle-class values including a decreased propensity to vote for parties of the Left. This change was very marked, for instance in the British Labour Party when the Party was presented by Harold Wilson between 1964 and 1970 as a 'party of government': it was regarded as electorally astute to be seen as being tough with the Party's traditional supporters and especially the trade unions over such issues as the seamen's strike of 1966 or the Government's proposals *'In Place of Strife'* for the reform of the trade unions.[10] This orientation was broadly true for most parties, including even the Italian PSI in its pursuit of a Centre-Left strategy.

There has been some change in recent years. The new membership of the parties has often attacked the purely electoral orientation of the parties and some concessions had to be made to them in order to integrate them. There have also been some other notable developments. In most countries the proportion of 'white-collar' workers who have become unionised has increased steadily. It is now fashionable to talk of a proletarianisation of the middle class and their adoption of weapons like the strike traditionally identified with the underprivileged class. At the same time the notion of embourgeoisement has come under critical scrutiny.

The target towards which many parties direct their recruitment activities is this new middle class, so defined by its income and its occupational pattern of employment in the 'soft professions', but probably also by a pattern of recent upward mobility and a retention of radicalised working-class values. The need to attract these new social groups while retaining the parties' traditional hard core support from manual workers has led parties such as the Swedish Social Democrats to adopt a 'hard/soft' strategy.

The SPD case shows the limits of a strategy directed towards winning middle-class votes. Absence of any serious competition on the Left led the party since Bad Godesberg to concentrate its efforts on the middle ground. For many years this brought electoral success, but at the 1976 election it became clear that little further progress could be expected in this direction: both the CDU and the FDP were firmly established in this section of the electorate. If the CDU/CSU split of 1976 had persisted then the CDU would have been an even more formidable competitor for the SPD in this area than in the past.

The parallel with the British Labour Party is clear. Working-class abstention, in 1970 and subsequently, has served as a limiting factor, ensuring that the party retains its explicit class appeal.

Alliances and Relations with Other Parties of the Left

The essential problem of the French, Italian, Finnish and Portuguese parties is that they face a powerful Communist party. In this situation the problem of alliances — for how long, on what conditions and, above all, with whom — becomes the main focus of political activity. They have the choice of joining a coalition with bourgeois parties which is normally avowedly anti-Communist: the Centre-Left coalition in Italy, the Portuguese Government of Mario Soares, or French Governments of the Fourth Republic. They can, on the other hand, form an alliance with the Communists and endeavour to play a leading role. This may be attractive in Finland, Iceland or France where there is some rough parity between the parties but is very difficult in Italy where the PSI is confronted by a dynamic PCI which is much larger and has adopted many of its specific policy proposals. In these countries there is a permanent danger of fission (as in Portugal, or with the PSIUP in Italy or the PSU in France) and desertion from one party to another, generating considerable movement between the parties of the Left.

Section Three: the Social Democratic Dilemma

The major problem for Social Democratic parties in Western Europe is the securing of not merely a political but also a social and economic consensus around the values of Social Democracy. This consensus was always difficult to achieve. It has become more difficult in an era when the changing party membership expects the party leadership to be more responsive to their demands. Since they are almost by definition atypical of the wider electorate, a tension arises between satisfying their demands and agreeing a wider consensus.

The onset of the world economic recession and its persistence especially on the economic periphery of Europe makes some of the tensions inherent in modern Social Democracy less easy to reconcile. We shall discuss five central dilemmas now facing Social Democracy in Western Europe. This list is by no means exhaustive. Many even in their own ranks would consider the devotion of Social Democrats to representative parliamentary institutions more out of place than at any time in the past, assuming the generally acknowledged failure of legislative bodies.

There appears to be a fundamental tension between many of the specific policy proposals of all the parties which demand greater central control over the economy and the strong currents within the various parties which demand greater decentralisation and the introduction of participatory democracy. This dilemma is seen at its clearest in France where within the united Left many elements are in favour of centralised control, while the *Parti socialiste* is committed to *autogestion* which envisages a great deal of autonomy and participation at the work place without ever satisfactorily explaining how the two are to be reconciled.

Another central dilemma is that between redistributive measures such as profit sharing, capital creation for workers (*Vermögensbildung* in West Germany, *økonomisk demokrati* in Denmark), high tax rates on the one hand and the commitment to full employment on the other, since these measures tend to depress investment. This dilemma was posed more starkly in the early 1970s between those who were in favour of zero growth and those who favoured full employment. In Britain the pervasive involvement of the trade unions in the Labour

Party gives a specific content to the British Social Democratic dilemma. 'This dilemma, in its simplest form is how to reconcile the maintenance of a full employment welfare state (the political objective of the trade union movement) with the maximum of money wages through free collective bargaining (the economic objective of the trade unions).'[11]

The fourth dilemma is one familiar from the world depression of 1929-30 and brought about the downfall of the last SPD-led cabinet of Weimar. This is the conflict between the interests of those at work and the unemployed and other welfare recipients. The forces of organised labour, the trade unions, normally represent most strongly the interests of those at work while the concern felt by social democratic politicians for the underprivileged often works in the contrary direction. This dilemma has been posed very strongly in Britain in 1975-6. The final dilemma for the Social Democratic parties involves their attitude towards energy. The cleavage here is between those Social Democrats (usually in office and with the support of the trade unions) who in pursuit of growth favour maximum exploitation of energy resources and those, usually on the Left, who for a variety of environmental reasons oppose massive exploitation of atomic and oil resources.

There is little that is fundamentally new in these tensions. Perhaps more importantly, however, there is even less that is novel in the response of Social Democratic governments to the challenges they face. There is little evidence from any of the parties analysed here of fresh thinking on these concerns. Their views on the central problem of the economy tend to assume that it is susceptible to domestic management through such devices as indicative planning. This fails to come to terms with the specific Western European situation of the increased internationalisation of the European economy. The consequent inability of Social Democratic Governments to respond to these pressures in a creative manner has led generally to some diminution of electoral support, notably in Denmark in 1973 and in the Swedish and West German general elections and British opinion polls and by-elections of 1976. Where the tensions have been resolved, as in West Germany, the solutions adoption have not been in accord with Social Democratic values. The replacement of Brandt by Schmidt is indicative of the replacement of a policy with some pretensions to reform (its achievements were less apparent): K.D. Bracher speaks of 'reform ruins'.

The massive participation of the Social Democratic parties in the Governments of Western Europe thus masks extensive problems as to their identity and direction. Yet tension between competing goals is a permanent condition of Social Democracy and there is little to suggest that the parties are about to suffer a dramatic erosion of electoral support. Their condition is perhaps best put by Wolfram Hanrieder in a phrase first used of the Federal Republic of Germany — 'a stable crisis'.

Notes

1. A representative view is given by Anthony Crosland in his Fabian pamphlet *'Social Democracy in Europe'* (London, Fabian Society, Fabian Tract No. 438, 1975).
2. Otto Kirchheimer, 'The Waning of Oppositions', in R.C. Macridis and B.E. Brown (eds.), *Comparative Politics: notes and readings* (Homewood, Illinois, The Dorsey Press, 1964), p.287.
3. For an extended consideration of the relationship of movement to party see Martin Kolinsky and William E. Paterson, *Social and Political Movements in Western Europe* (London, Croom Helm Ltd, 1976), especially the Introduction and the contributions by Hine, Paterson and Smith. See also Val R. Lorwin, 'Segmented pluralism: ideological cleavages and political cohesion in the smaller European democracies', *Comparative Politics*, January 1971.
4. As Melanie Sully shows in her chapter on the Austrian party, it has maintained a high ratio of members to voters into the 1970s.
5. D. Butler and D. Stokes, *Political Change in Britain* (London, Macmillan, 1969), p.116.
6. See Peter Byrd, 'The Labour Party and the European Community 1970 75', *Journal of Common Market Studies*, vol. XIII, no. 4 (1975), pp.469-83.
7. In Britain the composition of the party membership is obscured by the predominance of indirect membership, affiliated through the trade unions. The Conservative Party claims, with unquantifiable veracity, that the allegiance of many trade unionists to the Labour Party cannot be taken for granted. See the chapter on the British Labour Party by Minkin and Seyd, note 128, and the debate on this issue summarised by T. Forester, *The Labour Party and the Working Class* (Heinemann, London, 1976).
8. Frank Parkin, *Class Inequality and Political Order: Social Stratification in Capitalist and Communist Societies* (London, Paladin, Granada Publishing Ltd, 1972), p.132.
9. It was therefore a considerable shock for many members when the SPD leadership established a committee to look after the interests of workers and employers — Arbeitsgruppe für Arbeitnehmerfragen: many party members had assumed that was what the SPD itself was.
10. See, for example, the account by Peter Jenkins, *The Battle of Downing Street* (London, Charles Knight Ltd, 1970).
11. *New Statesman,* 20 September 1974.

Abbreviations

CDU   Christlich Demokratische Union (Christian Democratic Union) (West German)
CSU   Christlich Soziale Union (Christian Social Union) West German)
DGB   Deutscher Gewerkschafts Bund (German Trade Union Federation) (West German)

NVV	Netherlands Verbond van Vakverenigingen (Dutch Federation of Trade Unions) (Socialist)
PCI	Partito Comunista Italiano (Italian Communist Party)
PS	Parti socialiste (Socialist Party) (French)
PSI	Partito Socialista Italiano (Italian Socialist Party)
PSIUP	Partito Socialista Italiano di Unità Proletaria (Italian Socialist Party of Proletarian Unity): Italian Left Socialists
PSU	Parti socialiste unifié (United Socialist Party) (French)
PvdA	Partij van de Arbeid (Labour Party) (Netherlands)
SFIO	Section française de l'Internationale Ouvrière (French Section of the Workers' International) (French Socialist Party)
SPD	Sozialdemokratische Partei Deutschlands (German Social Democratic Party)

2 THE FRENCH PARTI SOCIALISTE

Byron Criddle

The awkward fate of the French Socialist Party[1] since its creation in 1905 has been formally to espouse radical Socialist objectives whilst being denied the means of attaining them. The denial derived essentially from the fragmentation in 1920 of the Party into rival Communist and Socialist parties; and from the lingering intrusion of religion into French politics. From 1920 onwards the Party was obliged to compete against Communist and Catholic-associated opposition for an urban industrial electorate already restricted in size as a consequence of the partial and incomplete nature of French industrialisation. Armed with anti-communist and anti-clerical weaponry in order to cope with its rivals, the Party, whilst never at any time severing its Marxist commitment to class struggle and defeat of the bourgeois state, provided evidence enough of its reformist orientation by justifying support for 'bourgeois' governments in terms of a pursuit of ameliorative reforms and the defence of the parliamentary republic. Léon Blum, the Party's parliamentary leader between the wars, differentiated between the 'exercise' and 'conquest' of power as a defence of collaboration with Centrist parties, and yet was able also with the formation of the Popular Front Government in 1936, to preside briefly over the only administration comprised solely of left (Socialist and Radical supported by Communist) parties in modern French republican history.[2]

Post-war the Party governed between 1944 and 1947 in a tripartite coalition, involving the Communists and the MRP (progressive Catholics).* This alliance born of war-time anti-Fascist co-operation broke up ostensibly over economic policy, though effectively over the worsening international climate which served to reopen the question of the Communist Party's *bona fides* as a defender of the parliamentary republic, simultaneously threatened by the new Gaullist (RPF) Party's campaign for a constitutional reconstruction involving substantial rejection of the traditional parliamentary model. Such a dual threat, underlined by the hard facts of parliamentary arithmetic, served to justify and indeed to oblige continued Socialist indulgence in coalition politics, but now solely with parties of the centre (Radical, MRP, etc)

*A list of abbreviations follows the Notes at the end of this chapter.

25

and in times of chronic difficulties with financial and colonial policy.[3] Graphically symbolic of the Party's fate after 1947 was the record of the Government of Guy Mollet,[4] the man who had ousted a reformist (Mayer) from the party leadership in 1946, rejecting Blum's call for an avowedly reformist Social Democratic Party shorn of Marxist rhetoric, calling indeed for 'condemnation of all attempts at revisionism, all forms of imperialist exploitation and attempts to mask that fundamental reality, the class struggle'.[5] In the event Mollet's Government spent almost all of its time stepping up a harsh campaign against Arab nationalists in North Africa and in planning the Anglo-French and Israeli invasion of Egypt in 1956, an act which the party press sought bizarrely to defend by reference to Marx.[6] By the time the Fourth Republic collapsed in 1958 the Socialists had participated in twenty-one of the twenty-seven Governments formed between September 1944 and June 1958, and provided the prime ministers of five. Yet the rewards for so much 'republican defence' were hard to detect. Little or no social reform reached the statute book; votes and membership declined continually. The PC on the other hand, for all Mollet's vigorous attempts to depict it as a Soviet trojan horse − 'a party of the East, not of the Left' − stood as the most stable formation on the political landscape, with roots sunk deep in parts of the country during the Occupation; confirmed at every election after 1945 as both the largest party on the Left and in the country as a whole; and claiming to be *the* party of the working class. Sustained by its possession of at least two-thirds of the regular Left voting section of manual workers and, after 1947, control of the largest trade union federation, the CGT, the PCF was able, shorn of governmental responsibilities, effortlessly to aggregate the votes of protest voters disillusioned with the record of the Socialists and other governing parties. Nor did the Marxist rhetoric with which the Socialists under Mollet after 1946 accompanied their participation in Government appear in effect to satisfy anyone: no working-class voters were weaned from the PCF; no radical Socialists (including those amongst the Party's own membership) were convinced; nor could confusion between theory and practice reconcile to the Party those voters who might have supported an unambiguously reformist Social Democratic stance.[7]

The coming of the Fifth Republic in 1958, however, put an end to both the opportunity and the necessity for Socialist participation in government, though not before Mollet divided the Party both inside and outside parliament by backing (even conniving at) de Gaulle's return, and participating in his 1958 government. (These acts precipitated a split in the Party and the setting up of a new though small rival party, which by 1960 was known as the *Parti socialiste unifié*).[8] The new regime however carried serious implications for the Socialists. The 1958 constitution seriously eroded the powers and significance of parliament in the formation and sustenance of the executive and by 1962 further buttressed executive power by providing for the election of the President by universal suffrage, a change which further reduced the role of parliament. Of equivalent importance was the transformation of the party system with the growth of the Gaullist UNR (later UDR), sufficient to enable it by 1962 with other conservative groups to dominate the National Assembly. Thus was destroyed the parliamentary environment through which Socialists had made and broken governments and gained access to ministerial spoils and influence. With parliament no longer playing a brokerage role the Socialist parliamentarians were left high and dry in what transpired after 1958 moreover to be permanent opposition. Institutional and electoral change had moved the political centre of gravity away from the Socialists to the Right, and to an important degree away from parliament.

Given the denial of power which the Fifth Republic implied for the Socialist Party, and the change to an electoral system[9] which (at both parliamentary and Presidential elections) implied — given a strong Gaullist pole — the need for a countervailing pole sufficiently attractive to beat the Gaullists (if not at the first then at least at the second ballot), Socialist history post-1958 was dominated, as it had to be for a party with only 15 per cent of the vote, by alliance strategy. The choice of alliances lay between centre-leftism (of the sort theoretically reflected in most of the coalition governments in which the Socialists participated before 1958) or united-leftism (an option which required a favourable international climate and one which had only ever been tried on a national scale at the Popular Front election of 1936). Centre-Leftism, or Centrism as it was described by its left-wing opponents, was advocated by Gaston Defferre,[10] prominent on the reformist wing of the Party, as the basis for his bid to become a candidate in the first Presidential election held under universal suffrage in 1965. The proposal involved concentrating on aggregating the Socialist, Radical and MRP votes in order to outdistance the Communist party and to obtain a good second place at the first ballot, and to assume Communist support at the second. Defferre's path was however blocked by, among others, Mollet, who invoked the traditional anti-clerical objection to Socialist collaboration with Catholic politicians. He was obliged to withdraw, soon to be replaced as the leading anti-Gaullist candidate by François Mitterand,[11] who became the agreed candidate of the Communist, Socialist and Radical parties. The relative success of this candidature (32 per cent at the first ballot, 45 per cent at the second) stimulated more Left-orientated alliance building for the 1967 and 1968 general elections. First the Socialists, Radicals and Mitterrand's small CIR group formed a loose confederation of parties known as the FGDS, under Mitterrand's presidency, the main purpose of which was to agree on a single non-Communist Left candidate in every constituency. The FGDS itself in turn negotiated an electoral pact with the PC whereby it was agreed that in the decisive second ballot of general elections the most successful Left candidate at the first ballot be given a clear run as the agreed candidate of the Left at the second. This arrangement was largely responsible for the doubling of Socialist and Communist seats in 1967. A repeat of such collaboration in the crisis election of 1968 was insufficient however to prevent a landslide defeat for all the Left parties. As a consequence of intra-Left antagonisms spawned by the events of 1968 in France and the crisis in Czechoslovakia, the FGDS collapsed in the autumn of 1968. Left collaboration temporarily ceased, and in the Presidential election precipitated in June 1969 by de Gaulle's sudden resignation, the Socialists fielded Gaston Defferre against both Communist and PSU rivals. His derisory 5 per cent of the poll confirmed the folly of such a fragmented approach to presidential electioneering.

After this debacle, with the prospect of a long respite before the next national elections, the Socialist Party resumed the task it had taken up at the end of 1968 when Mollet decided to stand down, of reforming itself in order to attract into the Party many who had left in protest against both its record in the Fourth Republic and the leadership style of Guy Mollet. One such refugee, Alain Savary, returned to become the new leader (or First Secretary), committing the Party to a rejection of all Centrist alliances and a resolute pursuit of Left-wing unity. This was less bold a gesture than it seemed: in effect the election results of 1967, 1968 and 1969 all served to confirm, with the continued absorption by the Gaullists of most that remained of the electorate and indeed leaders of non-Socialist Centre parties, that Centre-Leftism had, whatever the preferences of certain Socialists (such as Defferre), ceased to be a realistic option; leaving the pursuit of an alliance with the Communists as the only way either of increasing the number of Socialist seats in parliament or of maximising the effect of any challenge to Gaullist Presidential incumbency. In 1971 Savary was replaced as leader by Mitterrand, who in time opened negotiations, as Savary had done, with the Communist Party. In March 1972 the PS unveiled its programme of government, *Changer la Vie,* and in June of that year Mitterrand signed with the PC and left-wing Radical leaders the Joint Programme of Government of the Left, with which the next elections would be fought. For those (1973) elections the PS re-established its alliance with the small group of Radicals.[12] This along with the by now traditional second ballot arrangement with the Communists put the Left's representation in the National Assembly back almost to its 1967 level. A year later, in the Presidential election caused by Pompidou's death, Mitterrand, backed by all the parties of the Left, missed victory by the narrowest (49.2 − 50.8 per cent) of margins.

Electoral Performance

At the Popular Front election of 1936 the Socialist Party had been the largest party of the Left in terms both of votes (21 per cent) and of seats (146). In the first post-war election (1945) its vote increased (23 per cent) but was now lower than that of the PC (26 per cent), as was its total of seats. After 1945 the Socialist vote declined by about 3 per cent at every election until 1951 and then levelled off at 15 per cent in 1956 and 1958 (see Table 1). At both of these elections the party benefited from association with popular non-Socialist leaders (Mendès France in 1956 and de Gaulle in 1958). The year 1962 however saw the Party reach its electoral nadir with 12.6 per cent of the votes − representing less than one in ten of the adult population. Thereafter, in alliance with the Radicals (FGDS and UGSD) the share of the vote rose in 1967 to 19 per cent and in 1973 to almost 21 per cent. Taking PS votes out of the FGDS and UGSD totals however shows more accurately the extent of Socialist advance (ignoring the setback in the crisis election of 1968) from 15.5 per cent in 1967 to 19.0 per cent in 1973.[13]

With the ending of proportional representation in 1958 the Party found it difficult to get an equitable share of the seats, until it established not only the avoidance of vote splitting with Radicals on the first ballot, but also the alliance with the Communists on the second. Once intra-Left competition was ended the Left's share of seats rose, and the best year for the PS was 1967. That more votes in 1973 yielded fewer seats might be variously explained. Firstly, the possibility of an incomplete transfer of Communist first ballot votes to Socialist second ballot candidates in 1973 may be discounted, for the PC delivered its vote.[14] However whilst the Communists had made concessions to the PS (FGDS) in 1967 by allowing ten Socialist candidates who had been outdistanced by Communists on the first ballot to represent the Left on the second, so as to allow Socialists to win seats which the PC might lose, in 1973 the Communists did not renew such 'cadeaux' and consequently some seats were lost which the PS could have won. More important still however was the altered distribution in 1973 of the Socialist vote. A major feature of the election, building on trends manifested six years earlier was the deregionalisation of the Party's electorate. Traditionally it had known zones of strength and zones of weakness. The zones of traditional strength can be grouped into north, centre and south. In the north the Party's strength has traditionally been concentrated in the *North* region's industrialised departments (counties) of Pas de Calais and Nord. In the centre the Party traditionally polls well in the Puy de Dôme department of the *Auvergne* region, the Haute Vienne and Creuse departments in *Limousin,* and the Nièvre department of *Bourgogne.* In the south strength is concentrated in the Landes and Gironde departments of *Aquitaine*; the Haute Garonne, Ariège, Tarn, Tarn et Garonne and Gers departments of the *Midi-Pyrénées* region; the Aude and Hérault departments of *Languedoc-Roussillon* and the Bouches du Rhône, Vaucluse and Basses Alpes departments of *Provence-Côte d'Azur* region. In 1973 however it was precisely in these areas that the PS lost votes, and in some cases seats,[15] whilst gaining support in zones of traditional weakness: the east *(Lorraine)* and west *(Bretagne* and *Pays de la Loire).*[16] As a consequence of such movements the PS electorate was by 1973 a better distributed one but at a cost in terms of seats. Big leaps in support failed to yield seats: the growth from 10.2 per cent to 18.5 per cent in Lorraine for example, produced only one new seat for the party.[17] The trend however, towards making the PS a national rather than a regional phenomenon implied, if continued, major gains in the future. Deregionalisation of the PS vote in 1973 had another important aspect: growth of support in the big towns and cities, where with the exception of a few of the larger towns (Marseille, Lille, Limoges, Clermont-Ferrand, Bordeaux, Toulouse) the Party had traditionally never polled well.[18] By 1973 there had been a big improvement in the Party's showing in the conurbations (in part to offset a decline in rural and small town districts reflected in the loss of votes in the rural centre and south) (see Table 2). Big city growth (and rural retreat) mirroring national demographic trends was illustrated in the Party's success in the urban areas most commented upon for their rapid growth: Grenoble, Pau, Toulouse, Caen, Melun.

The sex composition of the Socialist electorate has also changed.

The Party in the 1950s and early 1960s was very heavily male-dominated (63 per cent in 1965), but by the late 1960s the pattern had settled down to one where only 53 per cent of Socialist voters were men. The decline in male support is best explained by seeing the change as an increase in female support, and this in turn has much to do with the decline of the barrier between Socialist voting and religious (Catholic) practice, in which women greatly outnumber men. The electoral growth of the PS in the old MRP strongholds of Bretagne, Alsace and Lorraine in 1967 and 1973 clearly owes much to the growing reconciliation between Catholics and Socialists, at both intellectual and electoral level.[19]

As far as the socio-economic composition of the Party's electorate is concerned (Table 2) the most striking feature is that whilst manual workers constitute the largest group among PS voters, they represent only one-third of the total Socialist electorate. This figure has been very steady since the 1950s, though at the time of the 1951 and 1956 elections it was closer to two-fifths. This relative weakness accounts for the difficulty the Party has had when contemplating its Communist rival, which has always been able to boast a greater dependence upon the votes of manual workers (in 1973 51 per cent of the Communist voters were in blue-collar occupations) as well as a deeper penetration of the sector, as evidence of its leadership both of the Left and of the popular classes.[20] Furthermore, whilst the working-class component in the PS electorate has expanded since the middle 1960s (and whilst its penetration of the blue-collar electorate has deepened), as important has been the increased proportion of the Socialists' electorate now contributed by white-collar workers. Significantly the latter are growing as a proportion of the French electorate, with the expansion of the tertiary sector of the economy, whilst the basically blue-collar secondary sector nationally has all but ceased to expand.[21] (Such a trend could serve to compensate for the continuing relative strength of the Communist Party's appeal to traditional blue-collar voters.) The Party's contemporary appeal to white-collar voters, and no longer solely to the legendary schoolteachers[22] and minor civil servants who have traditionally provided solid support — both as voters and activists and indeed parliamentary representatives (see below) — is not in doubt. By May 1976, poll data suggested that the proportion of the party's support represented by professional and managerial categories had almost doubled since 1973 (to 9 per cent),[23] and it is growth in all such strata that accounts for Socialist advance in the big cities. Effectively however, continuity of the socio-economic composition of the Socialist electorate (by 1973) was more apparent than change. The party — growing by a figure the equivalent of 30 per cent of its 1967 electorate — has extended its audience amongst both the blue, and the expanding white-collar sectors (including the professions) in almost equal numbers, whilst losing ground among the numerically declining rural and self-employed categories.[24] By paralleling such demographic trends the Party has managed, by advancing along a broad electoral front, to replace the Gaullist Party of the late 1960s as the party whose electorate in social composition most closely mirrors that of the electorate as a whole.

Most of the trends revealed in the 1973 election results were confirmed in the Presidential election a year later (although comparisons are not strictly appropriate given the inclusion in Mitterrand's following in 1974 of the Communist electorate). Mitterrand did better still than the parties of the Left had in 1973 in eastern and western France and continued to lose voters in areas of traditional Left strength. He outdistanced Giscard d'Estaing on the second ballot in Paris (55 per cent) and the big cities (52 per cent). He took 71 per cent of the blue-collar vote and almost half (49 per cent) of the white-collar/middle management sector; led amongst men (53 per cent) but not amongst women (48 per cent) and had over half (56 per cent, 51 per cent and 52 per cent respectively) of the three under-65 age groups: an electorate of much more healthy, dynamic aspect than that of Giscard d'Estaing.[25]

Organisation and Membership

As a democratic mass party, the PS has typically enough never, formally at any rate, defined its success entirely in terms of its capacity to aggregate votes. It has also sought to recruit members. The unit of organisation to which members adhere is the federation, which is based on the largest local government unit, the department. Within the ninety-five federations are sections, averaging by 1975 sixty per department (though that figure obscures substantial deviations from the mean in both directions). It is within sections — which correspond generally to a commune or to subdivisions in the case of a large town — that members' political activity takes place. Each federation, after holding a federal congress, elects delegates to the national congress of the Party which since 1961 has met biennially. The function of the national congress is to debate and decide major policy orientations and to elect the *comité directeur* (an executive committee with 81 members in 1971 and 1973, and 131 in 1975). This is done by voting for rival motions to which are attached lists of the names of contending candidates. The signatories of each motion obtaining more than 5 per cent of the votes have, since 1971, been accorded representation on the *comité directeur* in strict proportion to the percentage of votes cast for their motions.[26] The *comité directeur* in turn elects from among its number the first secretary (leader), the *bureau exécutif* and secretariat. The bureau (21 members in 1971 and 1973, 27 after 1975) is constituted on the same proportional basis as the *comité directeur*, but the secretariat (10 members in 1971 and 1973, 13 after 1975) is politically homogeneous: — all its seats occupied by representatives of the group securing a majority at the preceding congress. The members of the secretariat, all with the title of 'national secretary', look after specific briefs: party coordination, relations with other bodies, industrial activities, press, propaganda, international relations, finance, etc. Whilst the *comité directeur* has responsibility for running the Party between congresses, meets once a month, and has power to convene special national conventions in order to discuss particular matters of interest as they arise, the day to day running rests with the bureau and effectively the secretariat, which constitutes the inner cabinet of the Party.

The 30 per cent growth of the Socialist electorate between 1967 and 1973 was accompanied by a doubling of the Party membership between 1969 and 1975. Since the schism of 1920 (which reduced the membership from 180,000 to 49,000 by 1922) there have been five subsequent periods of membership growth, all associated with an upturn in the Party's electoral fortunes. Thus membership, after the Cartel des Gauches election of 1924, doubled from 50,000 in 1923 to 111,000 by 1925; after the victory of the Popular Front it trebled (from 110,000 in 1934 to 281,000 by 1937); in 1945/46 at the time of Socialist success in the first post-war election, it hit the all time high (1946) of 355,000; and a very slight increase accompanied Socialist involvement in the success of the Republican Front in the election of 1956. After the war the pattern was however one of progressive decline (see Table 3) from the post-war peak of one-third million to 81,000 on the eve of the Party's reconstruction in 1969. Once re-formed however, the growth in numbers was resumed and most especially, once more, after electoral successes in 1973 and 1974. In those two years alone a net gain of 40,000 members was registered, to take the figure by the end of 1975 to 149,623.[27]

Membership distribution has tended, naturally enough, to parallel zones of traditional electoral implantation, except in the greater Paris area where high membership figures have not correlated with electoral success. The Pas de Calais, Nord and Bouches du Rhône federations have each accounted for about 10,000 Party members throughout the post-war period.[28] Membership decline prior to reorganisation in 1969 did not affect these three big federations, whose power in the Party correspondingly grew. The 1970s' membership growth however has occurred in the smaller federations so that by 1973, where there had been 15 years earlier 7 federations with more than 1,000 members (excluding the big 3), there were now 17.[29]

The social composition of the membership has traditionally revealed, in its overwhelmingly white-collar character, the Party's lack of effective links with blue-collar trade unionism. A study in 1970 suggested that no more than 23 per cent of Party members were manual workers,[30] a figure slightly less than the estimate twenty years earlier.[31] Moreover the effect of renewal since 1969 has not been to increase blue-collar strength, but to recruit further among white-collar categories.[32] A study of delegates attending the Party congress in 1973 amplified a variety of trends affecting membership: its renewal, but also its 'bourgeoisification', and political heterogeneity. Forty-five per cent of the delegates had only joined the Party since the previous 1971 congress; and barely more than a third (36 per cent) remained from the pre-1969 period; 29 per cent had had no previous Party affiliation; 37 per cent had belonged to the SFIO, 18 per cent had belonged to Mitterrand's CIR, 8 per cent to the PSU and 7 per cent to various other Left or extreme Left-wing groups. In religious affiliation 60 per cent proclaimed no religion, whilst, proof of the growing support for the Party amongst Catholics, 37 per cent identified themselves as such (a majority of whom had only joined the Party in the previous two years). The union affiliations of the delegates also reflected a certain cosmopolitanism: 24 per cent were members of the teachers' union, FEN; 18 per cent belonged to the independent Socialist-inclined CFDT; 7 per cent to the Communist-influenced CGT; and almost 10 per cent were members of the intensely anti-Communist union federation closely allied to the old Socialist Party, the *Force ouvrière.* Alongside this heterogeneous group of unionists (accounting for two-thirds of the delegates) were a further 32 per cent who had no union or professional associational ties whatever. The delegates were predominantly young (almost 60 per cent were under 40) and came overwhelmingly from cities with more than 100,000 inhabitants (44 per cent) or from towns with 20,000-100,000 people (26 per cent), and were predominantly professional in occupation. Manual workers accounted for a mere 3 per cent, and routine white-collar workers for only 8 per cent; of the rest 51 per cent were in various professional and managerial occupations, excluding education which accounted for 25 per cent, whilst 8 per cent were students.[33]

Union-Party Relations

Since 1947, when Communists took control of the largest union federation, the CGT, the party has been without an effective union arm, cut off from the bulk of the skilled working class in steel-making, engineering and mining. The *Force ouvrière*, set up as a reformist alternative to the CGT in 1947, comprised mostly Socialist voters though on the whole in public service (e.g. postal workers) and civil service, rather than manufacturing occupations. The Right-wing orientation of the FO (claiming 600,000 members by 1973) has not enabled easy co-existence with the post-1969 PS. Instead the PS has sought to establish links with the third union federation, the radical Socialist, 725,000-strong CFDT. After the 1974 Presidential election this was made an especially strong priority as part of the drive to parallel Communist industrial strength, but doubts in the CFDT over what it saw as imprecise attitudes towards industrial democracy in the Socialist-Communist Common Programme and a traditional desire to stand aside from involvement, as an organisation, in party politics, caused such plans to abort.[34] It might be argued that since substantial PS support is drawn from all the union federations,[35] privileged links with any one might well not be in the Party's interests. The Party did, after 1971, try to compensate for its lack of strong union roots by forming industrial workplace sections, and from a base of 50 in 1971, a claimed 756 had been formed by 1976 – a substantial increase, but still a long way behind the PC's 7,439 (claimed) industrial cells.

Factionalism

Democratic in structure and reformist (as distinct from conservative) in aspiration, the Party has experienced a good deal of internal conflict. It was in order to discourage dissension and enhance efficient leadership that, on the recommendation of Blum and others, the proportional representation principle in election for the Party's leading organs was suspended between 1945 and 1971; the period covered more or less, as it happened, by Guy Mollet's leadership. Factionalism during the Mollet years was thus denied any encouragement from internal electoral procedures. Where it arose moreover it was resolutely discouraged by Mollet's appeals for loyalty to a leadership weighed down for most of the time before 1958 with governing responsibilities; by an outright ban on the expression of minority views in the Party press;[36] and by the run-down of membership in most of the smaller federations which provided much of the opposition to Mollet's rule. Mollet's domination of the Party's organisation rested to a great extent on his control of the votes wielded at congresses by the big Pas de Calais and Nord federations, and this domination became the more secure as membership dropped elsewhere. As those who lost their taste for Mollet's crafty manipulation of the Party withdrew, so it came to resemble nothing so much as an ageing reunion of the war-time generation, with so strong a stake in local office-holding that by the early 1960s Socialist councillors accounted for about 70 per cent of the Party's membership. A party of office holders had relatively little cause to argue amongst itself, especially with the departure of the radical dissidents after 1958. Factional strife, such as it was before 1958, occurred around one or two divisive issues (e.g. the European Defence Community proposal in the early 1950s; Algerian policy and the return of de Gaulle in 1958). After 1958 in the new political climate of the Fifth Republic and against the background of a personal antagonism between Mollet and Defferre, conflict involved dispute over alliance strategy, with Mollet claiming to favour a Left-wing alliance though not at the cost of sacrificing an ounce of the Party's independent identity; and Defferre arguing for a more ecumenical federation of the Centre-Left. With the Party preoccupied by this dispute between two ageing *caciques*, it required the emergence of Mitterrand, a neutral figure in Socialist Party terms, to demonstrate the importance of Presidential politics and to end, by his candidature in 1965 and the success of the FGDS in 1967, the prolonged debate on alliance options. Instead he favoured a strategy of rebuilding the non-Communist Left into a party capable of dealing on equal terms with the Communists and of appearing credible to an electorate becoming familiarised with stable one-party rule. Ironically enough, however, Mitterrand's remedy could only, given the heterogeneity of the various Left-wing groups that were to be drawn into the fold, involve an intensification of factional disharmony in the reconstituted Socialist Party he envisaged.

The reorganisation of the Party in 1969 put together an exceedingly cosmopolitan collection of people. Firstly there was the old SFIO ingredient, numerically (because of the votes of the big three federations) very important and aligned into pro-Mollet (Pas de Calais) and anti-Mollet (Defferre's Bouches du Rhône and Mauroy's Nord) factions. Mollet was anxious, though retired from the leadership, to be the king-maker, whilst Mauroy hoped to be the king. To these baronial rivalries were added a variety of incoming political clubs,[37] often

grouped around leading personalities, but all sharing a hearty distaste
for Mollet's sclerotic and bankrupt party: for its old-fashioned
anti-clericalism which served to isolate Catholic Socialists; its dull
routine civil service and schoolteaching personnel; its refusal to
promote within its ranks on any but the basis of 'buggins turn'; its
failure to adapt to the new Constitution; its intolerance of dissent. All
shared too in a desire to reunite the non-Communist Left. By 1969
most of the clubs had formed into three groups: the UCRG led by
Alain Savary, a former Minister in the 1956 Mollet Government who
had left to help found the PSU; the UGCS, led by Jean Poperen
(ex-PCF and ex-PSU); and the CIR led by Mitterrand. The UGCS and
UCRG were more theoretically inclined than CIR, having derived from
rival factions within the highly ideologically fragmented PSU.[38] CIR on
the other hand was much less radical politically and was suspected by
Left-wing Socialists of being little more than a vehicle for the
Presidential ambitions of Mitterrand, a man who had not even described
himself as a 'Socialist' until the early 1960s. (Whilst some CIR personnel
joined the new PS in 1969, Mitterrand, chagrined at having been denied
the Left's investiture as a Presidential candidate in the June 1969
election, did not). There was additionally the CERES group, which had
originated within the SFIO but had developed into a libertarian
Socialist group with strong extra-parliamentary tendencies, and a
younger age profile than the other formations, heavily influenced by the
May events of 1968; and most vitriolic in its condemnation of the old
Socialist Party which one of its activists denounced as representing
'Suez, CRS, and Centrism'.[39] These formations assembled at the Issy
congress in July 1969 and distributed their votes across four rival
motions; two of which – those of Savary and Mollet – were cautiously
or ambiguously Left-orientated (Savary's talking of making the 'union
of the Left the normal axis of Socialist strategy'); one of which
reflected the caution of the old Party's moderate wing towards Leftist
strategies (Mauroy); and one representing the uncompromisingly
pro-Left unity stance of CERES (backed by on this occasion the
other – Poperen and CIR – club elements). The Savary motion
obtained 11 per cent, Mollet's 28 per cent, Mauroy's 30 per cent and the
CERES 7 per cent. The continued absence of proportional representation
in election of the leading organs required the ambitious to join together
in a final 'synthesis (or composite) motion', which linked the moderate
Mauroy with the Left-wing Savary and the ostensibly Left-wing Mollet
to constitute a coalition which then occupied the *comité directeur*, and
proceeded, to Mauroy's annoyance, to elect Savary the new first

secretary. The renewal of the Party had thus only been partial: most of the formerly excluded elements (except for Mitterrand and the bulk of his CIR) had entered, but the power of the old Party's regional chiefs dominated through the weight of their federations, and most significantly, the influence of Mollet and many of his former assistants was still all too obvious at the heart of the Party.

A desire to dispose finally of the Mollet era formed the background to the next congress at Epinay in 1971. Five motions competed at this congress: that of *Savary-Mollet* which represented the status quo and pursuit of talks with the PC with a joint programme in mind; a *Defferre-Mauroy* motion (binding the two avowedly moderate regional *notables* of the old party) desiring, as before, a centrist strategy and only tentative talks with the PC; a *Mermaz-Pontillon* (Mitterrand-backed) call for continued PC-PS talks but with stress on 'concrete' rather than ideological problems; and finally two motions (in the name of *Poperen* and of the *CERES* leaders) both calling for a resolute Leftist strategy, but the latter the more radical in calling specifically for a joint PS-PC programme and for the reintroduction of PR in elections at Party congresses. The way votes were cast for these motions (Savary-Mollet 34 per cent, Defferre-Mauroy 28 per cent, Mermaz-Pontillon (ex-CIR) 16 per cent, Poperen (ex-UGCS) 12 per cent, Chevènement[40] (CERES) 8.5 per cent) revealed that the new post-1969/71 club-derived element in the Party was now commanding over 36 per cent of the votes as against less than 20 per cent at the previous congress, an increase explained largely by the adhesion with Mitterrand in 1971 of 10,000 former CIR members. Out of these fragments was formed an alliance which was no more than a coalition of 'outs': Mitterrand, anxious for power in the Party in order to acquire a viable base for his national political ambitions; Mauroy and Defferre, desiring finally to break Mollet's control and to slow down the growth of 'popular frontism'; and the CERES group, also with ambitions to get its hands on a viable political organisation to further the pursuit of its radical Socialist objectives. With the significant reintroduction at the 1971 congress of PR in elections for the *comité directeur* all factions secured representation, but the new alliance of Left, Right and Centre, after electing Mitterrand to replace Savary, voted, in its own interests, to oppose proportional representation of all groups in the secretariat. Thus the ten-man secretariat after 1971 was composed according to the relative strengths of the three factions within the new governing *majority*: 4 members (including Mitterrand) from the CIR faction; 4 from the Mauroy-Defferre ex-SFIO (but all anti-Mollet) faction; and 2

(Chevènement and Sarre) representing CERES. Even if this represented a highly ambiguous alliance of pragmatists, anti-Communists and Popular Frontists, it certainly also signified extensive leadership renewal: all but four of the secretaries being new to the leadership, and the new leader himself new to the Party. Three of the new secretaries were in their thirties and only two were over fifty: in Mitterrand's words, it was possible to talk of 'the accession to leadership responsibilities of a new political generation'.[41] The potentially strong centrifugal tendencies within this alliance were counteracted by Mitterrand's subtle leadership and by the onset (1971-3) of a period of electoralism. The two potentially awkward CERES secretaries were given important responsibilities (for drawing up a Party programme and for industrial organisation), whilst Mauroy was put in charge of the Party organisation, and satisfied by a delay in the negotiations with the PC, until the Party had a programme with which to confront the Communists. Once the Party programme was agreed (March 1972) the presentation of a united front in PC-PS negotiations for a joint programme became important. As important were the constraints on factionalism imposed by the approach of the 1973 legislative elections, in which all factions (even CERES with their anti-electoralist tendency) desired success in order to extend the Party's audience. The duly delivered electoral success involved four members of the secretariat joining Mitterrand in the National Assembly, including Chevènement, though not (and significantly in terms of intra-party factionalism) Georges Sarre, who failed to win a traditional Socialist seat in Limoges where the power of the local Right-wing Socialist mayor and deputy Longequeue was effectively employed against him.[42]

By 1973, at Mitterrand's first congress (at Grenoble) as leader, his (Mitterrand-Mauroy-Defferre) motion was endorsed by 65 per cent of the congress delegates, whilst the remainder voted 8 per cent for a motion supported by friends of Mollet; 5 per cent for one backed by Poperen; and 21 per cent for a motion proposed by CERES who, whilst remaining in the secretariat (1973-5) decided to test the growing popularity of their group by detaching themselves at congress from the Mitterrand majority. Mitterrand's dominance without the Left wing, however, was very apparent; he had in fact been able to obtain majorities in Party conventions without CERES, and indeed opposed by them, from early 1972 onwards. His power had come to rest on the votes controlled by Mauroy and Defferre,[43] and on those provided by his own ex-CIR faction in departments of growing membership weight (Isère, Nièvre, Drôme, etc.) whilst CERES strength was concentrated in other areas of recent membership growth: the Catholic east and west, Paris and the *Rhône–Alpes* region. By the following congress (at Pau) in 1975, after another important electoral success, this time for Mitterrand personally in the Presidential election, the leadership's conference motion obtained 68 per cent of the delegates' support, with 25 per cent going to CERES. Dominance assured, Mitterrand, encouraged by Mauroy, the leader of the Right wing of his alliance and by his own CIR faction, broke finally with the CERES group, ousting them from an enlarged secretariat and replacing them with representatives of other minor factions including the PSU (3,000 of whose members joined the PS with their former leader Rocard in early 1975) and more members of his own CIR group.

The gap between CERES and the 'majority' of the party was at once generational, ideological and tactical, and once the Party moved away from the electoral preoccupations of the 1972-4 period, after which relationships with the Communists deteriorated, containment of the conflicts became more awkward. The steadily increasing congress vote of CERES, and their capture by 1975 of thirteen federations,[44] their penetration of others (including even Nord and Pas de Calais), their heavy dependence on recently recruited, young, highly educated, previously politically unattached activists, made them a very unknown quantity.[45] Dominant amongst the socialist students and young Socialists and responsible for the Party's industrial implantation until 1975, they appeared to envisage a massive membership recruitment. In Chevènement's words, 'To cope with the resistance there will be to the joint programme (of the Left) as in Chile, it is very important that the greatest possible number of *militants* engaged in the unions and in the daily struggles, rejoin and reinforce the Socialist party'.[46] Remarks such as this encouraged Mitterrand and Mauroy both to put a brake on new section formation during 1974, and to counter CERES activity amongst youth and workers by putting both areas under reliable Mitterrand supporters in 1975. The tendency for CERES to organise national meetings without seeking the sanction of the bureau of the Party was also checked by the *comité directeur* in 1976. Poor relations between Mitterrand and CERES at national level were also reflected in the federations: in the Isère for example where control by the middle-aged Mitterrandist, Louis Mermaz, was resented by the expanding young CERES group in Grenoble. There was evidence moreover that men like Mermaz, a deputy and a mayor, though part of the 'modernist' wave that swept over the Party after 1969/71, were installing themselves as new *notables* surrounded by exclusive cliques of supporters for whom

membership growth could only constitute a threat. In dealing with
CERES Mitterrand did not rely solely on the exchange of insults, though
that certainly took place,[47] but wisely used both discipline and
conciliation, involving them in important committees even after dropping
them from the secretariat in 1975, and balancing any rough treatment
of them with equally stern treatment of Right-wing dissidents.[48]
Mitterrand has thus affected to preside as an impartial judge, involving
as many of the Party's factions as possible in decision-making. In effect
the leadership technique is as arbitrary as many critics have claimed. It
is based on the old CIR style where the leader surrounds himself with
coteries of advisers and experts, many of whom in Mitterrand's case are
élite corps civil servants. Given the degree of intra-factional mistrust at
the heart of the Party, Mitterrand, by virtue of his unassailable position
based on his leadership skills, his not inconsiderable oratorical ability
and his highly successful electoral performances, is able to call the
tune.[49]

Issues Involved in Party Factionalism

Two definable issue areas emerged in the early years of the reformed
Party: European integration and *autogestion* (workers' control). At the
1973 congress these proved the two issues about the importance of
which delegates of rival factions were least in agreement (see Table 4),
with CERES seeing *autogestion* as of high importance and Europe of
little importance; whilst the dominant Mitterrand group ranked Europe
of greater importance than did CERES or indeed the delegates as a
whole.[50] Both issues clearly carried much potential for division and
indeed both were subsequently made the subject of special Party
conventions in 1973 (Europe) and 1975 (*autogestion*).

   Autogestion is the issue that most distinguishes the new Socialist
Party from its predecessor. It was introduced into Party debates by
CERES spokesmen (frequently former members of the PSU, a party
which gave a good deal of thought to the question in the 1960s), and
was written into the 1972 Party programme, the co-ordination of which
Mitterrand entrusted to Chevènement as part of the spoils of victory
and faction balancing in 1971. The intensity of commitment to the
autogestion concept amongst the CERES group is not unrelated to the
youthfulness of the group's membership (with recollections of 1968)
and their heavily white-collar professional background, which renders
them of all party factions the least familiar with traditional blue-collar
trade unionism. The Communist Party on the other hand, with close
union links, has little interest in workers' control. Had the Socialist

Party substantial union associations, its leaders doubtless would be better able to repel the advanced anti-statist case made out by CERES for *socialisme autogestionnaire.* For CERES 'to control the government is not to take power'; for that, and for the avoidance of 'bureaucratic and technocratic' deviations, the popular masses had to be mobilised through workers' councils outside the structure of existing institutions and of political parties and unions. The former PSU leader Rocard,[51] endorsing before a Party convention in 1975 the proposals which had been drawn up under the eye of ex-PSU member of the Party secretariat Martinet, also spoke approvingly of the passing of a 'too purely electoralist heritage'. Against that, another former PSU and former PCF Left-wing statist, Poperen (by this time also in the secretariat), wanted *autogestion* defined strictly to mean workplace decision-making relating only to routine questions such as conditions of work (rather than the early soviets envisaged by CERES),[52] whilst another secretariat member, Mermaz (one of the technocratically-inclined ex-CIR members of Mitterrand's immediate entourage, and the man to whom Mitterrand had entrusted the industrial affairs brief inside the secretariat after the 1975 congress) emphasised the need to preserve good relations with the PC (which were threatened by the *autogestion* issue). Mauroy, second man in the secretariat to Mitterrand and leader of the relatively unreconstructed Social Democratic wing of the Party, observed drily that the *autogestion* proposals (prepared under the aegis of a fellow member of the secretariat) were not worth the Party dividing itself over.[53] Mitterrand for his part, circumspect on *autogestion* as on much else, and varying his comments according to his audience, observed that many delegates found the CERES arguments esoteric and accused the group of indulging in 'science fiction' in wanting to define what a PS Government would do in the first twenty-four hours after coming to power. Whilst congress delegates taken as a whole had ranked *autogestion* as the second most important issue, that it was not a priority for the Mitterrandist element had been confirmed in 1973 when amongst delegates supporting Mitterrand at the congress the subject ranked seventh in their estimation of importance, on a par with farming problems, and behind the more down-to-earth matters of urban environment, retirement, immigrant workers, incomes, European unification and telephone tapping (see Table 4). For Mitterrand and the majority *autogestion* is something to try out piecemeal, without compromising the need for central planning and state control. For CERES, and for the former PSU leaders it is an article of Socialist faith: the only way of escaping the failure of Social Democracy and statist technocracy.[54]

The European question divided the new party in a way it did not (except when it became involved with the issue of German rearmament) divide the party of Guy Mollet, the man who as Prime Minister signed the Rome Treaty on behalf of France.[55] The perceptible shift to the Left by the Party in the 1970s, both in its congressional motions and policy statements as well as alliance strategy, has destroyed the previous consensus on the European issue. Party motions on the questions have suffered in clarity as the number and variety of people they have sought to please has grown. Most declarations have come to see the EEC as a counterweight to American-based international capitalism (as represented by multinational companies); to ensure its openness toward Comecon; to require the powers of its Parliament to be extended; but to prevent any interference in the economic policies of a Left-wing French Government. Late in 1973 Mitterrand chose to engage his authority on the issue and threatened to resign unless accorded a majority at a special congress due to debate the matter in December. The anti-EEC CERES case which confronted Mitterrand was essentially based on the view that a party which had turned its back on Centrism and capitalism in its alliances and programme since 1971 had no business in the Common Market, which, as an expression of American economic imperialism was incompatible with Socialism, and would interfere with the freedom of a French Government of the Left. Mitterrand's rebuttal of this view entailed an appeal for recognition of the Party's governing vocation, which could only involve acceptance of the reality of French membership of the EEC, and the claim (traditionally made by those in the Party whose motivation in supporting integration was founded on more than anti-Communist sentiment) that Europe was a prerequisite of, rather than a barrier to the construction of Socialism (*Il faut faire l'Europe pour faire le socialisme*). Eighty per cent of the delegates supported Mitterrand, and in a final motion agreed unanimously the delegates blandly acknowledged the reality of interdependence – as natural as had been the affirmation of nationality in its day – and envisaged a democratised, third force Europe, avoiding policies which would lead to a reduction in workers' living standards. The need to accommodate the Communists was clearly reflected in the partial retreat from enthusiastic support for supranationalism in the Party, but in February 1976 Mitterrand got a 97-34 vote in the *comité directeur* in favour of direct elections to the European Assembly. The CERES group, attracted by developments in Spain and Portugal pursued in 1975/76 the idea of a *Europe du Sud*; anxious to express an identity different from that of the Nordic Social Democratic one prevalent in the Socialist International and unsympathetic to the problems of Socialist parties having to work with Communists; but the attempt to establish an organisation of Socialist parties to that end foundered on the realisation that economic disengagement from the rest of Western Europe was impracticable.[56] There can obviously be little doubt about the Party leadership's enduring commitment to European integration, and it is only in the interests of party management or of easy relations with the Communists that critical notes are occasionally sounded.

Local Election Strategy

An additional major area of dispute between CERES and the Mitterrandist majority prior to the municipal elections of March 1977 involved electoral alliances. The Leftist strategy and the renunciation of Centrism, laid down in 1969 and reaffirmed in 1971, put CERES on the side of the angels in arguing for an undeviating implementation of PS-PC alliances at local (as well as at national) level. In focusing upon the issue CERES was striking at the heart of the alliance between the Social Democratic municipal wing of the Party — led by Mauroy and Defferre who themselves presided over councils in Lille and Marseille which included in the PS-led majority Centrist councillors — and Mitterrand who was seeking carefully to end that tradition. Nor was PS-Centrist collaboration in local government exceptional. In 1975 the Party was participating in running 312 councils in towns of over 10,000 inhabitants. Of those 312, only 15 were run by an entirely Socialist majority; 118 were run by a PS-PC alliance, and 179 a PS-Centrist alliance.[57] At big city level the PS occupied the mayoral chair in 4 towns (Marseille, Lille, Limoges and Clermont Ferrand — the last two without Centrist support), and was involved in the non-Communist Left alliance running Grenoble. Only in Le Havre and Amiens, where the Party supported PC mayors, was there a straight Communist-Socialist alliance, and apart from the prominent cases of Lille and Marseille, the PS was involved (as part of the ruling group) with Centrist mayors in Nantes and Nancy. Whilst all these Centrist alliances dated from the 1971 municipal elections, and thus predated both the signing of the Common Programme of the Left in 1972 and the incorporation of the Centrist Party leaders into the government in 1974, they did reflect the enduring disinclination of the PS to share power locally with Communists.

Given that the Mitterrand coalition which captured control of the Party in 1971 was committed to eschew Centrism, notwithstanding its

substantial dependence for congress majorities on the votes wielded by
the Party's two Social Democratic big city *notables,* Defferre and
Mauroy, the question was not one of opposing the demand for joint
PC-PS lists but of deciding how extensive such a strategy should be and
what sort of exceptions might be tolerable. The matter was resolved,
once more, by a special congress at Dijon in May 1976, where CERES
spokesmen argued that Socialists and Communists had to learn to
govern together at local level and that there should be no exceptions.
Mitterrand accepted that the strategy would apply everywhere and that
in towns over 30,000 it would be policed by the *comité directeur,* and
that in towns of smaller size the local federations would see the
strategy was observed (thus affording the possibilities of deviations for
which the central organs of the Party would not have responsibility).
The Communists would have to give and take also however; there
should be no rejection by Communist councillors of local budgets (as
had happened in places during 1976) and PC mayors should be as
prepared to open up Communist town halls to Socialist participation.

Programmes and Alliances

The consistent strategy of Mitterrand since the mid-1960s — to make of
the non-Communist Left a flexible instrument capable of equalling in
weight of numbers the Communist Party, and thence, with a negotiated
programme, to make a credible bid for power — had by the mid-1970s
been accomplished.

The need for a Socialist programme (as a prelude to negotiation with
the PC on a joint programme), followed logically once the alliance
option had been decided. Its appearance in January 1972 represented
the first attempt in the history of the Party to present a programme
shorn of the traditional Marxist vocabulary, yet explicitly radical in
some of its propositions. It was an intelligent invitation to the electoral
consumer rather than a traditional rallying cry to the faithful, and as
such represented the difference between Fourth and Fifth Republican
politics. In addition to achieving a synthesis clearly weighted in a
moderate direction on controversial areas (*autogestion,*[58] Europe and
defence) it comprised a specific list of reforms in social and economic
policy, a nationalisation policy based on three criteria (commanding
heights, monopoly situations and reliance on public funds), and a
clarification on one or two constitutional questions, such as the
electoral system and use of the dissolution power in the event of a
government defeat. From the Socialist point of view the ensuing joint
programme of government[59] which was negotiated with the PC (and

then signed by the Left Radicals) by 27 June 1972 (and which
represented the first occasion on which the parties of the Left had
agreed on a five-year government programme), served the purpose of
enhancing its own electoral potential by obtaining Communist
endorsement of certain essential liberal democratic norms
(multi-partyism and alternation of parties in Government) which
heightened the credibility of a Socialist-led Left alliance. Suitably
capable of both reformist and radical interpretations, the programme
contained a nationalisation shopping list whose length represented a
compromise between the two parties; and whilst nationalisation by
popular demand was envisaged, so also (with an eye on Radical as well
as Socialist support) was the persistence of an 'important private
sector'. Open disagreement on *autogestion* was written into the
programme. In the awkward area of foreign policy (a significantly short
section of the programme) the EEC was to be 'democratised' (but not
opposed outright as was PC tradition), with the right of veto retained
(on PC insistence, though CERES was also anxious for this);[60] France
was neither to rejoin, nor yet formally to withdraw from, NATO
(simultaneous dissolution of NATO and the Warsaw pact was to be
pursued); nuclear force as 'at present conceived' was 'renounced'. The
barely concealed and serious lack of agreement reflected in this section
of the programme led in the elections that followed (1973, 1974) to a
much-repeated charge by Government spokesmen that a government of
the Left armed with such a common programme would be a government
without a foreign policy. In matters of defence policy this became a less
justified jibe; by 1976 both parties had drawn closer together, endorsing
a basically gaullist consensus; but on European policy the PS's gaullism
(defence of the veto) did not go so far as the PC's attack on a directly
elected Assembly as 'a crime against the French people'.

   The period after the 1974 Presidential election saw both a worsening
in PC-PS relations, coupled with further liberalisation of the Communist
Party's public face. The worsening of relations with the PS was
triggered off by the realisation, confirmed in by-elections after 1974,
that the PS had managed to attain its objective of overtaking the PC as
the largest party of the Left.[61] PS leaders were verbally attacked,
accused of incipient Centrism, and early in 1975 Mitterrand was
attacked as being arrogant and overbearing by Marchais himself, despite
the formerly good relations established between Mitterrand and the
Communist leader in the 1972-4 period. The continued liberalisation of
the PC served however to compensate for the coolness of PC-PS relations,
and by early 1976 a declaration of conventional civil liberties had been

outlined and the dictatorship of the proletariat renounced as part of party doctrine. In effect the Party had little choice, affected as it was more adversely by the institutions of the Fifth Republic than other parties: in a system personalising executive power it of all the parties could hardly expect to see a candidate of its own installed in the Elysée; and the electoral system obliged it, as it did the PS, to make an alliance which, given its position on the political spectrum, could only be with the Socialist Party, and which could not avoid entailing a dilution of the Party's independence and identity. Social and economic change furthermore together involved simultaneously both a stagnation in the growth of the Party's traditional blue-collar electorate and its greater integration in society as a whole. Still more worrying for the Party was the possibility that in responding to these developments, by opening itself outwards to the electorate and by burying its Stalinist and pro-Soviet past, it ceased to perform the function ascribed to it by one writer as that of a secular church and undermined the emotional security of its activists.[62] The signs indeed of an identity crisis could be read in the verbal assaults made on the PS after 1974.[63]

Prospects

The essential problem of the *Parti socialiste* remained, of course, its very existence as no more than a proportion of what in most northern European industrialised countries would be the single party of the Left. Whatever the nature of the social and economic forces that precipitated an important segment of the working class into the arms of an unconventional and semi-isolated party, once they *had* been so precipitated the problem of the French Left became chronic; with every attempt at a united strategy greeted at the hustings by the declaration that no change of government was possible without it being accompanied by a change of society. It is for this reason that the Centrist temptation lingers in Socialist thoughts. The evolution of the Communists, however, would appear logically to destroy to some degree Right-wing recourse to the 'red bogey' at every electoral opportunity,[64] though no party with such a title will ever cease to be something of an electoral liability nor fail to confirm what has become one of the most venerable clichés of contemporary French politics, that whilst on the Left nothing can be done without the PC, nothing can be done with it either. This credibility problem aside moreover, there are still serious *institutional* roadblocks erected by the Right in the last twenty years, the most-discussed being the crisis provoking potential of a political discordance between the National Assembly and the Presidency. To an extent the country came to live with this very situation after 1974 but clearly the co-existence of a Left and Right would make for more problems than that of Giscard with the Gaullists since the Presidential election of 1974.

Given Presidential authority and power it was understandable that Mitterrand's post-1965 strategy was based on an attempt to enter the Elysée in order to be the master of his own fate. That option closed, after 1974 and until 1981, it was necessary to envisage the possibility of a Left parliamentary majority confronted by Giscard d'Estaing. Giscard was as circumspect in answering questions about his reactions to such a situation as Pompidou had been, but Mitterrand after 1974 was realistic enough to defend a dualistic interpretation of the constitution – involving an accommodation of each (Assembly and President) by the other, which would inevitably involve a much less presidential interpretation of the constitution than hitherto had been possible. The problem, however, with this scenario was the declared Communist opposition to governing under Giscard's Presidency. Furthermore should such a situation present itself it seemed possible that the unity of the PS could not survive such a crisis. Opposed to those who would argue that the PC-PS alliance was irreversible and in terms of political and economic theory unassailable, would be those who have a stronger preference for wheeling and dealing, and it is in that context that the overwhelmingly conventional nature of the Party's parliamentary personnel, somewhat eclipsed at present, would be of great significance and the radical excesses of its militants less salient.[65] Notwithstanding the latter, Centrist temptations could prove hard to resist. It is possible, after all, to represent the Socialist party as the most bourgeois of the parties of its type in Europe, from its barrister leader down to its overwhelmingly 'middle class', or at any rate, white-collar, membership. Lacking a leavening of blue-collar trade unionists or even men from manual occupations among its parliamentary personnel,[66] the occupational composition of which (see Tables 5 and 6) has changed relatively little in twenty years, it would appear well placed, with its lawyers, doctors and senior civil servants, to confirm Communist suspicions. With leadership being recruited from among graduates of the ENA; with financial policy allegedly being written for the Party by civil servants in the Finance ministry; and with the influx after 1974 of former Gaullist technocrats, such as Delors (one-time adviser to the former prime minister Chaban-Delmas) and Pisani (a former Gaullist minister), outsiders could be forgiven for assuming that the Party was preparing, come what may, for Government.

The alternative view, and one popular with Left-inclined political sociologists, is to see the PC-PS alliance as the political expression of a social and economic transmutation which renders collaboration complementary rather than competitive and logically irreversible. Such a view sees the existence of a 'sociological majority' for the Left as a consequence of the decline of the agricultural and self-employed sectors of the economy and the expansion of tertiary sector employment, a process which by 1973 had led to 80 per cent of the active population being paid workers. The rapid increase in the numbers of the white-collar salariat and the collectivisation and bureaucratisation of their employment is held to provoke a decline in status, which in turn awakens a consciousness of a community of interest between themselves and the traditional blue-collar working class. This process has, moreover, supposedly been hastened by both the economic crisis and the simultaneous decline of a Right-wing governing coalition unable to cope with the contradictions between its technocratic ideology and its highly traditionalist electorate. Such an analysis had, by the mid-1970s, come to be accepted not only by the new left of the Socialist Party, but also by the Communist leaders who had traditionally resisted any but an *ouvrieriste* conception of the working class.[67] How, serious constitutional problems aside, the PS and PC as the political representatives of this 'natural' alliance would work together in Government, as distinct from a traditional and undemanding association as opposition parties, would be impossible to foresee. A further surrender by the Communists of more of their doctrine, notably those parts conditioning the Party's monopolistic attitude toward the manual working class and its continuing belief in the virtues of democratic centralism, could be seen as a minimum requirement.

The Socialist Party in the early 1970s appeared to have made, consciously or otherwise, a series of major adjustments: to its political and constitutional environment; to demographic growth and social change; and to a more contemporary corpus of ideas. In effect however, the major agent of socialist growth and transformation had been the bipolarisation of French political life, itself the product as much of presidentialism and new electoral laws as of social and economic change. Bipolarisation, involving the erosion of a centre placement of parties, is accompanied by the substitution of centripetal pulls for the centrifugal strains characteristic of polities in which a dominant Centre effectively isolates from office, as in the Fourth Republic, the 'extremes' of Left and Right.[68] Thus in the bipolarised system of contemporary France the overwhelming necessity for the broadest possible electoral aggregation requires and encourages not only the peaceful co-existence of groups within an enlarged Socialist Party, but also the close collaboration of the Socialist and Communist parties, with deeper integration of the latter party as a major consequence. Both parties thus found themselves propelled along a road not entirely of their choosing, yet one appearing to lead, given the effects of wear and tear on the governing Right-wing coalition, to eventual electoral success. Beyond that point however the future appeared unclear. The fragility of the Socialist Party's new-found strength made it a profoundly unpredictable force, with an unhealthy dependence upon one particular Presidentially credible leader; an indifferent penetration of the industrial working class; and a lack of homogeneity or coherence of the kind required to cope with its powerful and omnipresent neighbour. To make of the Party, in Mitterrand's phrase, a party of Government, and to take office either with or without the Communists, would be to venture into the unknown. In no other comparable country could so buoyant a party be said to face so uncertain a future.

Notes

1. The party was known as the PS (SFIO) *Parti socialiste: Section française de l'Internationale ouvrière* until 1969. and thereafter as the *Parti socialiste.*
2. On the party during these years see D. Ligou, *Histoire du socialisme en France,* (Paris, P.U.F.), 1962; N. Green, *Crisis and Decline: the French Socialist Party in the Popular Front Era* (New York, Cornell University Press, 1969); C. Audry, *Léon Blum ou la politique du juste* (Paris, Editions Denoel, 1970).
3. Seats in the first two Assemblies of the Fourth Republic were distributed thus: 1946-51 (%) PC 30; Soc. 17; Rad. 10; MRP 29; Ind. 14.
   1951-56 (%) PC 18; Soc. 18; Rad. 10; MRP 15; Ind. 16; RPF 20.
4. Guy Mollet: 1905-75, schoolteacher (*professeur*), son of a weaver. Deputy (Pas de Calais: Arras) 1945-75. Secretary-General of PS (SFIO) 1946-69. Minister in five governments between 1946 and 1958 including de Gaulle's (1958-9). Prime Minister 1956-7. Foreign affairs and Defence spokesman in FGDS (Fédération de la gauche démocrate et socialiste) shadow cabinet 1966-8. For a critical obituary see J. Julliard 'Contradictions de Guy Mollet', *Le Nouvel Observateur,* 13 Oct. 1975.
5. D. Ligou, op.cit., pp.544-7.
6. See H.G. Simmonds, *French Socialists in search of a role 1956-67* (Ithaca, Cornell University Press, 1970), pp.35-6. Idem, 'The French Socialist Opposition in 1969', *Government and Opposition,* vol.4 (1969), pp.294-307.
7. On the party during the Fourth Republic see P.M. Williams, *Crisis and Compromise* (London, Longmans, 1964).
8. The PSU had as its mission the purification and reunification of the French Left. By the mid-1970s it was virtually defunct, its former leadership having joined the PS; and in the 1960s it was never more than an electorally insignificant force with a claimed membership of 15,000. In 1967 it had four deputies and in 1969 its leader (Rocard) won 3.6 per cent of the votes in the

presidential election.
9. The post-1958 electoral system operates within single member constituencies. Two ballots are held where no candidate obtains an absolute majority of the votes cast on the first ballot or where the leading candidate's votes constitute less than 25 per cent of the registered electors. In such cases candidates obtaining less than 10 per cent of the registered electorate are eliminated, and at the second ballot, one week after the first, the candidate with a plurality of the votes cast wins the seat. In all elections since 1958, the overwhelming majority of constituencies have experienced two ballots. Presidential elections also involve two ballots (two weeks apart) where no candidate obtains an absolute majority on the first ballot. Only the candidates coming first and second at the first ballot are allowed to contest the second.
10. Gaston Defferre, b. 1910, newspaper proprietor (*Le Provençal*) and lawyer; son of lawyer. Deputy (Bouches du Rhône: Marseille) 1945-58 and 1962-. Senator 1959-62. Mayor of Marseille 1944-5 and 1953-. Minister in five governments between 1946 and 1957, notably as Colonies Minister in Mollet government 1956-7. Designated (1964) candidate for 1965 presidential election but withdrew before election. Presidential candidate in 1969 (June): 1,133,222 votes (5.0 per cent). President FGDS/UGSD group in National Assembly 1967-. President Provence-Côte d'Azur Regional Council 1974-. Member *Comité directeur* and *Bureau executif* of PS 1973-.
11. François Mitterrand: b. 1916, lawyer, son of businessman. Deputy (Nièvre) 1946-58; 1962-; Senator 1959-62. Mayor of Château-Chinon 1959-; President of Nièvre General Council 1964-. During the Fourth Republic leader of Left wing of UDSR (*Union démocratique et sociale de la Résistance*), a heterogeneous party of non-Marxist, non-laicist notables. Minister in nine Fourth Republic Governments, notably Minister of Interior in Mendès-France Government (1954-5) and Minister of Justice in Mollet Government (1956-7). Presidential candidate Dec. 1965: 1st ballot 7,694,005 votes (31.7 per cent); 2nd ballot 10,619,735 (44.8 per cent). President of FGDS Dec. 1965-Nov. 1968. President of FGDS 'shadow cabinet' 1966-8. President of CIR (*Convention des institutions républicains*) 1970-1. Joined PS June 1971. First Secretary of PS June 1971-. Co-signatory of *Programme commun* of the Left June 1972. Presidential candidate May 1974: first ballot 11,044,373 (43.2 per cent); second ballot 12,971,604 (49.2 per cent). For earlier career see R. Cayrol, *François Mitterrand 1945-67*, Fondation nationale des sciences politiques, 1967.
12. The *Radicaux de gauche* comprised a small group of Left-wing Radicals who rejected the leadership of Jean Jacques Servan-Schreiber.
13. Comment and analysis relating to the 1973 elections may be found in J. Hayward and V. Wright, 'Presidential Supremacy and the French General Elections of March 1973', *Parliamentary Affairs*, vol. 26, no. 3, pp. 274-306; and no.4, pp.372-402. J. Ozouf, 'Geógraphie des élections législatives de mars 1973', *Esprit*, June 1973, pp.1295-1317. C. Ysmal, 'Des élections sans surprise mais non sans changements', *Revue politique et parlementaire*, Apr. 1973, pp.2-12. J. Charlot, *Quand la gauche peut gagner* (Paris, A. Moreau, 1973). 'Les forces politiques et les élections de mars 1973', *Dossiers et documents du Monde*, Mar. 1973.
14. Virtually all (98 per cent) of first ballot PC voters transferred their support where required to second ballot PS candidates. Only 61 per cent of first ballot PS voters, however, were prepared to assist in the election of Communist deputies at the second ballot. See SOFRES survey, *Le Nouvel Observateur*, 28 Mar. 1973.
15. In Bouches du Rhône, the Party in 1973 had 4 seats where it had had 6 in

1967; in Pas de Calais, 6 seats where in 1967 it had 8. Such losses were attributable to the desertion of the Party by an anti-Communist element in its electorate, who were most numerous in areas where competition between the two parties had traditionally been strong.

16. Decline: (1973/1967) Auvergne −4.2 per cent; Bourgogne −4.0 per cent; Limousin −3.8 per cent. Growth: 1967/1973) Lorraine +8.3 per cent; Bretagne +7.9 per cent; Basse-Normandie +5.7 per cent; Pays de la Loire +5.5 per cent; Rhône-Alpes +4.3 per cent; Alsace +3.7 per cent.

17. Elsewhere: Bretagne, +2 seats; Basse Normandie, +2; Rhône-Alpes, +4.

18. Socialist weakness in the big cities was evidenced in 1962 by a complete absence of Socialist candidates in 18 of the 56 constituencies of the Paris conurbation (Seine department); and in 3 of the 5 constituencies in Lyon. Elsewhere, the party left some seats uncontested in the cities of Nice, St. Etienne, Bordeaux and even Lille. Only in Marseille were all seven constituencies fought. (See F. Goguel, *Le référendum d'octobre et les élections de novembre 1962*, (Paris, Colin, 1965, pp.332-3.)

19. A SOFRES poll in 1972 found 77 per cent accepting that it was possible 'to be a Christian and the supporter of a socialist society'; see 'L'Eglise et les élections', *L'Express*, 16-22 Oct. 1972. On the selection of a priest as the *suppléant* of a PS candidate in Angers see *Le Nouvel Observateur*, 19 Feb. 1973. More priests (24 per cent) supported the PS than any other party in 1973; see J. Charlot, op.cit. pp.67-9. Of the most regular (mass at least once a month) practising Catholics, 13 per cent voted PS. See SOFRES survey in *Le Nouvel Observateur*, 28 May 1973. For other comment on Catholics and the Left see *Le Nouvel Observateur*, 6 Mar. 1973 and 26 Mar. 1973; *L'Express*, 6-12 Nov. 1972 and 19-25 Mar. 1973; and *Le Monde* ('Les catholiques et la politique'), 6 and 7 Feb. 1973.

20. The PC electorate in 1973 was thus: farmers 5 per cent; businessmen 5 per cent; professional-higher managerial 3 per cent; white collar workers 17 per cent; manual workers 51 per cent; retired 19 per cent. Of the entire working class electorate the PC had 35 per cent and the PS 27 per cent.

21. The French labour force in 1974, by sectors, with 1962 figures in brackets, was composed thus: primary 12 per cent (21 per cent); secondary 39 per cent (39 per cent); tertiary 49 per cent (41 per cent). (See 'Faits et chiffres 1973', *Le Nouvel Observateur*, and *The Economist*, 29 Nov. 1975.)

22. More teachers (48 per cent) voted PS in 1973 than voted for any other party. (See J. Charlot, pp.74-6.)

23. 'Les nouveaux électeurs socialistes', *L'Express*, 10 May 1976.

24. Compared with 1967, the UGSD electorate gained net approximately 330,000 votes amongst white-collar and professional and higher managerial categories, and approximately 345,000 votes amongst blue-collar workers.

25. IFOP, *Le Point*, 21 May 1974. See also: H.R. Penniman, *France at the Polls: The Presidential Election of 1974*, (Washington, American Enterprise Institute, 1975), and 'L'Election présidentielle de mai 1974', *Le Monde Dossiers et Documents*.

26. The proportional representation principle operates at all levels of the party.

27. On the extreme rapidity and heterogeneity of growth in these years see: R. Ferretti, 'Les militants de la fédération du Bas Rhin du PS', *La nouvelle revue socialiste*, vol. 14-15 (1975), pp. 8-16; and H. Portelli and T. Dumias, 'Les militants socialistes à Paris', *Projet*, vol.101 (Jan. 1976), pp.35-43.

28. These federations were controlled respectively by Guy Mollet, Pierre Mauroy 1961-) and Gaston Defferre.
    Pierre Mauroy, b. 1928, teacher (*professeur*), son of teacher (*instituteur*). Mayor of Lille 1973-, Deputy (Nord) 1973-. President of Nord-Pas de Calais

Regional Council 1974-. Sec.-Gen. Nord federation of PS (SFIO) 1961-.
Deputy Sec.-Gen. PS (SFIO) 1965-8. National Sec. Young Socialists 1950-8.
Deputy Sec.-Gen. SFIO 1966-8. Exec. Com. FGDS 1965-8. Political Bureau
SFIO 1963-8. Member *Comité directeur, Bureau exécutif* and Secretariat of
PS 1971-.

29. In traditional areas some growth occurred (Haute-Garonne and Aude) though
decline was also common (Haute-Vienne and Gironde). Previously weaker areas
saw substantial growth: e.g. Drôme from 200 (1965) to 1,150 (1973); Isère
from 600 to 1,170; Nièvre from 400 to 1,200. See J. Derville, 'La féderation
socialiste de l'Isère depuis 1969', *Revue française de science politique,* vol.26,
no.3 (June 1976), pp.568-99.

30. Of the rest 7 per cent were farmers, 54 per cent 'lower middle class' (i.e. small
traders, middle managers, non-lycée teachers, routine white-collar workers)
and 16 per cent 'middle class' (i.e. higher professional, managerial and
businessmen). See M. Kesselman, 'Recruitment of Rival Party Activists in
France: Party Cleavages and Cultural Differentiation', *Journal of Politics,*
vol.35, no.1 (Feb. 1973), pp.2-41.

31. In 1953 blue-collar workers accounted for 24 per cent of the Party's
membership (See C. Hurtig, *De la SFIO au nouveau parti socialiste* (Paris,
Colin, 1970), p. 28.)

32. Two per cent of Paris federation members and 4 per cent of Bas-Rhin
federation members were manual workers. See Portelli, op.cit and Ferretti, op.cit.

33. See R. Cayrol, 'Les militants du parti socialiste', *Projet,* vol. 88, Sept.-Oct.
1974, pp. 929-40. Whilst this is a study of *delegates,* it can be assumed to
reflect strong trends in the composition of membership after 1971.

34. See interviews with Edmond Maire, secretary-general of CFDT, in *Le Nouvel
Observateur,* 9 June 1973 and 10 Nov. 1975; E. Maire and J. Julliard,
La CFDT aujourd'hui (Paris, Seuil, 1975).

35. In the 1973 elections the following proportion of union members voted PS:
CGT 29 per cent; CFDT 30 per cent; FO 43 per cent; Other 23 per cent.
(SOFRES, *Le Nouvel Observateur,* 28 May 1973.) In the 1974 Presidential
election (second ballot), for Mitterrand: CGT 90 per cent, CFDT 73 per cent,
FO 52 per cent, Other 64 per cent. (SOFRES, *Le Nouvel Observateur,* 10-16
June 1974.)

36. *Le Populaire,* – ended production in 1969. Replaced (1971) by the weekly *L'Unité.*

37. On the clubs see F.L. Wilson, *The French Democratic Left 1963-69: toward a
Modern Party System* (Stanford, Stanford University Press, 1971), pp. 77-107.

38. UGCS: Union des groupes et clubs socialistes; UCRG: Union des clubs pour
le renouveau de la gauche; CIR: Convention des institutions républicaines.
On UCRG see A. Savary, *Pour le nouveau Parti socialiste* (Paris, Seuil, 1969).
On CIR see F. Mitterrand, *Un socialisme du possible* (Paris, Seuil, 1970).
See also J. Poperen, *Une stratégie pour la gauche* (Paris, Fayard, 1969), and
L'Unité de la gauche 1965-73 (Paris, Fayard, 1975).

39. CERES: Centre d'études de recherches et d'éducation socialiste. See
P. Guidoni, *Histoire du nouveau parti socialiste* (Paris, Tema, 1973).
(The 'CRS' riot police, were used by the Socialist Minister of the Interior,
Moch.) See also M. Charzat, *et al., Le CERES: un combat pour le socialisme*
(Paris, Calman Lévy, 1975).

40. Jean-Pierre Chevènement, b. 1939, higher civil servant, son of teacher
(*instituteur*). Graduate of ENA. Joined PS (SFIO) 1964. Sec.-Gen. CERES
1965-71. Political secretary PS Paris federation 1969-70. Member Secretariat
of PS 1971-75; member, *Comité directeur* and *Bureau* 1971-. PS national
secretary in charge of Party programme 1971-3. Responsible for negotiating
'economic democracy' section of the *Programme commun,* 1972. Deputy

(Belfort) 1973-. Author of various books including *Socialisme ou socialmédiocratie* (Seuil, 1969); and *Le Vieux, la Crise, le Neuf* (Paris, Flammarion, 1975).

41. *Le Monde*, 18 June 1971.

42. Longequeue resented the selection of the Left-wing Sarre and contributed to his defeat by ensuring through control of the local paper poor press coverage of Sarre's campaign, and as mayor, the last minute reversal of meeting hall lettings. See *Le Nouvel Observateur*, 12 Feb. 1973.

43. At the 1973 congress 94 per cent of the Bouches du Rhône and 75 per cent of the Nord votes went to Mitterrand as did big majorities of all traditional (pre-1969) federations. Only in Mollet's Pas de Calais and Longequeue's Haute-Vienne was there resistance to the new leadership from old-style SFIO *notables*.

44. Essonne, Ille et Vilaine, Loire, Marne, Haute-Marne, Meurthe-et-Moselle, Meuse, Moselle, Paris, Haut-Rhin, Haute-Saone, Savoie, Belfort.

45. Sixty per cent of CERES delegates in 1973 had joined the Party since 1971, 42 per cent had no previous political affiliation; and 45 per cent were under thirty. See R. Cayrol, *Projet*, 1974, op.cit.

46. *Le Monde*, 9 Oct. 1974. Note also Gilles Martinet (ex-PSU) '51 per cent of the vote would not be enough; it would be necessary to effect a popular mobilisation' (*Le Monde*, 15 Oct. 1974).

47. Mitterrand called CERES 'a communist-Leftist *pot pourri*'. Chevènement retorted 'We are not the cardinal's musketeers'.

48. Thus in 1976 Paul Alduy, an old-style local *notable* and deputy with strong Centrist leanings who refused to collaborate at the second ballot of the cantonal elections with the PC, was expelled. (*Le Monde*, 6 Apr. 1976.) With another Centrist-inclined PS deputy, Chauvel, Alduy joined a group of ten former Socialist deputies, most of whom had been elected as 'social democrats' under the Réformateur (Centrist) label in 1973. (See *Le Monde*, 26 May 1976.)

49. In a debate on local election strategy Mitterrand put down critics by declaring: 'If there's any doubt about the text of the motion, ask me – I wrote it.' (*Le Monde*, 15 May 1976.)

50. R. Cayrol, 'L'univers politique des militants socialistes', *Revue française de science politique*, vol. 25, no. 1 (Feb. 1975), pp. 23-50.

51. Michel Rocard. b.1930, *Inspecteur des finances* (higher civil servant), son of teacher (*professeur*). Graduate of ENA (*Ecole nationale d'administration*). National Secretary of Socialist (SFIO) students 1955-6. National Secretary (Leader) PSU (*Parti socialiste unifié*) 1967-Nov. 1973. Presidential candidate 1969: 816,470 votes (3.6 per cent). Deputy (PSU) (Yvelines) Oct. 1969-73. Resigned from PSU 1974. Joined PS. Member, *Comité directeur*, and *Bureau exécutif* of PS, Feb. 1975-. On period as PSU leader see R. Cayrol, *Le PSU et l'avenir socialiste de la France; histoire et sociologie d'un parti* (Seuil, 1969). On reasons for leaving see 'Je quitte le PSU', *Le Nouvel Observateur*, 2 Dec. 1974.

52. See text of CERES motion at national convention on *autogestion, Le Monde*, 21 June 1975.

53. Mauroy had before the convention suspended the vote of his own Nord federation, claiming that in pre-convention meetings in the Nord only intellectuals, notably teachers, had contributed to the discussion, and manual worker activists had not been called. (*Le Monde*, 24 June 1973.)
    Defferre had elsewhere explained that there was no *autogestion* in his business, for if there was the workers would choose him. (*Le Point*, 5 Feb. 1973.)
    Martinet argued, however, that to avoid a Chilean fate, (1) the Left's

joint programme had to be made more explicit on *autogestion,* (2) new democratic structures were required to prevent falling into the trap of suicidal respect for institutions destined to assure the stability of the existing social system, but not permit its transformation, and (3) a policy had to be defined that was capable of 'rallying to the Left an important fraction of the army'. (*Le Nouvel Observateur,* 24 Sept. 1973.)

54. For further discussion of *autogestion* see J.P. Chevènement, *La Vieux, La Crise, Le Neuf* (Paris, Flammarion, 1976), M. Duverger, 'Une nouvelle base pour le socialisme démocratique', *Le Monde,* 21 June 1973. See also F. Mitterrand, op. cit. p. 66; M. Charzat, op. cit.; and A. Datraz *et al., La CFDT et l'autogestion* (Paris, Cerf, 1973), esp. ch. 7.

55. Continuity was reflected in the presence in the Secretariat after 1971 of Gerard Jaquet, a leading European integrationist of long standing, and of Robert Pontillon, who had had responsibility for foreign policy matters in the Party during Mollet's leadership.

56. See 'La rupture d'Elseneur', *L'Express,* 26 Jan.-1 Feb. 1976; and 'Mitterrand contre Schmidt', *Le Nouvel Observateur,* 28 Jan. 1976. In Dec. 1975 the Comité directeur disavowed by 3:1 an attack in the CERES review *Repères,* on the Portuguese PS and its leader Soares. *Le Monde,* 31 Dec. 1975.

57. In the 118 PS-PC towns, the PS led (i.e. provided the mayor) in 30, the PC in 88; in the 179 PS-Centrist towns, the PS led in 77, the Centrists in 102. See *Socialisme 2000,* Jan. 1975, organ of *Centre d'étude pour le socialisme.*

58. The commitment to *autogestion* was as a long-term objective with short-term experiments to be tried with workers' agreement in public sector enterprises. See *Changer la vie: programme de gouvernement du parti socialiste* (Paris, Flammarion, 1972).

59. See *Programme commun de gouvernement du parti communiste et du parti socialiste* (Editions Sociales, Paris), pp. 53-192.

60. So indeed had Mitterrand been in his CIR's *Contrat socialiste* of 1969; see Mitterrand, op. cit. pp. 97-9. Socialist-Communist divergence on the EEC had been demonstrated in the referendum on its enlargement in 1972 when the PC advocated No and the PS abstention.

61. Mitterrand's May 1974 second ballot vote of 13 million, whilst not to be taken as a vote for his *party,* did, with the 5 million Communist votes subtracted, create an impression of Socialist hegemony, and was certainly interpreted as threatening by the Communist leaders who had not forgotten the remark made by Mitterrand at a meeting of the Socialist International in Vienna in June 1972: 'Our fundamental objective is to reconstruct a large Socialist party on the ground occupied by the Communist party itself', 30 June 1972. On the question of relative electoral strengths of the two parties see G. Le Gall and M. Riglet, 'La gauche a-t-elle été rééquilibrée? ', *Etudes,* June 1973.

The rebalancing of the Left very much in the Socialist Party's favour, was apparently confirmed in parliamentary by-elections after 1973. By the end of 1976 the PS had won four by-elections, two in traditional areas (Landes and Haute Loire) and two in areas of recent growth (Savoie and Rhône). (The party's Left Radical allies also won a seat in Côte d'Or in 1974.) Inter-general election gains by one opposition party on such a scale were unprecedented. The extent of PS growth, moreover (a first ballot vote increased on average by 8 per cent) compared starkly with Communist stagnation. See, e.g. *Le Monde,* 16 and 23 Nov. 1976.

62. A. Kriegel, *Les communistes français* (Paris, Seuil, 1968). On the evolving PC see F. Bon, *et al., Le communisme en France* (Paris, Colin, 1970); A. Laurens and T. Pfister, *Les nouveaux communistes* (Paris, Stock, 1973) and A. Harris

and A. de Sédouy, *A l'intérieur du parti communiste* (Paris, Seuil, 1974).
63. For such an analysis see A. Duhamel, in *Le Monde*, 30 May 1976.
64. Recent examples being the 1973 leaflet bearing a photograph of the three leaders of the Left (PC, PS and Radical) shaking hands after signing the joint programme, with the caption 'Qui triomphe?'. In 1974 a common slogan was 'Oui à liberté; Non à Mitterrand'; in 1972 a Gaullist minister coined the celebrated phrase about the Socialist-Communist relationship being that of 'the rabbit and the cobra' (A. Peyrefitte, *Le Monde*, 2 Dec. 1972.)
65. The radical wing of the party is not well-represented in the National Assembly, Chevènement being a relatively isolated figure. The pre-1969 pattern of moderate mayor-deputies is however, prominent; over half the parliamentary group dates from that period, and a fair number of the 1973 intake, such as Mauroy, were very much in the same mould. Even among the more keen advocates of the PS-PC alliance, most of whom belonged to the 1973 intake (though some had been deputies briefly in 1967-8), a number, such as the Mitterrandists Mermaz, Fillioud and Labarrère were, as mayors, taking on the aspect of new *notables* as well as reflecting in their attitudes the ambiguity and circumspection of their leader.
66. The Popular Front election of 1936 saw the election of twelve manual workers as Socialist deputies. Since then however there have never been more than four returned at any election, and in 1973 there were none. The PC by contrast rarely has fewer than two-fifths of its deputies drawn from manual worker backgrounds; in 1973 the figure was 44 per cent.
67. See F. Mitterrand, op. cit. pp. 46-54; R. Garaudy, *The Turning Point of Socialism* (London, Fontana, 1969), pp. 188-232; J.-P. Cot, *Le Monde*, 22 June 1973; M. Cotta, 'Où en sont les communistes?', *L'Express*, pp. 34-7, 1-7 Nov. 1976.
68. See G. Sartori, *Parties and party systems: a framework for analysis* (Cambridge University Press, 1976), ch. 6.

Abbreviations

CD	Centre démocrate
CDP	Centre démocrate et progrès
CEDEP	Centre national d'études et de promotion
CERES	Centre d'études, de recherches et d'éducation socialistes
CFDT	Confédération française démocratique du travail
CGT	Confédération générale du travail
CIR	Convention des institutions républicaines
ERIS	Association d'études de recherches et d'informations socialistes
FEN	Fédération de l'éducation nationale
FGDS	Fédération de la gauche démocrate et socialiste
FO	Force ouvrière
MRP	Mouvement républicain populaire
PCF	Parti communiste français
PDM	Progrès et démocratie moderne
PS	Parti socialiste

PSU Parti socialiste unifié
RI Républicains indépendants
RPF Rassemblement du peuple français
SFIO Parti socialiste (Section française de l'Internationale ouvrière)
UCRG Union des clubs pour le renouveau de la gauche
UDR Union des démocrates pour la République
UDSR Union démocratique et sociale de la Résistance
UDV^e Union des démocrates pour la Ve République
UGCS Union des groupes et clubs socialistes
UGSD Union de la gauche socialiste et démocrate

Table 1. Socialist votes and seats won in elections
for the National Assembly 1945-73

Election	Votes	% Electorate	% Voters	Seats
21 Oct. 45	4,491,152	18.2	23.4	146
2 June 46	4,187,747	16.9	21.1	128
10 Nov. 46	3,433,901	13.7	17.8	102
17 June 51	2,744,842	11.1	14.6	107
2 Jan. 56	3,247,431	12.1	15.2	93
23 Nov. 58	3,193,786	11.7	15.7	44
18 Nov. 62	2,319,662	8.4	12.6	65
5 Mar. 67	3,481,261	12.3	15.5	93
23 June 68	2,966,482	10.5	13.4	44
4 Mar. 73	4,515,322	15.2	19.0	89

Figures for 1967 and 1968 represent votes cast for and seats won by PS (SFIO)
and CIR candidates as part of the FGDS alliance; those for 1973 represent the
contribution of the PS to the UGSD alliance of that year. If Radical votes and
seats are included for each year the results are thus:

1967	4,277,785	15.1	19.1	116
1968	3,632,322	12.9	16.5	57
1973	4,933,967	16.6	20.8	100

(Votes recorded from 1958 onwards are those cast at the first ballot)

Table 2. Composition of Socialist electorate 1965-73*

	1965 %	1967 %	1968 %	1973 %	French electorate %
Sex					
Men	63	53	55	53	48
Women	37	47	45	47	52
Age					
21 - 34	27	30	57	31	29
35 - 49	55	27	57	31	29
50 - 64	55	27	43	22	22
65+	18	16	43	16	20
Occupation of head of household					
Farmers	15	14	18	11	12
Businessmen	6	9	9	5	6
Professional/senior managerial	4	5	3	5	9
Other white-collar workers	19	18	16	22	17
Manual workers	33	33	34	36	32
Retired/no occupation	23	21	20	21	24
Size of place					
Rural communes	34	33	41	28	30
Towns with less than 20,000 inhabitants	15	12	10	15	14
Towns with 20,000 - 100,000 inhabitants	13	17	18	17	14
Towns with more than 100,000 inhabitants	22	22	20	27	25
Paris conurbation	16	16	11	13	17

*After Sondages 1966, no. 2, pp. 13-14 and J. Charlot, *Quand la gauche peut gagner* (Alain Moreau, 1973).

Table 3. PS membership 1945-75

	No: of members (to nearest 1,000)		No: of members (to nearest 1,000)
1946	355,000	1964	88,000
1948	223,000	1966	84,000
1950	140,000	1968	81,000
1952	116,000	1970	71,000
1954	115,000	1971	80,000
1956	118,000	1972	92,000
1958	115,000	1973	108,000
1960	100,000	1974	131,000
1962	91,000	1975	150,000

Sources: C. Hurtig, *De la SFIO au nouveau parti socialiste* (Colin, 1970), and *Le Poing et la Rose* (PS bulletin)

Table 4. Ranking of issues judged 'very important' by party factions;
Grenoble Congress 1973*

	All	Mitterrand group	CERES group	ex-Mollet group	Poperen (ERIS) group
	%	%	%	%	%
Quality of big city life	71	76	70	75	59
Construction of workers' control (socialisme autogestionnaire)	56	41	86	63	47
Immigrant worker problem	56	54	66	50	47
Retirement at 60	54	59	47	50	59
Wage/salary claims	52	54	50	44	59
Abortion	43	46	42	25	38
Telephone tapping†	41	42	43	31	38
European unification	41	51	25	81	27
Farming problems	40	41	41	31	41
State aid for culture	36	37	36	44	29
Israel-Arab conflict	26	27	28	6	24

*Table adapted from R. Cayrol, 'L'univers politique des militants socialistes: une enquête sur les orientations, courants et tendances du parti socialiste', *Revue française de science politique,* vol.XXV, no.1 (Feb. 1975).
Respondents were allowed the opportunity to name more than one issue as 'very important'. It is assumed that when an issue is named as 'very important' this implies a desire for positive or ameliorative action in connection with that issue.

†A matter of topical concern at the time.

Table 5. Occupational background of Socialist deputies elected in 1973, by year of first election

	All		Before 1958	When first elected — 1958-72		1973	
	No:	%	No:	No:	%	No:	%
Farmers	4	4	—	3	8	1	3
Owners, merchants, employers, industrialists	6	7	2	3	8	1	3
Senior civil servants	9	10	2	4	11	3	7
Doctors and pharmacists	8	9	—	3	8	5	12
Lawyers	4	4	1	1	3	2	5
Journalists	3	3	—	1	3	2	5
Engineers and other professionals	3	3	1	—	—	2	5
University lecturers	5	6	—	2	6	3	7
Teachers	28	31	3	11	30	14	34
Executives	7	8	2	4	11	1	3
Minor civil servants	4	4	1	2	6	1	3
White-collar employees	7	8	—	2	6	5	12
Manual workers	—	—	—	—	—	—	—
No information	1	1	—	—	—	1	3
Total	89	98	12	36	100	41	102

Source: *Who's Who in France 1975-76* (Lafitte, 1976).

Table 6. Occupational background of Socialist deputies 1956-73

Occupations	1956 (N=93)	1958 (N=44)	1962 (N=65)	1967 (N=93)	1968 (N=44)	1973 (N=89)
	%	%	%	%	%	%
Farmers	3	—	5	4	5	4
Owners, merchants, employers, industrialists	4	2	2	6	9	7
Senior civil servants	4	4	11	10	9	10
Doctors and pharmacists	10	21	12	6	11	9
Lawyers	14	9	8	9	7	4
Journalists	7	4	5	2	—	3
Engineers and other professionals	1	7	5	3	2	3
Teachers and lecturers	33	32	28	33	30	37
Executives	5	11	6	8	7	8
Minor civil servants	10	4	9	11	14	4
White-collar employees	3	2	3	6	5	8
Manual workers	4	2	5	1	2	—
Total	98	98	99	99	101	97*

*Excluding one (1 per cent) deputy whose occupation was unknown.
Source: *Who's Who in France* (Lafitte (various editions)).

Table 7. Changing configuration of the French party system 1946-76

			Votes cast for the main parties			
	PC %	PS %	Rad %	MRP %	Ind %	Other right %
1946 (June)	26	21	11	28	13	
1956	26	15	14	11	17	16
1967	22		19	Centre 15	UDR-RI 38	
1976*	20		30	13	RI 22	UDR 15

*An assessment based on parliamentary by-elections 1974-6, and on the cantonal election results and various IFOP opinion surveys in 1976. This configuration — involving Communist stagnation/decline, PS growth and a bipolarisation of the right between Giscardian and Gaullist factions — remained to be tested at the general election due to be held by the spring of 1978.

Table 8. Results of Elections for the National Assembly: 1967-73

	% votes	% seats
1967		
PCF	22.5	15.0
PSU	2.2	0.8
FGDS	19.1	23.8
of which PS (SFIO)	15.5	18.7
Parti radical	3.6	5.1
CD	14.6	8.4
UDV[e]	31.6	41.1
RI	6.1	8.6
Divers	3.9	2.3
1968		
PCF	20.0	6.9
PSU	3.9	—
FGDS	16.5	11.7
of which PS (SFIO)	13.4	9.0
Parti radical	3.1	2.7
PDM	11.3	6.8
UDR	37.6	60.2
RI	8.3	12.5
Divers	2.4	1.9
1973		
PCF	21.4	14.9
PSU	1.9	0.2
Ext. Left	1.2	0.4
UGSD	20.8	20.6
of which PS	19.0	18.2
Rad. de gauche	1.8	2.4
Réformateurs	12.9	6.3
CDP	4.0	4.7
UDR	25.5	37.9
RI	7.1	11.1
Divers	5.2	3.9

Votes recorded are those cast at the *first* ballot, whereas the seats recorded are those awarded after *both* ballots, and indeed largely at the *second* ballot.

Table 9. Presidential Election May 1974

	Votes	%
First ballot		
François Mitterrand	11,044,373	43.25
Valéry Giscard d'Estaing	8,326,774	32.60
Jacques Chaban-Delmas	3,857,728	15.11
Jean Royer	810,540	3.17
Arlette Laguiller	595,247	2.33
René Dumont	337,800	1.32
Jean-Marie Le Pen	190,921	0.75
Emile Muller	176,279	0.69
Alain Krivine	93,990	0.37
Bertrand Renouvin	43,722	0.17
Jean-Claude Sebag	42,007	0.16
Guy Héraud	19,255	0.08
	25,538,636	100.00
Second ballot		
Valéry Giscard d'Estaing	13,396,203	50.80
François Mitterrand	12,971,604	49.20
Total	26,367,807	100.00

Further Reading

Bizot, J.F. *et al. Au parti des socialistes: plongée libre dans les courants d'un grand parti.* Grasset, 1975.

Borella, F. *Les partis politiques dans la France d'aujourd'hui.* Seuil, 1973.

Charlot, J. *Quand la gauche peut gagner.* A. Moreau, 1973.

Guidoni, P. *Histoire du nouveau parti socialiste.* Tema, 1973.

Hurtig, C. *De la SFIO au nouveau parti socialiste,* Colin, 1970.

Ligou, D. *Histoire du Socialisme en France.* P.U.F., 1962.

Mitterrand, F. *Un socialisme du possible.* Seuil, 1970.

Philip, A. *Les Socialistes.* Seuil, 1967.

Simmons, H.G. *French Socialists in search of a role.* Cornell, 1970.

Wilson, E.L. *The French Democratic Left 1963-69: Toward a Modern Party System.* Stanford, 1971.

3 SOCIAL DEMOCRACY IN ITALY

David Hine

The Scope of Italian Social Democracy

Italy provides perhaps the least fertile political terrain in Western Europe for social democracy. In the post-war period social democratic parties, however broadly defined,[1] have never received the backing of more than a fifth of the electorate, and in recent elections they have been reduced to between 13-15 per cent of the vote. The major governmental role has consistently been filled by the Christian Democratic Party (DC), while the opposition role has been increasingly dominated by the Communist Party (PCI). Whether posing as a party of government in an unequal coalition with the DC, or trying to compete with or complement the opposition of the PCI, Italian social democracy has been conspicuously unsuccessful in establishing a distinctive and independent political identity for itself.

In fact, in the light of recent changes in the Italian Communist Party, it might plausibly be argued that social democratic status could be attributed with almost as much reason to the PCI as to the socialist and social democratic parties themselves. For the PCI is today the market leader in 'Eurocommunism' — the new brand of allegedly moderate, responsible, non-dogmatic and national Communism which has emerged in the last three or four years in the Latin countries of Western Europe. On policy issues the Party could hardly serve as a better guide for social-democratic moderation. It urges self-imposed wage restraint on the trade union movement; it accepts the need for a mixed economy 'in which forms of private and public initiative co-exist together';[2] and it makes a virtue of its commitment to the values of liberty and political pluralism. On international issues the Party is increasingly critical of the Soviet political system and Soviet domination of Eastern Europe; at times it appears more pro-European than the Labour Party, and in the last couple of years has even come round to accepting Italy's presence in NATO. Finally, the Party enjoys the lion's share of the support of the Labour movement, and in electoral terms it occupies a space not substantially smaller than that of the British Labour Party (34.4 per cent in the 1976 elections, against 39.3 per cent in the British general election of October 1974).

If today we still draw back, as I shall do in this chapter, from

67

identifying social democracy with the PCI, it is due as much to the weight of the past as it is to present realities. Historically, the PCI is the inheritor of a tradition which in philosophy and method is the complete antithesis of democratic socialism. Since its creation in 1921, it has been firmly identified with the Soviet world; only in the last few years has the *via italiana* led the PCI to diverge from the Moscow line on any significant scale. It is, in fact, the very recentness of the Party's apparent conversion to the principles of liberal democracy, together with lingering doubts over the sincerity of this conversion – which a still highly centralised and undemocratic party organisation does nothing to dispel – that arguably constitutes one of the main reasons for refusing to recognise the PCI as a 'social democratic' party.[3]

The focus of this chapter will therefore follow convention and centre upon those parties which are the more obvious candidates for social democratic status, and in particular the Socialist Party (PSI). But it is not inappropriate that the chapter has begun by considering the claims of the PCI as well, for its presence has had a dominating influence on the strategy of the Socialist Party throughout the post-war period. Nor is it difficult, in the light of recent changes in Communist policies, to understand the PSI's resentment of an electorate which today seems to choose, in increasing numbers, essentially social democratic policies, without at the same time endorsing social democratic *parties*.

While it is thus important to remember that social democratic ideas may be more widespread in Italy than election results would seem to suggest, it is equally important to bear in mind that even the two social democratic parties themselves are, each in different ways, unlike equivalent parties in the United Kingdom, West Germany, or Scandinavia. To begin with, the PSI, like the French and Iberian Socialist Parties, is, at the level of ideology and party symbolism, a great deal more 'Marxist' than the SPD or the Labour Party.[4] Clearly, to a large extent this is the result of the existence of the Communist Party at the PSI's side. The PCI draws its electoral strength from the Marxist political subculture,[5] and the PSI cannot afford to weaken its chances of successfully competing with the Communists within this sector of the electorate by abandoning any pretence of an explicitly Marxist ideological framework.

The PSI also departs from Anglo-German models of Social Democracy in its relations with the Communist Party. More will be said about this in the next section, but here it should be noticed that partly because of the PSI's more explicitly Marxist ideology, it has only briefly in the post-war period sought to isolate and reject the Communists, and even then (during the mid-sixties) only incompletely.[6] In general the PSI has regarded the Communists as misguided brethren who share the same ideological purpose but who adopt mistaken and potentially dangerous means, rather than as totalitarian enemies to be opposed at any cost.

At a superficial level, the Marxist nature of the Party expresses itself in the preservation of the hammer and sickle in the Party's crest, and the ubiquity of *'compagno'* (comrade) as the form of address inside the party. But it goes deeper than mere symbolism and 'revolutionary' rhetoric, and, I would argue, has a substantive effect upon Party thinking and party behaviour. It has inhibited the PSI from putting its full weight behind an incremental approach to the building of Socialism, at times when the Party has had a foothold in power (such as during the Centre-Left governments of the sixties). The tendency to spurn compromise solutions and to see policy problems in idealistic and over-ambitious generalities, which is present to some degree in social democracy the world over, is extremely marked in the PSI. Combined with an obsession with theoretical frameworks at the expense of detail, it has led to a poverty in the Party's policy-formation process which has left it, when in Government, ill-equipped to combat the political opposition from its conservative coalition partners, and the bureaucratic opposition of the Italian public administration.[7] Such tendencies have also severely damaged Party morale, for the more ambitious and idealist the Party's aspirations (and the claims made on behalf of the Centre-Left in the early sixties were ambitious in the extreme) the greater the sense of frustration and failure when faced with the results.

While the PSI is thus more Marxist than many social democratic parties, the PSDI (Social Democrat Party) is, despite its name, a very great deal more conservative than almost all. Indeed, today it is very difficult to justify its inclusion among the parties of the 'non-Communist' Left. Its main contribution to Italian Social Democracy has been a consistent and virulent anti-Communism, which enabled it, in the immediate post-war years, to inherit the small but significant tradition of the moderate, lay (but not militantly anti-clerical) Left. This electoral foundation was gradually overlaid in the 1950s and 1960s by the middle- and lower middle-class political clienteles which the PSDI was able to build, thanks to the access to government patronage at local and national level (but especially the latter) which its strategic position in ruling coalitions gave it.[8] However, it is true to say that until the mid-1960s, while the Party was still led by Saragat, it retained a residual tie with the moderate Left, and, at least at the level of public utterances, supported the Centre-Left and the reforms which it promised.

Ironically, the period of re-unification with the Socialists, from 1966 to 1969, which should perhaps have brought the Party back into the mainstream of social democracy, had quite the opposite effect. The more militant demands made upon the Centre-Left coalition by the new Socialist Party leadership after 1968 persuaded the Social Democrats, who were already feeling themselves swamped by the numerical superiority of the Socialists, that they would lose touch entirely with their more conservative clienteles if they remained in the unified Party.[9] As a result, in 1969, the PSDI was re-established as a separate party, and thenceforth it played an increasingly conservative role, acting as spokesman for a very diverse range of interests which were opposed to the reforms then being demanded by the labour movement[10] and even more opposed to Communist participation in government. Since the end of the sixties, therefore, the PSDI can only be counted as part of Italian Social Democracy in a very nominal sense. In any case, the 1976 elections reduced the Party to a mere 3.4 per cent of the vote and fifteen seats in the Chamber; its future viability must therefore be in considerable doubt.[11]

It can thus be seen that there are considerable problems in defining the scope of Italian Social Democracy; none of the various Italian parties provides a perfect fit, although clearly the PSI is the nearest candidate. In the following sections I shall attempt to analyse how the PSI set out to deal with the complexities which arose from its peculiar position on the Italian Left, and what the results have been.

Social Democratic Strategy in a Multi-Party System

The major problem which arguably faces social democratic parties in most European societies is to secure not merely a political, but also a social and economic consensus around the values of social democracy: put briefly, the 'social-democratic dilemma'.[12] In essence, this problem may be reduced to that of reconciling the various and seemingly mutually incompatible goals of social democracy — the extension of social welfare provision, a more egalitarian distribution of income, and the creation of labour market conditions favourable to the organised working class.

Where, as in Italy, the social democratic party operates in a multi-party system, and has little immediate, or perhaps even long-term prospect of securing a parliamentary majority, nor even of dominating a governing coalition, another problem arises which logically precedes those just outlined. This is the problem of alliances: for how long, on what conditions, and above all, with which parties? It is no exaggeration to say that given Italy's traditionally low level of electoral mobility the possibility of gaining an electoral or parliamentary majority has long since disappeared from the horizons of even the most optimistic in the PSI, and that as a result the problem of political alliances has at times dominated debate in the Party to the virtual exclusion of substantive policy issues. For this reason, I shall deal largely with the political aspects of the PSI's strategy in this section, and leave until later consideration how far, in economic and social terms, social democracy is a suitable instrument for tackling the problems faced by contemporary Italy.

An intimate relationship exists between the various splits and re-unifications experienced by Italian Social Democracy and its attempts to solve the problem of alliances. The PSI's post-war history has been the tortured search for a satisfactory relationship with the two major parties of the political system which leaves it with a distinctive political identity of its own. As various alliances have been tried, so a particular wing of the party has become estranged and has broken away, or more rarely, the conditions have been created for the reconciliation and re-integration of a hitherto alienated group.

Broadly speaking, the Party has experimented with three types of alliance. The first of these has been a leftward alliance with the Communist Party: a 'socialist alternative' platform such as that established by Mitterrand and Marchais in France. In the most intense years of the Cold War, from 1947 until the mid-1950s, such an alliance was pursued by the PSI (at a time, incidentally, when French Social Democracy was vigorously anti-Communist). It led to the breakaway of Saragat's Social Democrats – the PSDI – in 1947, and also to electoral defeat in the 1948 general election.[13] Much more recently the concept of the 'socialist alternative' has again found a place in PSI thinking, but under very different conditions: with the Italian Left clearly in the ascendancy; international circumstances a great deal less tense; and the PCI offering an entirely different public image. Since the successive defeats suffered by the DC in the divorce referendum and in the 1975 regional elections, the prospect that this greater electoral volatility might allow the Left to come to power in Italy has led many in the PSI to the conclusion that the 'new' PCI should once again be courted. The *'alternativa'* lobby in the PSI in fact got so far as to have its solution espoused by the Party as its official long-term policy aim at the March 1976 PSI congress; but only at such time as the democratic development of the PCI (conceded to be well advanced) was deemed irreversible.[14]

The second type of alliance tried by the PSI has been in quite the opposite direction: an alliance towards the Centre with the Christian Democrats — the Centre-Left coalition. This policy, developed with great caution over the years from 1955 onwards — when the crisis in the international Communist movement provided the PSI with exactly the justification it needed for breaking away from its former collaboration with the Communists — came to fruition in 1963 with the entry of the Party into Government with the DC. It paved the way for a reconciliation with the moderate elements of Italian Social Democracy; various small groupings joined the Party in 1959 and 1960,[15] and eventually the PSI and PSDI merged in 1966. On the other hand, the rupture of relations with the PCI implied by the entry into Government led to the breakaway of the Party's left, which in 1964 formed the PSIUP.

In the third section the effect on both the Party as an organisation, and upon its electoral following, of the Centre-Left experience will be examined in greater detail; but suffice it to say here that in electoral terms the experience was not successful: in 1968, as may be seen from Table 1, the combined PSI-PSDI vote was 5.4 per cent down on the figure for the two parties running separately in 1963.

Disillusionment with such a performance led the Party, at the end of the 1960s, towards a third type of alliance strategy which in some ways can be considered 'consociational'.[16] The PSI abandoned its hopes of creating a dominant Social Democratic movement which, by extending its appeal over a wider area of the Italian Left, would isolate the Communists. Instead, in the wake of the massive increase in working-class unrest at the end of the decade, it strove to re-establish its links with the PCI while not actually rupturing those with the Christian Democrats. This approach had much in common with the 'Grand Coalition' of the three major parties (PCI, PSI and DC) which ruled Italy from the Liberation to 1947. It was based on a formula known as the *'equilibri piu avanzati'* ('more advanced balances'): the idea being that Communist support in parliament would push the Socialist/Christian Democratic coalition in a more advanced (i.e. more leftward) direction. The PCI itself, has, of course, been pursuing a similar objective; Berlinguer's 'historic compromise' is based on the same concept except that it envisages not merely Communist external support for a Government, but Communist participation in it.

The first consequence, as we have already seen, of the PSI's change of strategy in the late 1960s was the alienation of the Social Democrat group, and in 1969 the PSDI was re-established as a separate party.

There were few compensatory gains, however, on the Left; the rapproachement with the PCI failed to attract back to the Socialist Party in any great numbers those who in 1964 had broken away to form the PSIUP. When the latter party finally broke up in 1972 the majority of its followers went to the PCI, and only a few returned to Socialist ranks.

Socialist demands for the Communist Party to be associated with Government have become even more insistent as the seventies have progressed, but they have not been couched in entirely unambiguous terms. The great danger for the PSI is that if the Communists do actually enter Government the 'historic compromise' thus consummated between two such giants as the PCI and the DC would leave precious little room in the bed for third parties. For the great difference between the PSI's first pursuit of a 'consociational' strategy — during the years from 1944 to 1947 — and its more recent attempts, is that *then* the PSI was one of the three mass parties (in 1946 it got over 20 per cent of the votes to the PCI's 18.9 per cent), while today it is dwarfed by the Communist Party. The latter already has a great deal more influence over government policies than the Socialist Party.

Indeed, in many ways the 'historic compromise' has already come about. Even before last June's election the economic strength wielded by the PCI, as a result of its control over the trade union movement, put the Party in a very powerful position indeed. And since the election the Party's parliamentary position has been much enhanced. As long as the PSI sticks by its current demand that Government policies be discussed with and be acceptable to the PCI as well as itself, then no Government can be formed against the will of the Communists.[17] But herein lies the great difficulty for the PSI. If it pursues the 'consociational' strategy, the logical conclusion is Communist participation in Government, which would leave little room (inside the Government at least) for the Party. But to abandon such a strategy in favour of a Socialist 'alternative' alliance, with the Communists alone, is not possible either; the PSI itself is not yet ready to admit that the PCI is completely 'democratic', and many of its more moderate supporters would be frightened by such a step. More importantly, the PCI itself rejects the proposal — still pursuing its own 'consociational' strategy: the 'historic compromise'. There would thus be a considerable danger of a Communist-Christian Democrat administration coming about against the will of the PSI, and without its participation.[18]

The PSI's solution to this dilemma — an exquisitely *political* dilemma — is to try to walk a delicate tightrope between two different strategies, the 'alternative' and the 'consociational', while committing itself to neither. Thus the Party, as was pointed out above, has accepted the former strategy as its long-term goal, while in the meantime pursuing a version of the latter strategy, but one which does not exclude a role for itself, because it appears to stop short of full Communist participation in Government.

The Consequences: Dimension of Party Support

Judging from the results of the 1976 general election, however, the policy has not yielded dividends. Under circumstances favouring an advance of the Left as a whole, the PSI's vote remained stagnant at 9.6 per cent while the PCI surged forward to over 34 per cent. The PSI's figure was identical to its showing in the 1972 election, which was held in circumstances decidedly *un*favourable to the Italian Left. The inescapable conclusion was that in the four intervening years the Party had lost ground seriously.[19] The problem was precisely that by identifying too closely with the Communists (refusing to support future Left-wing governments unless they also enjoyed the support of the Communists) the PSI convinced many voters that if the two parties were going to work together closely anyway, and if the PCI really had changed sufficiently for the PSI to now find it a respectable coalition partner, then it made more sense to vote for the Communists – a 'serious' and uncompromised party – than for a small party like the PSI which was so demoralised and compromised by its years in power as to be no longer politically credible.

The Socialist Party, then, despite its years of 'autonomy' from the PCI during the sixties (or perhaps paradoxically, as we shall see in a moment, *because* of it) has once again suffered from being too closely identified with the Communist Party. Unable to isolate and defeat the PCI, it has fallen victim to the latter's moral ascendancy over the whole Italian Left. Its failure to create a strong independent Social Democratic force in the 1960s has left it with an unwanted legacy: the inability to undertake any political initiative of its own without first ensuring that it is 'covered' on its left from the criticism of the PCI, and that the initiative has, at the very least, the benevolent neutrality of the larger party. And this, of course, stems from the structural and organisational consequences which the PSI's participation in Government has had, as well as the purely electoral consequences.

The years since the early sixties have had a profound effect upon the PSI's organisational strength. The Party is based on individual (i.e. direct) membership, and was reconstituted on a highly centralised basis by Morandi in the years after the 1947 split. It never matched the size or efficiency of the PCI's organisation, but nevertheless by the mid-fifties it had re-established for itself a national network of some 450-500,000 predominantly working-class members, based, for the most part in the North (especially the industrial triangle) and the Red Belt regions of central Italy.[20]

However, from the 1957 Congress of Venice organised factions emerged, divided over the question of the Party's relationship with the PCI and the DC, and this internal conflict had a damaging effect both on party organisation, which was all but ignored except in so far as members were enrolled to support one or other faction, and on party morale. The split in 1964, which resulted in the creation of the PSIUP, took away a significant number of Party members, as may be seen from Table 2, but its effects were even more serious in qualitative than in quantitative terms; it took away a large proportion of the Party's more militant activists, especially in the Red Belt regions, and of its middle-level (i.e. provincial) leadership, and it cost the Party very dearly in terms of its followers in the CGIL — the Communist trade union confederation.[21]

Factionalism, however, did not end with the 1964 secession of the Party's left. Instead, over the following years it increased quite dramatically, especially during and after the years in which the PSI was re-united with the PSDI, from 1966 to 1969. And unlike the previous, left-right, division in the Party, the cleavages which developed in the middle and late sixties were no longer about ideology; they were now, in the main, purely personal struggles for power and influence in the Party. They were battles for preference votes in local government and national elections, for control of the party organisation, and the PSI's share in the patronage which it obtained through participation in Government.[22]

These developments changed the whole shape of the Party. The concept of collective leadership, and of a unified direction to Party policy, disappeared entirely. While in the early fifties the PSI had been very similar in structure to the Communist Party, by the later sixties, at least in terms of the behaviour of Party activists, officials and leaders, it was far more like the DC.

The geographical and social composition of the PSI's membership also came increasingly to resemble that of the DC. By the early seventies, at least half the members were southerners, and the South is an area in which Party membership is traditionally based upon clientelistic methods of enrolment. The high turnover rates in membership emphasise this characteristic. In 1972 (a congress year, when individual leaders are particularly anxious to enhance their following among the party rank and file so as to enhance their power in the Party) membership rose to at least 575,000, and according to one estimate a great deal more.[23] The following year membership fell by over 100,000 (see Table 2). There has also been a significant shift in the social composition of the PSI's membership. From Table 3 it may be seen that the industrial and agricultural working class (blue-collar workers) constituted just under a third of the total membership in 1973, and this compares with estimates of nearly a half for the fifties and early sixties. As the report prepared by the Party for its 1975 Conference on Party Organisation put it:

> The process of geographical dislocation of the Party membership from the North to the South has in fact brought about a profound change in the social composition of the Party. The traditional working-class character of the PSI has become ever weaker, with the progressive loss of support among the working-class groups of the North and Red Belt area, and the entry into the party, in the Southern regions, of social groups which have traditionally been in a minority in the social composition of our party: white-collar groups, professional classes, small farmers, artisans and shop-keepers, and especially the non-active (housewives and pensioners).[24]

A further indication of the extent of the change in the Party's structure brought about by the Centre-Left is to be found in the new role played by the NAS (*Nuclei Aziendali Socialisti* or Socialist Factory Cells). Originally, these were bodies established to ensure a workplace presence for the Party, and to keep it in touch with the organised working class. By the early sixties they had largely shown themselves to have failed in this task; Landolfi estimates that there were probably little more than 1,000 in existence.[25] But they did not disappear. Instead, as a result of the Party's entry into Government, their role changed. They became concentrated in the state sector — in the civil service, and other administrative bodies, in local government and municipal corporations, in the health service and public enterprise of various sorts: anywhere, in fact, where the PSI had a share in the administration of the organisation in question, and in the patronage it offered.[26] The NAS became, like the *sezioni* (the ward organisations — the basic units of the Party) the battleground for the internecine factionalism which has racked the Party over the last ten years.

Participation in Government has therefore weakened the PSI's capacity to maintain contact with the working class, and to respond to the PCI's increasing dominance of the Italian Left. The Party's public image has suffered irrevocable damage from the years of collaboration with the Christian Democrats. It has not merely been shown to be incapable of pushing the coalition in a progressive direction (economic planning floundered from the start, and a host of other reforms have failed to materialise – not the least of which the long overdue reform of Italy's elephantine and hopelessly inefficient public administration). It has also given the impression of being heavily involved in the less savoury side of party life in Italy – graft, the systematic exploitation of patronage for party and indeed personal ends, and so on. And the development of highly articulated factions vying for position, and power, but no particular principle, has re-inforced the public impression that the PSI has become more and more like the Christian Democrat Party.

Since the early seventies the Party has tried hard to rectify this image, and the rapprochement with the Communists forms part of an attempt to reassert traditional Socialist values, and in particular the class basis of the Party. Particularly since the 1972 election, there has been a painful process of self-examination taking place, as the pages of *Mondo Operaio,* the Party's theoretical monthly, confirm. But the constant pious hopes that the factionalism may come to an end, and that the Party will then rediscover its vocation, have come to nothing. After the disappointment of the 1976 election result, the factions were officially declared 'dissolved' at a traumatic meeting of the Party's Central Committee, but as an official of the Party remarked to the author rather wryly, '*Ci sono ancora le amicizie*' (The friendships remain').

The Relevance of Italian Social Democracy

In the light of these facts it is not difficult to understand why, at the moment of the greatest popular demand for political, economic and social change since the Liberation, it should have been the Communist Party and not the Socialist Party which reaped the impetus and the electoral benefit. Voters in the June 1976 elections regarded with profound suspicion a party which, having blamed the failures of successive Governments in which it participated on circumstances beyond its control (and in particular upon the opposition of the DC), should now be proposing a different policy, the Socialist Alternative, which once again seemed to depend upon circumstances beyond the

Party's control. For the whole force of the Party's professed desire for
an eventual alliance solely between the two parties of the Left, was that
it would only come about when the PCI's democratic maturity was
beyond doubt. In the meantime the suspicion remained that in the
absence of suitable changes in the PCI, the Socialists might, as in the
past, be tempted back into a Centre-Left coalition which would do no
more than its predecessors.[27] And to the extent that, in the PSI's view,
to prevent this happening the Communists must be allowed to
contribute — externally if necessary — to a Centre-Left coalition, this
was an acknowledgement that what really counted was not the
contribution of the Socialists but that of the Communists. The whole
point, therefore, of distinguishing itself from the PCI by claiming
better democratic credentials was neutralised by the PSI's insistence
on the key role of the PCI. The electorate might have been willing to
write a blank cheque to a party whose public credibility was less
compromised than that of the PSI, but for the latter to claim a
'guarantor' role in the party system after a long record of self-confessed
failure was stretching the gullibility of even the Italian electorate.

At the level of electoral and trade union support, therefore, orthodox
social democracy has been conspicuously unsuccessful in recent years.
But at the level of ideas the judgement should not, perhaps, be
entirely unequivocal. For it may be argued that it is substantially
through the contribution of the PSI that the Communist Party has — *if*
it has — been gradually re-integrated into Italian political life. In other
words, the PSI's rapprochement with the Communists after 1969 gave
the Communist Party's self-professed desire for a share in responsible
goverment the credibility which it previously lacked. That someone
was trying to unlock the door on which the PCI was knocking, even if it
was not yet open, seems to have encouraged and strengthened those
elements in the Communist Party which were in favour of the moderate
strategy.

Where, then, does this leave the PSI, and — since the two are clearly
no longer identical — what does it mean for Italian Social Democracy?
As far as the Party is concerned, it seems likely that the maxim of
'politique d'abord' will continue to be paramount, if only because
where the leadership of any Italian party is concerned, the survival of
the Party as an organisation takes precedence over the pursuit of the
Party's goals, if and where the two collide. For this reason alone, despite
the PSI's recognition that the *'area Socialista'* in Italy is now vastly
greater than the area occupied by the PSI, it seems improbable,
especially after De Martino's replacement as Party Secretary by the

allegedly more moderate Bettino Craxi,[28] that for a while at least the two parties will take any further steps toward collaboration. Indeed, the first edition of *Mondo Operaio* after the election (*La Questione Socialista dopo il 20 guigno*),[29] after acknowledging that partly through the PSI's own tactics the election had turned into a referendum for or against the Communist Party, went on to stress the great differences between the democratic nature of the PSI and the rigid and centralised structure of the Communist Party, and to criticise most bitterly the historic compromise, which was based on a 'totalitarian' view of the Italian political system, and the PCI's role in it.

This criticism of the Communist Party may well grow in the future, as the PSI tries to win over certain voters — especially in the trade unions — who are unhappy about the restraint which the PCI is urging, where it is not imposing, upon the trade union movement, in order to display its moderation and responsibility, and to impress upon the Government that it is an indispensable element in maintaining social and industrial peace. The temptation for the PSI to do this — to try to outflank the PCI on its 'Left', by demanding union autonomy and free collective bargaining — will be very great indeed.

This, of course, raises the thorny issue of the extent to which orthodox social democracy has any relevance to the problems of contemporary Italy. For there can be little doubt that the real problems are economic and social, even more than they are political; yet it is the political issues which substantially exercise the PSI. It is by no means clear that it has any distinctive solution to the economic issues. All parties proclaim the need to expand the productive base of the economy, and to channel resources in this direction and away from what is universally regarded as Italy's large and politically subsidised parasitic sectors. But there is no suggestion that any of the parties is yet prepared to incur the unpopularity that this would bring among those hardest hit by such a change. Nor does any of them have any clear idea of how to maintain social stability while engaging in such a policy. The PCI's 'historic compromise' is probably the most constructive solution in this area, but even this is fraught with problems.

Equally, if any of the values of social democracy are to be translated into practice in Italy — the expansion of social welfare (housing, education and health) and a further redistribution of income in favour, not of the prosperous organised section of the working class, but of the unemployed and the very large sector of low-paid workers in insecure jobs — then the support of the bulk of the trade union movement has to be obtained. For such measures require real sacrifices of present consumption — either through income transfers to others, or to social and productive investment. Once again it must be conceded that there is little likelihood that the PSI possesses the moral or political authority to obtain a consensus of this type, and indeed short-term political considerations may induce the party to work in quite the opposite direction by opposing the one party — the PCI — which may perhaps have this authority. The conclusion must therefore be that in policy terms, as well as in electoral terms, orthodox social democracy is today a marginal force in Italian society, and that despite all its political ambiguities, the future of social democratic values may well lie far more with the Communist Party than with the Socialists.

Notes

1. The nature of both the PSI (*Partito Socialista Italiano* — Italian Socialist Party — and the PSDI (*Partito Socialista Democratico Italiano* — Italian Social Democrat Party) and the extent to which each can be defined as social democratic are discussed in the first section of the chapter. For reasons of space the PSIUP (Socialist Party of Proletarian Unity), which broke away from the PSI in 1964, and survived for eight years until the elections of 1972, is not dealt with here. For a brief note on it see the present author's 'Italian Socialism and the Centre-Left Coalition: Strategy or Tactics?' *Journal of Common Market Studies,* vol. XIII (1975), no. 4, pp. 440-1.
2. Alfredo Reichlin, *Rinascita,* 25 July 1975, p. 1. See also the leading article by the PCI's chief economist, Eugenio Peggio, in *L'Unita,* 29 Apr. 1976.
3. It is arguably doubtful that the ideological traditions of fifty years can be swept away by the public utterances of the party leadership (not necessarily shared by the rank and file, but accepted because of the demands of party discipline) over a mere five.
4. Article 1 of the PSI Constitution states that Marxism is 'fundamental' to the party's doctrine. It also goes on to state that ' . . . The Party aims to create a society liberated from the contradictions and coercions deriving from the division into classes produced by the capitalist system . . . ' (*Statuto,* S.E.T.I., Roma, 1973, p. 3.)
5. For those interested in the electoral basis of the Italian Left and in the concept of the Marxist political subculture, the fundamental work is G. Galli *et al.* (ed.), *Il Comportamento Elettorale in Italia* (Bologna, Il Mulino, 1968). The results are summarised in English in G. Galli and A. Prandi, *Patterns of Political Participation in Italy* (Yale, New Haven, 1970).
6. Although alliances with the PCI were broken in many of the local governments in the Red Belt regions the rupture was never complete. Even if Nenni sought to make it so the then Party Secretary, De Martino ensured that it was not. At trade union level, although there was talk of creating an entirely Socialist trade union confederation, presumably based on the UIL, this never came about and most Socialist trade union members remained in the Communist-Socialist CGIL throughout the sixties. See D.L.M. Blackmer, *Unity in Diversity: Italian Communism and the Communist World* (MIT Press, Cambridge, Mass., 1968), pp. 266-76.
7. Probably the two clearest examples of this are to be found in the PSI's

formulation of economic planning policy in the period 1962-4 (at a time when economic planning was increasingly popular among a number of Western European social democratic parties) and in the extremely ambitious approach which the party had to the control of town planning, urban building and housing programmes. Antonio Giolitti, the PSI's chief authority on economic policy, and Minister of the Budget and Planning in several Centre-Left Governments, has conceded that the overtly ideological terms in which both these policies were conceived acted as a barrier to detailed policy formulation which might have led the party to less ambitious but more successful approaches. A. Giolitti, interview with author, 16 Sept. 1976. See also G. Tamburrano, *Storia e Cronaca del Centro Sinistra* (Feltrinelli, Milan, 1971), pp. 276-8. Giolitti also pointed out that the PSI's aversion to anything that smacked even remotely of an incomes policy, and hence a restriction on the power of organised labour, was a major barrier to the successful implementation of the planning mechanism.

8. See, *inter alia*, P.A. Allum, *Politics and Society in Postwar Naples* (Cambridge UP, London, 1973), pp. 157-8 and 239-40.

9. For a fuller discussion of this question see my 'Italian Socialism and the Centre-Left Coalition', pp. 449-50, and F. Rizzi, 'Dall Unificazione alla Scissione Socialista', *Rivista Italiana di Scienza Politica*, no. 2, 1973.

10. On the consequences of and demands thrown up by the increase in labour militancy at the end of the sixties see the present author's 'The Labour Movement and Communism in France and Italy', in Martin Kolinsky and William E. Paterson (eds.), *Social and Political Movements in Western Europe* (Croom Helm, London, 1976).

11. The fall in the PSDI's share of the vote from 5.1 per cent to 3.4 per cent is an indication of the fundamentally conservative nature of much of the party's former electorate. The DC, which prior to the elections was under fire from all quarters and widely expected to fare very badly indeed, managed in the event to hold its support steady, while the smaller parties, Liberals and Social Democrats, were the ones who lost. The general interpretation put on this, supported by the direction in which the DC campaign was aimed was that while the latter party lost many progressive voters to the PCI, especially among the working class, it gained from the smaller centre parties, whose electors, in the last analysis, recognised that the DC was a better defence against the Left and the reforms it might introduce, than any of the smaller parties.

12. For a perceptive and stimulating discussion of the 'social democratic dilemma' as it applies to Britain (though the argument is applicable to any industrial society in which the power of organised trade unionism is increasing) see Peter Jenkins, 'The Social Democratic Dilemma', *New Statesman*, 20 Sept. 1974, pp. 373-8.

13. In the 1948 election the PSI ran joint lists of candidates with the PCI, and was heavily defeated as a result. Not only did the joint list obtain only 31 per cent of the vote, but the Communist voters, with superior discipline, concentrated their preferences on a few party leaders in each constituency, and thus were able to elect far more deputies and senators than the PSI.

14. De Martino, leader of the largest faction within the PSI, and Party Secretary since the 1972 Congress, emerged from the PSI's 40th (1976) Congress with a resounding vote of confidence in his leadership. Party morale and party expectations for the forthcoming general elections (based on the PSI's showing in local and regional elections in 1975) were high, and, capitalising on this, De Martino was able to win the approval of the Congress for a formula which recognised the legitimacy and desirability of the *'alternativa socialista'*, but

left the party leadership free to determine when conditions were ripe for such an enterprise. The 'conditions' were basically twofold: firstly, the balance of forces on the Left was to be 're-equilibrated' (i.e. the PSI had to gain in strength relative to the PCI) and secondly, the PCI had to give further proof of its new approach to 'proletarian internationalism' (i.e. it had to move yet further away from Moscow, and give a greater commitment still to pluralist democracy). The electoral tactic involved in this formula was the attempt to persuade those voters frustrated with Christian-Democrat government, and who sought change and reform, but who were still apprehensive about voting PCI, to support the Socialists as 'guarantors' of democratic stability.

15. Among the most important of these were the *MUIS* (Italian Movement for Socialist Unity) and *Unità Popolare* (Popular Unity). See A. Benzoni, *Il Socialismo Italiano nel Dopoguerra* (Marsilio, Padova, 1968), pp.88-101.

16. See, *inter alia*, the article by A. Lijphart, 'Consociational Democracy', *World Politics*, XXI (1969), pp. 207-25. The chief characteristic of consociational democracy, according to Lijphart's classification, is the ability of leaders of different sub-cultures in a culturally fragmented society to join together in government to stabilise an otherwise insoluble problem of obtaining consent.

17. On the problems of coalition building after the 1976 general election see David Hine, 'Italian Compromises: Historical and Necessary', *Contemporary Review*, vol. 229, no. 1329 (Oct. 1976), pp. 182-8.

18. The 'historic compromise' is now so well known and discussed that there is little need to explain it. For those interested in its original formulation, see the articles by Enrico Berlinguer, *Rinascita*, 28 Sept., 5 and 12 Oct. 1973.

19. See Sisinio Zito, 'Per il Rinnovamento del PSI', *Mondo Operaio*, 7/8 (July/Aug. 1976), pp. 20-3.

20. The details of party organisation contained in the following paragraphs come from my own research on the structure of the PSI in the years from 1962-72, as yet unpublished, and shortly to be submitted as a thesis for the degree of D. Phil. in the University of Oxford. A summary of party membership trends can be found in a document prepared by the Organisation Office of the PSI for the party's 1975 Conference on Organisation (Florence, 6-9 Feb. 1975): 'Base Sociale e Strutture del Partito', *Quaderni della Sezione Centrale di Organizzazione*, No. 1, (SETI, Roma, 1975). See especially pp. vi to xi. I should like to express my thanks to the Organisation Office for the help given to me over several research visits to Rome.

21. See A. Benzoni, 'Il Socialismo Italiano Nel Dopoguerra', pp. 177-80.

22. See, *inter alia*, G. Tamburrano, 'Autonomia del partito e lottizzazione del potere', *Mondo Operaio* (May 1975), pp.78-82.

23. See note 1, Table 2.

24. 'Base Sociale e Strutture del Partito', op.cit. pp.vii-viii.

25. A. Landolfi, 'Il Socialismo Italiano', ed. Lerici (Rome, 1968), pp. 141-5.

26. PSI, 'Documenti PSI; Proposte per la riforma dello statuto del partito' (Roma, SETI, 1971), pp. 3-4. Of 157 NAS attached to the Rome Federation of the PSI, at least 123 were in the public sector.

27. Zito, 'Per il Rinnovamento', p.20.

28. Craxi was a close supporter of Nenni, and was regarded as his successor as leader of the Autonomist wing of the party. His appointment as Secretary was widely regarded as have been engineered by Giacomo Mancini, De Martino's great rival during the late Sixties and the Seventies. See my 'Italian Socialism and the Centre-Left Coalition', pp.446-50.

29. *Mondo Operaio*, 7/8 (July/Aug. 1976) pp.2-4.

Table 1. Electoral support: Chamber of Deputies 1953-76

	1953		1958		1963		1968		1972		1976	
	%	Seats	%	Seats	%	Seats	%	Seats	%	Seats	%	Seats
PSI	12.9	75	14.2	84	13.8	87	} 14.5	} 91	9.6	61	9.6	57
PSDI	4.5	19	4.5	22	6.1	33	}	}	5.1	29	3.4	15
PSIUP	—						4.5	23	1.9	—		
'Non-Communist Left'	17.3		18.7		19.9		19.0		16.6		13.0	
PCI	22.6		22.7		25.3		26.9		27.2		34.4	
Total 'Left' vote	39.9		41.4		45.2		45.9		43.8		47.4	

Table 2. PSI membership 1961-73*

	Total Membership	Percentage Distribution		
		North	Centre	South
1961	465,000	45	22	33
1963	491,000	42	22	35
1965	437,000	37	21	42
1967	633,000	37	21	42
1970	537,000	33	17	50
1972	575,000	38	18	44
1973	463,000†	43	19	38

*These are the official figures provided by the PSI's *Sezione Centrale di Organizzazione,* and come from 'Il Partito Socialista, Struttura e Organizzazione', *Quaderni della Sezione Centrale di Organizzazione,* No. 5 (Marsilio Ed., Venezia, 1975), p. 326. They provide an approximation of the membership returns from the provinces to the National Party Offices in Rome, but the latter cannot easily check their accuracy. Individual federations inflate membership, particularly in Congress years (e.g. 1972) to increase their relative strength. Benzoni estimates that the 1972 figures returned to Rome, before the latter 'adjusted' it downwards, was actually 654,000! (A. Benzoni, 'L'Organizzazione Socialista Dopo Morandi', *Mondo Operaio,* no. 7, 1974, p. 25.)

†Because of severe factional conflict in the two provinces of Cosenza and Pescara, the figures for 1973 do not include these two federations (approximately 18,000 in previous years).

Table 3. Social composition of PSI membership 1973

Professional/managerial groups	1.5%
White collar/teachers	12.5%
Shopkeepers/artisans	8.7%
Small farmers/share croppers	7.1%
Blue-collar workers	32.1%
Apprentices/students	1.5%
Pensioners	8.3%
Housewives	10.0%
Others	8.3%

Source: 'Il Partito Socialista', p. 331.

Further Reading

Very little of value has been written on either the PSI or PSDI in English. Among the few works, the following are worthy of note:

Barnes, S.H. *Party Democracy. Politics in an Italian Socialist Federation.* Yale, New Haven, 1967.

Hine, David 'The Italian Socialist Party and the Centre-Left Coalition: Strategy or Tactics?' *Journal of Common Market Studies.* Vol. XIII. June 1975.

Stern, A.J. *et. al* 'Factions and Opinion Groups in European Mass Parties: Some Evidence from a Study of Italian Militant Socialists.' *Comparative Politics.* Vol. III. July 1971.

Zariski, Raphael 'The Italian Socialist Party: A Case Study in Factional Conflict.' *American Political Science Review.* Vol. LVI. June 1962.

For readers of Italian:

Averardi, G. *I Socialisti Democratici.* Edizioni di 'Corrispondenza Socialista', Rome, 1971.

Benzoni, A. and Tedesco, V. *Il Movimento Socialista nel Dopoguerra.* Marsilio, Padova, 1968.

Cazzola, F. *Il Partito Come Organizzazione: Studio di un Caso, Il PSI.* Tritone, Rome, 1969.

4 SOCIAL REVOLUTION AND DEMOCRACY IN IBERIA

Jonathan Story

This essay on social democracy in Iberia uses Karl Kautsky's distinction between revolution and reform.

> Measures which seek to adjust the juridical and political superstructure of society to changed economic conditions are reforms if they proceed from the class which is the political and economic ruler of society. They are reforms whether they are given freely or secured by the pressure of the subject class or conquered through the power of circumstance. On the contrary, those measures are the result of revolution if they proceed from the class which has been economically and politically oppressed, has now captured political power and must in its own interest more or less rapidly transform the political and juridical superstructure and create new forms of social cooperation.[1]

But, he adds in *The Social Revolution,*

> . . . anyone is a revolutionist who seeks to conquer the political power for a hitherto oppressed class and he does not lose this character if he prepares and hastens this conquest by social reforms wrested from the ruling classes. It is not the striving after social reforms but the explicit confining oneself to them that distinguishes the social reformer from the social revolutionist.

The value of Kautsky's definition is that it avoids the contentious problem of labelling one or other political party, personality or movement as 'social democratic'. In the case of Iberia, this renders a valuable service, given the wide spectrum of candidates. Obviously, the Portuguese Communist Party (PCP),* with its adherence to Lenin's principle of the revolutionary élite and Stalin's method of democratic centralism, is not a candidate. But the Spanish Communist Party (PCE), with its advocacy of political parties and parliamentary liberties, may

*A list of abbreviations is given at the end of this chapter, on p.99.

be one. Secretary-General Santiago Carillo appears on better terms with Dr Mário Soares, leader of the Portuguese Socialist Party (PSP) than with his colleague, Secretary-General Cunhal of the PCP. The PCE has joined a Platform of Coordination, with the Spanish Socialist Worker's Party (PSOE), minus a number of groups which call themselves 'Social Democratic'. Similarly, Soares as Prime Minister has excluded from governmental responsibility the Popular Democratic Party (PPD) of Sá Carneiro, and the Democratic and Social Centre. The PPD has described its policies of a mixed economy membership, in NATO and in the EEC, and in defence of private property as 'Social Democratic'. The Democratic Centre by the 1976 elections had altered the positioning of Social from descriptive of Centre to qualifying Democratic.

The value of Kautsky's definition is even greater in the case of Spain than of Portugal, due to the political fragmentation of parties over the forty years of Franco's autocracy and the search for unity since his death on 20 November 1975. Thus, as the regime eroded slowly over the 1960s and early 1970s, members of the Falange or of the state syndicates sought ways of converting the régime to some form of Social Democracy on the Western European pattern. Cantarero Castillo, in his book *Falange and Socialism,* published in 1973, declared the urgency of 'redirecting the social ideology of Falangism towards a democratic overture and its theoretical revolutionism towards a practical, realist and daily reformism'.[2] He had been preceded in that path by Dionisio Ridruejo who founded the Social Democratic Union now led by García López under the name of the Spanish Social Democratic Union (USDE). Well outside the regime's ranks of semi-dissidents is one of the longest standing proponents of Western Socialism, Professor Tierno Galván, leader of the small but influential Popular Socialist Party (PSP). In size and financial support, the PSP is overshadowed by the PSOE whose secretary-general is the Andalusian lawyer, Felipe González. The PSOE is allied with a variety of regional parties and to two trade unions, the General Union of Workers (UGT) and the Workers Sindical Union (USO). Both PSP and PSOE are members of the Convergence, together with Christian Democrats, Carlists, various Maoists and the PCE.

Furthermore, the upheaval in Iberia over the past two or three years has been accompanied by a torrent of talking. Socialism is a word with a multitude of meanings from the participation of the Carlist leader, Prince Charles Hugo de Borbón, through the statism of Cunhal or the political pluralism of Soares to the revolutionary action of Maoists. Not surprisingly, Social Democracy is a label both shunned and courted. It is shunned as smacking of compromise with the existing social or international order, whereas the Iberian experience for Socialists is more one of resistance. On the other hand, the label of Social Democracy is courted as non-Marxist or as moderate in word and deed compared to the intransigence of Fascism and Communism. Whatever the meaning attached to the word though, those subscribing to some branch of the broader Socialist movement in Spain and Portugal have been precipitated into action since 1974.

In other words, Kautsky's definition allows for a discussion of a situation rather than of an identity. In Iberia, there is no party which neatly corresponds to West Germany's Social Democrats, but rather there is a seeking for political power by people formerly excluded, and a series of concessions by ruling classes either to preserve as much as possible of what has to be shared, or to rewin eventually what has been abandoned under duress. Thus, in the case of Spain, King Juan Carlos intends to modernise rather than liquidate the state cobbled together by Franco over the forty years of his autocracy. The King's action represents a political response to changed economic and social conditions after the industrialisation of the past years; in this sense, he is a reformer. Yet the far-reaching changes demanded of the regime by the Spanish opposition may place them in the category of Kautsky's revolutionaries. The Spanish opposition offers to co-operate in an eventual stabilisation of the Spanish economy in return for political concessions and an equal sharing of burdens. In Portugal, the situation is reversed: the new constitution is installed, but Premier Soares is imposing a stabilisation plan, returning expropriated land, and attempting to oust Communists from the single union, the InterSindical. In other words, concessions have still to be won in Spain whereas victories are being defended or reversed in Portugal.

However divergent the timing of revolution between Portugal and Spain, one overriding factor has conditioned developments in both countries. Both Iberian economies are integrated into the global economy, over which they exercise marginal influence but that exercises maximum influence over them. Thus, the conquest of state power by the Spanish and Portuguese Socialist movements may prove an empty victory, if that power has to be exercised according to the rules of the international economic system, rather than in response to the demands of domestic populations.

To trace what has happened, how and with whom, this essay will deal with the reform movements of Portugal and Spain separately. This means an account of the past, the main actors, their rivalries and their programmes, as well as a brief discussion of the economic and social problems which they face. For reasons of space, little room can be given to the complex involvement of external interests and powers in the process of Iberia's transformation from autocracy of one sort to autocracy of another.

Portugal and Social Democracy

Reform of the corporate state, an end to economic stagnation, and self-determination for the African possessions constituted the main themes of the opposition leader, General Delgado, in his candidacy for Portugal's Presidency in 1958. The themes recurred in increasingly radical guise over the following seventeen years. They were incorporated in the 1961 Programme for the Democratisation of the Republic, and in the platform of the Democratic Social Action set up in 1963. But a split ensued in this organisation over relations with the PCP. Soares founded the Portuguese Socialist Action (ASP) with a view to forming a common front, while the Social Democrats hoped forlornly that the regime was able to reform from within. Sá Carneiro became a deputy to the National Assembly but was soon disappointed by the inability or unwillingness of Caetano to reverse the regime's policies.

Schism recurred among Portugal's Socialists following the Soviet invasion of Czechoslovakia and the PCP's endorsement of Moscow's action. At the Congress of Averro in 1969, Soares' ASP, which favoured a common front for the forthcoming elections to the National Assembly, stated that 'the socialism for which the ASP struggles differs as much from (Western European) social democracy as the totalitarianism of the popular democracies. ASP struggles for a socialism in freedom'.[3] Subsequently, Soares founded the Electoral Commission of Democratic Unity which won 2 per cent of the restricted votes cast. The PCP supported the rival opposition group which won 10 per cent of the vote. Soares nonetheless was invited as Portuguese delegate to the Socialist International and in 1972 founded the Portuguese Socialist Party (PS) with the support of the West German Social Democrats.

Modifications in PCP tactics in the early 1970s, and the continued need for co-operation among opposition groups led to the sinking of PCP and PSP rivalries in 1973, and to their agreeing on common candidates to the 1973 elections for the National Assembly. But the regime's overthrow was the work of the officer corps, aroused by the futility of the African wars and by the country's social and economic inadequacies. Thus, while the programme of the Armed Forces Movement included all the themes for which Portugal's Socialists had struggled, it also stated the armed forces' claim to be the revolution's ultimate source of legitimacy as representing 'the aspirations and interests of a vast majority of the Portuguese people'[4] in the overthrow of the Caetano regime. Therein lay the struggle for power between rival factions with distinct definitions of legitimacy and of the role of the state in a modern society. Preoccupation with the struggle deflected all contenders[5] — General António de Spínola's followers, the Communists, the radical praetorians and the Socialists — from concentrating their attention on the equally burning issue of economic policy.

In the first government of Spínola, elected President of the Junta of National Salvation by the Armed Forces Movement, the PSP had three ministries — including the crucial Ministry of Information — and the PPD were given the Ministry of Interior. Sa Carneiro was minister without portfolio and attached to the Prime Minister, Palma Carlos. The PCP, however, held the Ministry of Labour, where its policy at first was to resist strike pressures for fear of playing into the hands of 'reaction'. But Spínola's attempt to establish a Presidential régime, to delay decolonisation in Africa, and to curb the liberty of the Press and the right to strike, alienated both the PSP and the PCP. Premier Palma Carlos' proposals for presidential elections in October and a postponement of general elections to the Constituent Assembly until 1976 were rejected by the AFM, but also by the PSP and the PCP. There followed the nomination of the pro-Communist Vasco Gonçalves as Premier, and of Major Otelo de Carvalho as Commander of the Operational Command of the Continent (COPCON). Portugal lurched rapidly towards revolutionary conditions with each major political force contending for the ear of a population depoliticised over the years of the Salazar and Caetano régimes.

In this turmoil, the Socialists were precipitated into rivalry with the PCP over African policy and domestic liberties. Once Spinola had resigned as President in September 1974, the PCP pressed its advantage of superior organisation, consolidated in the clandestine labour movement during the years of opposition. Communist cadres penetrated the local authorities and central administration. Sympathisers surfaced in radio, press and television while the 5th Division of the General Staff served as an effective propaganda instrument. Spínola's supporters were purged, businessmen were imprisoned and civil servants dismissed. By contrast, Soares as Foreign Minister and Sá Carneiro as leader of the PPD nailed their flags firmly to the mast of a liberal constitution. Appeals were made for Western financial support,[6] and an economic plan proposing a reorganisation of Portugal's industrial structures and an open door to foreign investors was drawn up.

The Communist bid for power gathered force in December 1974 and during the first half of 1975. Power-sharing with other parties in the civilian government was mitigated by penetration of the AFM, embellished with its own Supreme Council of the Revolution and a General Assembly of officers, non-commissioned officers and ranks. Against both the PPD and the PSP, the AFM, with Communist support, pushed through a single labour union — the InterSindical. Nationalisation of the monopolies and credit institutions followed, along with a revoking of the existing economic plan. The PSP and the PPD were invited early in April 1975 to sign a Platform of Agreement codifying military power at the heart of the State over the next five years. This institutionalisation of the AFM's claim to legitimacy provided the PCP with an excuse not to accept the electoral verdict of April 1975. In the elections, the PSP received 37.9 per cent of the votes and 115 seats in the Constituent Assembly. The PPD received 26.4 per cent and 80 seats, against 12.5 per cent and 30 seats for the PCP. The PCP's ally — the PDM — received only 4 per cent of the votes and 5 seats.

Communist flouting of the electoral verdict through alliance with the radical military meant riding roughshod over PSP and PPD preferences, but also alienated broad sections of the Portuguese population. Communist power in the Lisbon work-force was strengthened by the setting up of the InterSindical, so that PSP militants struck periodic alliances with radical groups opposed to Stalinist centralisation, while the PPD strove to consolidate its electorate in northern Portugal by establishing its non-Marxist identity. Furthermore, nationalisation of the banks secured for the State a commanding influence over the country's newspapers, as in the time of Salazar, leading to the PS's championing of a free press in the *República* affair. Simultaneously, the Communists took over the Portuguese Church's Radio Renascença, while the Government announced the first steps towards the expropriation of lands. A movement for the independence of the Azores gathered strength. In these conditions, the country began to disintegrate. The Church, Spínola's Army of National Liberation stationed in Spain, the Centre Democrats and the PPD rivalled for the loyalty of the property-owning peasantry of northern Portugal where two-thirds of the country's population lived. Lisbon and Oporto, the two industrial cities, were courted by the PCP and the PS, while the PCP managed to consolidate its position among the landed proletariat of the Alentejo, in southern Portugal.

This almost nineteenth-century conflict between land and town, and propertied and propertyless peasanty, was translated into a sharpening of rivalry over the form of the state. On 23 May 1975, the AFM announced 'that the alliance of the people and the AFM is the foundation of the Revolution and the only possible way to Socialism'. In June, the radical AFM Assembly demanded the collectivisation of the means of production and government by grass roots democracy. Soares resigned from the Government and announced in late July a popular mobilisation to have the 'popular will' of April respected, a curtailment of military power and a campaign against the reintroduction to Portugal of a dictatorship whether of Stalinist or Castroite nature. There followed Soares' alliance with Major Antunes, Antunes' denunciation[6] early in August in the Council of the Revolution of Portugal's move to 'bureaucratic dictatorship', mass demonstrations in Lisbon and Oporto and the resignation of Premier Gonçalves. The new government of Admiral Azevedo included four Socialist ministers, two from the PPD and Antunes at the Foreign Ministry.

The tide of revolution in Portugal ebbed as quickly as it had flowed. As the time for Angola's independence in November approached, refugees flooded back to Portugal, swelling the ranks of those discontented at radicals of any ilk. The Western powers withheld loans for which there was an increasingly desperate need, on condition that the Constituent Assembly resume its deliberations without military interference. Since Azevedo's government was unable to fulfil its programme for the defence of political union and press liberties, the initiative passed from the political parties to the more conservative military. On 25 November the crisis came to a head. A radical military attempt to seize the bases around Lisbon, possibly with a view to dominating the capital, was quashed by disciplined troops. The instigator of the counter-coup, Eanes, was promoted to Commander in Chief. There followed a purge of the Revolutionary Council and of the armed forces, a revocation of the April 1975 Platform of Agreement with the political parties, and partial steps towards setting the country's finances in order through a combination of foreign loans and a stabilisation plan.

The constitution, as finally accepted by the electorate in the April 1976 elections, may not prove a victory for Portugal's Socialists or Social Democrats in the longer term. First of all, the Presidency is the preserve of a military purged of its radical elements. The President has the power to dissolve the National Assembly, to appoint Cabinets and to send legislation back for consideration. Secondly, the constitution may become a football in political battles. Thus, the PS with PCP backing, but against the opposition of the PPD, inserted articles in the text on worker participation and central planning. This was not harmful immediately to the PSP, as the Party received 35 per cent of votes cast, the PPD 24 per cent, the Social Democratic Centre 16 per cent and the PCP 15 per cent. A similar result was recorded in the election of General Eanes to the Presidency in June. Thus, the PS is the largest party in Portugal, but alternately seeks support to its right or to its left. Socialist cohesion is threatened not only by the Party's tension between non-Stalinist Marxists and those attracted to the PPD, but also by the policies which it is implementing in Government.

Prime Minister Soares has inherited an economy, 55 per cent of whose GNP is engaged in the external sector and where industrial equipment is antiquated. Up to 1968, Portugal invested only about 10 per cent of its GNP, a fraction which rose sharply in the late 1960s and early 1970s, but sank over the course of the revolution. Furthermore, much of its imports are in the form of foodstuffs. This excludes an easy return to autarchy. Given the need to reduce unemployment from 15 per cent and inflation from an annual average of about 60 per cent, the Soares Government has chosen austerity, and an appeal to domestic and especially foreign capital. Without modernisation of plant and equipment and the long-term boost for exports which is supposed to follow, the trade deficit may never be filled and Portugal may fall into a permanent dependence on foreign creditors. Therefore he is seeking to dislodge the Communists from the InterSindical, and to introduce a pluralist union system. Also, he is having property returned that was expropriated from previous owners during the heyday of the revolution. Once the PSP has accomplished that task, the non-Marxist PPD and SDC may be well placed to form a government under the aegis of a conservative President. Alternatively, the PS may split with one wing joining the PPD and the other strengthening the anti-Cunhal elements in the PCP. Whatever happens, all parties must address the economic problems. Their survival depends on its successful resolution.

Spain and Social Democracy

Probably one of the most momentous developments in Spain since the Civil War of 1936 to 1939 has been the renewal, under changed circumstances, of the alliance between those political tendencies which fought under the banner of the Republic. They had come together for a brief moment after 1945 in the hope of Franco's voluntary demission and of a United Nations intervention in Spain. But they were separated again under the influence of the cold war and Western acquiescence in the régime as an ally in the containment policy. The Socialists, based mainly in Toulouse, lost touch with political realities in Spain, leading to a split between the older generation of exiles and the younger generation of militants. The PCE abandoned guerilla activities in the late 1940s and attempted to win over other parties to a policy of national reconciliation.

The opposition's demands on the regime were first formulated in 1962 four months after Spain's application for associate status with the European Economic Community. The European Movement, meeting in Munich, invited all opposition groups, excluding the PCE, to express their view on the terms to be imposed. Their terms amounted to a proposal for the EEC to pursue a revisionist policy. Spain would be accepted given the establishment of authentic representative and democratic institutions, a guarantee of human rights, recognition of Spain's regional communities, free trade unions and freedom to form political parties.[7] Subsequently, the Socialists faded from public view as the regime's propaganda focused on the Basque nationalists and the PCE. Only at the congress of the PSOE at Toulouse in 1972 was renewal initiated. Two years later, in October 1974, Felipe González was elected Secretary-General. He enjoys the patronage of the SPD.

Meanwhile, the PCE, riven by factions over domestic and external policies, underwent metamorphosis. Domestic division centred on relations to other political tendencies, on the illegal worker commissions, and the practicability of a general strike. Foreign affairs assumed an increasingly significant role with the Sino-Soviet rift, revolutionary developments in Latin America and the regime's growing disquiet over the American bases. Unlike the PCP, the PCE denounced the Soviet invasion of Czechoslovakia, leading to Moscow's attempt to set up a rival party. The effort met with failure and the Soviets had to accept the PCE leadership of Santiago Carillo and Dolores Ibarruri. With the signing of the German treaties and of a Soviet-Spanish commercial agreement in October 1972, the PCE evolved rapidly towards political options identified with the phenomenon of Euro-Communism.

These political options were developed at the Eighth Party Congress in 1972, the Brussels Conference of Western European Communist Parties in January 1974 and a PCE Central Committee meeting of April 1974. A number of points may be made. First, the PCE gave priority to the attainment of Socialism in Spain over its international affiliations. 'Each Communist Party must show its capacity to unite the greatest of national forces in the struggle for Socialism accentuating its independence and applying Marxist methods to the concrete conditions of each revolution.'[8] Secondly, the PCE came to advocate the formation of a common front leading to a broad coalition government and the drawing up of a new constitution. The PCE backed an Italian Communist Party proposal for a similar alliance at the level of the EEC and a 'democratisation' of the Brussels institutions. Thirdly, the Central Committee meeting of April 1974 urged 'an offensive of the masses against the cost of living'[9] in order to secure a 'democratic rupture' with the Franco regime and the peaceful setting up of 'a provisional government of national reconciliation'. A step in this direction was taken with the creation of the Democratic Junta in July 1974, joined by Christian Democrats, Carlists and Professor Tierno Galván's Popular Socialist Party (PSP).

Unlike the PCE, the various Socialist groups in Spain were caught unprepared by the rapid decline in the regime's authority over 1974. No clear policy was elaborated by the PSOE at its Congress of Suresnes in October, but a series of talks was subsequently held with Christian and Social Democrats. The result was a formal secretariat — the Democratic Platform — and help in the elaboration of a policy sufficiently common to embrace Christian Democrats, Carlists, regionalists and Maoists. Membership of the Democratic Platform was left open, a hint to the PCE of willingness to dialogue.

Movement of the Democratic Junta and of the Democratic Platform towards co-ordination was slow. Probably one influence was the coincidence of the Spanish opposition's desire for a relatively bloodless revolution and the interests of the Western powers in a stable transfer of power from Franco to Juan Carlos. After the failure of Spínola's coup in Portugal on 11 March 1975, and Cunhal's flouting of the electoral verdict in April, President Ford's administration moved to overt support for Juan Carlos. At the same time Junta and Platform began to harmonise their demands, including a general amnesty, the concession of political and trade union liberties and a 'transitional compromise' with the regime as a step to the elaboration of a new constitution. Also, the PSOE wanted to offset the PCE's strength in the labour commissions by emerging as the main opposition political party in the manner of the Portuguese Socialists. The PSP of Tierno Galván served as a valuable liaison. Eventually a union was consummated in March 1976 when both Junta and Platform formed a Democratic Co-ordination — or the Plata-junta as it is called. The Co-ordination represents 'a unitary organism of all the opposition at all levels'; the objective is to open 'a period of constitutional reform that ends in a popular consultation to determine the form of state and government'.[10]

Convergence was also promoted by Western European reaction to developments in Iberia. The scene was set by the Portuguese revolution and the marked swing to the left throughout Europe in 1974. With the rapprochement between President Giscard d'Estaing and Chancellor Schmidt, M. Mitterrand – leader of the French Union of the Left – sought to organise a common Socialist policy for Southern Europe distinguishable from the Social Democratic orientation of West Germany, Scandinavia and Britain. González accepted Mitterrand's invitation of April 1975, as did Soares; but González also went to Bonn for discussions with SPD leaders while Soares' hopes for a loan for Portugal from the EEC were dashed by French opposition at the Council of Ministers in July. As the leading party in the government of the main European power in the Atlantic alliance, with large financial reserves, the German Social Democrats had the most to offer. Communist activity in Portugal further sharpened Schmidt's hostility to Mitterrand's idea and in June SPD leader Brandt met in Vienna with Premier Palme and Chancellor Kreisky where co-operation between Socialists and Communists was roundly criticised.

Nonetheless, the differences between French and West German Socialists over Iberia may be exaggerated. Both supported the PSOE as the kernel for a Socialist rassemblement in Spain; both condemned Cunhal's tactics in Portugal though for different reasons. West Germany's Social Democratic leadership pointed to Portugal as proving the incorrigibility of Communists; the French Socialists exploited events in Portugal to push the French Communists towards renouncing the dictatorship of the proletariat. Furthermore, West Germany's desire for a peaceful transition in Spain was hardly compatible with preserving the PCE in clandestinity. That is where it operates best, and at maximum advantage over the PSOE, in view of the PCE's strength in the worker commissions. There was little for foreign parties to accomplish in Spain other than hope, in Mitterrand's words at the Paris Conference of Socialist Parties of Southern Europe, that the PSOE would be 'the crystalliser of the process of union between Spanish Socialist groups'.[11]

In the last resort, regime and opposition are alone to work out their own dialectic of *ruptura* and *apertura*. In this, the Spanish Socialists have met with success. They have embraced the PCE in the Democratic Convergence; the Socialist General Union of Workers (UGT) held its first public conference for forty years in April; in May, the PSOE opened negotiations with the PSP for a united Socialist party. As the Socialists have organised, they have developed sufficient confidence openly to accept the monarchy. King Juan Carlos, in turn, has identified his throne with a move to wide-ranging reform. After his return from the United States at the end of June, Juan Carlos dismissed his Prime

Minister, Arias Navarro, who had balked on even minor modifications to Franco's institutional heritage. In September, the King steered to the Cortes a draft law proposing a Lower House composed of 350 members elected by proportional representation and an Upper House with a maximum of 244 members, 40 of whom may be directly appointed by the King. If the Cortes rejects the proposals they may be submitted to referendum in November; elections have been promised for June 1977.

But the task of creating a coherent party, capable of holding together, let alone acting as an efficient instrument for government, is immense. One outstanding weakness of the Spanish Socialists is in the labour unions. The Communists, with their hold in the workers' commissions, are reputedly the strongest and claim to have infiltrated the official syndicates. Though a meeting was held in July 1976 to form the Co-ordination of Sindical Organisation latent suspicions of Communist intentions have been roused. The workers' commissions propose a single labour organisation in the manner of the InterSindical in Portugal and may hope to inherit the regime's existing structure. (Indeed one of the major points of contention within the regime is whether the Communists should be given a *de facto* share in power through alteration of the syndical law rather than legitimising them as a political party.) The commissions' proposal, not surprisingly, has been sharply criticised by the UGT and by the revived Anarchist movement, the Confederación Nacional de Trabajadores (CNT). Another small Socialist union, the Unión Sindical Obrero (USO) emphasises that any move to a single union should await the achievement of full democratic rights and an extensive debate at grass roots level. Thus, there can be little doubt that the regime's main interlocutor on the side of labour in the implementation of an economic policy is the network of worker commissions.

That leaves the PSOE and the PSP as essentially political organisations with the prospect — like the PS in Portugal — of exerting power through their strength in parliament. How successful they prove depends to a certain extent on their ability to forge a viable political programme capable of being implemented in government, but sufficiently vague to embrace their own heterogeneity. This heterogeneity is expressed in innumerable Socialist or Social Democratic groups, each anxious to preserve its identity and each with its own preferred formulations. It is further expressed in the variety of Socialist regional parties eager to assert local rights against centralising tendencies from whatever quarter. González' difficulties may be depicted by a remark in Barcelona, in April 1976. When asked what he considered was the clientele of the PSOE in Catalonia, he answered that the Party 'could include consequential sociodemocrats – not the liberals who call themselves sociodemocrats – to non-Leninist Marxists'.[12]

All this is a far cry from Spain's economic problems. Though the economy developed faster and over a longer period of time than that of Portugal, the problems are not dissimilar. Oil and raw material price rises aggravated the balance of payments deficit and led to the Government resorting to foreign loans. Investment has lagged, jeopardising long-term productivity and hence competitivity on world markets. Unemployment is about 6 per cent, and inflation runs at around 20 per cent. A severe deflationary policy risks jeopardising the process of political evolution, but further devaluation resulting from trade deficits and high inflation rates entails equal uncertainty. Similarly a return to autarchy is ruled out, as much of the economy is dependent on imports. The opposition therefore concentrates on institutional reform, rather than tackle the thorny economic problem. There, it is as vulnerable as the regime.

In conclusion, then, the future of Socialism or of Social Democracy in Iberia looks bleak. In Portugal, the PS, together with the PPD and assorted Maoist groups, preempted the seizure of the State by the Stalinist PCP. But the PS, as the Government party, is implementing a policy of which, for want of any other, a conservative regime could be proud. In Spain, the PSOE, the PSP and the PCP are pushing the regime towards reforms of 'the juridical and political superstructure'. No doubt, the intention is to hasten the conquest of political power; but there is little sign of any party knowing what to do with the power once attained. For the essential problem of Socialism or Social Democracy in Iberia is not only the setting up of new constitutions – that mirage of nineteenth-century reformers – but the working out and implementation of an economic and social policy suited to the peculiarities of both countries. That task is as perplexing as the global economic situation is threatening.

Notes

1. Karl Kautsky, 'The Social Revolution', quoted in C. Wright Mills, *The Marxists* (London, Pelican, 1975), p. 158.
2. Cantarero Castillo, *Falange y Socialismo* (Madrid, 1973), p. 18.
3. *Portugal Socialista*, 20 July 1969.
4. *República* (Lisbon), 26 April 1974.
5. See my 'Portugal's "Revolution of Carnations" ', *International Affairs*, vol.52, no. 3 (July 1976).

6. For instance, interview in *Le Monde*, 24 December 1974.
7. From Jacques Georgel, *Le Franquisme, Histoire et Bilan 1939-1969* (Paris, Editions du Seuil), p. 207.
8. *Manifesto: Proyecto programma del partido Communista de España* (Belgium, Harmel Press, 1974), p. 28.
9. Santiago Carillo, *Hacia el Post-franquismo* (Paris, Librairie du Globe, 1974), p. 15.
10. *Cambio 16*, 29 March 1976.
11. *Cambio 16*, 2 February 1976.
12. *Cambio 16*, 25 April 1976.

Abbreviations

Portugal

AFM	Armed Forces Movement
ASP	Portuguese Socialist Action (Dr Mário Soares)
COPCON	Operational Command of the Continent
PCP	Portuguese Communist Party
PDM	
PPD	Popular Democratic Party (Sá Carneiro)
PS	Portuguese Socialist Party (Dr Mário Soares)
SDC	Social Democratic Centre

Spain

CNT	Confederacion Nacional de Trabajadores (Anarchist)
PCE	Spanish Communist Party
PSOE	Spanish Socialist Workers' Party (Felipe González)
PSP	Popular Socialist Party (Prof. Tierno Galván)
UGT	General Union of Workers
USDE	Spanish Social Democratic Unión (García López)
USO	Workers' Syndical Union/Union Sindical Obrero

Table 1. Portugal: election results

Elections to a constituent Assembly were held in April 1975.
Elections to a 263-member Legislative Assembly were held on 25 April 1976.
At both elections there was a very high turnout: 91.7 per cent in 1975 and 83.3 per cent of an electorate of 6,481,352 in 1976.

The votes, percentages and seats gained by the 14 parties which contested the elections (compared with 12 in 1975) are given below, together with corresponding figures for 1975:

	1976 Votes*	1976 Percentages†	1976 Seats[∞]	1975 Votes	1975 Percentages	1975 Seats[ɸ]
Portuguese Socialist Party (PSP) :: :: ::	1,887,180	34.97	107	2,145,392	37.87	116
Popular Democratic Party (PPD) :: ::	1,296,432	24.03	73	1,494,575	26.38	81
Social Democratic Centre (CDS) :: ::	858,783	15.91	42	433,153	7.65	16
Portuguese Communist Party (PCP) :: ::	785,620	14.56	40	709,639	12.53	30
Popular Democratic Union (UDP) :: ::	91,383	1.69	1	44,546	0.79	1
Popular Socialist Front (FSP) :: ::	41,954	0.78	0	66,161	1.17	0
Movement for the Reorganisation of the Proletarian Party (MRPP) :: :: ::	36,237	0.67	0	–	–	–
Movement of the Socialist Left (MES) :: ::	31,065	0.58	0	57,682	1.02	0
Christian Democratic Party (PDC) :: ::	28,226	0.52	0	–	–	–
Popular Monarchist Party (PPM) :: ::	28,163	0.52	0	31,809	0.56	0
International Communist League (LCI) :: ::	16,235	0.30	0	10,732	0.19	0
Portuguese Communist Party (Marxist-Leninist) (PCP-ML) :: :: :: ::	15,801	0.29	0	–	–	–
Alliance of Workers and Farm Labourers (AOC) ::	15,671	0.29	0	–	–	–
Workers' Revolutionary Party (PRT) :: ::	5,182	0.10	–	–	–	–

*Excluding the overseas vote.
†Percentages, which do not take account of the overseas vote, calculated on basis of actual votes cast, of which 4.78 per cent were invalid.

[∞] Including four deputies representing (i) emigrant workers in Europe, who returned one Socialist and one PPD deputy, and (ii) emigrant workers in the rest of the world, who returned one PPD and one CDS deputy.
[ɸ] Final distribution.

Source: Keesings Contemporary Archives, 25 June 1976, 27792.

5 THE BRITISH LABOUR PARTY

Lewis Minkin and Patrick Seyd

I would offer, if I may, one word of counsel to delegates on this matter. When you are dealing with such a sensitive subject . . . make certain that you are clear in what you intend to do; that people understand what you intend to do, and do not haver and waver. (James Callaghan. The Labour Party Conference 1962.)

In Search of an Identity

Since its formation in 1900 the Labour Party has been undeviating in its adherence to Parliamentary democracy. That apart, its fundamental commitments have been marked by a range of subtle ambiguities and its political identity has often been uncertain. As with all Social Democratic parties, that identity emerged from the purposes the Party sought to achieve and also from the development of three crucial relationships: that with organised industrial labour, that within the Party between its constituent elements, and that with the electorate. Was the Party a trade union party? Was the Party internally a democratic party? Was it a Socialist party? Was it a working-class party? There was no unambiguous tradition of belief or action which made the answer to any of these questions either simple or immediately clear. And it has been a significant feature of the Party's history that its identity has regularly drawn conflicting perceptions and prescriptions from the various members of 'the great alliance'.

It is our intention here to analyse the recent history of the Party in terms of the development of these ambiguities. To do this we will first indicate their character in the period up to 1955 and then explore in more detail the Party's behaviour in the past two decades. Whilst political history, particularly the development of ideas and traditions, can rarely be divided satisfactorily into tidy periods and compartments, as we shall indicate the many changes in the Party and its political environment after 1955 give this departure point more than mere analytical utility.

The Ambiguities

1. Relations with Industrial Labour

I want to say to our friends who have joined us in this political

movement, that our predecessors formed the party. It was not Keir
Hardie who formed it, it grew out of the bowels of the Trades Union
Congress. (Ernest Bevin, 1935.)

The most obvious characteristic of the Labour Party was that it was a
trade union party in the sense that historically and by association there
was a high degree of formal interconnection between the Party and
trade unionism. This association had seven features: the Party was the
product of an initiative taken at the Trades Union Congress of 1899[1]
and owed its survival in infancy to an infusion of trade union support.[2]
Throughout its history most of the Party's members have been trade
unionists.[3] Structurally, individual unions were affiliated to the Party
at all levels from local to national. The unions held formal majorities at
the Annual Conference[4] – the Party's supreme policy-making authority
– and in elections for the NEC[5] – the Party's administrative and
governing body. Individual unions sponsored a number of Labour
candidates and thereby ensured that a block of trade unions' sponsored
MPs were part of the Parliamentary Party.[6] Financially, the unions via
affiliation, sponsorship and campaign contributions were major
contributors to the Party's funds.[7] Lastly, union members provided the
solid base of the Party's electoral support.[8]

   On the face of it, this interconnection appears to indicate a high
degree of integration and identification between the Party and the
unions. In practice the relationship was much more flexible and
complex. From the earliest days the idea of a structural attachment
between the Party and the TUC was rejected. They were linked only
loosely through a bridging council (the National Joint Council – later
the National Council of Labour) and other policy links were fluid and
ah hoc.[9] Members of the TUC General Council were prohibited from
nomination for Labour's National Executive Committee.[10] Overlapping
composition of the industrial and Parliamentary leadership was reduced
after 1923 when the TUC General Secretaryship became a full-time
trade union post[11] and after 1931 when there was a tendency for senior
union officials to keep out of the Parliamentary arena.[12] The common
facilities and common headquarters shared for a period by the Party and
the TUC were eventually divided.[13]

   For most of the Party's history the majority of trade union leaders
have exercised considerable restraint in their relationship with the Party
leadership and in the performance of Party roles. This restraint was to
some extent a product of compositional difference: the TUC affiliated
membership was always wider and greater than that committed to the

Labour Party.[14] But it was also related to fundamental issues of function and purpose. The unions aspired to a proper representation of the interests of labour in the government of the country but their concern with their own organisational integrity, their concern with the priority of industrial issues, their desire to preserve their industrial unity, their sensitivity towards the Party's viability, and their sense of constitutionality, all inhibited a full 'colonisation' of the Party.

From the Party side, too, the union connection has never implied a full commitment to the idea of a trade union party. The ambiguities inherent in the idea of representation of 'the interests of labour' were brought out not only in the Party's electoral appeal (see below) but in the behaviour of Ministers towards the unions when Labour formed minority Governments in 1924 and 1929. It was made clear immediately by the MacDonald Governments that Labour in office was a party of the nation not of the sectional trade unions; in industrial disputes it was prepared to behave in much the same way as previous Governments.[15] Even the consultation which might have been expected of partners in 'the Labour movement' was not forthcoming under MacDonald. The policy of the 1929 Government towards unemployment generally, and cuts in unemployment benefit specifically, caused a rift with the TUC which was to end in the departure of MacDonald and two other senior leaders into a National Government and their subsequent expulsion from the Party.[16]

With Labour back in Opposition in the 1930s the unions and the Party moved in closer policy harmony. There was a common interest in reversing the Conservatives' 1927 trades union legislation.[17] The rapport built in that period between Clement Attlee, the Party's Leader, and Ernest Bevin, the General Secretary of the largest affiliated union – the Transport and General Workers – helped cement relations when Labour once again took office in 1945, this time as a majority Government. With Bevin (now Foreign Secretary) playing a major brokerage role in relation to the unions and with a much greater degree of direct consultation with the unions than the MacDonald Government had sought, the two generally moved together towards a considerable social and economic achievement. But the ambiguity remained. The fundamental stress for this Government as for all Labour Governments was on the national interest. The Government's independence of the unions was shown in controversial initiatives on major industrial questions,[18] including the prosecution of striking dock workers.[19]

Nevertheless what was most characteristic of the relationship between Labour and the unions then and in Opposition after 1951 was the degree of accord – particularly between the majorities of the PLP leadership and the TUC General Council. This accord was based upon solid achievement. Access to Government by the unions, nationalisation of some basic industries, a welfare state, full employment and rising living standards bred both satisfaction and a common conservatism amongst the majority of the leadership. And their strong anti-Communism proved to be an effective cement to the close relationship. But there were problems which were to emerge with some sharpness in the 1960s. What was to be the relationship between the Party and the unions now that the unions had won direct access to the Government regardless of its political complexion? And how would a Labour Government relate to the unions if its policies undermined the support normally given by a loyal group of union leaders?

2. Internal Relations: Democracy, Power and Authority

> ... the Labour Party is a collective expression of democratic sentiment based on the working class movement and on the constituency organisations of the workers by hand or brain. Accordingly, in the Labour Party, the final word rests with the Annual Party Conference ... (*The Rise of the Labour Party,* Labour Party Publication, 1948.)

The genesis of the Labour Party as an extra-Parliamentary organisation and the traditions that it inherited shaped an organisational structure which in principle operated according to rules of intra-party democracy. The supreme policy-making authority of the Party was the Annual Conference of delegates from affiliated organisations.[20] These delegates, in the main, cast their votes in accordance with the prior mandates established by the members of their own organisation. The decisions of the Conference were in theory binding upon the Party's administrative body – the National Executive Committee[21] – upon those staffing the Party's machinery under the control of the General Secretary and, with qualifications,[22] upon the Party's representatives in Parliament. In principle, therefore, policy-making in the Labour Party was democratically produced by the Party's members.

In practice the Party's behaviour has never been as coherent or as democratic as this format might indicate. From the first there was a complex of conflicting loyalties and obligations. The Party remained a federal body and its affiliated trade union and Socialist organisations jealously guarded their independence from any dictation, including that of the Party Conference. The Party's representatives in Parliament were

subject to a variety of cross pressures from the Labour movement —
obligations to unions and the local parties always vied with that to the
Party Conference. Further, there was persistent tension between the
open and often rumbustious factional dissent characteristic of the
Party, and adherence to concepts of Party and working-class unity
which were often the basis for an authoritarianism and intolerance
which sought to limit that dissent.

Within the affiliated organisations there were always problems of
representation. The vast bulk of the Party's membership was indirect
through an affiliated union: levy-paying exhausted the political
commitment of most of them. And it was also the case that although
the unions remained firmly committed to the principle of internal
democracy there did tend to develop a concentration of power amongst
the unions' national officials. This concentration varied according to
the union's structure, traditions and countervailing forces. But it meant
that union leaders could sometimes exercise considerable sway over the
union and discretion in the application of its mandates.

But the greatest representational problem emerged in relation to the
authority of the Party Conference and the role of the PLP. How was
intra party democracy to be reconciled with Parliamentary democracy?

In practice a delicate *modus vivendi* developed. To a considerable
extent it was based on the accumulation of power at leadership level
within the Party and the unions and the development of a division of
authority. One facet of this was the discretion allowed to the PLP
leaders in policy implementation and their general pre-eminence in
Party policy formulation. The mechanisms through which this worked
involved an influential PLP leadership role in relation to the NEC and
an influential NEC leadership role in relation to the Conference. These
institutionalised leadership roles were, in part, facilitated by the behaviour
of the unions within the Party. Each union cast its votes at the Party
Conference in a block which did not register minority opinion and the
block votes regularly produced majorities in support of the Parliamentary
leadership.

But this was only one facet of the Party's behaviour. The history of
the Party has also involved a subtle interaction between this overt policy
pre-eminence of the Parliamentary leadership and an important,
though typically covert, trade union policy role. Thus there evolved a
complex and dynamic power situation — a dialectical power relationship
— characterised by a rhythmic pattern of action and reaction prior to
the public emergence of policy proposals, and by a subtle juxtaposition
of negative and positive roles. Thus alongside the policy pre-eminence

and apparent Government independence of the Parliamentary leadership must be noted: the long-term interaction between the unions and the Parliamentary leadership over policy initiatives taken by the unions and accepted as party policy during the Party's formative years; the 'closure' of key areas of policy-making from Party initiative, notably the industrial and political freedom of the unions as they defined them; the negative and boundary-setting role of the unions in policy consultations which took place prior to the emergence of NEC policy proposals; and the long-term reaction of the unions to what was perceived as the failure and lack of principle of the 1931 MacDonald Government — they moved to a more positive policy role when the Party returned to Opposition in the 1930s.

The delicacy of this relationship, resting as it did on a range of unwritten conventions and customary constraints, required some degree of consensus. Here the factional element was important. Though the unions reached their greatest unity on issues which touched upon the 'closed' areas and the Parliamentary leaders achieved their greatest homogeneity when collective responsibility was imposed upon them as Government Ministers, typically both were divided along factional Right/Left lines.[23] These factional divisions enhanced Party-union cohesion because the Right was normally in a majority in each of the major committees of the Party and the TUC and aware of their common differences with the Left. Also, the apparent fragility of the Party with its divided authority, confederal structure and factional conflict led to a section of the broad 'centre' of the Party consciously acting as a reconciling force. The dominance and cohesion of the Right was clearest in the late 1940s and 1950s. By 1955 three large unions, the Transport and General Workers, the General and Municipal Workers and the National Union of Mineworkers were regularly casting in support of 'the platform' at the Party Conference 2,328,000 votes out of a total union vote of 5,552,000 and a total Conference vote of 6,773,000.[24] A majority of the medium-sized and smaller unions were prepared to follow their example. Thus between 1948 and 1960 with the exception of one minor vote in 1950 'the platform' at the Party Conference was undefeated.[25] And elections for the National Executive Committee revealed a similar dominance of the Right in the Trade Union and Women's sections.

Thus behind the rhetorical commitment of the Party and its Parliamentary leadership to intra-Party democracy and the role of the Party Conference as 'the final authority' was a set of relationships which solidified the position of the Right-wing leadership. The formal deference they paid to the Conference accorded with the Party's traditional antipathy to élitism — an antipathy strengthened by the experience of MacDonald. But it was also a handy instrument to use against dissent.

Thus the ambiguities of power and democracy remained. How would the Parliamentary leadership react to a major shift in the political alignment of the unions? And how would they respond to an adverse Conference decision on a major issue having for years upheld its 'final authority'?

3. Purpose and Policy

The Labour Party is a Socialist Party. (*Labour and the Nation,* Labour's programme 1928.)

The coalition of forces which produced the Labour Party involved the Fabian Society, the Independent Labour Party and the Social Democratic Federation, as well as forty-one trade unions, but the pre-war policy of the Party was predominantly derived from the individual and collective claims of the unions. From one perspective the behaviour of the Party after 1918 marked a major change in this position. It adopted a new constitution with a specific commitment to 'the common ownership of the means of production' and it adopted a programme 'Labour and the New Social Order' which was avowedly Socialist and distinctly anti-Capitalist. However, the adoption of Socialism had ambiguous features which were to have reverberations throughout the subsequent history of the Party. For one thing much of the new programme was adapted from the policy resolutions of the non-Socialist Party Conferences of the pre-war years. For another it is unclear to what extent the acceptance of Socialism as a goal involved the acceptance of Socialism as a philosophy by the bulk of the trade union affiliated membership.[26] And in many ways the Party's Socialism drew from complex and varied traditions to a degree which left its meaning indistinct.[27]

In spite of this ambiguity there can be no doubt that the language of equality and transformation was more acceptable to a wider audience within the Labour movement following 'the war to end all wars'. And if the commitment of Socialism was vague in its policy concomitants it is certainly the case that what had hitherto been a factional position was now a firm Party commitment taken increasingly for granted.

For the Parliamentary leadership it involved a complex and variable mixture in which probably the dominant elements were a combination of collectivism (directed towards ensuring a humanitarian redistribution of income and a rationalisation of the economic resources of society) and a vague conception of the moral and social transformation of man. For the growing body of Socialist opinion at all levels within the Party these goals were seen as attainable only within a programme for the common ownership of the means of production. For others ownership remained of less significance.[28]

One feature which united the vast majority of the Party regardless of faction or section was the belief that transformation could and should be affected through Party activity in Parliament. Though many in the Party, particularly those on the Left, were likely to sympathise with labour's involvement in industrial conflict there was always among the Party leadership an unwillingness to utilise industrial conflict for political ends and an ideological inhibition against the waging of class struggle. Class conflict would be diminished by state activity designed to eliminate social injustice and transform Capitalism into Socialism.

During the 1920s the Party leaders constantly employed the rhetoric of transformation yet their policies, both in Opposition and Government, were essentially pragmatic and cautious. The world crisis of 1929 left them in a dilemma in which their response was to continue to voice the old rhetoric whilst implementing orthodox economic policies in an attempt to alleviate the slump. These orthodox policies inevitably resulted in sacrifices being demanded of the working class; sacrifices which in 1931 the TUC finally refused to accept. The consequent formation of a National Government, and the defections and expulsions of the Parliamentary leaders, had a considerable impact — both long and short term — on the Labour Party.

The immediate impact was to discredit the policies pursued by the Labour Government. And this, combined with the obvious international crisis of Capitalism, provided an ethos in which more Left-wing ideas could flourish. In ensuing years the Labour Party was prone to stress not only the systemic character of the crisis but also to differentiate sharply the distinctive systems of Capitalism and Socialism. From both Right and Left of the Party came detailed and specific proposals for public ownership. Nevertheless the extent of the shift in the Party's programme was limited by the inability of the Left to gain leading positions in the major unions and on the policy-making NEC.

The ILP, disillusioned by the Labour Government's actions, disaffiliated in 1932 and, waging an independent Socialist campaign, went into permanent decline.[29] This and the limited electoral success of the Communist Party[30] was to be a salutary reminder to the Left of the Party of the difficulties involved in operating outside the mass Party.

Thus Left factions have always had to face the dilemma of either operating under the constraints of Party membership or seeking an independent base in a class which appeared unwilling to support them. In 1937 the Parliamentary Left joined the overwhelming support given to *Labour's Immediate Programme* on the basis that it gave a clear indication of the Socialist measures which a majority Labour Government would implement.

And Labour's first majority Government in 1945 did in fact implement almost in full the programme it had formulated in Opposition in the 1930s and during the war years At the time, and certainly in the minds of some of Labour's leaders, the consequent transformation appeared comprehensive and far reaching. Subsequently the Attlee Government has entered the legends of Labour's folklore as the embodiment of a radical Socialist Government. But was it?

In retrospect as one historian has pointed out this became the 'incredible shrinking social revolution'.[31] For one thing the changes no longer looked quite so far reaching when viewed from the late 1950s. For another it became clear that in several respects the Government's policies reflected a measure of political consensus between the parties on the rationalisation and humanisation of British Capitalism. Unquestionably the crucial element was the acceptance of Keynesian techniques of economic management, particularly towards the purpose of full employment. And Labour's social programme was to some extent anticipated in proposals produced during the Coalition Government.

Further, a degree of consensus also developed between the Labour and Conservative Party leaderships over defence and foreign policy. The concept of a Socialist foreign policy was soon superseded by a concern for practicality and the national interest. And the hope of a new relationship — 'Left talking to Left' — with the USSR soon developed into the 'Cold War'. There was increasingly a stress on anti-Communism and the Soviet threat to Western Europe. With this went a growing closeness to the USA, the formation of the NATO Alliance, and an increasing economic interdependence by the members of that alliance within the hegemony of the USA. A rapid increase in defence expenditure upon the outbreak of the Korean War led to the resignation of three of the Party's Ministers and the opening of the Bevanite revolt.[32]

This issue soon spread to the whole field of Government policy. The specific focus of conflict was in practice usually particular issues of defence and foreign policy. But of more fundamental importance was the response to the achievements of the 1945 Government. What gave that Labour Government its distinctive ideological character was the nationalisation programme, a programme advocated on grounds of immediate efficiency but also as part of the transformation towards a 'Co-operative Commonwealth'.

The Party now faced some basic questions about its purpose. Had this been so carried into practice that for the immediate future it required only consolidation? Alternatively did the Party need to press forward with a further 'shopping list' of industries to be taken into public ownership? This was the great ideological dilemma which separated 'consolidationists' from 'Bevanites'. But, in addition, within this division there were those on the Right who were prepared to state the case for a completely new social analysis and a bold restatement of Socialist purpose.

4. Relations with the Electorate

> . . . the Party of the Producers by hand or by brain . . . (*Labour and the New Social Order,* 1918.)

A party born out of the unions, with an affiliated membership which consisted mainly of manual worker trade unionists and with an electoral support which had grown mainly amongst the same constituency, naturally made its primary appeal to the manual working class. But after 1918 there was also a conscious attempt to broaden the appeal of the Party. The 'workers by hand or brain' and 'the producers' could imply a much wider section of the population including the white collar, professional and small business groups.[33] Though the Party's manifestos were often critical of the idle or privileged rich and of the economic and industrial system of which they were a part there was a specific denial that the Party was a sectional Party and there were regular references to the Nation and the People. Thus, there was always an element of ambiguity to the Party's identity and its social allegiance.

The social composition of Labour's parliamentarians was another expression of the ambivalence of its appeal. As Labour moved towards major party status in the early 1920s, the class composition of the parliamentarians shifted with a substantial minority component now from middle-class backgrounds.[34] The shift in social composition was also marked at Cabinet level in the three Labour Governments. These Cabinets were initially a balance of social elements in which those drawn from working-class backgrounds via a career as an official of a trade union or other working-class organisation or in a purely manual occupation made up only approximately 50 per cent of the membership.[35]

But there was a trend noticeable in the 1945 Cabinet for the manual worker trade unionist to decline leaving as the dominant element the university-educated middle-class from the professions.[36]

The ambiguity of the Party's appeal was also embodied in the content of its manifestos. Typically they included measures of nationalisation defended both on specific grounds of their contribution to efficiency and on the grounds of their general role in the scheme of social transformation. They also included measures of social reform suggested as both practical and just. Thus Labour's appeal always had both the face of amelioration and the face of transformation. There were times such as in 1929, when the ameliorative face was presented with excessive moderation and vagueness. Times also, like 1931, when the appeal was more ideologically distinctive and the rhetorical anti-Capitalism pronounced.

In general the Party's electoral performance between 1918 and 1940 reinforced the optimism which was always a by-product of the Party's social philosophy. Its total vote rose at each election until 1931. Even then the result in terms of votes was nothing like as disastrous as the drop in seats.[37] With support rising again in 1935 it was possible to see the 1931 election result as an unfortunate aberration ensuing from treacherous leadership. In the late 1930s the Party generally looked with confidence towards the probability of a majority Labour Government.

As a result of the experience of the Second World War and a reflective perception of the depressed 1930s, Labour's first majority Government took office in 1945.[38] It came to power on the basis of its largest-ever working-class support — but also its largest share of middle-class support.[39] Thus the 1945 victory — a victory gained on the basis of a Manifesto which was a subtle blending of immediate and long-term purposes — was also ambiguous in social terms. It was a confirmation of the Party's long-held belief that ultimately the working-class majority would increasingly swing their support behind the party of labour. On the other hand the new support from the middle class encouraged some in the Party leadership to believe that the Party's most viable electoral strategy involved preserving a broad national appeal and in the context of the late 1940s a moderate consolidationist appeal.

Labour in Opposition after 1951 faced some major problems of adjustment. First, though it lost the election the Party had attained its highest-ever total of votes.[40] If it was to retain and expand this support the Party had two possible electoral strategies it could explore. Should it seek to maximise the manual working-class vote, or should it seek to pursue more strongly a broader social appeal? Its 1955 election campaign embraced neither alternative full-heartedly.

Secondly, the Party confidently expected that the Conservative Government would put the clock back politically by exacerbating industrial conflict, dismantling the Welfare State and increasing the level of unemployment. When none of this occurred the ideological dilemma for Labour's leadership appeal appeared acute. How could a moderate Party leadership differentiate its ideological appeal in a period of inter-party consensus?

The Watershed

The party inherited by Hugh Gaitskell at the end of 1955 was in many ways a mature party. It had replaced the Liberals as the second major party, it had held Office as a majority Government. It had seen 'betrayal' by the leader it most revered and it had seen the implementation of its original programme under the leader that perhaps it least appreciated. It had in great measure accepted and been integrated within the procedures of British Parliamentary Government but it had also retained its distinctive internal pattern of authority based on the sovereignty of the Annual Conference. It was now a large party with an individual membership of nearly a million and an affiliated membership over five times that figure.[41] Further it had now a considerable party bureacracy when measured against its pre-war days.[42] Though it had lost the 1955 election it was still a confident party. Much had been achieved in a manner consistent with the Party's purposes and democratic philosophy. And the old optimism still encouraged the belief that it would see even better days.

But much was changing — both within the Party and external to it. Not only was the 1945 generation of senior leaders now in retirement or on the back-benches but new faces were appearing in the trade union leadership. Most of these faces would take the trade union movement further to the Right but one at least — that of Frank Cousins in the Transport and General Workers Union — was to strengthen the position of the Left.

The environment within which the Party was operating was in a process of rapid change. With the death of Stalin the worst of the 'Cold War' was over. Internationally, the revelations of the 20th CPSU and the Hungarian revolution were to have major repercussions for the international Communist movement and indirectly for the British Labour Party also.[43] There was the failed venture at Suez, with a retreat which symbolised both Britain's declining status in the world and the formal end of Empire.

And the withdrawal from Suez was an indicator also of Britain's financial vulnerability to political pressure. The next four years were to be years of unprecedented affluence and social change — years in which the manual working class from which Labour took the bulk of its electoral support 'never had it so good'. But they were years also in which Britain was rapidly losing ground to faster-growing Continental competitors in France and Germany and the first stages were under way of a series of economic crises which were to have crucial consequences for the role of Labour Governments.

New Developments

1. Relations with Industrial Labour

The Labour Party's relationship with the unions is the most fundamental element in its political life. The changing form, tone and temper of the relationship determines the pattern of power and democracy within the Party. It affects the Party's purpose and policy and it contributes to the Party's electoral image and support. In turn, developments in these areas have reverberations which are felt in the relationship with the unions. Thus the interrelationship is complex and there are times when participants are in the grip of powerful cross-pressures. In the two decades since 1956 these cross-pressures resulted in some major oscillations in behaviour and three distinct phases — differentiation and loyalty to 1966, degeneration and estrangement from 1966 to 1969 and a new accommodation and loyalty from 1970 to the present.

The first phase was in some ways the most subtle. On the surface in the period after 1956 the relationship looked settled and close. The behaviour of the Conservative Government was still well within the post-war Welfare State consensus but there were sufficient points of friction on industrial, economic and wages policy issues for the unions to be aware of their traditional ideological differences. The development of Labour's domestic policies — particularly on pensions, land and housing — also served to differentiate the parties. And (during the Party's internal convulsions over nuclear disarmament between 1960 and 1962) there was sufficient involvment in the Party by the majority of TUC General Council members for them to produce a remarkable degree of organised support for Hugh Gaitskell.[44] Whilst unwilling to concede wage restraint to the Conservative Government the unions were prepared in 1963 to agree to a proposed voluntary incomes policy with a Labour Government, provided it was within the context of an expanding economy with some degree of price control and a commitment to social justice for the lower paid. The meaning and terms of this proposed incomes policy varied union by union and union leader by union leader, but the loyalty which always accompanies the election of a Labour Government was sufficient for most of them to overcome their misgivings at the first emergence under the 1964 Labour Government of statutory elements in the policy.

Nevertheless alongside this pattern of accord between the majority of unions and the Party leadership there were other developments which were to be the basis of estrangement. From their side after 1959 the Labour leadership sought to clarify the Party's electoral identity. As will be explored in the section below, the new Party strategy was concerned to appeal to the new white-collar salariat. This meant shedding the Party's 'cloth cap' image and reducing the extent to which the Party was closely identified with the manual worker unions.[45] The stylistic differences of the electoral appeal were heightened by changes taking place in the composition of the PLP leadership. Whilst the leadership of the majority of unions remained overwhelmingly manual working-class, the leadership of the Party became increasingly middle-class. Thus both in electoral identification and in social composition the political leadership was moving away from the affiliated unions.

For their part the unions through the TUC were in the process of clarifying their direct relationship with Government. In the context of growing doubts about Britain's economic performance the Conservative Government was anxious after 1961 to involve the TUC in a new tripartite economic body, the National Economic Development Council. The majority of the TUC led by the General Secretary, George Woodcock, went along with this new movement of the unions 'from Trafalgar Square into Whitehall'. This first phase of TUC 'incorporation' into Government policy formulation had some significant concomitants in TUC attitudes and composition and some major consequences for the trade union relationship with the Party. In an attempt to broaden the composition of the TUC and bring in more of the white-collar unions there was an increasingly 'neutral' political tone given to the TUC's image. The proportion of TUC membership which was not affiliated to the Labour Party rose considerably as its white-collar composition increased.[46] In several ways there was an increase in the differentiation of trade unionists from Party members[47] and there was a decline in the significance of Party-trade union forums, particularly the National Council of Labour.[48]

These developments both from the Party side and from the union side served for the moment to clarify their functional differences. They were of considerable long-term significance for the form and cohesion of the traditional relationship. But in the short run also they tended to exacerbate the tensions arising from the behaviour of the Labour Government after 1966.

Britain's financial, economic and industrial problems loomed large and put a strain on the Labour Government-union relationship so great that it caused the most serious confrontation in the history of the alliance. The attempt by Labour's Prime Minister Harold Wilson to make Labour 'the Party of Government' involved an assertion of the Labour Government's independence of industrial labour to a degree which eventually rivalled that of the MacDonald Governments. In an attempt to establish clearly an unambiguous 'national' image for the Government there were times when it appeared to be claiming a positive virtue for its unwillingness to court the popularity of some of its most loyal trade union supporters. Thus substantial sectors of the mining industry were closed,[49] there were some tense industrial disputes in which the Government was closely involved,[50] and unemployment was allowed to rise to new post-war levels.[51] The voluntary incomes policy agreed with the unions in Opposition soon turned into a statutory policy and many of the benefits claimed for it in Opposition failed to materialise. As a consequence one major union after another slowly turned against the policy.

The culmination of a growing conflict over inflation, wage levels, shop floor militancy and strikes was an attempt by the Labour Government to bring in legislation to cover industrial relations. The proposals in the White Paper 'In Place of Strife' included elements which under other circumstances would have appealed to the unions. But there were clauses which involved penal sanctions upon offending trade unions and trade unionists and the vast majority of unions reacted strongly against this intrusion by a Labour Government into the 'closed' areas.

After months of internal conflict, opposition to the penal clauses was so great within the Parliamentary Party that the Government was forced to retreat. The TUC gave a 'solemn and binding' undertaking to try to prevent and settle industrial disputes; the Industrial Relations Bill which the Government eventually produced in April 1970 was emasculated of the offending proposals. This conflict had several psychological effects. It heightened the sense of estrangement which union leaders were already feeling from the Labour Government. It fed the current of militant Left-wing opinion running within the unions and it increased the resentment of those on the right of the Parliamentary leadership who saw the union connection as both an electoral handicap and a Governmental hindrance. Given the sense of industrial self-sufficiency of the trade unions at this point and their reliance on the direct relationship with Government it might well have threatened the Labour Government - Labour Party - trade union relationship in a more fundamental way — had the Labour Government been re-elected.

But Labour was replaced by a Conservative Government with an ideological programme which challenged some fundamentals of the post-war consensus. Its actions within that programme, including the promulgation of a complete framework of law to cover the field of industrial relations, led to a halting and embittered dialogue between the TUC and the Government — a 'cold war' in which the unions again looked to the Labour Party to protect their fundamental industrial functions. Reacting to the Conservative Government and reacting to the behaviour of Labour's ex-Ministers when they were in Office the affiliated unions moved to a much more positive role in Party policy-making and a re-establishment of the national linkage between the Party and the TUC.

In retrospect the majority of both the union leaders and the Parliamentary leaders drew from the experience of the period from 1966 to 1970 the lesson that it was imperative that a Labour Government and the unions work in closer consultation and harmony. From the unions advance consultation was demanded so that the Labour Government could clear away the industrial legislation of the Conservatives and protect the unions from further legislative measures. From the Party leadership the consultation was accepted because it was realised that incomes policy of any kind could only be practical if it involved consent. The result was the formation of a body which in practice replaced the National Council of Labour as a consultative forum — the Liaison Committee.[52] From it came in February 1973 the document *Economic Policy and the Cost of Living* — the 'Social Contract' as it came to be known. This embodied a commitment by the political leadership that they would abolish the legal framework for industrial relations, promulgate various measures of economic, industrial and social reform, and respect the unions' concern with free collective bargaining. For their part the unions gave a somewhat vague undertaking to exercise a measure of restraint in that bargaining. This formal accommodation between the two leadership groups was reinforced by the emergence of a new troika of key personnel. The links between

Harold Wilson, the Party Leader, Michael Foot, one of the most senior of the Party Left-wing MPs and Jack Jones, the General Secretary of the Transport and General Workers Union, were a cementing force of the Party-union relationship in this period and in Government after 1974.

The circumstance in which Labour again took Office were such as to solidify the relationship. Conservative Government policy had pushed the Party and the unions closer together in policy and the confrontation between the Conservatives and the National Union of Mineworkers which led to the General Election pushed the two into closer electoral identification. There developed a much closer understanding between the Labour Government and the unions than was seen in the later years of the Wilson Administration. It was based on a determination to avoid the ruptures of the past and to avoid the return of the Conservatives. In policy terms the unions won a range of major industrial gains.[53] And there was a respect from the Government for the union's abhorrence of a statutory incomes policy. Further, sensitivity to the union connection was reflected in the personnel of the Wilson and particularly Callaghan Cabinets.[54] It was reflected also in the preservation of the Liaison Committee as a regular linkage between Party-TUC and Government and above all it was reflected in the central place which the Government gave publicly to its connection with the unions.

Nevertheless, as before, the trade union-party relationship had another face. The price for the unions of this co-operation and legislation was very high. After fifteen months of escalating wage settlements the TUC, frightened by the rise in unemployment and inflation[55] and its international repercussions, accepted a voluntary wage restraint policy of unparalleled severity.[56] And in 1976 it renewed the commitment.[57] Further, though there were differences between the TUC and the Government over economic policy these were pressed very gently. The TUC was even muted in its criticism of major public expenditure cuts and of Government policy which necessarily increased the level of unemployment. Indeed in 1976 the co-operation and loyalty given to the Labour Government by trade union leaders was every bit as conscientious as that given by the post-1945 generation, with much less to show for it except the hope that the economic recovery with Labour in Office would sustain both the Labour Government and in the long-term the economic aspirations of the unions.

2. Internal Relations: Democracy, Power and Authority

The pattern of power in the Party often involved a heavy-handed centralism with considerable partiality between the competing factions. Control over the National Executive Committee gave control over its Organisation sub-committee, the National Agents Department and the Party regional machine. This gave a position of leverage over the process of candidate selection: in principle it was the prerogative of the constituency parties but in practice it was subject to some close supervision.[58] This gave a position of control over dissent within the Party: in principle there was free and open discussion but in practice there was a list of proscribed organisations, a close observance over groups which might form 'parties within the Party', a ban on Parliamentary factions, and considerable pressure upon Parliamentary dissidents. This gave also a role in the management of the Annual Conference: in principle the agenda was decided by the freely elected committee of Conference delegates but in practice Party officials played an important part in the links between the Parliamentary leaders and the Conference Arrangements Committee which established an agenda which sometimes gave crucial advantages to the Party leadership.[59]

So much of this pattern depended on the fact that the majority in each of the major forums was held by those from the Right of the Party and particularly on the alignment of a majority of the unions with the Parliamentary leadership. In 1956 the advent of Frank Cousins as a Left-wing General Secretary of the Transport and General Workers Union brought a new possibility of instability to the 'block vote' base. For the moment it remained only a possibility because, contrary to myth, the behaviour of the T & GW delegation in the next three years was consistent with the position it had taken throughout the 1950s.[60] And in any case the leadership of three other unions which had occasionally supported the dissenting Left — the Engineers, the Shop Workers and the Railwaymen — was moving to the Right. Thus not only did elections for the NEC follow the pattern of Right-wing dominance but the controversial domestic and defence policies of the new Party leadership secured majorities at the Party Conference on every occasion that they were debated.

The position of the Parliamentary leadership began to look different following the General Election of 1959. Gaitskell's failure to secure change in the Party constitution (discussed below) and the growing strength of the Left-wing movement towards Britain's unilateral nuclear disarmament produced a crisis of authority within the Party. Matters were brought to a head at the 1960 Party Conference when the unilateralists won[61] and the central issue became: should the Conference be able to determine the policy of the Parliamentary leadership?

Gaitskell said no. And for twelve months he fought — and fought
successfully — with the aid of a new Right-wing factional machine[62]
to win union support and reverse the Annual Conference decision.

This was a clear attempt to establish once and for all the independence
of the Parliamentary Party from the Annual Conference but as usual
with the Labour Party there was more than a hint of ambiguity to a
pattern of behaviour which appeared open and uncomplicated. The
defiance at the Conference implied that the Conference had no
authority. Twelve months of seeking to reverse the decision implied
that it had. Nevertheless in numerical terms[63] the victory was Gaitskell's
and there were many repercussions for intra-Party democracy. For a
start it broke the taboo of Conference supremacy. Even at the height
of their power as Government Ministers the Attlee generation had
genuflected towards the final authority of the Conference. Now, for a
decade the authority of the Conference diminished and though in the
early 1970s there was to be some re-establishment of its position it
never returned to the situation of the 1940s and 1950s when the
wording of its decisions was subject to the most dexterous management
and exegesis. Further, with the victory of multilateralism went also the
dominance of the Gaitskellites and the ascendancy of revisionism, in
spite of Gaitskell's failure to change the Constitution and in spite of
the evidence of considerable support for traditional Socialist measures
within the affiliated organisations. Finally Gaitskell himself took on a
new stature and the office of Leader was enhanced in prestige to a
degree which allowed him an independence even of the factional
machine which had sustained him in his critical hour.[64]

The election of Harold Wilson following the sudden death of
Gaitskell made remarkably little immediate difference to the relations
of power and authority established during the period of Gaitskell's
leadership. The ex-Gaitskellites continued to dominate other senior
positions within the Parliamentary Party and the Labour Government.
And in the Government's early years the majority of trade union
leaders continued to ensure that their votes went in support of
Wilson's political leadership.

But the actions of his Government from 1966 were to have
momentous consequences for the Party's power structure and its
internal democracy. As Government policy increasingly departed from
that of the affiliated organisations so the Party Conference began to
register a range of defeats for that policy.[65] The Government to the
consternation of many party activists responded by virtually ignoring
the decisions. Thus by the end of 1968 the Labour Conference appeared

an impotent ceremonial assembly, intra-Party democracy an empty
procedure, and the authority of the Party Conference superseded by
the permanent authority of the Parliamentary leadership. It seemed
that at least one ambiguity had been erased: Labour in Opposition and
in Government appeared virtually indistinguishable from its political
opponents in its internal distribution of power.

But the appearance was misleading. Labour's internal relations are
uniquely affected by the changing role and behaviour of the unions.
By the end of 1968 the Conference decisions which the Government
was ignoring included some which were of central concern to the unions.
Their resentment at Government policy, particularly over incomes, led
to a renewal of the strength of the Left. New Left-wing officials were
elected in four of the six largest unions in the period from 1967 to
1969.[66] The most significant of these was Hugh Scanlon who replaced
a formidable loyalist Lord Carron in the Amalgamated Engineering
Union. The alliance of Scanlon with Jack Jones of the Transport
workers became a central feature of union politics in the next few
years. Their position as leading trade unionists of the Left was
enhanced by the pattern of union growth, amalgamations and
occupational changes which affected both their unions and others to
the overall advantage of the Left.[67] Thus by 1969 the Right-wing block
vote was no longer the dominant feature of 'floor' politics at the Party
Conference, and the trade union Left was in a more powerful position
than it had been at any time in the Party's history.

In the short run the new strength of the Left and the increasing
hostility of the unions to Government policy had no immediate effect
in producing compliance with the policies of the Conference. And the
rather more assertive NEC was unable to force a radical election
Manifesto. But considerable changes were under way and some were
already obvious. The Government had lost that control over the
extra-Parliamentary party so evident under previous Labour
Governments. The Party machine under a new General Secretary and a
new National Agent[68] began to establish a more liberal relationship
with the much depleted Party in the country. And the NEC was
beginning a compositional shift to the Left which ultimately by 1975
enabled Left-wing MPs to take the Chairmanship of both its policy
sub-committees.[69]

In Opposition after 1970 the full extent of the changes became
apparent. The NEC became a more important policy-making body with
a far greater independence of the Parliamentary leadership than when
the Party last moved from Government into Opposition nearly twenty

years ago. A new 'political' General Secretary, Ron Hayward, was appointed in 1972 and he took seriously his designated role as defender of the policy of the extra-Parliamentary Party.[70] The Conference itself was now less subject to agenda manipulation than it had been for many years and more assertive in its attitude towards the Party leadership. The new strength of the Left-wing at the Conference and the new ethos in which traditional Socialist proposals were far more acceptable was reflected in a range of policy defeats inflicted by the Conference on even the Leftward-moving NEC.[71] By utilising the Clause V procedure of the Party Constitution[72] the NEC had room for manoeuvre with some of these decisions. Nevertheless the Conference had more authority in this period than it had done in the previous decade.

Once again the old rhetoric of respect for the authority of the Conference and the policy-making sovereignty of the members was prominent in Party documents. As usual this idealised the reality but it was certainly the case that now in Opposition the position of the Parliamentary leadership was clearly circumscribed. It was limited by the normal processes of consultation which accompany NEC policy-making but there was also the Liaison Committee upon which the union leaders played a more initiating role in policy-making. As a result much of the Party's policy in Opposition came from extra-Parliamentary sources.

There were changes also in the Party's treatment of dissent. Since 1966 factions had been allowed to operate within the PLP and discipline became much less rigid than it had been in earlier periods. In spite of major revolts against Labour Government policy there was little in the way of disciplinary action and no suspension of the Parliamentary Whip. A similar pattern emerged with the treatment of dissent from the Right after 1970. The Pro-Marketeers broke a major Party taboo by voting with the Conservative Government over the terms of entry.[73] But then and subsequently there was no attempt to enforce discipline over them. The new liberalism and tolerance was extended to the behaviour of the Organisation sub-Committee and the National Agent's Department which grew less prone to pursue organised Left deviants in the constituency Parties.

Subsequently, there was a remarkable new development in the relationship between MPs and their constituency Parties. With the NEC exercising a purely legal check on the re-selection process, four prominent Right-wing MPs were rejected on political grounds by their local parties in the period from 1972 to 1976.[74] Thus the members of a PLP which was still predominantly Right-wing under Harold Wilson and then James

Callaghan[75] had much greater reason to look over their shoulders at the party activists.

The changing role of the NEC was also evident in its relationship with the Labour Government after 1974. It became much more ready to pursue the Government in support of Annual Conference decisions and much more independent of the Government in formulating the new Party programme. The Government's rapport with the TUC (in which several of the major union leaders appeared after 1974 to be moving to the Right) was much greater than that with the NEC. The complexity of this situation was indicated in the clear divergence of style and content between the new 'social contract' of 1976 and the new Party programme the same year. At the same time the Conference was diverging from the Government to a degree which still outflanked the position of the NEC and there were substantial defeats for the Government at both the 1975 and 1976 Party Conferences.[76] As with the previous Labour Government, Ministers avoided most of these decisions. Thus there was now a considerably policy divergence not only between the Labour Government and the various extra-Parliamentary bodies but between all the major committees and forums of the Labour movement, and a remarkably fluid pattern of alignment.

3. Purpose and Policy

The environment in which Gaitskell was elected to the leadership was one in which all the ingredients favoured the emergence of a powerful movement of Right-wing Socialist revisionism. The Conservative Governments of 1951 and 1955 had made little attempt to dismantle the foundations of the Welfare State. There was an unprecedented growth in general affluence and a period of relative industrial and international peace. In these circumstances the dichotomy of Socialism and Capitalism no longer presented itself with the stark clarity of the past. The traditional Socialist critique of Capitalism appeared to be outmoded and even the Socialist goal itself no longer had quite the same utopian appeal after the experience of public corporations at home and the dead winter of Stalinism in 'the home of Socialism'.

In this situation revisionists[77] brought forward a new analysis of the social and economic system. It was presented as a humane post-Capitalist 'mixed economy' in which, with the State playing a positive role in economic life and with the application of Keynesian techniques, the old instabilities had been eradicated. The pattern of booms and slumps was a thing of the past; structural unemployment and primary poverty had been abolished. Within industry the divorce of ownership and control had led to a new ethic moderating the pursuit of profit maximisation. And the trade unions now had a major countervailing power. With sensible economic management and the rise of meritocratic forces there was no reason why rapid economic growth should not produce continuously rising living standards and the resources on which to base a governmental policy of social justice.

Revisionists brought to bear on this diagnosis a reinterpretation of the Party's fundamental purposes. Socialism, since the 1930s generally accepted to involve a structural theory of change and a goal defined in terms of common or public ownership, was now defined as a syndrome of values. The three given emphases were equality, social justice (or welfare) and personal freedom. Public ownership was relegated to the status of being just one means amongst several for the achievement of the Socialist ends.

This revisionism was to achieve an overwhelming influence on the Party's official policy for the next fifteen years but its introduction encountered strong resistance. The Left opposition to Gaitskell and his allies took regular factional form[78] based not only on a traditional Socialist rejection of revisionism but also on a defence and foreign policy perspective in which there was a strong tinge of neutralism, an antipathy to the level of defence expenditure and, particularly, a growing opposition to the idea that Britain should have, or be a base for, nuclear weapons. The conflicts over defence policy were fought with high emotion and great commitment from both sides. Nevertheless it is arguable that some of the verbal disputes over the meaning of Party policy were fed by the resentment which had built up over the new drift of domestic policy.

We can trace three tactical approaches of the Gaitskell leadership as they attempted to come to terms with this resentment. The first attempt was embodied in the 1957 document *Industry and Society*. It was characteristic of the document and the period that an analysis of the economy which revealed the dominance of large firms and the obsolescence of ownership was accompanied by an acceptance that in the main these firms were 'serving the nation well'. Where public ownership was to be extended apart from re-nationalisation it was to be mainly through the mechanism of purchasing equity shares. How much and in what form was left vague and opponents of the change were reassured by the promise that this was to be a corollary of full-scale public ownership not a replacement of it. The ambiguities inherent in this prescription helped to give it substantial support at the Party

Conference.[79]

In the aftermath of the Party's 1959 election defeat Gaitskell moved towards an open rejection of the clause in the Party's constitution – Clause IV (4) – which embodied the traditional Socialist goal, and sought instead to replace it by a wider statement of values and an unambiguous acceptance of the mixed economy. The attempt was rebuffed and *Labour's Aims* which was the final product of this manoeuvre was accepted by the Conference only on terms which gave it little constitutional legitimacy.[80]

It is an irony of this period that the Gaitskellites who had been forced to retreat in their attempt to rid the Party's purpose of ambiguity should achieve much of what they wanted via a document which was in ideological terms ambiguous to an extent unusual even by Labour Party standards. *Signposts for the Sixties* (following *Labour in the Sixties*) appeared to be an attempt to straddle both Party traditions. In style and language it was a new mutant and was accepted at the Party Conference without even a card vote. On the one hand it was more critical of the failure of post-war private enterprise than the 1950s Party documents and in various indefinite ways offered the possibility of substantial advancement of public ownership. But its main motif was the Galbraithian diagnosis of 'private affluence and public squalor'. And the concentration of attention in the document was on taxation, education and social welfare. Specific commitments on public ownership were limited to the renationalisation of the steel industry.

The success of *Signposts for the Sixties* can to some extent be accounted for by the Party's preoccupation with the defence policy conflict. But it was also a reflection of the intellectual weakness of the Left's case in a period when all the social and economic trends appeared to be strengthening the revisionist perspective. An optimist of the Left might take much from the possibilities inherent in the new strategy of *Signposts for the Sixties*. But one man's new strategy for achieving Socialism is another man's strategy for avoiding it. For the next decade the Party's policy was to be interpreted by a leadership which was revisionist in philosophy and then under Wilson increasingly pragmatic in practice. Further it was a leadership which in Government became preoccupied with the problems of national economic management.

In retrospect this preoccupation can be seen in the Party documents of 1960 and 1961 with their stress on science and technology as forces of economic regeneration. But the central figure in the change of emphasis was Harold Wilson. Elected in 1963 at a time when Britain's economic record and institutions were coming in for increasing criticism

Wilson stressed the themes of modernisation, planning and advancement by merit. The egalitarianism involved in the latter and the continued emphasis on social justice preserved an ideological appeal differentiated from the Conservatives. But there were times in 1963 and 1964 when 'a breakthrough in the production barrier'[81] appeared to be the central goal.

This concern with giving a 'sharp cutting edge' to Britain's economic performance was accompanied by an insularity which now appears remarkable. Few envisaged the degree to which Britain's international and financial vulnerability would limit the freedom of action of even a government as cautious as that of Wilson. But the constraints were apparent within twenty-four hours of taking office.

Facing a balance of payments deficit of what seemed at the time astronomical proportions the new Wilson Government made defence of the £ sterling axiomatic to its policy and the central purpose became the rectification of the deficit. Subsequently the Government was caught in a repetitive series of crises of confidence in which in order to protect sterling it was forced into increasingly deflationary measures. These deflationary measures, affecting as they did the level of public expenditure, undermined the Party's social programme to an extent that it was possible to argue in 1970 that relative poverty had increased rather than diminished.[82] Concern for the confidence of the international financial community and for investment at home led to the avoidance of major egalitarian measures — such as the wealth tax — and even a new concern for the high level of standard tax rates. The only full public ownership measure enacted was the renationalisation of steel. In order to stimulate rationalisation the Labour Government encouraged the monopolies they had suggested in Opposition might be brought into public ownership and they handed out major subsidies to private industry without any of the share purchase implied in the 1961 Programme. Thus by the end of the Government's period of office, although some revisionists claimed that they had finally achieved their hegemony over the Party.[83] Socialism, whether defined in revisionist or traditional terms, was very much a subordinate element in the Government's purpose.

Perhaps the Government's greatest achievement lay in its liberal humanitarianism. It presided over an impressive spate of radical social and penal legislation covering abortion, capital punishment, homosexuality, divorce law and theatre censorship. These were mainly initiated from the back benches and to some extent cut across Party lines. But they were very much in line with the personal freedom emphasised by revisionist Socialism. History may judge that this was the one area where revisionists were as radical in practice as they claimed in theory.

Pragmatism in much of the Government's domestic policy was paralleled by pragmatism in defence and foreign policy. The ideologically distinctive elements of defence and foreign policy were soon reduced. Under the pressure of economic exigency the Government eventually set a firm date for a withdrawal from bases east of Suez but the nuclear capacity was retained and the Government's policy towards Vietnam, Rhodesia and Greece aroused considerable anger within the Party. The European Economic Community in which Labour had shown only reluctant interest since the 1962 Party Conference was made the object of a firm application for membership, an application which, though rejected, was left to lie on the table.

By 1969 the balance of payments deficit had been rectified and in 1970 the Government could argue that Britain was now strong and the time was opportune to make it 'great to live in'.[84] But the purposes inherent in the Wilsonian definition of greatness appeared to be only vaguely related to the ideological purposes debated so fiercely in the 1950s. And for many in the Party a favourable balance of payments was inadequate when set against the policy failures of the previous six years. Consequently in the aftermath of Labour's election defeat in 1970 there was a major ideological reaction within the Party, with a critical re-examination of the purpose and strategy which had formed the basis of policy in the previous decade.

By this time the ethos of British politics had changed considerably from that so congenial to revisionism in the middle 1950s. Gone was the optimism about economic management, the achievement of high growth rates and the effectiveness of fiscal measures to reduce inequality — all fundamental elements in the revisionist case. At a time when rising unemployment was combined with rapid inflation Keynes no longer appeared to be the saviour of advanced capitalism. And with the Conservative Government seeking to implement an ideological programme the post-war consensus was threatened for the first time since 1950.[85] Suddenly the language of capitalism, crisis and class appeared more relevant than it had done for three decades.

In this new phase traditional Socialism appeared to many within the Party to be of greater relevance to the problems of what was now more widely acknowledged as a capitalist economy. The change was most marked in the many resolutions submitted to the Party Conference demanding massive extensions in public ownership and industrial democracy. It was marked in the tendency for some of the more Right-wing unions to adopt a Left-wing position on public ownership and in the willingness of union leaders after 1970 to give their public ownership mandates a Left-wing interpretation. Symbolically, the Conference which had only reluctantly accepted commitment to the mixed economy in the statement of *Labour's Aims* in 1960, now reaffirmed unequivocally Clause IV of the Party's constitution.

Whilst revisionists appeared to have nothing new to offer in the way of an intellectual diagnosis[86] there was rather more fertility on the Left. One stream of thought, involving a leading member of the PLP, Anthony Benn, stressed the populistic character of the 'new politics' and made industrial democracy the central theme of its Socialist prescriptions.[87] A more sustained critique of the revisionist position which strongly influenced the Party's new industrial policy was one which stressed the growth of the multinationals and the need for public ownership and control to secure democratic accountability.[88] In general there was a much greater acceptance of the idea that the inefficiencies and inequalities of British Capitalism could only be rectified by a major extension of the public sector of the economy and a major extension of state control.

As always in the Labour Party the National Executive Committee played a brokerage role between the various intellectual tendencies. Thus what emerged from the complex and to some extent incoherent process of policy-making on the NEC after 1970 was a series of programmatic documents based around yet another unifying formula – 'a fundamental and irreversible shift in the balance of wealth and power in favour of working people and their families'.

The new documents reflected the Party's Leftward movement in several ways: in the language of Socialism and nationalisation, in the indictment of irresponsible capitalism and in the substantial list of public ownership commitments. But alongside this there was a concern with practical measures of immediate social, economic and industrial reform and the preservation of elements of the revisionist perspective of the late 1950s including, most paradoxical of all, the proposal for the National Enterprise Board to purchase equity shares in the twenty-five largest firms. This was seen as a Left-wing measure in 1976; in 1957 it would have been interpreted as merely a bold form of revisionism. Thus as always the Party's programme produced a radical base for Party unity which papered over the wide divergences of tactics and traditions.

The programme was one thing; the actions of the Labour Government were another. That Government was constrained by a variety of political forces unsympathetic to Labour's various social purposes. It required the goodwill and co-operation of private capital for investment. It required the understanding and sympathy of international capital to protect the pound. And its measures had to be consistent with obligations under a variety of organisational treaties of which the EEC now loomed largest.

In the early months of the Labour Government Left-wing Ministers at the Department of Industry[89] presented an industrial strategy based upon an extension of public ownership and control and industrial democracy. At Cabinet level these purposes were much weaker and they were under severe pressure from the City of London and the CBI. There was soon a clear and major shift. The National Enterprise Board was limited in its funds and powers and the Government's first priority became the stimulation of an expanding and profitable manufacturing base to the economy regardless of ownership.[90]

The Government did attempt to implement some of the more controversial elements in its election manifesto. The ferocity of the conflict in the House of Commons was indicative of ideological divisions on public ownership and social equality which continued to differentiate the major parties. But in a situation of extreme economic and financial vulnerability with a syndrome of fundamental problems — a massive balance of payments deficit,[91] escalating inflation,[92] the highest level of unemployment since the war[93] and a pound sterling rapidly diminishing in value[94] — the Government was prepared to launch major cuts in proposed public expenditure on the social services on a scale which far surpassed that of the previous Wilson Government.

Thus in 1976 not only was the Party's fundamental ambiguity of purpose unresolved but also the Labour Government was managing the economy through policies which were in fundamental conflict with the revisionist Socialism which was the formal commitment of the majority faction of the Cabinet.

4. Relations with the Electorate

Labour's defeat in the 1959 election was its third election defeat in a row and the second consecutive defeat in which the Party's share of the national vote had declined. (See Appendix I.) For a Party which had throughout much of its history taken an optimistic view both of its own inevitable organic growth and the inevitable germination of the values for which it stood, this defeat was quite traumatic. It followed three years of unprecedented social change and economic prosperity and it was these features to which attention was drawn in the subsequent post mortem.

Attention was particularly focused on two 'trends'. One was the *'embourgeoisement'* of the manual working-class, i.e. their alleged tendency to accompany their acquisition of increased material goods with an aspiration towards middle-class values and Conservative voting. Election studies carried out at the time [95] and the work of academics some of whom were sympathetic to revisionism[96] appeared to support the *embourgeoisement* thesis. Another trend to which attention was also drawn was that of the declining size of the blue-collar section of the workforce and the increasing number of white-collar workers. This was alleged to give the Conservative Party an increased potential constituency whilst diminishing Labour's traditional base of support.[97] From this diagnosis it was proposed that the Party should try to shed its 'cloth cap' image and adopt a clear 'people's party' identity.[98] Further the Party was urged to shed its inhibitions at utilising new techniques of electoral appeal and to shape that appeal by reference to what the electoral consumers found acceptable, and unacceptable.[99]

One consequence of this new diagnosis was to raise again the question of the distribution of authority within the Party. The desire of the Parliamentary leadership to reshape the Party's style and strategy seemed everywhere to be frustrated by the Party's structure and its format of intra-Party democracy. Hence the crisis over the Conference authority in 1960. Another consequence was to raise the problem of the degree to which the Party's connection with the manual worker unions gave the Party the same social identity at a time of increasing unpopularity of the unions.[100] Awareness of both these electoral 'costs' of the union connection shaped the attitude of Labour Ministers to the issues affecting the unions after 1966. A third consequence was to focus attention on the issue of nationalisation, found to be a significantly unpopular electoral policy.[101] Not only did this lead to an increased determination on the part of the leadership to avoid any further specific commitment on nationalisation but it also led Gaitskell to attempt for public consumption to repudiate the Party's commitment in Clause IV of the Constitution.[102]

The attempt to achieve the latter failed but having secured a victory over the unilateralist Left the Gaitskellites with support from ex-Bevanites like Harold Wilson and Richard Crossman could go ahead with the reform of the Party's electoral strategy. The result was that under Harold Wilson's leadership the Party could fight the 1964 election as a people's party in a modern 'classless style' and with a special appeal to the new

middle class. The strategy appeared to be extremely successful and
Wilson a particularly skilful mass media exponent of it. The Party
secured only a narrow majority at the 1964 election but then won a
clear victory in March 1966 in which Labour's share of middle-class
voters reached its 1945 level and its share of working-class voters
reached a new peak.[103]

But in the by-elections of the next four years the Wilson Government
staggered from one disaster to another.[104] Seeking now to establish its
image not only as a people's party but as the country's natural 'Party
of Government' the Wilson Government emphasised its responsibility
and made successful economic management its primary appeal. The
Government sought clearly to differentiate its national orientation from
that of 'sectional' trade union labour. There was no special attempt to
nourish the manual worker base of the Party nor was there any concerted
effort to halt the massive drift of Party membership (see Appendix II
and note 129). It was anticipated that the Government would
eventually make its appeal directly through the media on the basis of
its record. And it was anticipated that its record of 'painful responsibility'
would have its electoral reward. In the event the Party lost the 1970
election on the lowest poll since 1951.

There was none of the detailed post mortem of 1959 perhaps because
of the fear of tearing the Party in half, perhaps because those who had
used the data of political sociology in that period no longer found its
findings palatable. A major academic re-assessment had taken place of
the views accepted so readily in the early 1960s about working-class
political behaviour and electoral change.[105] For one thing, the
embourgeoisement thesis was shown to have much less impact than had
been thought;[106] the changing occupational structure likewise.[107] For
another thing there was now solid evidence that for demographic
reasons unexplored in earlier studies Labour's manual working-class base
was an increasing electoral asset.[108]

The 1970 defeat tended to be interpreted within the Party as the
consequence of a failure to nourish the working-class base of the Party
and particularly the hard core of active trade unionists.[109] There was
some evidence to support this belief [110] but, true or false, it had its effect
in a post-election situation where in any case the manual worker trade
unions were becoming more assertive within the Party.

Thus in by-elections after 1970 there was more of a stress in the
Party's electoral campaigns on bringing out the traditional Labour
voter. But the Party's changing electoral appeal was shaped by forces
which to some extent were no longer under its control. British politics

suddenly took on the aura of the 1920s as an ideological Conservatism
faced a militant trade unionism and the future of free collective
bargaining was at stake. Further, the rise of unemployment and the
confrontation with a more militant National Union of Mineworkers
raised all the class symbols of half a century previously. Labour fought
the February election in 1974 on ground chosen by the Conservative
Government and feared by Labour moderates, i.e. a 'who governs
Britain?' election in which the unions were seen as challenging national
governmental authority and the Party was seen as closely linked to the
unions.

The result from two perspectives was remarkable and unpredictable.
For one thing, to the surprise of many, the Conservatives lost much
ground and were replaced by Labour in office, but it was a Labour
Government with a diminished share of the national vote — a share
which increased only slightly in a further election held in October that
year (see Appendix III). The major surprise was the resurgence of the
Liberal Party[111] and the rise of Nationalism.[112] The Scottish Nationalists
in the wake of the election appeared poised to shatter the position of a
Labour Party which in Scotland had developed serious organisational
weaknesses 'and considerable insensitivity'.[113] Whilst the racialist
National Front established itself as the fourth party in England[114]
candidates from parties to the Left of Labour polled very badly even in
industrial areas deeply involved in the miners' dispute with the
Government.[115]

The results of these elections left Labour solidly entrenched in
industrial areas but with a declining proportion of the national,
working-class[116] and even trade union vote:[117] Class-party alignment has
weakened considerably[118] and, except amongst young voters, the
overall level of subjective class consciousness appears not to have
increased even during this period of confrontation between the
Conservative Government and the unions.[119]

There is room for considerable argument about the causes of the
phenomenon. On the surface it appears to bear out much of the general
diagnosis made in the late 1950s and early 1960s that the intensity of
class feelings and the influence of class as a force shaping voting
behaviour were diminishing as a result of various processes of social
change. But political parties are themselves major factors determining
the way in which the electorate defines their society.[120] And the
changes in the Labour Party have tended to transform the character of
the electoral competition.

This was not only a matter of the 'classless' strategy and of the 'national' policies consequent upon them but also important was the composition of Labour's leadership. The Parliamentary Labour Party has become increasingly a middle-class party. The working-class element has diminished to a minority of just over a quarter of the PLP. And the biggest rise has taken place amongst the university-educated middle class from the professions.[121] The change at leadership level is even more striking. By 1969 the Wilson Cabinet had only one manual worker in its ranks and only two other members who had come up through the trade union movement. There was some rectification in the mid-1970s but still the Callaghan Cabinet of September 1976 had only three ex-manual workers and only two others who had come up through the trade union movement.[122] Thus the appeal that the Labour Party presented was predominantly by Parliamentarians who were in social terms indistinguishable from the meritocratic section of the Conservative leadership.[123] Thus the developments in the Labour Party have played a considerable part in undermining the sharp contours of class-party politics.

A similar point could be made about the Party's ideological relationship with the electorate. There is evidence to indicate that on a range of major policies associated with the Party's Socialist purposes working-class support for the Party is becoming less and less enthusiastic: the Party has lost support in recent years for its committed position on racial integration, public expenditure on the social services and on public ownership.[124] At a time when Labour's Government is preoccupied with establishing its credential as a Government of sound economic management it is difficult to escape the conclusion that much of the educative Socialist case is going by default. This has important long-term consequences for the character of the Party's radicalism. If the overall shift of working-class opinion is politically to the Right it leaves them open to long-term mobilisation by forces very hostile to the Party. And even their continued support for the Labour Party as the Party of sound economic management is one which lays down narrow constraints on the radical alternatives that the Party can successfully adopt.

Appraisal

In the past two decades several attempts have been made to eradicate some of the Party's long standing ambiguities. Significantly, all these attempts were, in the end, unsuccessful. In the middle 1970s the ambiguities were if anything more profound than ever.[125] The Party is balanced uneasily between the forces of traditional and revisionist Socialism with some representatives of the latter now preferring to be known as 'social democrats'. The Party is balanced also between on the one hand powerful forces which have put the relationship with the unions under considerable strain and on the other hand urgent considerations which have stimulated a new accommodation and a remarkable sensitivity to trade union traditions. Electorally the Party has lost its 'cloth cap' image and it no longer commands the support of a majority of the manual working class; yet it is now more closely identified with the trade unions than a decade ago and is predominantly a party of the largely working-class conurbations. In spite of the growth of white-collar trade unionism the Party's affiliated membership remains overwhelmingly manual in occupation whilst the Parliamentary Party becomes increasingly drawn from the university-educated professional groups. These Parliamentarians have shown that when they form a Government they can ignore wide policy divergences between themselves and the extra-Parliamentary party, but in Opposition the strength of assertive trade unionism and extra-Parliamentary institutions forces a redistribution of power. It is arguable that the majority of the PLP have never been less sympathetic to the concept of intra-Party democracy but the fact remains that not since the Party's earliest years have they been under the pressure they now feel from the Party's constituency activists.

The complex interplay of these cross-pressures makes for a high degree of confusion in the Party's identity and ambivalence to its commitments. Probably the most acute ambiguity lies in the relationship between the Party and the unions. Arguably it is now the most important relationship in British politics; the future of the British economy and of the Labour Party may hinge upon its continued resilience. Awareness of this has led to a determination amongst both the political and the industrial leadership that the accommodation between them be preserved. From the union side this is grounded in an appreciation of the industrial legislation secured through the Labour Government and in a fear of the return of the Conservatives. From the Government side it is based on an understanding that either an industrial relations and incomes policy work in harmony with the unions or in the long run they will not work at all.

But from both sides there is an underlying ambivalence. In the case of the Parliamentary leadership it arises predominantly from electoral considerations. The Labour Government's unique capacity to invoke sympathetic support from the unions gives the PLP special election appeal as the one group of Parliamentarians who are likely to pull off a deal with the unions. And it is still the case that Labour's electoral

support has a bedrock of committed trade unionists. On the other hand
the unions continue to be unpopular with a majority of the electorate.
Their political power, real or imaginary, is resented (even by many rank
and file trade unionists)[126] and there is some evidence to suggest that
the Party's close attachment to the unions is a source of electoral
disadvantage amongst those who reject class politics.[127]

From the union side the doubt arises from a feeling that the Labour
Government is 'cashing cheques at the bank of loyalty' and that a rigid
incomes policy is storing up considerable industrial problems. Given
the determination of the unions to see a 'planned return to free
collective bargaining' and a diminution of unemployment the
short-term relationship between them and the Government is likely to
see an increase in tension. And in the long term the changing
composition of the TUC threatens its traditional political
commitments.[128] The development of the unions, continued
'incorporation' into Government, the changing electoral loyalties of
sections of the working-class, the growth of 'neutral' trade unionism
and the continuing atrophy of Labour's grass-roots,[129] could mean
eventually a much looser Party-union relationship.

Not only is the Party's long-term relationship with industrial labour
problematic but if anything its purposes are more uncertain. Indeed in
1976 it is arguable that the Party is in the throes of considerable
ideological fragmentation. A Party which in the late 1960s was held by
many to be a 'modern Revisionist' Party, after 1970 rediscovered its
official antipathy to Capitalism, reaffirmed the traditional Socialism of
Clause IV of its constitution and took on an extensive public ownership
programme. But in Government since 1974 there have been
developments which utterly confuse the ideological clarity of the Party
and its factions. Some of the Left-wing union leaders have begun
playing a role associated with the traditional Right, some on the Left
of the Party have adopted radical revisionist measures for state
intervention and are advocating them for radical Left-wing purposes,
and finally the Parliamentary Left and the trade union Left are divided
over the compatibility of incomes policy and Socialism and over the
extent of trade union co-operation with the Government. And, both
within the CLPs and amongst a minority of the Parliamentary Left,
Marxism has a greater appeal than at any time since the 1930s. Yet on
the Right of the Party there are those for whom a cautious reformism
in liaison with the unions defines their Socialism, those who have
consciously shed Socialism for a 'Social Democracy' which places
definite limits on the desirable extent of state ownership and some who

have even placed limits on the desirable level of public expenditure. Thus behind the central preoccupation with the management of an ailing economy there are divergences of purpose as great as any the Party has experienced. The situation is made even more acute by the fact that large sections of the Party have only reluctantly accepted the Government's crucial decisions to keep Britain in Europe and to devolve constitutional power on to national assemblies for Scotland and Wales. Each of these decisions could have fundamental and irreversible consequences for British politics and for the alignment of the parties. But the manner of the Party's commitment makes it likely that neither will be pursued with great conviction and both will continue to be a focus of bitter internal dispute.

These tensions over the Party's purposes are reflected in the differing perspectives on its electoral situation. Labour's return to Office in 1974 masked a considerable slippage of support. Its strength is now concentrated in the large conurbations and the broad classless appeal of the middle 1960s has faded. And yet at least part of the explanation for Labour's declining base of electoral support may be a deep ideological inhibition on the part of its leadership to the sharpening of its class image even when it appeared electorally valuable. It is arguable that the findings of the authoritative Butler and Stokes survey gave the Party good grounds for consolidating its appeal to the manual working class. But compared with the electoral studies of the late 1950s which appeared to show the reverse, comparatively little attention has been paid to this. Certainly on the basis of the evidence of generational displacement and working-class fertility it may well have been the case that Labour's movement away from its working-class base in the 1950s was a major error of strategy and one whose consequences cannot easily be undone. The move towards 'classless' Liberal and Nationalist and even racialist parties has been made that much easier by the weakening of class perceptions and attachments and consequently the Party is being forced into a position of running hard to follow the currents. Given the diversity of claims being expressed in the electoral arena and evidence of the fragmentation of the Party's class base it now seems likely that in the next decade we will see a further move towards making the Party a party 'of conscience and reform' — a 'catch-all' party of the moderate Left.

Much depends on the changing pattern of power within the Party. It remains to be seen whether the present fluid and confused situation will end in a consolidation of the position of the Right or Left. In spite of proposed constitutional reforms which would make CLP rejection of a sitting MP easier[130] and also make the Party Leader electable by the wider Party membership,[131] it looks as if for the moment the movement to the Left in the Party has reached its peak. The ambiguities inherent in the position of union leaders still associated with the Left but carrying out a Right-wing trade union role in conditions of extreme economic fragility may be resolved by adoption of the old 'praetorian guard' role. On the other hand if the Party moves back into opposition to a very Right-wing Conservative Government the Left may once again be strengthened — as will the forces of intra-Party democracy.

With so many unresolved dilemmas and ambiguities it is little wonder that the Party's long-term cohesion should appear problematic. In the short-term the forces of reconciliation and accommodation are extremely powerful. The uniting formula of 'a fundamental and irreversible shift in the balance of wealth and power in favour of working people and their families' clearly differentiates the egalitarian Party from its Conservative opponents. The Party has in James Callaghan a Party manager of exceptional adroitness. And the stigma of 1931 still commands considerable force in Party mythology. The Party is probably most vulnerable to a cleavage in which sections of the Parliamentary Right move into electoral and/or governmental coalition with national-minded centrist forces of other parties. A change in the electoral system, a governmental crisis culminating in a National Government, even a change in the financing of political parties could facilitate this development. For the Left of the Party, thwarted by so much that has happened in the past decade, there is no obvious re-alignment to the Left which would not involve a major weakness since independent parties to the Left of Labour have all suffered major electoral disaster.

But so much in the Party's development is dependent upon the experience of economic crisis. From 1964 it became apparent that there were major constraints upon the pursuit of Socialist goals in a mixed economy based on a weak international economic position. Even the more limited goals of 1950s revisionism now look visionary in a situation where Government policy is facing major obstacles of financial and economic stringency; not to mention the reconciliation of egalitarianism with the profit motive, 'financial confidence' with the pursuit of radical social justice. There is optimism that (when it arrives) North Sea Oil may change the financial situation. But otherwise Britain's economic and financial situation has not looked so precarious for nearly half a century. The Labour Party's own internal situation looks almost equally vulnerable and the future of the two are now inextricably intertwined. The Party has in the past emerged from critical periods with its basic strength intact and its sense of purpose replenished. It may well do so again. But not before it has taken decisions which will once again test its fundamental ambiguities.

Notes

1. The resolution calling for a special congress of 'co-operative, socialistic, trade union, and other working organisations' came from the Railway Servants although members of the Independent Labour Party appear to have played a role in its initiation. H. Pelling, *The Origins of the Labour Party* (London, Oxford University Press, 1965), p. 205.
2. Decisions of the courts undermining the collective bargaining position of the unions – particularly the Taff Vale judgement – stimulated trade union affiliation which rose from 41 unions and 353,070 members in 1900 to 181 unions and 1,049, 673 members by 1907.
3. It is part of the Constitution of the Labour Party that even individual members of the Constituency Labour Parties 'eligible for trade union membership must also be members of a union and contribute to its political fund'. (Clause III, 3 (b).) This clause was adopted in its present form in 1929 but the 1924 Party Conference had approved a constitutional amendment making trade union membership obligatory for individual party members. (*Labour Party Annual Conference Report* (hereafter LPACR) 1924, pp. 152-4.)
4. In 1918 the trade unions cast 2,471,000 votes out of a total conference vote of 2,746,000. The largest Socialist organisation, the ILP, cast 35,000 votes and the total constituency party vote was only 115,000. Even in 1953 at the height of constituency party representation out of a total conference vote of 6,417,000 the trade unions cast 5,086,000 votes, the CLPs only 1,307,000 and the Socialist, Co-operative and Professional organisations only 24,000 votes.
5. In 1900 the trade unions agreed to an allocation of seats on the new Executive Committee on which they had 7 seats and the Socialist societies 5 seats. By 1914 the National Executive Committee had grown to a membership of 16 – 11 representatives of the Trade Unions, 3 representatives of the Socialist Societies, 1 representative of Trade Councils, Local Labour Parties and Women's Organisations, and the Treasurer. Apart from the Treasurer all were elected at annual conference by the respective sections. In 1918 a major change in the method of election was approved and there was a significant change in the NEC's composition. The NEC comprised 23 members – 13 from affiliated organisations, 5 from local Labour Parties, 4 women, and the Treasurer – elected by the Party Conference as a whole making the NEC subject to the voting preponderance of the trade unions. Since 1937 the Constituency Labour Parties have elected 7 representatives, the Socialist organisations 1, and the trade unions 12 but in addition the 5 Women's representatives and the Treasurer are elected by the whole conference. Thus the trade unions could command 18 of the 27 positions on the NEC. In 1953 the Deputy Leader of the Party joined the Leader with ex-officio status on the Committee. In 1972 the Young Socialists secured 1 representative since then the NEC has had 29 members.
6. Up to and including the Parliament of 1918 the PLP was overwhelmingly trade union sponsored. In 1922 there was a significant increase in the unsponsored

component and generally between the wars the percentage ranged from 39 per cent in 1929 to 76 per cent in 1931. Since the Second World War approximately one-third of the PLP has been sponsored by the trade unions. In October 1974 it was a figure of 127 out of a total of 319.

7. Estimates of the trade union financial contribution to the Party vary widely because of the difficulty of assessing the source of income at the local and regional level. Overall estimates have varied between 40 and 70 per cent. (M. Harrison, *Trade Unions And The Labour Party Since 1945* (London, Allen & Unwin, 1960), p.100. R. Rose, *Influencing Voters* (London, Faber, 1967), pp. 250-60.) The Party is most reliant on the unions for its General Election Fund and for the financing of its national organisation. The Party's accounts for 1975 reveal that of the £1,246,978 received by the Party nationally in affiliations and contributions no less than £1,117,515 came from the unions.

8. Until the 1974 General Elections it was a feature of Labour's electoral support that there was a strong correlation between trade union membership and Labour voting. J. Blondel, *Voters, Parties and Leaders* (Harmondsworth, Penguin, 1974), p. 65. For recent changes see p.131 of this article.

9. V. Allen, *Trade Unions And The Government* (London, Longmans, 1960), pp. 221, 222, 239 and 240.

10. *Labour Party Constitution and Standing Orders*. Standing Order 4, iii (d).

11. W. Citrine, *Men and Work* (London, Hutchinson, 1964), pp. 74-5.

12. V. Allen, *Trade Union Leadership* (London, Longmans, 1957), p. 142.

13. Between 1921 and 1926 the Labour Party and the TUC shared common research facilities. And from 1927 to 1956 they both occupied Transport House as their respective national headquarters. It was intended that the Labour Party should follow the TUC to their new headquarters at Congress House but in the end the Party could not afford the rent and therefore the Party remain tenants of the Transport and General Workers' Union.

14. Between 1902 and 1956 the percentage of union members affiliated to the TUC varied between the low point of 64.7 in 1914 and the high point of 85.7 in 1946. Union membership affiliated to the Labour Party varied between 27.4 in 1943 and 65.8 in 1927. This difference reflected both the larger number of unions affiliated to the TUC and the larger membership on which unions affiliated. Derived from Table 4.13 in G.S. Bain, R. Bacon, and J. Pimlott, 'The Labour Force', in A.H. Halsey (ed.), *Trends In British Society Since 1900* (London, Macmillan, 1972), p. 125.

15. V. Allen, *Trade Unions And The Government,* pp. 230-5, 241-5.

16. The other two were Philip Snowden, Chancellor of the Exchequer, and Jimmy Thomas, Secretary of State for Dominion Affairs. MacDonald became Prime Minister in the National Government.

17. Under the terms of the 1913 Trade Union Act it was made legal for unions to incur political expenditure provided that this came out of a special political fund and any member who did not wish to participate could 'contract out' of the political levy: i.e. the proportion of his dues paid into the political fund. In 1927 the Trade Disputes and Trade Unions Act changed the basis from 'contracting out' to 'contracting in'. In 1946 the Labour Government's Trade Disputes and Trade Unions Act returned it to a basis of 'contracting out'.

18. On 4 February 1948 the Government produced a new White Paper – *The Statement on Personal Incomes, Costs and Prices*. This wages policy document was issued without prior consultation with the TUC.

19. On 8 February 1951 seven members of the TGWU were arrested under war-time legislation remaining on the statute book for conspiring to incite dockworkers to take part in strikes in connection with trade disputes. Eventually after strikes and protests the prosecutions were withdrawn.

20. The sovereignty of the Party Conference was asserted in Clause 5.1. of the 1918 Constitution. 'The work of the Party shall be under the direction and control of the Party Conference . . . '
21. Clause 6 (a). *The Constitution & Standing Orders of the Labour Party*, 1918.
22. These qualifications were contained in phrases like 'with a view to giving effect . . . ' (Clause 4 (c)) and 'as the occasion may present itself . . . ' (Clause 4 (a)). A resolution of the 1907 Party Conference referred to 'the time and method of giving effect to (Conference) decisions . . . ' as a matter for Parliamentary discretion. (*LPACR*, 1907, p. 49.)
23. Put simply, the distinction was between those who took a militant/visionary and those who took a moderate/practical approach to the Party's policy and strategy – particularly over public ownership. But there were many other points of difference. In Office there was a distinction between those who wanted to exemplify 'socialist principles' and those who wanted to exemplify 'fitness to govern' and there was a difference in the stress placed upon working-class as opposed to national interests. There were differences also in the industrial arena where the Left's militancy was sometimes accompanied by support for industrial action for political purposes. This reflected itself in attitudes towards the Communist Party which the Left was prepared to treat as a deviant part of the working-class movement whilst the Right would have nothing to do with what was considered an alien and undemocratic force. International policy differences were even more complicated. Both Left and Right supported the concept of a 'socialist' foreign policy but this involved a complex range of perspectives – ethical, humanitarian, pacifistic and 'labour united with labour'. In practice in the 1930s the two wings divided over the issue of collective security and over the form and content of various anti-Fascist alliances.
24. *LPACR*, 1955, pp. 106, 277-82.
25. There were several votes in which 'the platform' came close to defeat, particularly that on German rearmament in 1954, and often the NEC had to amend its policies in anticipation of the mandates of the unions. The Left was strong in several smaller unions but also in three large ones – the Amalgamated Engineering Union, The Union of Shop, Distributive and Allied Workers and the National Union of Railwaymen.
26. McKibbin raises doubts about the extent to which the unions supported this new commitment. R. McKibbin, *The Evolution of the Labour Party 1910-1924* (London, Oxford University Press, 1974), pp. 91-106.
27. It is possible to distinguish various strands of British Socialism. An ethical concern with social injustice; a sentimental and optimistic concern with the spiritual and moral regeneration of man leading to harmony and brotherhood; a trade union concern with solidarity and the freedom of industrial labour; a technocratic concern with efficiency, planning and rational collectivism; and a class concern asserting the position of labour in a Capitalist system based upon property relationships. These were not mutually exclusive and the personnel of Labour's leadership drew from what Cowling has described as 'a ragbag of attitudes, purposes programmes and intentions . . . '. M. Cowling, *The Impact of Labour 1920-1924* (London, Cambridge University Press, 1971), p. 28.
28. Throughout the history of the Party there have been those in the Leadership who regard it, in Sidney Webb's words as a 'shibboleth', *(LPACR*, 1918, p.44.) In the 1920s it was given little emphasis by Labour's Parliamentary leadership but it became more central to the Party's policies in the 1930s.
29. The ILP's membership declined from 16,773 to 4,392 between 1932 and 1935. See R. Dowse, *Left In the Centre* (London, Longmans, 1966), p. 193.

In 1935 the ILP put up 17 Parliamentary candidates but only 4 were elected. By 1951 there were only 3 ILP Parliamentary candidates and they all lost their deposits.

30. The Communist Party had only 4 MPs between its inception in 1920 and the General Election of 1950. Since 1950 there have been no Communist MPs and the Party's vote has sunk almost to insignificance.

31. A. Marwick, *Britain In The Century of Total War* (London, Bodley Head, 1968), p. 389. For a discussion of the significance of the 1945 Labour Government see P. Addison, *The Road To 1945* (London, Cape, 1976); Marwick, pp. 329-60; A. Marwick, *The Explosion of British Society 1914-1970* (London, Macmillan, 1970), pp. 111-21.

32. The Bevanites became associated with the Left-wing demand for a new nationalisation programme but the main confrontations between them and the Right took place over the level of defence expenditure (which the Bevanites argued was crippling the nation's social policy) and over foreign policy.

33. On this see S. Webb, *The New Constitution of the Labour Party* (Labour Party pamphlet, 1918), p. 2.

34. W. Guttsman, *The British Political Elite* (London, MacGibbon & Kee, London), 1965), p. 237.

35. Derived from tabular matter in Guttsman, W. op. cit. p. 242. The figures given are 10 of 20 (1924); 9 of 19 (1929); 11 of 20 (1945) and 9 of 18 (1950). Allen, *Trade Unions And The Government,* gives the number of trade unionists as 7 in 1924, 6 in 1929, and 6 in 1945. (pp. 238, 259, 291.)

36. Allen points out that by 1951 the number of trade unionists had dropped to 4 out of 17. (pp. 292-3.)

37. Labour's vote had risen from 2,385,472 in 1918 to 8,389,512 in 1929 when the Party won 288 seats. Though it won only 52 seats in 1931 it received 6,649,630 votes.

38. Labour won 393 seats in the House of Commons, an overall majority of 146.

39. See H. Durant, 'Voting Behaviour in Britain 1945-1964', in R. Rose (ed.), *Studies in British Politics* (London, Macmillan, 1969), p. 123.

40. Labour secured 13,948,605 votes. This was the highest number of votes received by any single party before or since. Nevertheless the Party won only 295 seats as against the Conservatives' 321.

41. The individual Party membership in 1955 was 843,356; this had been dropping since 1952 when it peaked at 1,014,524. The trade union affiliated membership was 5,605,988 which was, up to that point, the highest in the Party's history.

42. The policy-making staff at Labour's headquarters had risen from 8 in 1939 to 27 in 1958. In 1955 there were 227 Party Agents compared with 125 in 1937.

43. Several of the Left-wing trade union leaders who emerged in senior positions in major unions in the late 1960s had broken with the Communist Party in this period. They included Lawrence Daly who became General Secretary of the National Union of Mineworkers, High Scanlon who became President of the Amalgamated Engineering Union, and Richard Seabrook who became President of the Union of Shop, Distributive and Allied Workers. In addition Les Cannon and Frank Chapple of the Electrical Trades Union broke with the Communist Party in 1956 and subsequently waged a successful battle to overthrow the Communist leadership of the union; by the late 1960s they had emerged as the most Right wing of the leaders of unions affiliated to the Party.

44. A secret committee of twelve members of the TUC General Council organised support for Gaitskell in his attempts to reverse the 1960 Party Conference

decision. See P. Seyd, *Factionalism Within the Labour Party: A Case Study of the Campaign For Democratic Socialism* (M. Phil thesis, 1968), p. 139.

45. In 1959 Labour's affiliated unions were made up predominantly of manual workers. There was very little change in this position in the decade between 1960 and 1970 when the total vote of the white-collar unions was still less than 5 per cent of the total union vote of 5,473,000.

46. Between 1964 and 1970 there was a 75 per cent increase in the affiliated TUC membership of white-collar unions to 2,046,137. By the end of 1971 the 2,916,000 non-manual trade unionists made up 30 per cent of the TUC's total membership.

47. In 1962 there was a constitutional amendment that only trade unionists who were individual members of the Party could be trade union delegates to the Party Conference. (Clause VII (i) of the *Constitution and Standing Orders of the Labour Party,* 1962.) In 1965 the provision was extended to trade union delegates attending constituency party meetings. (Model Rules, clause vii(i).)

48. On this see L. Minkin, 'The British Labour Party and The Trade Unions: Crisis and Compact', in *Industrial and Labour Relations Review,* vol.28, no.1 (Oct. 1974), pp. 19-20. In this period an attempt was made to wind up the remaining local joint Trades and Labour Councils.

49. Between 1966 and 1970 a total of 187 pits was closed and the labour force declined by 150,000. (*Digest of Energy Statistics* (HMSO, 1970), pp.39-40.)

50. The two most significant disputes were the Seamens' Strike of July 1966 and the Dock Strike of July 1967.

51. Unemployment rose to a monthly average of 559,300 (2.7 per cent) by January 1970.

52. The Liaison Committee was set up in January 1972. It initially had a membership of 18 − 6 from the PLP, NEC, and TUC respectively − plus an additional 3 office staff from Transport House and 3 from Congress House. There was some change in the composition of the Liaison Committee. In 1975 it was composed of 6 members of the TUC, 7 members of the NEC and 9 members of the PLP plus an office staff of 1 from Transport House and 1 from Congress House.

53. The Conservative Government's Industrial Relations Act was repealed as was the legislative and institutional framework of its prices and incomes policy. New Trade Union and Labour Relations Acts were introduced in 1974 and 1975 as well as an Employment Protection Act and an Industry Act in 1975 both of which included provisions which the unions wanted. To these can be added the Equal Pay and Sex Discrimination legislation and the introduction of a Manpower Services Commission, a Health and Safety Commission and an Advisory, Arbitration and Conciliation Service.

54. In the Callaghan Cabinet of September 1976 there were three ex-manual workers (Roy Mason and Eric Varley − mineworkers − and Stan Orme − engineer). There was also one ex-draughtsman (Albert Booth) and one former official of the Inland Revenue Staff Federation (James Callaghan). In addition Michael Foot and Tony Benn strongly identified themselves with the trade unions. Foot in particular was a vital link between the Cabinet and the unions, first as Secretary of State for Employment and then as Leader of the House of Commons.

55. Between January and June 1975 the retail price index rose by 31 per cent. In January 1975 unemployment was 742,000 (3.3 per cent).

56. The TUC agreed that all wage rises should be limited to £6 per week whilst for those earning over £8,500 no increase would be allowed.

57. In 1976 wage rises were limited to 5 per cent up to a maximum of £4 per week.

58. It was particularly significant that although the CLPs had the formal right to refuse reselection to their sitting MP, in practice where an attempt was made to unseat a Right-wing MP on purely factional grounds the NEC stepped in and gave protection. Conversely, the NEC was occasionally prone to use its discretionary power in relation to selection where a candidate was defined as being too far to the Left.

59. See L. Minkin, *The Labour Party Conference* (London, Allen Lane, forthcoming), chs. 3 and 5.

60. Ibid. chs. 4 and 6.

61. At the Labour Party conference the Party leadership was narrowly defeated in 4 votes on the subject of unilateral nuclear disarmament. (*LPACR,* 1960, p. 202.)

62. The Campaign For Democratic Socialism, founded in September 1960, was a unique phenomenon. It was the first occasion on which the Right had organised as a formal faction independent of the Party machine. It was a highly centralised organisation, issuing instructions to 260 'whips' in the constituencies. It was well financed and it had the support of senior members of the PLP and the NEC and members of the General Council of the TUC. See Seyd, op.cit.

63. The voting for Policy For Peace was an impressive 4,526,000 for the document and 1,756,000 against. (*LPACR,* 1961, p. 194.) But some of the largest unions were mandated to support any policy which would unite the Party and in any case this new policy statement involved some significant concessions to unilateralism notably the commitment to renounce a specifically British nuclear deterrent.

64. On the Common Market issue in 1962 Gaitskell adopted a negative stance which caused considerable dismay to the mainly pro-Market supporters of the Campaign For Democratic Socialism.

65. In 1966 and 1967 the Party Conference rejected the Labour Government's policy on three separate policy issues. In 1968 the Conference rejected the Government's policy on five issues. One of these votes involved a 5:1 majority against the Government's legislative incomes policy and there was a unanimous hand vote against the reintroduction of prescription charges.

66. The union leaders involved were Lawrence Daly, General Secretary of the National Union of Mineworkers from 1968; Jack Jones, General Secretary of the Transport and General Workers Union from 1969; Richard Seabrook, President of the Union of Shop, Distributive and Allied Workers from 1968; and Hugh Scanlon, President of the Amalgamated Engineering Union (and subsequent titles of the union) from 1967. In addition in 1967 Tom Jackson became General Secretary of the Union of Post Office Workers with Left-wing support but after 1970 he moved rapidly to the Right after the union had been involved in an unsuccessful national strike.

67. These changes are explored in Minkin, 'The British Labour Party and Trade Unions: Crisis and Compact', pp. 22-4.

68. Harry Nicholas was elected General Secretary in 1968; he was a trade union official and therefore outside the established Party machine. In 1969 a new National Agent, Ron Hayward, was appointed; he was the Party's Southern Regional Organiser and defeated an established member of the National Agents Department for the post.

69. The Home Policy and International Policy sub-committees of the NEC had normally been chaired by those from the Right of the Party. In 1972 Ian Mikardo replaced Joe Gormley as Chairman of the International Policy sub-committee and in January 1975 Tony Benn became Chairman of the Home Policy sub-committee.

70. The job specification stipulated that the General Secretary should 'bear first-line responsibility for propagating, and seeking the implementation of, the policies of the Party as laid down by Conference and the National Executive Committee ... '.
71. Between 1970 and 1974 the NEC was defeated 10 times in policy votes.
72. Clause V of the Party Constitution distinguishes the Programme from the Policy. 'The Party Conference shall decide from time to time what specific proposals of legislative, financial or administrative reform shall be included in the Party Programme. No proposal shall be included in the Party Programme unless it has been adopted by the Party Conference by a majority of not less than two-thirds of the votes recorded on a card vote.' (*The Constitution And Standing Orders of The Labour Party*.) The focus on this procedure meant that the NEC was less narrowly bound by each and every Conference decision.
73. On 28 October 1971 69 Labour MPs voted with the Conservatives and against the Labour Party in the crucial vote over the principle of entry into the EEC.
74. In 1972 Lincoln CLP rejected Dick Taverne; in 1974 Sheffield Brightside CLP rejected Eddie Griffiths; in 1975 Newham North East CLP rejected Reg Prentice; and in 1976 Hammersmith North CLP finally rejected Frank Tomney.
75. James Callaghan was elected leader of the Labour Party in April 1976 when he secured 176 votes against 137 votes for Michael Foot. Foot's vote and the general increase in the size of the Tribune Group since 1970 indicated some change in the balance of the PLP towards the Left; but voting for the Liaison Committee of the PLP and the election of Callaghan as Leader indicated the continuing predominance of the Right. Foot's vote for the Leadership and for the Deputy Leadership in October 1976 (166 votes to 128 votes for Shirley Williams) was inflated by the wish of some of those in the Centre of the PLP to preserve Party unity and to stabilise the relationship with the unions.
76. In 1975 the NEC was defeated in 7 policy votes and in 1976 again in 7 policy votes at the Party Conference.
77. Revisionism can be traced to two intellectual streams of thought. One derives from an Oxford group meeting in the 1930s, which included Hugh Dalton, Evan Durbin, Hugh Gaitskell, and Douglas Jay. The other emerges from a group of German emigrés – the Socialist Vanguard Group – who formed *Socialist Commentary* in 1942. By the mid-1950s the most prominent revisionists were Gaitskell, Gordon Walker, Jenkins and the most influential revisionist thinker of the next two decades, Anthony Crosland. The revisionists' case was put with considerable force reaching a peak in 1956 with the publication of Crosland's *The Future of Socialism*, Gaitskell's Fabian pamphlet *Socialism And Nationalisation*, the Socialist Union's *Twentieth Century Socialism*, and John Strachey's *Contemporary Capitalism*.
78. Central to Left factionalism within the Party was the role of the weekly journal *Tribune*, edited by Michael Foot to 1960 and then by Richard Clements. Between 1956 and 1964 the Left was also organised into two formal factions; one was Victory For Socialism and the other was the Unity Group (an offshoot of the Appeal for Unity Behind Conference Decisions, formed in 1960). After 1964 when both VFS and the Gaitskellite organisation CDS were wound up formal factionalism tended to wither away. There was a revival in 1966 when formal factionalism was allowed within the PLP and the Tribune Group was formed; in 1968 the Socialist Charter organisation was established to mobilise Left-wing activists in the constituency parties.
79. *Industry And Society* was carried at the 1957 Party Conference by 5,309,000 votes to 1,276,000 votes. (*LPACR*, 1957, p. 161.)
80. *Labour's Aims* was not moved as an amendment or addendum to the Party Constitution but was merely commended to the Party Conference as 'a

valuable expression of the aims of the Labour Party in the second half of the 20th century . . . ' (*LPACR*, 1960, p. 13).

81. Harold Wilson, *LPACR*, 1963, p. 134.
82. See P. Townsend and N. Bosanquet, *Labour And Inequality* (London, Fabian Society, 1972); this view is challenged by Michael Stewart in W. Beckerman (ed.), *Labour's Economic Record 1964-1970* (London, Duckworth, 1972), pp. 75-117.
83. S. Haseler, *The Gaitskellites* (London, Macmillan, 1969), ch. 11.
84. The Labour Party election manifesto of 1970 was entitled 'Now Britain's Strong Let's Make It Great To Live In'.
85. The Conservative Government of 1970 sought to disengage from industry, to give tax incentives to the high income earner, to raise substantially the level of council house rents and, as already noted, to produce a complete legislative framework for industrial relations. There were some measures of denationalisation and, after 1972, the Government turned full circle on its commitment to avoid any incomes policy and produced a complete legislative policy covering prices and incomes.
86. See A. Crosland, *A Social Democratic Britain*, Fabian Tract 404, 1971; also *Socialism Now* (London, Cape, 1974).
87. See A. Benn, *The New Politics*, Fabian Tract 402, 1972; also *Speeches* (Nottingham, Spokesman Books, 1974).
88. S. Holland, *The Socialist Challenge* (London, Quartet, 1975).
89. The senior Ministers in the Department were Tony Benn and Eric Heffer. Heffer resigned from the Department in 1975 and Benn was moved from the Department in the wake of the EEC Referendum result.
90. See the Papers by the Chancellor of the Exchequer and the Secretary of State for Industry on industrial strategy. Reprinted in *The Times*, 6 Nov. 1975.
91. In 1974 the current account deficit was running at approximately £900 million a quarter. In 1975 the Government managed to reduce the annual current account deficit to £1,700 million, under half the annual total for 1974.
92. The rises in the retail price index escalated until between January and June 1975 the figure was 31 per cent. As a result of the new incomes policy it rose by only 13.4 per cent from June to December 1975.
93. Unemployment averaged 4.2 per cent of the total workforce during 1975.
94. In January 1974 the pound was valued at 2.34 against the dollar. By November 1976 it had shrunk to below 1.60.
95. D.E. Butler and R. Rose, *The British General Election 1959* (London, Macmillan, 1960), pp. 15 and 197.
96. M. Abrams, R. Rose, R. Hinden, *Must Labour Lose?* (Harmondsworth, Penguin, 1960). Rita Hinden was the editor of the journal *Socialist Commentary* — a journal which had consistently supported the revisionist position. It was her contribution to *Must Labour Lose?* which gave the most extreme interpretation of the data.
97. H.A. Turner, 'Labour's Diminishing Vote', *The Guardian*, 20 Oct. 1961 quoted in A. Crosland, *Can Labour Win?*, Fabian Tract 324, 1960, p. 10.
98. A. Crosland, *Can Labour Win?* p. 20.
99. Ibid. The topic is discussed in R. Rose, *Influencing Voters* (London, Faber, 1967), pp.60-86.
100. A well-publicised Gallup Poll found that just prior to the 1959 General Election criticism of the trade unions by non trade unionists was greater than at any time since Gallup began polling twenty-two years previously. (*News Chronicle*, 7 and 8 Sept. 1959.)
101. M. Abrams *et al.*, *Must Labour Lose?* especially the section written by

Rita Hinden.
102. *LPACR,* 1959, pp. 105-14.
103. Derived from tabular data in H. Durant, 'Voting Behaviour in Britain 1945-1966', in R. Rose (ed.), *Studies in British Politics* (London, Macmillan, 1969), p. 166.
104. See D.E. Butler and M. Pinto Duschinsky, *The British General Election 1970* (London, Macmillan, 1971), pp. 14, 21, 34-5. By 1968 also the Conservative lead in the opinion polls was a record 28 per cent (ibid. p. 35).
105. See particularly J.H. Goldthorpe, D. Lockwood, F. Bechhofer, and J. Platt, *The Affluent Worker: Political Attitudes and Behaviour* (London, Cambridge University Press, 1968). Also D.E. Butler and D. Stokes, *Political Change in Britain* (London, Macmillan, 1969).
106. There was no necessary progression from rising material wealth to the adoption of middle-class life styles and thence to Conservative voting. See Goldthorpe *et al.*, op. cit. p. 73. Also Butler and Stokes, op. cit. 2nd edition 1974, p. 133.
107. See Butler and Stokes op. cit. 2nd edition, pp.130-2 for the factors ors which mitigate this tendency.
108. The factor of physical replacement of the electorate was 'easily the largest contribution to Labour's return to power (in 1964) . . . ' Butler and Stokes, op. cit. p. 350. There was a higher birth rate amongst Labour's working-class voters and a higher death rate amongst Conservative voters.
109. E. Heffer, *The Class Struggle in Parliament* (London, Gollancz, 1973), p. 169.
110. A National Opinion Profile of the electorate indicated that between 1966 and 1970 the greatest swing away from the Labour Party took place among the unskilled working class (a 7.4 per cent swing). The Party did less poorly among the skilled working class (2.7 per cent swing) and actually held its support among the lower-middle class (−0.1 per cent swing). Support declined among the rest of the middle class (6.0 per cent swing). The impact on the result of abstentions by workers who usually voted Labour is not altogether clear. (Butler and Pinto Duschinsky, op. cit. p. 342.) See Hugh Berrington 'Riddle of the Turnout', *Sunday Telegraph,* 17 Feb. 1974, p. 19.
111. The Liberal Party's share of the total vote was 19.3 per cent in February and 18.3 per cent in October 1974.
112. The Scottish Nationalist Party share of the total Scottish vote was 21.9 per cent in February and 30.4 per cent in October 1974. Plaid Cymru's share of the total Welsh vote was 10.8 per cent in both elections.
113. In the critical arguments over devolution there was a breakaway from the Labour Party in Scotland led by two Labour MPs, J. Robertson and J. Sillars which resulted in the formation of a small independent Scottish Labour Party. Under various pressures the Labour Party in Scotland was pushed into support for a devolved Scottish Parliament.
114. The National Front was represented by 54 candidates in February and 90 in October. The average National Front vote was 3.3 per cent in February and 3.1 per cent in October.
115. Ten Workers' Revolutionary Party candidates averaged 0.9 per cent in October compared with an average of 1.0 per cent for the nine who fought in February.
116. I. Crewe, J. Alt and B. Sarlvik, 'The Erosion of Partisanship 1964-1975' (paper presented to the PSA Conference, Nottingham, 1976), p. 18.
117. Ibid. p. 18.
118. Ibid. p.18.
119. Ibid. p. 19.
120. F. Parkin Class, *Inequality and Political Order* (London, MacGibbon & Kee,

1971), p. 99. For a discussion of the relative influence of socio-economic and political factors see Butler and Stokes, op. cit., 2nd edition, pp. 193-9.

121. See D.E. Butler and D. Kavanagh, *The British General Election of October 1974* (London, Macmillan, 1975), pp. 212-16.

122. The three ex-manual workers were Roy Mason, Eric Varley and Stan Orme. The only two other trade unionists were Albert Booth and James Callaghan himself. (See note 54.)

123. In addition it has been argued that a significant feature of recent developments in the Party has been the *embourgeoisement* of the Party membership and the decline of working-class politics. See B. Hindness, *The Decline of Working Class Politics* (London, MacGibbon & Kee, 1971). This view has been heavily criticised. For empirical evidence to the contrary see particularly T. Forester, *The Labour Party And The Working Class* (London, Heinemann, 1976), pp.117-23. It is important to point out that the changing social composition of the Party tells us little about its trade union membership. See note 3.

124. I. Crewe *et al.*, op. cit. p.23; derived from tabular data presented there.

125. The ambiguities are most apparent in the conviction with which contrasting writers view the strength of the traditional Socialist Left in the Labour Party. Some observers, e.g. S. Haseler, *The Death of British Democracy* (London, Paul Elek, 1976), see the Left as now being the dominant influence in the Labour Party. But Coates, Howell and Panitch all address themselves to the Left's fundamental weakness within the Party. D. Coates, *The Labour Party And The Struggle For Socialism* (London, Cambridge University Press, 1975); D. Howell, *British Social Democracy* (London, Croom Helm, 1976); L. Panitch, *Social Democracy and Wage Militancy* (London, Cambridge University Press, 1975). Barratt Brown and Forester are optimistic about the prospects of Left-wing Socialism through the Labour Party, whilst Coates and Panitch, following Miliband, see its failure as inevitable. M. Barratt Brown, *From Labourism To Socialism* (Nottingham, Spokesman Books, 1972); Forester, op. cit.; R. Miliband, *Parliamentary Socialism* (London, Merlin Press, 1973). From the other wing of the Party Taverne is pessimistic about the possibility of pursuing revisionist Social Democracy through the Labour Party. D. Taverne, *The Future of the Left* (London, Cape, 1974). Howell believes that both traditional and revisionist Socialism are in decay.

126. I. Crewe *et al.*, op. cit. p. 23.

127. Ibid. pp. 10-11.

128. As a result of the continuing infusion of the white-collar unions into the TUC by 1976 the point was approaching where the non-Party affiliated members of the TUC would be in a majority. TUC membership (31 Dec. 1975) − 11,036,326; Labour Party affiliated trade union membership (31 Dec. 1975) − approx. 5,600,000.

129. For various reasons the official figure for individual Labour Party membership grossly overstates the real membership and overstates still further the active membership. Nevertheless it is indicative that the individual membership of the Labour Party as at 31 December 1975 was 674,905, a decrease of 16,984 when compared to the 1974 figure and that 523 constituency parties are affiliated on the compulsorily minimum number of 1,000 members. By comparison in 1952, when individual party membership was at its peak, the total was 1,014,524. During the period of Office of the two Wilson Governments formal individual Party membership dropped from 830,116 (1964) to 690,191 (1970).

130. At the 1976 Party Conference for the second year running the Party leadership managed to avoid a debate on this contentious issue but there is

considerable, and very vocal, support.

131. At the 1976 Party Conference the NEC accepted a resolution 'to consider appropriate means of widening the electorate involved in the choice of Leader'. This proposed reform, like the reform of candidate selection procedure, has been instigated from the Left but has wider Party support.

We are grateful to Royden Harrison, David Howell and Philip Williams for their comments on the final draft of this chapter and we thank Ivor Crewe, Jim Alt and Bo Särlvik for permission to cite from their unpublished paper.

Appendix 1. Labour Party electoral support and seats 1900-1970

	Total Votes	Percentage Share	Seats
1900	63,304	1.8	2
1906	329,748	5.9	30
1910	505,657	7.6	40
1910	371,772	7.1	42
1918	2,385,472	22.2	63
1922	4,241,383	29.5	142
1923	4,438,508	30.5	191
1924	5,489,077	33.0	151
1929	8,389,512	37.1	288
1931	6,649,630	30.6	52
1935	8,325,491	37.9	154
1945	11,995,152	47.8	393
1950	13,266,592	46.1	315
1951	13,948,605	48.8	295
1955	12,404,970	46.4	277
1959	12,215,538	43.8	258
1964	12,205,814	44.1	317
1966	13,064,951	47.9	363
1970	12,178,295	43.0	287

Source: Derived from D. Butler and P. Sloman, *British Political Facts 1900-1975* (London, Macmillan, 1975), pp.182-6.

Appendix 2. Labour Party membership 1945 to 1975

	Constituency Parties No.	Total Individual Membership Men	Women	Trade Unions No.	Membership	Socialist and Co-operative Societies, etc. No.	Membership	*Total Membership
1945	649	291,435	195,612	69	2,510,369	6	41,281	3,038,697
1946	649	384,023	261,322	70	2,635,346	6	41,667	3,322,358
1947	649	361,643	246,844	73	4,386,074	6	45,738	5,040,299
1948	656	375,861	253,164	80	4,751,030	6	42,382	5,422,437
1949	660	439,591	290,033	80	4,946,207	5	41,116	5,716,947
1950	661	543,434	364,727	83	4,971,911	5	40,100	5,920,172
1951	667	512,751	363,524	82	4,937,427	5	35,300	5,849,002
1952	667	594,663	419,861	84	5,071,935	5	21,200	6,107,659
1953	667	584,626	420,059	84	5,056,912	5	34,425	6,096,022
1954	667	544,042	389,615	84	5,529,760	5	34,610	6,498,027
1955	667	488,687	354,669	87	5,605,988	5	34,650	6,483,994
1956	667	489,735	355,394	88	5,658,249	5	33,850	6,537,228
1957	667	527,787	385,200	87	5,664,012	5	25,550	6,582,549
1958	667	515,298	373,657	87	5,627,690	5	25,541	6,542,186
1959	667	492,213	355,313	87	5,564,010	5	25,450	6,436,986
1960	667	459,584	330,608	86	5,512,688	5	25,450	6,328,330
1961	667	434,511	316,054	86	5,549,592	5	25,450	6,325,607
1962	667	444,576	322,883	86	5,502,773	5	25,475	6,295,707
1963	667	480,639	349,707	83	5,507,232	6	20,858	6,358,436
1964	667	478,910	351,206	81	5,502,001	6	21,200	6,353,317
1965	659	475,164	341,601	79	5,601,982	6	21,146	6,439,893
1966	658	454,722	320,971	79	5,538,744	6	21,175	6,335,612
1967	657	427,495	306,437	75	5,539,562	6	21,120	6,294,614
1968	656	401,499	299,357	68	5,364,484	6	21,285	6,086,625
1969	656	387,856	292,800	68	5,461,721	6	21,505	6,163,882
1970	656	394,290	295,901	67	5,518,520	6	23,869	6,222,580
1971	659	699,522		67	5,559,371	6	25,360	6,284,253
1972	659	703,030		62	5,425,327	9	40,415	6,168,772
1973	651	665,379		60	5,364,904	9	42,913	6,073,196
1974	623	691,889		63	5,787,467	9	39,101	6,518,457
1975	623	674,905		61	5,750,039	9	43,930	6,468,874

Source: Report of the National Executive Committee 1976, p. 59.

Appendix 3. United Kingdom General Election results, February and October 1974

		Electorate and Turnout	Conservative Party	Labour Party	Liberal Party	Plaid Cymru & Scottish Nationalists	Communist Party	Others (mainly Irish parties)
February	%	78.1	37.8	37.1	19.3	2.6	0.1	3.1
	Votes	39,770,724	11,872,180	11,646,391	6,058,744	804,554	32,743	958,293
	Seats		297	301	14	9	0	14
October	%	72.8	35.8	39.2	18.3	3.5	0.1	3.1
	Votes	40,072,971	10,464,817	11,457,079	5,346,754	1,005,938	17,426	897,164
	Seats		277	319	13	14	0	12

Source: D. Butler and D. Kavanagh, *The British General Election of October 1974* (Macmillan, London, 1975), pp. 293-4.

Appendix 4. Votes* of Affiliated organisations at the Labour Party
  Conference of 1975

Transport and General Workers	1,000,000	
plus† Vehicle Builders	58,000	1,058,000
Engineers (all sections)		986,000
Two largest unions		2,044,000
General and Municipal Workers		650,000
Public Employees		400,000
Electricians		350,000
Shopworkers		299,000
Mineworkers		253,000
Post Office Workers		186,000
Scientific Technical and Managerial Staffs		185,000
Construction Allied Trades and Technicians°°		183,000
Ten largest unions⌀		4,550,000
Total votes cast by all unions represented at the Conference (52 orgs.)		5,725,000
Total vote cast by all Constituency Labour Parties represented at the Conference (512 orgs.)		634,000
Total vote cast by all Socialist Co-operative and Professional organisations represented at the Conference (9 orgs.)		47,000
Total Conference Vote		6,406,000

*Derived from Labour Party Conference Information Department News Releases
  Nos. AC 5/75 and AC 16/75.

†Union amalgamated with the Transport Workers but retaining separate
  affiliation.

°°Union formed in 1972 as a result of the merger between the Associated Society
  of Building Trade Workers and the Amalgamated Society of Woodworkers.

⌀By 1975 the National Union of Railwaymen had dropped to an affiliation of
  157,000 and was the 11th largest union. Next in size was the Professional
  Executive and Computer Staffs (previously the Clerical and Administrative
  Workers Union) with 100,000.

Further Reading

Bealey, F. *The Social and Political Thought of the British Labour Party.* London, Weidenfeld & Nicolson, 1970.

Beer, S.H. *Modern British Politics.* 2nd edition. London, Faber, 1969.

Coates, D. *The Labour Party and the Struggle for Socialism.* London, Cambridge University Press, 1975.

Crosland, A. *The Future of Socialism.* 2nd edition. London, Cape, 1964.

Haseler, S. *The Gaitskellites.* London, Macmillan, 1969.

Holland, S. *The Socialist Challenge.* London, Quartet, 1975.

Howell, D. *British Social Democracy.* London, Croom Helm, 1976.

McKenzie, R.T. *British Political Parties.* 2nd edition. London, Heinemann, 1963.

Miliband, R. *Parliamentary Socialism.* 2nd edition. London, Merlin, 1973.

Minkin, L. *The Labour Party Conference,* London, Allen Lane, forthcoming.

Panitch, L. *Social Democracy and Industrial Militancy.* London, Cambridge University Press, 1976.

Pelling, H. *The Origins of the Labour Party.* 2nd edition. Oxford, Clarendon Press, 1965.

6 THE IRISH LABOUR PARTY

Andrew Orridge

The Irish Labour Party is among the smallest in Europe in terms of both its proportion of the vote and of parliamentary seats. It has never held more than 15 per cent of the seats in the Dail (the lower house of the Irish parliament) and has sunk as low as 4.6 per cent, while its share of valid first preferences has never stood higher than the 21.1 per cent gained in the first election it contested in 1922 and has at times fallen below 10 per cent.[1] Yet there is no competition with Communists within a splintered Left as in France, Italy and Finland, where the Socialist parties are of a similar proportional size. An exploration of the reasons for this smallness is at the same time a useful vehicle to describe the milieu in which the Party operates and serves to demonstrate that in a comparative European perspective contrasts are more obvious than comparisons. The Irish Labour Party exists in a political world unlike that of any other Social Democratic party in Europe.

Contrasts

Firstly and most obviously the socio-economic structure of the Republic has not contained enough groups to which the Party might appeal for it to gain a very large share of the vote.[2] If a considerable exaggeration may be permitted to make the point clearly, the twenty-six counties entered upon independence as an agricultural region of the United Kingdom, earning its living by selling cattle and dairy produce to the larger island and buying manufactures.[3] Total employment in the secondary sector, mining and manufacturing, was only 13 per cent in 1926 and had increased to 30.6 per cent in 1971, and these figures include management. The industrial working class, the 'natural' constituency of the Party, has thus been small throughout the Party's history and in any case the Party has failed to gain its support on a large scale until recently, as we shall see. Agriculture has been the backbone of the Irish economy, although in a state of slow relative decline from 53.4 per cent of the working population in 1926 to 25.9 per cent in 1971.[4] An agricultural economy can, of course, be a source of extremely radical politics; no one living in the century of peasant revolutions should be blind to this. And the Irish agricultural economy might seem promising material for discontent at first sight.

153

It is characterised by many small holdings, 24 per cent between 1 acre and 15 acres and 49 per cent between 16 acres and 50 acres in 1970;[5] by a population pressure that has led to a continuous fall in total population from the 1840s until very recently and an emigration rate that did not fall below an average of five persons per thousand per annum in any five-year period since independence until 1966;[6] and by a long history of agrarian violence and discontent up to the beginning of the twentieth century. However the root causes of past agrarian discontent had been largely eliminated before the emergence of the Irish Labour Party. The Great Famine of the 1840s set in motion a restructuring of rural society that drastically reduced the large classes of landless labourers and dwarf tenants of the early nineteenth century and replaced them with an economy consisting mainly of small to medium-sized farms worked largely by family labour and maintained in size by the export of those who could not inherit or marry an inheritor.[7] Secure tenure for these holdings was achieved before independence by a series of Land Acts passed by the British Parliament from the 1880s onwards in an attempt to meet Irish grievances. The ex-landlords received British Government stocks and the ex-tenants were required to repay the purchase price through annuities that were less than the rent.[8] Rural Ireland on the eve of independence was very largely a society of independent proprietors of modest plots. Finally these proprietors have possessed secure incomes for most of the period since independence. Apart from a period of acute disagreement between the British and Irish Governments in the 1930s, the Irish farmer has been well placed geographically, climatically and economically to provide one of the major export markets for food in the developed world with one of its major demands — beef. This has by no means provided large incomes, but given a willingness to accept low living standards, especially in the west of the country, the Irish holding has up to now escaped being placed in a position of marginality. It would be wrong to say that there has been no tension in this agrarian society since the 1920s. The average size of farms increases steadily from west to east across the country, coinciding roughly with variations in support for the two larger parties,[9] and in the twenties and thirties there was hostility towards the larger farmers from some quarters.[10] Also the sixties have seen an increase in the militancy of the farming community as its relative position has declined. But in a comparative perspective these incidents seem minor and the overall picture is of a rural society lacking those besetting sources of agrarian discontent: landlord-tenant relations, landlessness and subdivision, and economic marginality. It is difficult to imagine a more conservative political animal than an independent rural proprietor with a secure income[11] and certainly the Labour Party has not found support over much of rural Ireland.

However, while the Party has not found widespread support in rural areas, it is nonetheless only in certain largely agricultural counties that it has found consistent support. Although its vote in the two major urban centres of Dublin and Cork has varied greatly over the last fifty years, the Party has always been able to depend on the election of a number of deputies in certain counties in the east and south of the country. If four widely spaced elections are examined — 1923, 1933, 1948 and 1973 — there are fourteen counties excluding County Dublin and Cork County Borough which have returned at least one Labour deputy on at least two of these occasions. In 1923, the year of the first general election under anything resembling settled conditions in the new state, Labour won 13 of its 15 seats and 60.1 per cent of its total valid first preferences in these counties; in 1933, the year of Labour's lowest ebb, it won all 8 of its seats and 72.4 per cent of its vote in these counties; in 1948 it won 14 of the 19 seats going to Labour candidates and 65.6 per cent of its vote in them; and even in 1973, the last general election, it won 12 of its 19 seats and 48.3 per cent of its vote in these areas.[12] It is suggestive that these counties contain larger numbers of agricultural labourers working on farms not owned by relatives than elsewhere in Ireland. Busteed and Mason's ecological regression analysis of the relation between Labour voting and the strength of the rural 'proletariat' for the general elections of 1965 and 1969 produced correlation coefficients of 0.54 and 0.61 respectively. A similar analysis by this writer for the general elections of June 1927 and 1933, the high and low points of Labour's early history, produced coefficients of 0.76 and 0.43 respectively, indicating that this association has been a consistent feature of the Labour vote.[13] However, as with most Irish deputies, it is probably true that personal relations between the TD (*Teachta Dala* — member of the Dail in Irish) and his constituents have a great deal to do with the election of these Labour members.

The second feature of the Irish political climate that explains Labour's small size is the massive influence of nationalism in Irish politics. Ireland holds the dubious distinction of being one of the only two Western European countries to have fought a war of independence in the twentieth century (Finland being the other) and this is symptomatic of the importance of national feeling in Irish politics. The emergence of the Irish Labour Party coincided with the most traumatic and formative period of modern Irish nationalism, culminating in the war of independence and its aftermath, and the conflicts and atmosphere engendered by these events have been the controlling factors in moulding the rest of the Irish party system and of the content of politics in the first thirty years of independence. This has damaged the prospects of the Labour Party in numerous ways.

Even before the Easter Rising of 1916, nationalism was the dominant force in Irish politics in the shape of the Irish Parliamentary Party, established in the 1870s and 1880s and devoted to a federal solution to the problem of Irish national aspirations. This party was virtually wiped out in the 1918 general election by Sinn Fein, the umbrella secessionist movement which grew up in the wake of the Easter Rising. Secession was gained by the combined efforts of Sinn Fein and the original Irish Republican Army, but was followed within a year by a civil war between the now divided nationalists over the terms of the Treaty with the British, which had established the Irish Free State as a British Dominion. The opponents of the Treaty lost the war, but the political conflict between these two factions over the issues of the civil war dominated Irish politics until the Second World War and ended in the almost complete triumph of the anti-Treaty faction under the leadership of Eamonn de Valera. His party, in the eventual guise of the Fianna Fail Party, became and remains the only party capable of forming a government alone, while their opponents, in the eventual form of the Fine Gael Party, are next largest. Nationalist divisions have thus become institutionalised and have been the dominant organising force in Irish politics despite the resolution of the original conflicts by the end of the 1940s. For Labour to flourish issues and divisions needed to be arranged in terms of class, but all attempts to do this have failed until recently. If, to use Schattschneider's phrase, politics is the 'mobilisation of bias' by which some issues are organised into politics while other issues are organised out, those definitions of issues that would have favoured the Labour Party have been largely organised out of Irish politics.[14] The damage can be documented.

Although an Irish Trade Union Congress was formed in 1894, on the model of the British Trade Union Congress, any political aspirations were confronted by the massive power of the Irish Parliamentary Party, which held virtually every seat in Ireland outside of Ulster. Trade union sponsored candidates stood at local elections, occasionally with some success, but the ITUC was actively discouraged from contesting parliamentary elections by the Irish Parliamentary Party, which possessed its own 'Labour Nationalist' MPs, on the lines of the Liberal-Labour MPs in Britain. Also the important Belfast element in the ITUC was attached to the idea of affiliating with the emerging Labour representation in Great Britain. It was not until 1912, under the combined stimulus of dissatisfaction with relations with both the Irish Parliamentary Party and the British Labour Party, the emergence of a more militant unionism associated with the Irish Transport and General Workers Union and James Larkin, and the prospect of an Irish parliament of some kind, that the ITUC finally decided to establish an Irish Labour Party. However, there was not to be another general election until 1918 and the Party only contested one by-election in the meantime, with a respectable showing.[15] In the meantime the Easter Rising occurred and Sinn Fein became a major force in Irish politics. The Labour Party considered contesting the election of 1918, but this was also the scene of the decisive battle between Sinn Fein and the more moderate and long-established Irish Parliamentary Party to choose which brand of nationalism was to dominate Ireland and, after considerable pressure from Sinn Fein, the Labour leaders decided to stand aside and let the nationalist issue be resolved. This was, in effect, to let nationalism organise the issues in the major twentieth-century restructuring of Irish politics.[16] By the time that Labour did put forward candidates for the first time four years later in 1922, a war of independence had been fought and a civil war was imminent: the nationalist issues were deeply engraved. Labour gained 17 seats at that election, roughly 13 per cent of the Dail, but it found that support difficult to build on in the following years of civil war and reconstruction, despite the loss of the war by the anti-Treaty opposition, the imprisonment of its leaders for a year and a half, and the refusal of its TDs to take their seats in a Dail they regarded as illegitimate. The real issue overshadowing parliamentary politics in those years was whether or not the representatives of some 30 per cent of the voters would enter constitutional politics. Legislation intended to unseat abstentionist TDs compelled them to do so in 1927 and if Labour had found it difficult to make headway against the dominant nationalism with the anti-Treaty party out of the Dail it was to find the battle altogether unequal when they entered it. Not only was the nationalist conflict the meat of parliamentary politics, Fianna Fail as the more radical of the two big parties also had the greatest following among the rural and urban poor and capitalised upon this with promises of better housing, improved social security and industrial development. This cut into the issues of Labour's basic appeal and arranged them around a populist nationalism rather than class. The first years of Fianna Fail dominance after its victory in the election of 1932 were also the years of Labour's lowest ebb, with only 7 seats and 7.7 per cent of the valid first preferences in that election and only 8 seats and 5.7 per cent of valid first preferences in the 1933 election. Although the intense nationalism of those years is long past, the points of substantive division long settled, and the radical populism of Fianna Fail a very faded flower, it is only in the last decade that Labour has been able to erode their institutional results. Perhaps the most remarkable tribute to the influence of nationalism on Irish politics is the fact that it captured the political allegiances of the working class in the Dublin area, by far the largest urban agglomeration in the country, to such an extent that only recently has Labour begun to win consistent and considerable support there. In the general elections of 1923, 1932, 1948 and 1957, Labour won only 4.6 per cent, 6.3 per cent, 10.4 per cent and 8.1 per cent respectively of the valid first preferences in the area, while the two major parties won between them 67.6 per cent, 73 per cent, 63.5 per cent and 73.3 per cent respectively.[17] More recent results are discussed below (page 164).

Intertwined with the influence of nationalism has been the peculiar nature of the political influence of Catholicism in Ireland, the third major element of the Irish political climate. Alone among the largely Catholic countries of Europe the Church has always been identified with the 'out groups' rather than the dominant groups. This is clearly because of Ireland's history as a largely Catholic region of a Protestant metropolitan state. For centuries Catholicism has been the church of the oppressed native Irish, and indeed the reason for much of that oppression. The result has been that when independence came it came to a country in which no large group felt deeply alienated from the Church, despite the hostility of the Church to all forms of violent nationalism. There is no equivalent in Ireland to the radical peasant anti-clericalism of France and Italy. Indeed the slightest whiff of any tendencies contrary to the teaching of the Church has been and still is a danger to Labour.[18] It is necessary to be quite clear about the nature of this influence. It is not only the influence of a powerful church organisation with a wide following and a readiness to step on any form of social radicalism, although this description fits the Irish Church with some accuracy, it is also the influence of a deeply Catholic social environment in which there are few votes at all in an anti- or even non-Catholic Socialism. The power of the hierarchy is supplemented by the character of a Catholic society.[19]

Other factors have been advanced as explanations for the size of the Irish Labour Party. Left-wing parties and their supporters are given to lengthy discussions of alleged lost opportunities for the advancement of their cause and the Irish Labour Party is no exception. One of these opportunities was the general election of 1918 and the results of the failure to contest it have already been discussed briefly in note 16 above. Another popular candidate is the effect of Partition on the fate of the Labour Party. Some writers have argued that by cutting off the industrialised area of Belfast, Partition greatly reduced the 'natural' constituency of the Party.[20] Although supporters of this position can point to the success of trade union candidates in certain local elections in Belfast in the first quarter of this century,[21] the fact of the matter is that at all important times the working class of Northern Ireland has divided along lines of nationality and religion. It is difficult to imagine any way in which re-unification could have been, or might be, achieved which would not have reinforced that division. Certainly it is difficult to see how it might have benefited the Irish Labour Party.

It is thus clear that the Irish Labour Party has had to operate in a very different set of circumstances from that of most European Social Democratic and Labour parties, and this has had a deep influence on its character and its role in the polity.

Firstly the Party has rarely been a source of radical policy. Despite its early associations with James Connolly, the most famous Irish Socialist revolutionary and one of the martyrs of the Easter Rising, and with the militant unionism of James Larkin, the Party has shown few signs of deep Socialist commitment from the 1920s until very recently. The radical 'Democratic Programme' of the First Dail, set up by Sinn Fein MPs who refused to sit at Westminster in 1919, owed much to Labour leaders who were invited to draw up a programme in return for their withdrawal from the election of 1918; but it is generally agreed that the programme was an aberration for the socially conservative factions of Sinn Fein and Labour made little of it during the twenties.[22] The only other veer to the Left occurred in the thirties under the pressure of competition from Fianna Fail. Under a new leader, William Norton, in an attempt to differentiate themselves from Fianna Fail, and also influenced by the disrepute into which Capitalism had fallen in those years, the Party adopted a more radical constitution in 1936. This document declared the commitment of the Party to 'the public ownership by the people of all essential sources of wealth'[23] and to the 'establishment in Ireland of a Worker's Republic founded on the principles of social justice, sustained by democratic institutions and guaranteeing civil and religious liberty and equal opportunity to all citizens who render service to the community'.[24] A moderate enough

statement, one might have thought, for a European Labour party in the
thirties, but the phrase 'a Worker's Republic' was closely associated with
the name of James Connolly and had been the title of periodicals he had
edited. It was thus suspect to certain elements in the Party, especially
the Irish National Teacher's Organisation and its secretary, M.P. Linehan,
an expert on Catholic social teaching. The teachers decided to seek the
advice of the hierarchy on the compatibility of the constitution with
the teaching of the church and, after reference to a Committee of
Experts, the aims were declared contrary to Catholic teaching. At the
conference of 1939 the Administrative Council of the Party undertook
to redraft the Constitution and the new version of 1940 abandoned the
controversial clauses and replaced them with phrases such as 'a
Republican form of government' and sentences such as, 'The Labour
Party believes in a system of government which, while recognising the
rights of private property, shall ensure that, where the common good
requires, essential industries shall be brought under public ownership
with democratic control'.[25] Norton proposed the changed Constitution
from the platform:

> The Labour Party is a political party and objection has been taken
> by the hierarchy to the term Worker's Republic. If the conference
> wants to avoid the deliberate misrepresentations which opponents
> would employ against us, it is necessary to delete the term from the
> Constitution. Conference will have to make up its mind whether it is
> not wiser for the party to drop the term.[26]

Conference decided it was wiser by 89 votes to 25. Since then until
recently the Party has retained its allegiance to 'pale, pink, bourgeois
objects'.[27] Perhaps the clearest indication of this occurred in 1951 when
the Party was part of a coalition government that found itself involved
in the most overt clash between State and Church since independence,
over a proposed maternity and child health scheme popularly known as
the 'Mother and Child Scheme', put forward by the Minister of Health,
a member of the short-lived reformist republican party, Clann na
Poblachta. Despite the apparent relevance of this kind of issue for a
Labour Party the leadership stayed well clear of the crisis and played
little part in the acrimonious controversies that led to the downfall of
the Government.[28]

It might be added that there is a further influence of the Irish milieu
that helps to explain Labour's lack of radicalism. As I wrote above,
until recently the Party has not drawn much support from areas

populated by the urban working class, and a great deal of its support from the rural south and east. The nature of Irish rural TDs is by now fairly well established: they earn their political living by building up a personal relationship with constituents from one part of a multi-member constituency on the basis of acting as go-between in the constituents' relationships with the State. They devote themselves whole time to this activity, display little interest in policy-making, and are frequently the present member of a generation of TDs from the area in question.[29] There is no indication that Labour TDs differ from this general pattern, and this is not the kind of political material that produces radical policies, or indeed any policies at all. Dr Thornley, himself now a Labour TD, has written that most Labour TDs were 'somewhat to the right of Senator Fitzgerald' (a Liberal member of Fine Fael, now a TD and Foreign Minister of the Republic).[30]

A second effect of the character of Irish politics is that the Labour Party has rarely been in power. This is not solely due to its small size, for small parties in strategic positions can exercise considerable influence and the Labour Party has often been in apparently strategic positions. In 12 of the 18 Dails since independence, a total of 25 out of 55 years, no party alone has had an absolute majority, thus giving Labour a coalition-forming potential. But the logic of the rest of the party system has worked to deprive the Party of leverage in most of these instances. Formally no party had an overall majority from 1922 to 1932, but the absence of the anti-Treaty party until 1927 gave power to the pro-Treaty party by default. From then until 1932, apart from the short but tumultuous Dail of June to September 1927 in which Fianna Fail was forced to enter constitutional politics, Labour suffered from the existence of other small parties and independents who could together provide the pro-Treaty party with a majority. (Although Labour is the only long-lived small party to date, other parties have risen and fallen, at times becoming a little larger than Labour.[31]) After the election of 1932, Fianna Fail has had a majority for 24 of the 42 years, and when it has not held such a position it has preferred minority government or opposition to coalition. This leaves Labour the options of supporting Fianna Fail, as it did in 1932 to 1933 and 1937 to 1938, or forming a coalition with Fine Gael, as it did in 1948 to 1951, 1954 to 1957 and 1973 to date. (On other occasions Fianna Fail has been able to govern with the aid of independents.) When Labour gave support to Fianna Fail in the thirties, as the more apparently socially reforming of the two nationalist parties, it was rewarded with regular meetings between the party leaders on policy, and the Labour leaders of the time claimed this as the source of Fianna Fail's social conscience. However, the electors were clearly not impressed by this argument, and indeed the need of Fianna Fail to cement its own support among the less well off provided quite adequate independent motivation. After 1938 the formal co-operation was not repeated. But on the other hand, Fine Gael has in the past been regarded as the most socially conservative of the large parties, appealing to larger farmers and the urban middle class and, while Irish parties are far from ideological, the alliance has not always been comfortable, especially if economic policy begins to hurt the unions. It was not even considered until after the Second World War, when it became clear that an alliance of Fine Gael and Labour was the only possible basis for an alternative government to Fianna Fail, and in the sixties there was a considerable period when Labour made clear at elections that they would not go into coalition with Fine Gael. The net result is that to date the Irish Labour Party has only held office for 9 of the past 54 years, and has been formally involved in policy formation for only 2 years more.

Comparisons

The Party is at first sight more typical in its relations with the trade unions. As in Britain, the Party began as an offshoot of the trade union movement, and indeed at about the same time as related above. However its existence remained shadowy until after the First World War, owing to the absence of any elections to fight, and, as related above, it did not actually contest seats until 1922.

The connection with the unions has remained close. For the first twelve years of its substantive existence the Party was part of a united body called The Irish Labour Party and Trade Union Congress. In 1930 this arrangement ended and a formally separate Labour Party was established, supposedly to improve the organisation of the political wing, but the relationship remained close. Three out of the four leaders of the Party have been prominent trade unionists and the leadership as a whole has been predominantly trade unionist until recently. Of all those who had been Labour TDs up to 1948 47 per cent were trade union officials and in 1965 the proportion among sitting Labour TDs still stood at 45.5 per cent.[32] The majority of the delegates to the annual conferences have been trade unionists and the largest unions have usually been affiliated to the Party. However the unions have not been generous with direct aid. According to Chubb, the Party's largest source of income for its organisation is an annual collection at branch level. Affiliated unions do have to pay fees and they do have political funds, but the former are small, and the latter have gone to individual candidates directly rather than through the Party.[33]

In other more significant ways the connection with the unions has actively damaged the Party, in large part again because of the divisions produced by the intensely nationalist atmosphere of the first thirty years of independence. The Irish TUC covered the whole island, a heritage of the British connection, and this meant that there was a clear division of unions into those whose headquarters are in Dublin and whose members live mainly in the Republic, and those which are branches of British unions and often have the bulk of their members in Northern Ireland. This division has produced considerable tension in the movement. Associated with it in some ways was the personal and political hostility between two of the most prominent figures in the Labour movement, the radical socialist James Larkin, leader of the Workers' Union of Ireland, and William O'Brien, general secretary of the Irish Transport and General Workers Union. This dated back to a battle for control of the ITGWU in the early 1920s. O'Brien was also the foremost opponent of British-based unions in the Labour movement. In the 1940s these tensions split both Party and trade union movement in interlinked disputes. After many years absence, Larkin again became active in Labour politics and eventually, despite ITGWU opposition, stood successfully as a Labour candidate in the 1943 general election. In response the ITGWU disaffiliated from the Party, established a National Labour Party based on its affiliated TDs, and accused the Labour Party of communist infiltration. The split was healed only by co-operation in office between 1948 and 1951. In 1945 the ITUC also split and the Congress of Irish Unions was formed by the ITGWU and other Irish-based unions. This split lasted until the late 1950s and deprived the Party of much union support while it lasted.

In other respects the Party has not suffered from relations with trade unions in ways that other Labour and Social Democratic Parties have. There has rarely been tension between Party and movement over issues of industrial relations or economic policy. This is partly because the trade union movement itself has hardly been a radical body. But probably the main reason for these cordial relations is the fact that the Party has rarely had to bear the responsibility for official policy for long periods. The possible tension between executive responsibility and traditional loyalties was revealed at the end of the coalition government of 1954 to 1957. The balance of payments difficulties of 1956 led to a policy of deflation and trade control which hit living standards and employment badly. The Labour Party suffered some

pressure from the trade unions until the coalition Prime Minister, the
Fine Gael TD John Costello, put forward a set of largely cosmetic policy
proposals intended to meet the situation. However, trade union anguish
increased again over the next year and the Party was saved from
embarrassment only by the fall of the Government on another issue. As
we shall see below, similar difficulties are confronting the present
coalition Government.

The Future

The attentive reader will have noticed the frequent occurrence in this
essay of the phrase 'until recently' and indeed the Irish Republic has
been changing at a more rapid rate in the past fifteen years than at any
period since independence. The stagnation of the mid-fifties, symbolised
by an actual decline in the Gross National Product in 1956, brought
about a crisis of confidence in the future of the country and a major
re-alignment of Government policy. A mild form of indicative planning
was adopted and there was a change of emphasis in the Government's
capital spending from social to more productive expenditure. The
results of this, allied to a favourable period for the British economy,
were several years of a growth rate remarkable by Irish, and indeed
British, standards. Between 1958 and 1961 the growth rate did not drop
below 4 per cent p.a. Thereafter the troubles of the British economy
slowed down the progress, but not to pre-1957 standards, and the Irish
economy has continued to expand although events since 1973 have
dealt a considerable jolt to this progress. A large amount of the expansion
has come from an alliance between state and foreign capital in the form
of very generous aid to foreign investment. The Irish industrial economy
has accordingly been expanding very rapidly and, if one were to adopt a
crude materialism, one would expect this to lead to an increase in
support for Labour.[34] Not only is the 'natural' constituency expanding
but also the new commercially and economically orientated political
atmosphere should work in its favour. There is evidence to this effect.
In the 1965 and 1969 elections the Party began for the first time to
find considerable support in Dublin in both votes and seats and is now
the major opposition party to Fianna Fail in the city in both national
and local elections. At the same time its national vote has also showed a
considerable increase, as can be seen in Table 1. The largest party has
shown signs of alarm. Fianna Fail has not been enamoured of the
proportional representation multi-member constituency system of
election for some time. Its leaders have felt that the system leads to
frequent narrow majorities, minority Governments and repeat elections,

and that it allows parties they regard as being to the 'right' and 'left' of Fianna Fail to campaign on dissimilar platforms and then combine in coalition. An attempt to amend the Constitution to allow a single member 'first past the post' system was made by the Fianna Fail Government in 1959, but was rejected narrowly at the necessary referendum. In 1968 the Party decided to try again and the other parties made it clear that they thought the motivation was party political. Labour with the aid of the unions fought a vigorous campaign against the proposal and this time the referendum was a severe blow to the governing party, rejecting the measure by 657,898 votes to 423,498 votes in a 63 per cent poll.

However, premature conclusions should not be drawn. The increase in the Labour vote has not continued through the 1973 elections, although the drop in support has largely come from outside Dublin. Also established political parties have enormous potential for survival and adaptation. Fianna Fail especially is a formidable competitor for any growth in working-class voting power. It has a strong organisation, no commitment to anything but a largely achieved nationalism and can form Governments alone. And the small amount of survey evidence available shows that it has a strong base to build on for, while Labour is *a* working-class party, with 55 per cent of its support from the objectively defined working class, Fianna Fail has more claim to be *the* working-class party with 42 per cent of the total objectively defined working-class vote against Labour's 28 per cent.[35] The future of the Labour Party is thus better characterised as open and favourable rather than assured.

The last decade has also brought other changes for Labour. From the mid-sixties onwards it began to receive, at last, an influx of middle-class support and personnel. This had much to do with the feeling, after several years of sustained growth, that Ireland was on the move and that Labour was the party of the future, as well as being the most palatable of the existing parties. There was an upsurge in membership in the universities and, more visibly, several academics with some national fame as TV personalities and public figures stood for Dublin constituencies for the Party and gained election. The most famous of these was the ex-diplomat Dr Conor Cruise O'Brien.[36] For the first time there was a significant dent in the trade unionist character of the parliamentary party. Of the 19 TDs elected for Labour in 1973, 8 (42.1 per cent) called themselves trade union officials while 4 (21 per cent) had professional occupations compared with 9.1 per cent in 1965 and 6 per cent of the total number of Labour TDs up to 1948.[37] In the present Government two out of Labour's five ministerial posts have gone to this new element in the party.[38] At the same time the Party has committed itself more firmly to socialism with the New Republic programme of 1967.

However, tensions have followed these new developments, with older members preferring to campaign on records of personal service to constituents rather than the new programme, debate and doubt about the wisdom of coalition and its effects on the Party's new-found votes and socialism, and problems about Northern Ireland. Dr O'Brien was the party's spokesman on the North when in opposition and made clear his belief that reunification could only come about with the consent of the Protestants at a time when that view was much more unpalatable in the Republic than it now is. He was able to carry the Party with him but did meet opposition at Party Conferences from more traditionally nationalist elements. This nationalist viewpoint is to some extent associated with the left wing of the party and this also has strengthened in the past ten years. It is now organised in a body called the Liaison Committee of the Left and at least two of the new generation of Labour deputies, Dr David Thornley and Dr John O'Connell, have shown sympathy with the Left. Dr Thornley has recently had the Labour whip withdrawn from him for attendance at a rally against Government security legislation which was also attended by prominent members of the Provisional IRA. So far, the Party leadership have, while in government, controlled this internal opposition with little difficulty and have gained massively favourable votes at Party Conferences on all important matters. But Labour Left-wing doubts represent the greatest immediate threat to the tough security policy of the present Government and organised radical opinion in the Party is probably better organised now than it has been for many decades.

A further feature of the political climate of the 1960s in Ireland was the likelihood of eventual EEC membership. The Irish economy was closely tied to the British economy and if and when the British entered it was clear that the Irish would follow. However, when the point of decision was reached, during the 1971 entry negotiations, both the Labour Party and the Irish Congress of Trade Unions were opposed. The reasons advanced by the Party included the danger to national sovereignty, the effect on Irish price levels, and the inability of the Irish economy to soak up farmers who might be displaced by the Mansholt Plan. But the core of both Party and union opposition was the possible effect on employment. Much of Irish industry, especially consumer durables, had grown up behind tariff barriers laid down in the period of intense economic nationalism in the 1930s, and although efforts had been made to prepare industry for freer trade conditions since the first British EEC negotiations in 1961, it was clear that some jobs would be lost. It was also clear that the expansion in industrial output in the 1960s owed as much to higher productivity as to increased employment. The Party argued that associate membership would be more rational for a developing economy such as Ireland, but the ICTU preferred no relationship at all to full membership.

For membership were both Fianna Fail, then in Government, and Fine Gael, plus most farming interests; against were ranged Labour, the unions and both wings of Sinn Fein, the political wing of the IRA, all members of the Common Market Defence Campaign. The main scene of battle was the necessary referendum to amend the constitution on 11 May 1972. The weight of interests were for the EEC and their campaign was considerably better organised and financed. Also the Government attempted to meet Labour arguments about employment by announcing a drive to create 38,000 jobs net by 1977, taking maximum advantage of Community aid in doing so. The decision was expected to be in favour of the Community but the size of the majority was a surprise, with 83 per cent in favour in a 71 per cent poll and all constituencies registering large majorities for entry. Some argued that the electorate divided on party lines and it was true that the total vote against entry approximated to Labour's first preferences in the 1969 general elelction. But whereas Labour's vote is strongly regional, the anti-entry vote was much less so.[39]

The Party accepted the decision philosophically, with its leader Brendan Corish stating: 'The decision has now been made by the people. As a democratic party working within the context of a parliamentary system, the Labour Party accepts that decision.'[40]

Some sections of the Party were not enthusiastic anti-marketeers from the very beginning and neither Party nor unions have had difficulty in adjusting to entry. Both play a full part in the relevant Community institutions. Delegates at Party Conferences are occasionally deeply critical of the EEC, but there is no immediate threat to the Party's involvement in European institutions.

Labour's greatest contemporary problems and opportunities, however, are presented by its return to power, after seventeen years, as junior partner in the coalition government formed after the general election of 1973. The Party had rejected coalition for much of the 1960s but had entered the 1973 election campaign committed to the idea and the campaign was fought on a common fourteen-point programme with Fine Gael. The problems that the new Government has been faced with are familiar. The programme promised, among other things, reformed capital taxation, increased social security, reformed social welfare programmes and greater housing expenditure. At least part of many of these promises has been delivered, but overshadowing all else has been the economic effects of the energy crisis. A small open economy, closely tied to the weak British economy, has been hit harder than most in the period since 1973. Inflation hit levels above 20 per cent in 1975 and unemployment had been rising steadily. Open clashes between trade unions and the Government have so far been avoided. This is partly because of budgets which have increased social welfare payments and have run large deficits to help stem the rise in unemployment. But it is also because of the wage bargaining system in the Republic. Since 1970 wages movements have been governed by a series of National Wages Agreements negotiated voluntarily between the Irish Congress of Trade Unions and the Irish Employers Confederation through the non-governmental Employer-Labour Conference. There is no long-term commitment to this procedure and each set of negotiations has to be first sanctioned and then have its results submitted to conferences of the ICTU. The unions are deeply opposed to any direct Government involvement in this centralised free collective bargaining and the State is represented only as an employer, by civil servants, in the Employer-Labour Conference. This has provided some sort of wage restraint without statutory intervention, but it has become increasingly difficult to maintain as the problems of the economy have grown. Both the 1974 and 1975 agreements needed Government intervention at some point in their lives and the 1976 agreement took three months to negotiate and was then rejected by an ICTU conference. A rather looser version, proposed by the Irish Employers Confederation, was accepted by the ICTU in September 1976, three months after the final settlements under the previous agreement had expired. A substantial part of the difficulty which caused this delay was the Government's anxiety about the deteriorating economic situation. Inflation was again rising at a time when that of other countries was falling, unemployment in June 1976 was the highest in the European Community at 10.2 per cent,[41] and the government's borrowing requirements were assuming daunting proportions. Strains in the coalition partnership were becoming evident. The Government's original proposals for 1976, voiced in December 1975, were for a voluntary pay pause until the end of the year, and this was reinforced by ominous speeches from the Taoiseach, or Prime Minister, Mr Cosgrave, and the

Minister of Finance, Mr Ryan, both members of Fine Gael, which threatened draconian budgets and emphasised the necessity of a pay pause. This was interpreted by the Press as a threat of statutory control.[42] However, the Minister of Labour, Mr O'Leary, a Labour TD, publicly declared that the alternatives were voluntary agreement or chaos, and explicitly ruled out statutory controls.[43] In the event wage increases had to be accepted, although the tough line taken by the Government representatives on the employers' side of the Employer-Labour Conference caused much of the delay in the wage agreement.

At the time of writing, some way out of these tensions was being sought through tripartite negotiations between unions, employers, and Government to attempt to formulate an agreed four-year economic plan. This had been insisted upon by the Irish Employers Confederation as part of the eventual 1976 wages agreement and was to be accompanied by further wages talks in the Employer-Labour Conference. Much depended upon these linked negotiations, but given the attitudes of all parties concerned it is difficult not to see further tensions between the coalition partners and between the Labour Party and the trade unions.

Political prediction is a risky business but it is possible that much of what has been written here will soon apply to a departed version of the Irish Labour Party. It now has consistent support in urban areas, the country is changing rapidly in the direction of the Western European norm, and the Party is in office for the first time in seventeen years. Furthermore, Fianna Fail, the present opposition, has lost votes in Dublin as Labour has gained them, is troubled by leadership problems, and in by-elections since 1973 has lost support even in the areas of the western seaboard in which it has traditionally been impregnable. But the analyst should not be blind to other potential futures. The economic outlook for the Republic in the short and medium term is bleak and there are long-term problems for Party leaders in managing relations between Left and Right in the Party and between the Party and the unions. The next ten years will be as important for the Irish Labour Party as any since the founding of the independent state.

Notes

1. Irish parliamentary elections take place in multi-member constituencies using the single transferable vote system. The figures are taken or calculated from B. Chubb, *The Government and Politics of Ireland* (Stanford, Stanford University Press, 1970), Tables B4 and B5, pp. 333-4, as are all other election figures unless otherwise stated.

2. The political entity presently called the Republic of Ireland was called the Irish Free State from 1922 to 1937, Eire or Ireland from 1937 to 1948 and has been known as the Republic since the last date. I shall refer to it as Ireland or the Republic for the sake of convenience.
3. This is, in fact, a considerable exaggeration. Even in 1926 Gross Agricultural output was estimated at £57,837,000 while Gross Industrial production was slightly higher at £59,477,000. (See J. Meenan, *The Irish Economy Since 1922* (Liverpool, Liverpool University Press, 1970), Table 2.10, p. 52 and Table 2.12, p. 57.) But, on the other hand, in 1928, 42 per cent of exports by value were live animals while 57 per cent of imports by value were raw materials and manufactured goods. (See D. O'Mahoney, *The Irish Economy* (Cork, Cork University Press, 1967), Table I, ch.VI, p.122.)
4. See Chubb, op. cit. Table A.5, p. 327 and *Census of Ireland 1971*, vol. III (Dublin, Central Statistics Office, 1974), Table II.
5. Calculated from the *Statistical Abstract of Ireland, 1971* (Dublin, Stationery Office, 1974), Table 64.
6. See Chubb, op. cit. Table A2, p. 326 and *Census of Ireland 1971* (Preliminary Report, Dublin Central Statistics Office, 1971), Table G.
7. For accounts of this process of restructuring see L.M. Cullen, *An Economic History of Ireland Since 1660* (London, Batsford, 1972), pp. 134-6; F.S.L. Lyons, *Ireland Since the Famine* (London, Fontana, 1973), pp. 46-7. For accounts of emigration, see Lyons, op. cit. pp. 51-3, and C. Arensberg and S.T. Kimball, *Family and Community in Rural Ireland* (Cambridge, Mass., Harvard University Press, 1968). The best indicator of the entire process is the number of agricultural labourers which stood at 1,326,000 in 1841, 326,000 in 1841, 277,000 in 1911, and only 35,569 in 1971. The figures are from Lyons, op. cit. p. 53 and *Census of Ireland 1971*, vol. III, op. cit.
8. '. . . by 1917 almost two thirds of the tenants had acquired their holdings' (Cullen, op. cit. p. 154).
9. See E. Rumpf, *Nationalismus and Socialismus in Ireland* (Meisenheim am Glam, 1959), and the interpretation in Chubb, op. cit. pp. 77-82.
10. See, for instance, D. Thornley, 'The Blueshirts', in F. McManus (ed.), *The Years of the Great Test* (Cork, Mercier Press, 1967), p. 52.
11. 'No social group is more conservative than a landowning peasantry and none is more revolutionary than a peasantry which owes too much or pays too high a rental.' (S.P. Huntington, *Political Order in Changing Societies* (New Haven, Yale University Press, 1968), p. 375.
12. Figures compiled from the *Irish Times*, 3 Sept. 1923, 28 Jan. 1933, and 6 and 7 Feb. 1948, and *Trade Union Information*, Irish Congress of Trade Unions Research Service, March, 1973. In the 1948 election the Labour Party was split and the votes and seats for both wings have been included in the above figures. The figures are not, in fact, directly comparable because of changes in constituency boundaries which no longer exactly coincide with administrative counties, but the differences are not enough to alter the overall impression. The counties are Carlow, Kilkenny, Clare, Cork, Kerry, Kildare, Leix, Offaly, Limerick, Meath, Tipperary, Waterford, Wexford and Wicklow.
13. M.A. Busteed and H. Mason, 'Irish Labour in the 1969 Election', *Political Studies*, vol. 18 (1970), pp. 373-9. The correlations for 1927 and 1933 were calculated from figures in the *Irish Times*, 17 June 1927, and 28 Jan. 1933, and from the *Census of Population of Ireland 1926* (Dublin, Stationery Office, 1928), vol. II, Tables 3A and 5.
14. E.E. Schattschneider, *The Semi-Sovereign People* (New York, Holt, Rinehart and Winston, 1960), p. 71.

15. A. Mitchell, *Labour in Irish Politics, 1890-1930* (Dublin, Irish University Press, 1974), pp. 65-7.

16. The importance of the failure to contest this election has been emphasised by B. Farrell in 'Labour and the Irish Political Party System: a suggested approach to analysis', *Economic and Social Review*, vol. I, (1970), pp. 477-89, where it is pointed out that the combination of the extension of the franchise produced by the 1918 Representation of the People Act and the absence of a general election since 1910 meant that around two-thirds of the electorate were voting for the first time and furthermore at a critical period for the formation of party loyalties. However, Labour would have had to contest seats on a national scale to win major party status and it is clear from the information presented in the paper that Labour leaders were planning to field candidates in only fifteen largely urban seats. Thus, even if it had ignored the pressures from Sinn Fein, the Party could not have broken through on a massive scale.

17. From Chubb, op. cit. Table B6, p. 335.

18. For attempts to damage Labour with allegations of this sort in the 1969 general election see Busteed and Mason, op. cit. p. 378, and Conor Cruise O'Brien, *States of Ireland* (London, Panther, 1974), pp. 181-3.

19. The definitive and exhaustive treatment of the role of the Catholic Church in the Republic is J.H. Whyte, *Church and State in Modern Ireland* (Dublin, Gill and Macmillan, 1971).

20. See, for example, D. Thornley, The Irish Labour Party, *Irish Times*, 30 Mar. 1965.

21. See Mitchell, op. cit. pp. 20, 122-9.

22. See, for example, P. Lynch, 'The Social Revolution that Never Was', in T.D. Williams (ed.), *The Irish Struggle, 1919-1926* (London, Routledge and Kegan Paul, 1966).

23. Cited in Whyte, op. cit. p. 82.

24. Cited in D. Nevin, 'Labour and the Political Revolution', in McManus, op. cit. p. 64.

25. Whyte, op. cit. p. 84.

26. Nevin, op. cit. p. 65.

27. Ibid. p. 64.

28. See the account in Whyte, op. cit. chs.VII and VIII.

29. See B. Chubb, 'Going About Persecuting Civil Servants: The Role of the Irish Parliamentary Representative', *Political Studies*, vol. 11 (1963), pp.272-86; M. Bax, 'Patronage Irish Style: Irish Politicians as Brokers', *Sociologische Gids*, vol. 17 (1970), pp. 171-91; P.M. Sacks, 'Bailiwicks, Locality and Religion: Three Elements in an Irish Dail Constituency Election', *Economic and Social Review*, vol. I (1970), pp. 521-54.

30. 'The Challenge Now Facing Fine Gael and Labour', *Irish Times Annual Review*, 1968.

31. For an account of these parties, see M. Manning, *Irish Political Parties: An Introduction* (Dublin, Gill and Macmillan, 1972).

32. The figures for the 1922 to 1948 period are taken from J.L. McCracken, *Representative Government in Ireland* (London, Oxford University Press, 1958), pp. 114-15; those for 1965 from Chubb, op. cit. Table 3.5, p.96.

33. See Chubb, op. cit. pp. 92-3, where the Labour Party's published annual income in the late sixties is said to be about £8,000, of which £1,600 came from the affiliation fees of trade unions.

34. Employment in the secondary sector, mining and manufacturing, rose from 24.6 per cent to 30.6 per cent of the gainfully employed population between 1961 and 1971, compared with a rise of only 0.9 per cent of the total in the entire previous decade. Perhaps more impressively, industrial output rose by

47 per cent in value between 1957 and 1963 while agricultural output rose by only 1 per cent in value in the same period. (Sectoral employment figures calculated from *Census of Ireland 1971,* vol. III (Dublin, Central Statistics Office, 1974), Table I; output figures from G. FitzGerald, *Planning in Ireland* (Dublin and London, Institute of Public Administration and PEP, 1968, p. 45.)

35. These figures are from the Gallup Survey of April 1969 undertaken for the Irish Labour Party and reproduced in summary form as Appendix A, Manning, op. cit.

36. The others were Justin Keating and David Thornley, both lecturers at Trinity College, Dublin.

37. The figures are from the *Irish Times,* 3 Mar. 1973; Chubb, op. cit. Table 3.5, p. 96; and McCracken, op. cit. pp. 114-15. It is also worth noting that at least two of those Labour TDs elected in 1973 who are trade union officials, B. Desmond and L. Kavanagh, have had higher education. (See *Who's Who, What's What and Where's Where in Ireland,* 1973.)

38. Dr O'Brien is Minister of Posts and Telegraphs, a position that covers TV and broadcasting, and Justin Keating is Minister of Industry and Commerce.

39. For instance, in Mayo West, where Labour and minor parties won only 1.8 per cent of the first preferences in the 1969 general election, the anti-EEC vote held up at 12.2 per cent, while in Dublin North East, where Labour and minor parties won 57 per cent of the valid first preferences in 1969, the anti-EEC vote, although high, was still well below Labour's general election performance at 25.3 per cent. See *Irish Times,* 12 May 1972.

40. *Irish Times,* 24 May 1972.

41. *Irish Times,* 9 July 1976.

42. See, for example, the speech of Mr Ryan in Dublin on 9 Mar. 1976 *(Irish Times* 10 Mar. 1976) and the letter from Mr Cosgrave to the ICTU and the Irish Employers Federation later that month *(Irish Times,* 18 Mar. 1976).

43. *Irish Times,* 22 Mar. 1976.

Table 1. The Labour vote since 1948

General Elections	Seats* Total	Seats* Dublin°°	Votes† Total No.	Votes† Total % of total valid poll	Votes† Dublin°° No.	Votes† Dublin°° % of Labour vote
1948$	19		149,088	11.3		
1951	16		151,828	11.4		
1954	19		161,034	12.0		
1957	12		111,747	9.1		
1961	15	1	136,110	11.7	26,000	19.1
1965	21	6	192,740	15.4	55,030	28.6
1969	18	10	223,280	17.0	93,440	41.9
1973	19	7	185,117	13.8	78,347	42.3

*The total number of seats in the Dail was 147 from 1948 to 1957, and 144 from 1961 to 1973.

†Votes = valid first preferences.

°°Given separately only from 1961 onwards.

$The Labour Party was split in this election and all figures are totals for both wings of the party.

Sources: Chubb, 'The Government and Politics of Ireland', op. cit. pp. 333-4; Manning, op. cit. p. 79; *Irish Times,* 3 Mar. 1973.

Further Reading

There are few works concerned solely and explicitly with the Irish Labour Party. General introductions can be found in the relevant sections of,

Chubb, B. *The Government and Politics of Ireland.* Stanford, Stanford University Press, 1970.

Manning, M. *Irish Political Parties. An Introduction.* Dublin, Gill and Macmillan, 1972.

The most substantial piece of research on a particular period is

Mitchell, A. *Labour in Irish Politics, 1890-1930.* Dublin, Irish University Press, 1974.

Article-length discussion of aspects of the party's history and place in Irish politics can be found in,

Busteed, M.A. and Mason, H. 'Irish Labour in the 1969 Election.' *Political Studies,* vol. 18. 1970. Pp. 373-9.

Farrell, B. 'Labour and the Irish Party System: A Suggested Approach to Analysis.' *Economic and Social Review* vol. 1. 1970. Pp. 477-89.

Lynch, P. 'The Social Revolution that Never Was.' In T.D. Williams (ed.), *The Irish Struggle, 1919-1926.* London, Routledge and Kegan Paul, 1966. Pp. 41-54.

Nevin, D. 'Industry and Labour.' In K.B. Nowlan and T.D. Williams (eds.), *Ireland in the War Years and After.* Dublin, Gill and Macmillan, 1969. Pp. 94-108.

Nevin, D. 'Labour and the Political Revolution.' In F. McManus (ed.), *The Years of the Great Test, 1926-1939.* Cork, Mercier Press, 1967. Pp. 55-68.

A number of more general works on Irish politics and society contain important sections on aspects of the Labour Party.

Farrell, B. *Chairman or Chief? The Role of the Taoiseach in Irish Government.* Dublin, Gill and Macmillan, 1971.

Farrell, B. *The Founding of Dail Eireann.* Dublin, Gill and Macmillan, 1971.

Lyons, F.S.L. *Ireland Since the Famine.* London, Fontana, 1973.

McCarthy, C. 'From Division to Dissension: Irish Trade Unions in the 1930s.' *Economic and Social Review,* Vol. 5. 1973-4. Pp. 353-84, 469-90.

McCarthy, C. *The Decade of Upheaval. Irish Trade Unions in the 1960s.* Dublin, Institute of Public Administration, 1973.

McCracken, J.L. *Representative Government in Ireland: A Study of Dail Eireann, 1919-48.* London, Oxford University Press, 1957.
Whyte, J.H. *Church and State in Modern Ireland.* Dublin, Gill and Macmillan, 1971.

Mention should also be made of a number of biographical studies of important figures in the labour movement.

Greaves, C.D. *The Life and Times of James Connolly,* London, Lawrence and Wishart, 1972 (1962).
Larkin, E. *James Larkin, Irish Labour Leader, 1876-1947.* London, 1965.
Levenson, S. *James Connolly. A Biography.* London, Martin Brian and O'Keeffe, 1973.
Mitchell, A. 'William O'Brian, 1881-1968, and the Irish Labour movement', *Studies,* vol.XL, 1971.
Three recent studies of the social bases of Irish parties contain discussion of the Labour Party.
Gallagher, M. *Electoral Support for Irish Political Parties.* Sage Professional Papers, Contemporary Political Sociology Series, vol.2, no.06-017, London and Beverley Hills, Sage, 1976.
Rumph, E. and Hepburn, A.C. *Nationalism and Socialism in Twentieth Century Ireland.* Liverpool, Liverpool University Press, 1977. (This is a translation and updating of Rumpf's work of 1959 cited in note 9 above.)
Whyte, J.H. 'Ireland: Politics without Social Bases', in R. Rose (ed.), *Electoral Behaviour. A comparative handbook.* New York, Free Press, 1974.
One much older work should be mentioned:
Clarkson, J.D. *Labour and Nationalism in Ireland.* New York, AMS Press reprint, 1970 (1925).
Also:
Thornley, D.A. 'Development of the Irish Labour Movement', *Christus Rex,* vol.XVIII, 1964.

7 THE GERMAN SOCIAL DEMOCRATIC PARTY

William E. Paterson

The German Social Democratic Party (SPD)* is the oldest and most famous Social Democratic party in Western Europe. Its Party Chairman, Willy Brandt, is Europe's best-known Social Democrat. Its leaders and policies have traditionally played a key role in the various Internationals to which it has been affiliated. It is rivalled in strength and historical prestige only by the British Labour Party. The SPD has been in Government since 1966. And yet now as in the past the Party is prey to internal tensions about policy, strategy and timing and it is the aim of this article to analyse some of the more important conditioning factors. A fully comprehensive analysis would require a study of volume length. This study has yet to be written.

Historical Evolution

Among Social Democratic parties the SPD is probably uniquely conscious of being part of a historical tradition which reaches back to Ferdinand Lassalle. The modern history of the Party really begins with the creation of the Socialist Workers' Party of Germany, however. This was formed at Gotha in 1875 by the fusion of the *Allgemeiner Deutscher Arbeiterverein* (German General Workers Association) founded by Ferdinand Lassalle, with the *Sozialdemokratische Arbeiterpartei* (Social Democratic Workers Party), led by August Bebel and Wilhelm Liebknecht. The long-standing persecution by Bismarck, enacted in the Anti-Socialist Laws (1878-90), helped to consolidate the Party and to increase its support. In 1891 a new programme was ratified at Erfurt. The Erfurt Programme was divided into two parts, the first outlining a theory of social development and long-run objectives in Marxist terms, the second laying down a fairly familiar series of aims that the SPD would try to realise within the *status quo* of capitalist society. The programme, with its synthesis of revolutionary and reformist tendencies, faithfully mirrored the tension between contending groups in the Party. This tension, sometimes dormant, sometimes expressed in visceral conflict, has been a continuing feature of the Party's history.

*A list of abbreviations is given at the end of this chapter, on pages 206-7.

In the period between the adoption of the Erfurt Programme and the outbreak of the First World War, the SPD presented an outward picture of unparalleled success. Its electorate expanded from 3 to 4¼ million between 1903 and 1912, and by that time its total vote was twice that of any other party. This success was however accompanied by a constant conflict, between those like Rosa Luxemburg who stressed the revolutionary aspirations of the Party, and the 'revisionists', notably Eduard Bernstein, who wished the Party to adhere to its reformist course and to abandon its Marxist doctrine. The triad was completed by the Party Executive, who attempted to preserve the historic synthesis of reformist practice and revolutionary theory.[1] Despite some increased militancy among some sections of the party after the 1905 revolution in Russia and despite its great prestige in the international labour movement, the SPD in general lacked dynamism. Bismarck's social policy had absorbed some of the pressing demands of the German working class and the persecution of the Socialists had given the activists the feeling of having participated in a revolution — albeit an ersatz one imposed on them from above. What remained was an intense and active commitment to the forms and symbols of the movement, but only a passive orientation towards transforming the goals of the movement into practice.[2] This meant that, although the SPD officially remained an anti-system party (*diesem System keinen Mann und keinen Pfennig*), in practice it became ever more involved in the system. By 1913 there were nearly 11,000 Social Democrats on Municipal and District Councils. Even more strikingly, during 1910 an estimated 100,000 Social Democrats worked in the agencies and the administration of the workers' insurance systems, in trade and industrial courts, and in the municipal labour exchanges.[3] Moreover, the electoral success of the SPD in these succeeding years resulted in important changes which tended to bring the SPD more nearly into alignment with other political parties. In 1905, at the Party conference, it was decided to institute reforms in Party organisation. This led to three main changes. Firstly, the basic unit of the SPD was changed from the local association (*Ortsverein*), to the constituency association (*Wahlkreisverein*). This change presupposed that winning elections was the main focus of Party life, rather than the alternative 'movement model', where the apparatus was there to mobilise the masses in a much wider sense. Secondly, the informal system of *Vertrauensleute* dating from the period of persecution was jettisoned in favour of a more formalised hierarchical structure. A hierarchy of *Land* and regional organisations was created to act as intermediaries between the local and the national level. Perhaps even more significantly, these 1905 reforms created the institutional pre-conditions for the rapid growth in the power and influence of the Party bureaucracy. The reforms envisaged a uniform system of finance and established new requirements for full annual reports at all levels of the Party. In effect, these reforms presupposed the replacement of the old voluntary system by paid party officials. By 1909, almost all regional organisations and a majority of local associations had a paid party secretary. Since these secretaries (though subject to nomination by the association concerned) were appointed and paid for from the centre where the party bureaucracy, headed by Bebel, had succeeded in establishing a dominant position, they came to be identified very closely with the central bureaucracy.

The growth in importance of the Party Executive and party bureaucracy was accompanied by a marked growth in the importance and autonomy of the *Reichtagsfraktion*, a growth which went hand in hand with continued electoral success.[4] These developments tended to reduce the need for active commitment and participation by the individual member and to replace it by permanent and formal organisation, better adapted to the exigencies of elections. This developing tension between the formal commitment to participation and actual realities in the 1914 SPD was brilliantly analysed by Roberto Michels in his formulation of the 'Iron Law of Oligarchy'.[5]

The tension between revolutionary aspirations and reformist practice was finally resolved in the vote of the SPD *Reichstagsfraktion* on 4 August 1914 for war credits. It is likely that after the failure of Hermann Müller's mission to Paris the vote would have been in favour of war credits.[6] Nevertheless, an important factor in the decision was the action of the trade union leaders who, in a meeting on 1 August, issued a resolution calling off all strikes in progress and suspending strike payments for the duration. The funds were to be used instead for unemployment relief and to aid war victims. This is a particularly clear illustration of the way in which the trade unions tended to pre-empt the choices for the Party since the party leaders were unwilling to contemplate splitting the working-class movement.

The SPD in Weimar

The close of hostilities in November 1918 found the SPD about to be split into three parts. Most of the Party continued to support the official SPD which in turn had supported the war effort, albeit not so unreservedly as the trade union leaders. However, Party unity had come under increasing strain. The party leadership, which had tolerated a great deal of dissent in peace-time, was not prepared to let dissidents endanger their newly minted alliance with the ruling groups in German society. Accordingly, they forcibly took over *Vorwärts,* which had been pursuing a Left-wing line in 1916. The leadership policy of support for the war had become much less popular due to the lack of success at the front, the increasingly repressive nature of Government policy and the growth of annexationist demands. These developments drew many who had been previously in favour of the war into opposition. When the Party polarised into pro- and anti-war factions the majority expelled many of those opposed to the war. Accordingly in Easter 1917, at Gotha, those Socialists opposed to the continuation of the war, most already expelled from the SPD, met to form a new Independent Social Democratic Party, the USPD (*Unabhängige Sozialdemokratische Partei Deutschlands*). In December 1918, before the Communist International had been established, Rosa Luxemburg and Karl Liebknecht split off from the USPD to set up a new explicitly revolutionary Communist Party, the KPD (*Kommunistische Partei Deutschlands*). To complete the picture of fragmentation, the Free Trade Unions (ADGB) cut the organic bond with the SPD and proclaimed their neutrality *vis-à-vis* political parties in a resolution passed at the Nuremberg trade union congress in July 1919. This disunity was reduced somewhat after 1922 when the USPD rejoined the SPD. Following this, the ADGB modified its stance and, while still remaining officially neutral, supported the SPD in elections after 1924 and provided much of the financial support for the increasingly costly electoral campaigns.

The departure of the articulate critical left of the SPD, first to the USPD then to the KPD, accelerated the trends already visible in the pre-1914 SPD, in particular the trend away from participation and towards further bureaucratisation. The party institutions, like the Party Council and Control Commission, which were meant to control and monitor the Executive on behalf of the Party membership, ossified completely. Even the Annual Congress was a shadow of its former self and after 1925 its meetings were made biennial.[7]

The trend towards bureaucratisation was reinforced by the electoral system which tended to place the power of nomination and thus of election in the hands of the party 'Apparat'. The electoral system also tended to act in an anti-majoritarian manner and to discourage innovation in party policies since, given the exigencies of the electoral system, there was little likelihood that the adoption of new policies would enable the SPD to capture a majority.

Socially, too, the Party was changing. Many working-class members, especially in the large industrial centres, had joined the USPD after 1917 and had then gone over to the Communists. This trend was reactivated after the onset of the depression in 1929. By 1930, the best indications we have suggest that about one-quarter of the party membership was non-proletarian in origin.[8] This compared with about 10 per cent in 1905-6.[9] Moreover the working-class element in party membership was largely recruited from the skilled working class.[10] Even more striking was the percentage of parliamentary party leaders (35 per cent) whose social origins lay above the working class.

The failure of the Müller Government in 1930 and a continuous haemorrhage of the younger and more dynamic elements of the SPD into the KPD and after 1931 into the SAP left the Party seriously weakened.

These failings were glaringly apparent in the SPD response to the end of Weimar. Weakened by the attitude of the trade union leadership, which bordered on capitulation, harried by the Communists, and bound to a legalistic defence of the constitution, they remained committed to parliamentarism even when they knew that it was doomed to failure. The option of direct action through the Iron Front or armed resistance through the *Reichsbanner* (a Socialist militia founded in 1924) was never really seriously considered by the Party leadership and the initiative, despite the courageous opposition of the SPD to the 'Enabling Law', remained firmly in the hands of Hitler who brilliantly combined pressure in parliament with control of the streets through a dynamic movement.

Exile

After its forcible dissolution on 22 June 1933 the Party Executive was reconstituted in Prague. In 1937 it moved its headquarters to Paris and in 1940 after the collapse of France, the rump of the Party Executive reached London, though some members fled directly to the United States. There were also important centres of exiled SPD members in Stockholm and Zürich. London was, however, the most important centre because of the presence of the rump Executive; the importance SPD members accorded to contact with the Labour Party; and the fact that the SPD representatives in London were able to work with other exiled German Socialists in the framework of the Union of German Socialist Organisations in Great Britain. This had been formed in 1938 after a meeting of the exiled Party Executive (Vogel, Ollenhauer) with *Neu Beginnen* (Waldemar Von Knoeringen), SAP and ISK (International

Socialist Combat Group, Willi Eichler).

In exile the parliamentary Party role that had sustained the SPD for so long vanished. They were too largely bereft of the support and guidance of comrades in foreign Socialist parties — though the British Labour Party was a partial exception. They were forced back to aspirations of leading and organising a revolutionary movement (from what remained of the SPD) against National Socialism. This, however, remained merely an aspiration. Contrary to the initial views of some SPD leaders, who foresaw a repeat of the 1878-90 period where exiled leaders were able to direct an active though banned SPD, the exiled Socialists found themselves fairly quickly unable to exert any leverage on events inside Germany. Not only did communication become even more difficult and hazardous but Party members inside Germany were not disposed to accept direction from abroad. They remembered the failure of the SPD-led Government in 1930 and of the SPD itself after March 1933. Those who continued to be actively opposed to the regime generally ended up in concentration camps; and the great majority of the rest were persuaded at least to acquiesce in, if not to support, the regime by a combination of fear and the regime's success in alleviating unemployment. After war broke out direct communication ceased altogether and efforts were concentrated on aiding the Allied effort and planning the post-war Germany.

Despite the manifest failure to influence either Allied war aims or events inside Germany these years were important for the SPD since there was a continuous debate about the Party's future in terms of its past. This debate often degenerated into mutual recrimination but it was very important in the long term since out of it grew an informal consensus about what kind of party the SPD should become. The consensus was very close to the views developed by Schumacher inside Germany and was to provide a basis for the post-war collaboration between the exiles and Schumacher, the first post-war leader of the party.[11]

The Emergence of Schumacher

The future shape of the SPD was very unclear after the cessation of hostilities in Europe in 1945. There were three possible foci around which the SPD might develop. In terms of historical legitimacy, the strongest claimant was the exiled Executive Committee in London, some of whose adherents were sustained by Burnhamite notions popular in the 1930s that post-totalitarian leadership could only be provided by 'external elites', since those politicians who had not fled the dictatorship would either have been eliminated or discredited by collaboration. Despite these advantages, the exiles were handicapped by distance, by their obvious dependence on the Allies, and by the failing health of their Chairman, Hans Vogel. A second, stronger group formed themselves into a Central Committee (*Zentralauschuss*) of the SPD. This was based in Berlin and was led by a former Reichstag deputy, Otto Grotewohl. In mid-June this Committee issued a 'Manifesto of the German Social Democratic Party' which called for early fusion with the KPD. In the very early days after the end of the war, when it still seemed self-evident that Berlin would continue to be the focus of German politics, the Central Committee appeared likely to provide the dominant element in Party life.

The third centre was in Hanover, from where Dr Kurt Schumacher had begun to organise the SPD members in the Western zones. While this group lacked the legitimacy of the exiles and the central geographical advantages of the Central Committee, it possessed in Schumacher the most impressive of the survivors of the Weimar SPD. His anti-Nazi record of vehement opposition in Weimar, both in the Reichstag and the Iron Front, had led to his early arrest after the passing of the Enabling Law and he spent the next decade in Dachau. This gave him a moral and psychological advantage over both the SPD temporisers of April to June 1933, and those who had fled into exile. The moral authority conferred on him by his heroic past was heightened by his gaunt tortured appearance (he had lost his right arm in 1914 and he was to lose his left leg in 1948) and impressive rhetorical skills. This moral authority was accompanied by considerable intellectual ability and a passionate desire to rebuild the SPD.

In August 1945, fourteen of the nineteen *Bezirk* (District) leaders authorised Schumacher to convene a conference of Party leaders. This meeting took place at Wennigsen near Hanover in early October 1945. The conference was to prove crucial for the later development of the SPD. At this conference Grotewohl attempted to persuade the Social Democrats in the Western zones either to call an immediate national conference to choose a new Party leadership, or to confirm an expanded central committee as the provisional national leadership. Schumacher was able to block either option by pointing to the Allied decrees against national organisation of the political parties. Schumacher secured the support, not only of the Western Social Democrats but also of the exiles who were present, for an arrangement whereby the Central Committee would represent Social Democracy provisionally in the Soviet zone, while the *Büro Dr. Schumacher* represented it in the three

Western zones. It was also decided that Grotewohl and his Central Committee should take no further action that would commit the SPD to closer co-operation with the KPD. In the event, Grotewohl led the SPD of the Soviet zone into the SED in 1946 and Schumacher was left in control of the SPD in the Western zones of occupation and West Berlin.

In the first section the historical evolution of the Party was considered in a very general manner. In the remainder of the chapter the approach will be somewhat different and the post-war evolution of the Party and its present situation will be analysed from a number of different perspectives. For those totally unfamiliar with the post-war history of the Party, it is perhaps useful to point out that the SPD remained in opposition from the founding of the Federal Republic until 1966. From 1966-9 the SPD formed a governmental coalition, 'the Grand Coalition' with its main competitors the Christian Democrats (CDU/CSU). From 1969 until the present the SPD has been the dominant partner in a coalition with the Free Democrats (FDP).

The Internal Life of the Party

Party Organisation

The SPD, unlike the British Labour Party, is a direct party with no organic connections to the trade union movement or system of bloc membership. Ultimate authority, theoretically at least, resides in the Conference which meets biennially. In the period between conferences and in practice, the Party is governed by a thirty-six man Executive Committee. Traditionally, the SPD has been the prototype of an Executive-dominated party. In the immediate post-war period some attempts were made to revitalise the autonomy of the district level. Formerly, the key functionary in the Party, the District Secretary, had been a salaried official of the Executive Committee. Now he was to be selected and paid for by the district organisations. Control of the nomination process for elections which had rested with the Party Executive Committee was now located at the district level. Lastly, the national leadership was almost entirely dependent upon dues collected by the districts. Indeed, until 1950, it was the districts which set the level of subscriptions.

However these reforms did not prevail and within a fairly short time the SPD had begun to display the bureaucratisation and ageing that had been so marked in Weimar. Indeed in many ways the Party was the recreation of the Weimar SPD. When Schumacher was confirmed as

Party Chairman in 1946 about two-thirds of the members had belonged to the SPD in Weimar.[12] In these first post-war years the Party was dominated by Schumacher. He had a genuine wish for more participation at the grass roots. However he had an even stronger conviction that, just as the SPD was the only force morally and intellectually qualified to lead post-war Germany, so only he could lead the SPD. This inevitably meant that control of the Party became for him the main priority. This necessitated relying on the established Party leaders at the lcoal level. At the centre, Schumacher was supported by the ex-London emigrés Erich Ollenhauer, Fritz Heine, Willi Eichler and Herta Gotthelf, together with three associates from Hanover, Alfried Nau, Herbert Kreidemann and Egon Franke. Gradually they became indispensable aides to Schumacher and when the Party Executive Committee was formally re-established in 1946, they became its inner nucleus of salaried members. This meant that the Executive was dominated by people who relied totally for their eminence on Schumacher. Any innovation in policy or organisation could only come from Schumacher, as was dramatically demonstrated during his illnesses when the Executive was powerless to act.

It was, however, equally true that Schumacher's failing health induced him to rely increasingly on the bureaucracy in his dealings with the Party. This was especially true after 1949. In the period up until 1949 Schumacher relied on his authority as Party Chairman and succeeded in imposing it on SPD delegates to the Bizonal Economic Council and Parliamentary Council. However once the Bundestag was established Schumacher relied more on his position as parliamentary party leader.

If Schumacher's leadership tended to discourage participation and to stifle innovation in organisational questions, there is nevertheless an argument to be made that ideologically he made some innovations. These innovations were of a cautious nature. He refused to countenance a prolonged debate about a new Party programme, perceiving the damage that this might do to his position in the Party. In essence, he introduced a modest revisionism, while not directly attacking the traditional ideological tenets of the SPD. He rejected the idea of a party based on the workers alone: 'Socialism is no longer the affair of the working class in the old sense of the word. It is the programme for workers, farmers, artisans, tradesmen, and the intellectual professions.'[13] Marxism was rejected by Schumacher as the only legitimate basis for the party: 'It is no matter whether someone becomes a social democrat through the methods of Marxist analysis, for philosophical or ethic reasons, or out of the spirit of the Sermon on the Mount.'[14]

At the time of Schumacher's death in 1952, the organisation and programmatic symbols of the Party were still intact but they were decaying from within. Membership had fallen steeply since 1948 and the parliamentary Party was becoming the most influential organ of party decision. The Party Executive retained some importance but the Control Commission and Party Conference were if anything weaker than they had been in Weimar.

By 1952, the SPD was well on the way to becoming an electoral party in that its orientation was almost exclusively towards electoral success, but the Party had largely failed to extend its appeal much beyond the industrial working-class districts, whilst the Christian Democrats had consolidated their hold on the middle-class electorate. The apparent strength of its organisation and the uncompromising nature of its programme were becoming an embarrassment, making the SPD unable to escape from the image of a class party. It was also handicapped by the identification of Socialism with the GDR.

After the second electoral defeat of 1953, and after the banning of the Communist Party in 1956 had removed all competition on the Left, the efforts to change the Party accelerated, culminating in the adoption of a new Party programme against very little opposition at the special conference in Bad Godesberg in 1959.[15] This programme totally ignored Marx and accepted the principle of private ownership in so far as it did not hinder the creation of a just social order. Economic and social change, it was argued, had outstripped the old party doctrines. The SPD would now concentrate on improving and reforming rather than abolishing the system of free competition. At the same time in a famous speech in the Bundestag on 30 June 1960, Herbert Wehner on behalf of the SPD indicated its willingness to join with other German groups in defence of the Federal Republic against Communist threats by fully accepting NATO and its foreign policy postulates. These programmatic alterations were accompanied by the dropping of many of the old symbols associated with the party. The colour of Party membership books was changed from red to blue and Party members were expected to stop addressing each other as Comrade and to use the term 'party friend'. The flag of the Federal Republic was now flown alongside the traditional red flag above the party headquarters.

Taken together these changes represented a conscious choice by the Party leadership wholeheartedly to embrace the concept of a *Volkspartei*, to turn their back on 'the mass integration party model' of the past in favour of what Otto Kirchheimer has called 'the catch-all party model'. According to Kirchheimer, the success of one catch-all party (in West Germany the CDU/CSU) transforms the party system; other parties are forced to imitate it in order to compensate.[16] In this model the Party seeks to represent all social groups and to operate primarily as an electoral party, i.e. to seek to make appeals to all groups in the electorate. Emphasis is laid not on 'agitation or extra-parliamentary activity, but rather governing, research and expertise and a pragmatic – some would say technocratic – approach to the problems of the day' (Wolinetz). Given the historical strength of the organisation of the SPD; the class background of the members; and the formal procedures for participation by the party membership; it was never possible for the Party leadership to operate totally as a *Volkspartei* without reference to the Party membership, but in general terms this view of the Party remained the accepted one throughout the sixties.

The overriding aim of the Party leadership in the years after Bad Godesberg was to participate in Government. 'That the party exists not to sustain the organisation but that the organisation is there to attain and determine governmental power – to have made this clear is what is historically correct about the series of reforms associated with Bad Godesberg.'[17]

The attempts by the Party leadership especially identified with Herbert Wehner to create a coalition with the CDU finally succeeded in November 1966 when the so-called 'Grand Coalition' was formed. Although broadly accepted by the Party membership, it did lead to a crisis of legitimacy for what remained of the young Left in the SPD after the expulsion of the SDS in July 1960. These members of the extreme Left of the SPD coalesced with extreme Left groups outside the Party in what came to be known as 'the extra-parliamentary opposition' (APO).[18] Although this movement gained a lot of support among the critical young intelligentsia its social base remained very narrow. An attempt to form a new party to the left of the SPD known as the Action Community for Democratic Progress (ADF) which relied heavily on the newly legalised Deutsche Kommunistische Partei was a complete failure. The Soviet occupation of Czechoslovakia in August 1968 activated the latent conflict between the anti-authoritarian adherents of APO opposed to bureaucratic Socialism and the DKP supporters. In 1969, the ADF performance was derisory (0.6 per cent) and the SDS, which had been subject to increasing disarray, finally dissolved itself in March 1970.

The SPD as a Governing Party

After the Federal Election of 1969, the SPD and FDP were able to form a governing coalition and Willy Brandt became Federal Chancellor. This coalition has remained together since then, though Brandt resigned as Chancellor in May 1974 and was replaced by Helmut Schmidt.

Willy Brandt's accession to the Chancellorship in 1969 seemed to many observers both inside and outside the Federal Republic to be a triumphant vindication of 'the embracement strategy', of the SPD as a 'catch-all' party which had brought it such striking electoral gains in the 1960s. However, contrary to these expectations the period since 1969 has been one of intense programmatic concern and one in which both the values embedded in the Bad Godesberg Programme and the whole notion of a *Volkspartei* (catch-all party) have been fiercely debated. The main catalyst of this change has been the changing membership of the Party. The failure of the ADF and the break-up of the SDS, combined with the SPD victory and the promises of reform identified with Willy Brandt, led to a vast influx of young members in the period following 1969. There were 93,827 new members in 1969 and 155,992 new members in 1972.[19] In 1973 the number had dropped to 68,772 and fell further to 55,036 in 1974. The percentage of those who can class themselves as Young Socialists (i.e. party members under thirty-five years) rose from 54.6 per cent of new members in 1969 to 65.6 per cent in 1971. The most marked increase was in new members under twenty-one. They doubled in number from 10.4 per cent of new members in 1969 to 21.1 per cent in 1971. Similarly the percentage of new working-class members which had been 55 per cent in the period 1956-61 had fallen from 39.6 per cent in 1969 to 35 per cent in 1971. By 1974 it had fallen to 26 per cent. In the same year the percentage of new members under twenty-one had fallen to 14 per cent.

The demands of these new members were articulated primarily by the Young Socialists. Formally, all Party members under thirty-five are potentially at least *Jusos* (Young Socialists). In fact even at the height of *Juso* activity only about one-fifth of SPD members under thirty-five actively participated in any meaningful way in *Juso* activities.

The challenge from the Young Socialists first became apparent at their 1969 conference in Munich where the radical Karsten Voigt was elected as chairman. This conference passed a series of resolutions which were extremely critical of the SPD's failure in their view, to represent working-class interests. They attributed this failure to the idea of a 'catch-all party' associated with the reforms initiated by Bad Godesberg.

This attack produced an angry reply from the Party Executive and a reminder to the Young Socialists that Party decisions were binding.[20]

In the period following the Munich Conference, the Young Socialists concentrated on strengthening their position in the Party as well as continuing the theoretical debate. In this they were guided by two principles of action, 'the double-strategy' and 'the imperative mandate'.[21] Basically, the double strategy meant the Young Socialists involving themselves in the Party and indeed taking it over in the long run ('the SPD of the 1980s') but feeling themselves free to indulge in extra-Party co-operation with other groups when they considered it useful and necessary. In the Party, they pressed for the operation of 'the imperative mandate'. This would have meant a situation in which delegates to any of the higher Party bodies and to parliament would be controlled by those who elected them. If they wanted to diverge from a position that they had been mandated to represent, they would have to get a new mandate from 'the basis'. Such a notion, while clearly close to the ideas of participation implicit in the organisational structure of the SPD, was equally clearly unwelcome to the Party leadership.

The response of the Party leadership was not to expel them as they had done with the SDS but to attempt to integrate the *Jusos* into the Party. This was done in two ways. Firstly, many *Juso* activists were encouraged to become Party functionaries, since the post-war veterans were nearing retirement. This often led them to align their views more closely to the mainstream of party opinion. More ambitiously an attempt was made to involve the whole Party in programmatic endeavour and to project the discussion about the Godesberg programme into the future. At the Saarbrücken Conference of the Party in 1970, a long-term programme commission was established to draw up an *Entwurf eines ökonomisch politischen Orientierungsrahmens für die Jahre 1973-85*. Although this commission was safely under the chairmanship of Helmut Schmidt, several *Jusos* and leftists were given places on the commission.

The tension between the *Jusos* and the Party Executive was reduced by the polarisation of the years 1969-72 when the SPD/FDP Government was subject to the furious opposition of the CDU/CSU particularly over *Ostpolitik*. In this situation, the *Jusos,* while continuing to consolidate at the local level, were compelled to devote most of their energies to defending the SPD leadership.

At the Hanover Party Conference of April 1973 the Young Socialists were able to pick up some support from the old Left and from the left

centre of the Party. With this they were able to get an appreciable
number of Left-wing supporters elected to the Party Executive and to
have the first draft of the *Orientierungsrahmen* referred back. The
leadership on the other hand was able to defend most of its policies and
the Präsidium or inner-executive Committee, which in fact transacts
most of the Executive's business, remained firmly in the hands of the
established Party Leadership.

In the months following the Hanover Conference, the Young
Socialists were in a state of nearly constant battle with the Party
Executive. There was an almost continuous attack on Brandt by the
Young Socialists for his support for legislation designed to make
employment of radicals in the public service more difficult (the so-called
Radikalenerlass).[22] In early April 1974, partly to appease his Right-wing
critics like Schmidt and von Donhanyi, Brandt issued a ten-point appeal
for Party unity directed particularly at the Young Socialists.[23] This
appeal, which stressed the necessity of adherence to the Godesberg
Programme and the Governmental Declaration of 18 January 1973, was
rejected by the leadership of the Young Socialists.[24] The last months
of Brandt's Chancellorship saw an increase in tension between the
Young Socialists and leading figures in the Party accompanied by
increasingly strident demands for their expulsion.[25] These demands
were partly occasioned by awareness of the harm that the Young
Socialists were doing to the Party's electoral chances in a series of state
elections which went very badly for the SPD.

Willy Brandt resigned as Chancellor to be replaced by Helmut
Schmidt in early May 1974. This change coincided with a decline in
the influence of the Young Socialists and the Left which had gradually
become more marked. This failure of the Left is apparent in their
declining number of votes at the Mannheim Party Conference of
November 1975 and in the second version of the *Orientierungsrahmen*
presented at the same conference, in which many of the formulations
have a markedly less doctrinaire character. Perhaps of more practical
importance has been the restriction placed on publication of opinions
at odds with the line of the rest of the Party both at national and local
level.[26] Since then the Young Socialists have made very few attacks
on the leadership. The leadership in its turn has not proceeded with any
significant exclusions from the Party.

Why Did the Challenge from the Left Fail?

There seem to be four main reasons for the present failure of the Left
and the *Jusos* in the SPD. Unlike the new Left in Holland, they are

confronted with an electoral law which would make secession an unpromising alternative since they would have to clear a 5 per cent threshold for representation. There is no evidence that such a potential electorate exists in a country where suspicion of Socialism is rife. The slavish adherence of the DKP, the new German Communist Party, to the GDR renders it an unattractive alternative. The narrow middle-class social basis and the overwhelmingly academic orientation of the Young Socialists has tended to cut them off from other members of the party. In contrast to the situation in Holland, the trade unionists in the party have taken an explicitly hostile line and the *Jusos* have never established a successful industrial base.[27] Lastly and perhaps most importantly the onset of the world economic recession in 1973 deprived them of much of their potential support in the left centre of the party and rendered much less attractive their pleas for zero growth.

Although West Germany was less affected directly by the 1973 recession, its psychological impact was threefold: it undermined the position of Willy Brandt's government, unable now to carry through the reforms which it had promised; Brandt was replaced by Helmut Schmidt, whose priorities were clearly management of the domestic economy rather than reform, and who was therefore unwilling to accord any priority to Left-wing views. Secondly, with the change in the economy the job prospects of young people diminished and their radicalism tended to evaporate. Thirdly, the impact of economic recession correlated with a *Tendenzwende* to the Right in the political system as a whole, evidenced by generally adverse *land* election results and in waning support for Left-wing ideas within the SPD.

Factional Politics in the SPD at the Parliamentary and Governmental Level

At the governmental level the only Left-wing member of the cabinet, Erhard Eppler, resigned in early July 1974 as a protest against the decision to cut development aid. In the *Bundestagsfraktion* the Left remain a small and isolated minority of approximately thirty adherents. They meet on a regular but informal basis in the so-called *Leverkusener Kreis*. It has links with the *Frankfurter Kreis* which attempted to co-ordinate the left in the Party as a whole but which, despite meeting regularly every two or three months over a number of years, has failed to exercise any very marked influence.

Given its position of strength in the cabinet and parliamentary party the Right sees little need to organise at the level of the *Bundestagsfraktion*. This is likely to continue to be the case since the

Left representation there has if anything decreased after the 1976 election. There is however a so-called *Lahnsteiner Kreis* which attempts to ensure that the Party remains true to a Right-wing interpretation of the Godesberg Programme. This group published an important pamphlet *Godesberg und die Gegenwart* in 1974 and includes two very prominent members, H.J. Vogel and H. Ehrenberg.

Leadership Style and Factional Politics

Under Schumacher the leadership style was so authoritarian that factionalism or even individual dissent was a rarity.[28] Ollenhauer's style of leadership was much less authoritarian. He was rarely prepared to go faster than the party as a whole. The combination of prosperity and anti-Communism meant, however, that he had little problem in party management terms in moving the party on to a revisionist course, with the exception of defence.

Brandt's style as Party Chairman was, as befits the Chairman of a *Volkspartei,* an exceptionally loose one and he has on the whole been extremely reluctant to restrict discussion in the Party. This worked very well in the sixties when things seemed to be going the SPD's way whatever they did. Everything could safely be left to 'the trend'. In the period of turbulence between 1970-3 Brandt's loose style in dealing with the challenge from the Left was undoubtedly an electoral handicap. In a long-term perspective, however, his style and his encouragement of the programmatic debate did succeed in integrating the Left into the Party. In the changed situation after 1973/4 problems of party management are much less acute and Brandt's appeal to the ethical values of Party members acts as a foil to the uncomplicated pragmatism of Schmidt. If the set-back experienced by the SPD in the 1976 election continues in the *Land* elections and the next Federal election (a sort of *Genosse Trend* in reverse) then problems of Party management will become more acute and might demand a different, tighter, style of leadership.

The Party and the Trade Unions

The relationship between the SPD and the trade unions has often been an ambiguous one in the Federal Republic. When the united trade union movement (the *Deutscher Gewerkschaftsbund*) was formed in 1949, it was officially neutral on party political questions. Despite extensive interpenetration of membership with the SPD, its first Chairman, Hans Böckler, actually steered it in a direction where it could reasonably be seen as supporting the Christian Democratic

Government, particularly over the issue of European Integration. The importance of the rearmament issue led in 1952 to the removal of Böckler's successor, Fette, and his replacement by Walter Freitag, an SPD deputy. During Freitag's period as Chairman in 1952-5, the DGB was very closely identified with the SPD.[29]

Relations with the SPD have again been close since the late sixties, partly on account of their support for Brandt's *Ostpolitik,* but principally because the SPD has been more sympathetic, if not much more successful, in practice than the CDU/CSU in responding to demands for an extension of industrial co-determination beyond the coal and steel industry. The German unions do not have the same institutionalised access to the SPD that their British counterparts enjoy to the Labour Party, nor are they an important source of finance. Yet they can and often are an important source of support to the SPD in various ways.

How valuable this support can be in electoral terms can be seen in the 1972 election. The DGB gave more decisive support to the SPD than in any previous campaign, including that of 1953. The DGB's action was the product of four main factors. There was first, the tremendous sympathy for Brandt and his Government at the grass roots, demonstrated in the spontaneous pro-Government strikes particularly in the Ruhr at the time of the no-confidence motion by the CDU/CSU opposition on 27 April 1972. There was also the hope that an SPD victory would increase the chance of co-determination (*Mitbestimmung*) on the basis of parity being extended to all industries. The visible decline in the influence of the Catholic Social Wing in the CDU made it seem much less likely that the CDU would be accommodating in this respect. Finally, the clear identification of the business lobby with the CDU/CSU opposition helped to provoke the DGB support for the SPD. The backing by the DGB was very effective and was a major factor in the high degree of support that the SPD gained among working-class voters.

This backing was largely absent in the 1976 election. The General Secretary of the CDU, Professor Kurt Biedenkopf, waged a campaign against *Filzokratie,* i.e. using trade union positions to benefit the SPD. This campaign placed the DGB on the defensive and while many obviously worked as individuals for an SPD victory, there was very little of the public display of solidarity so characteristic of the 1972 election.

The DGB support is important to the governmental wing of the SPD in two further ways. Firstly, many of the SPD Cabinet members have backgrounds as trade union leaders. In the Schmidt Cabinet

Cabinet of 1974-6 there were five: Georg Leber (Defence), Walter Arendt (Labour), Helmut Röhde (Education), Kurt Gscheidle (Traffic and Post) and Hans Matthöfer (Research). Secondly, their support in not pressing for inflationary wage settlements is essential to the survival of the SPD in Government. One of the factors in Brandt's resignation as Chancellor was his inability to get his view of the correct level of wage settlements accepted by an important union.[30]

Although the DGB as such plays no recognised role in the factional balance inside the SPD, the role of trade unionists and trade union functionaries is a crucial one. At the local level many of the party office-holders are trade union functionaries. At the national level the major trade unions and the DGB are in a strategic position to influence the SPD leadership when the SPD is in government. Reflecting the generally conservative nature of the values held by the German trade unions, this weight is almost invariably exercised, as in the past, against the left of the party.[31]

Electoral Support

The SPD has traditionally relied for the overwhelming bulk of its electoral support on the urban working-class. Competition for this section of the electorate in the Federal Republic traditionally came not from the Communists (banned in 1956) but from the attraction of the CDU/CSU for working-class Catholics. This tended to confine the size of the SPD electorate. The SPD could mobilise the working-class electorate better than its competitors but it was not a party with a majority bent since it was unable to mobilise all the workers. The relationship between class and politics is shown fairly clearly in a study by Derek Urwin of the 1960s.[32] A series of surveys carried out in 1967 showed that farmers, members of the professions and the self-employed preferred the CDU/CSU to the SPD by a margin of 58.0 to 14.3 per cent, while the workers preferred the SPD by a majority of 49.5 to 32.6 per cent. Officials (who constitute a vast category in Germany) and the salaried classes were more evenly divided: 45 per cent supporting CDU/CSU and 33.9 supporting the SPD. The high percentage of workers voting CDU/CSU may be explained by the importance of religion. The CDU/CSU is preferred by two-thirds of all church-going Catholics. Non-church-going Catholics inclined towards the SPD. The changed circumstances of the 1969 election somewhat altered this situation, with the SPD making significant gains in working-class, Catholic, districts and among middle-class voters.[33]

The SPD's advance continued in 1972, confirming the *Genosse Trend* (the trend towards the SPD), which first became apparent in 1961 and was associated with the party's 'conversion to political cosmetics' at Bad Godesberg in 1959, i.e. its abandonment of Marxist terminology and its projection of itself as a 'catch-all' party. The SPD gained 4.4 per cent in 1961, 3.1 per cent in 1965, 3.4 per cent in 1969 and 3.2 per cent in 1972.

In 1969 there was evidence of SPD inroads into three groups traditionally loyal to the CDU/CSU: Roman Catholics, women and rural voters. In 1972 this breakthrough was decisively confirmed. For the first time, the Catholic Saarland cast a majority of votes for the SPD, and in other *Länder* the SPD gained important victories in traditionally Catholic/CDU constituencies such as Aachen-Stadt and Aachen-Land (Nordrhein-Westfalen) and Osnabrück (Niedersachsen). Women, too, who transnationally tend to have more conservative political habits than men, voted in increasing numbers for the SPD: in the four Cologne constituencies, for example, Infas estimated that 53.5 per cent voted for the SPD in 1972, compared with only 39.8 per cent in 1965. Finally, rural voters, both Protestant and Catholic, cast more ballots for the SPD than ever before – Infas estimating a 6.4 per cent increase in Protestant rural areas such as Schleswig-Holstein and Niedersachsen, and 4.9 per cent in Catholic rural areas such as Bayern. One other group successfully mobilised by the SPD in 1972 was unskilled industrial workers (hitherto a group with a relatively high abstention rate), 3.9 per cent more voting for the SPD than in 1969. In some major cities, notably Munich (0.8 per cent loss) and Hamburg (0.2 per cent gain), the SPD did relatively badly. In the case of Munich this may have been a reaction against the high level of *Juso*, i.e. Left-wing, activity. The supposition that there was a reaction to radical tendencies in the SPD is strengthened by the fact that these were areas with a high incidence of vote splitting (in Munich the FDP second votes were 4 per cent higher than first votes at 10.6 per cent, and in Hamburg 4.9 per cent at 11.2 per cent).[34]

Somewhat unexpectedly the SPD became the largest party in the Bundestag, not by continuing its advance into the middle classes, but primarily by mobilising its traditional adherents. In one sense the SPD became more of a *Volkspartei* through its further penetration into the Catholic working-class, Protestant and Catholic rural voters and the female electorate. This was balanced, however, by the loss of further refugee votes (1972 was the first campaign in which the SPD did not have a prominent refugee candidate) and its failure to sustain the high rate of advance into the middle-class electorate characteristic of the

1969 election.

In 1976 the *Genosse Trend* was reversed and the SPD slipped back 3.3 per cent. There were some marked differences in the percentage swing against the SPD. In south Germany and in Nordrhein-Westfalen the SPD lost 3.5 per cent, while in the north its overall average loss was 2.4 per cent. The Saar was the exception to this rule with the SPD only losing 1.8 per cent. The most dramatic decline was in Bayern where the SPD, already in a weak position, lost a further 5 per cent. Of the fifteen constituencies in which the SPD lost more than 5 per cent, fourteen were in Bayern.

In the large urban concentrations there were comparable differences. In Munich and Frankfurt the SPD lost 8.2 per cent and 5.2 per cent respectively, whilst in cities like Hamburg, Hanover and Düsseldorf the reverse was quite small. In the face of these very diverse results any explanation of voting behaviour must be very tentative. It does seem, however, that this time as in the past the possession of the Chancellorship proved to be an important advantage.

Question: Whom would you prefer as Chancellor?

	Chancellor Candidates in office	Percentage of respondents in favour	Chancellor Candidates not in office	Percentage of respondents in favour
1961	Adenauer (Erhard)	22% (28%)	Brandt	21%
1965	Erhard	38%	Brandt	15%
1969	Kiesinger	40%	Brandt	21%
1972	Brandt	58%	Barzel	26%
1976	Schmidt	53%	Kohl	34%

Source: *Comparative Politics,* July 1970, p. 598; *Die Zeit,* 24 Nov. 1972, *Der Spiegel,* 27 Sept. 1976.

The problem for the SPD was that Schmidt ran continually ahead of his party not only in terms of his general popularity (the normal situation) but also in relation to his competence in particular areas. We can see this clearly if we look at the public opinion figures on dealing with inflation, where 39 per cent of those polled thought Schmidt more capable than Kohl (30 per cent) whilst 49 per cent thought the CDU/CSU was likely to combat inflation more effectively (35 per cent).[35] The difficulty for the SPD was twofold. Firstly, Schmidt was not very closely identified in many voters' minds with the SPD since he always presented himself as Chancellor rather than as Vice-Chairman of the SPD. On the other hand if he were to identify himself too closely with the SPD he would lose the advantage he possessed as Chancellor. Secondly, with the possible exception of Walter Arendt no other member of the SPD ministerial team enjoyed widespread public support or recognition.

It is unlikely that the activities of the Young Socialists and the Left wing of the party had a significant effect outside Bayern and Hesse. The advent of Helmut Schmidt as Chancellor in May 1974 with his well-known aversion to Left-wing theory, and the subsequent generally successful integration of the radicals into the mainstream of the party dramatised at the Mannheim Party Conference of November 1975 meant that the Young Socialists were much less visible than in the 1972 election.

In contrast to 1972, foreign policy issues played a relatively insignificant role. In 1972 the SPD had made significant advances into social groups previously hostile to it: Catholics, especially Catholic workers, women and rural voters. In 1976 the Catholic hierarchy took a much more moderate though still anti-coalition line because of the reform of Paragraph 218 of the *Grundgesetz* relating to abortion. Despite this all the analyses seem to suggest that the SPD lost all the gains it had made among Catholics including Catholic workers in 1972.[36] The evidence also tends to suggest that women voted disproportionately in favour of the CDU/CSU.[37] In agricultural areas the SPD losses were in conformity with its general reverse.[38]

Groups Favourable to the SPD

In the 1972 election two groups voted particularly strongly for the SPD: young voters and workers. In the 1976 election the picture changed somewhat. The generation of first voters who had voted for Brandt in 1972 remained loyal to the coalition.[39] However, in the succeeding generation, although a majority voted for the coalition the disproportion was not nearly so marked.[40] Analyses suggest that the political attitudes of school children are even more conservative. This change obviously has much to do with disappointed expectations and a changed intellectual climate in the wake of the *Berufsverbot*,[41] the *numerus clausus*,[42] and a gradual shrinking of opportunities.

In 1972 the SPD increase was three times as high in areas with a large working-class population. This time its losses in working-class areas were the same as the national average. Clearly the rather conservative policies of the last two years could hardly have been expected to mobilise the workers in the same way as in 1972.

The SPD and Europe

A characteristic and novel feature of the post-war policy of the SPD has been a new interest in external policy.[43] Since 1949 the predominant focus of the foreign policy of the Federal Republic has been Western Europe. After opposing the various attempts at European integration during the period of Schumacher's leadership (1945-52), the Party under Ollenhauer began to revise its policy at least as far as the economic integration of Western Europe was concerned.[44] This process culminated in Ollenhauer's acceptance on behalf of the SPD of membership in Jean Monnet's 'Action Committee for the United States of Europe'. Thereafter the SPD was a fairly enthusiastic supporter of the European Communities.

SPD support for European integration was particularly marked in the early 1960s for two reasons. First, the *Deutschlandplan*, on which it had staked so much, was reduced to ruins by the development of the Berlin crisis. Secondly, leading members of the *Bundestagsfraktion*, particularly Herbert Wehner, were attracted by the prospect of a coalition with the CDU/CSU and a pro-European policy was likely to help in this. This 'pro-European' phase in SPD policy probably reached a peak in 1965 when the SPD was conspicuous among European political parties by the depth of its support for the Commission in its confrontation with de Gaulle.[45]

The formation of the Grand Coalition in 1966 led, however, to some change in priorities. Policy in external affairs was articulated by Willy Brandt rather than by Herbert Wehner and Fritz Erler, as had often been the case in the early 1960s. Brandt, a long-time supporter of European integration, had been forced to rethink some of his former policy positions as a result of the erection of the Berlin Wall in 1961. He was greatly aided in this process of reformulation by constant contact with the agile mind of Egon Bahr, press-spokesman of the Berlin Senate. It was Bahr who signalled the way Brandt was thinking in a famous speech at the Protestant Academy at Tutzing. In this speech, Bahr called for an end to the policy of confrontation, of all or nothing, with respect to the German Question. Rather than working to overthrow the GDR, attempts ought to be made to change it. This would only be possible through a policy of *rapprochement*. This concept of *Wandel durch Annäherung* (change through *rapprochement*) was to be extraordinarily influential and provided the *leitmotiv* in SPD policy after 1966. Such a policy towards the East, unlike the former policy of confrontation, was likely to have a marked effect on *Westpolitik* since it implied a de-emphasising of the single-minded pursuit of Western unity and an emphasis on solutions that would include the whole of Europe.

After the SPD joined the government in 1966 to form the Grand Coalition, it becomes useful to distinguish between different levels (arenas) of party activities and particularly between the governmental and party level, the Government level being the more important for two reasons. Firstly, it is Governments rather than parties that participate directly in the European integration process. Secondly, in the Party at large interest in European integration became less intense during the late 1960s and the focus shifted to domestic reform, programmatic questions and *Ostpolitik*.

The Government Level

As Foreign Minister of the Grand Coalition, Brandt was mainly concerned with *Ostpolitik*. At a more general level, he was preoccupied with the modalities of the interaction of the problems of peace and the German Question. The problem as he saw it was to find 'an orientation which places the German Question in its European context and for this we need a concept which contains the basis of a European Peace Order'.[46]

The precise contours of the 'European Peace Order' were indistinct and were delineated differently at different times. It was always clear, however, that this 'European Peace Order' was not regarded by Brandt as an alternative to the EEC but assumed that West Germany would remain within the framework of the EEC.

> We are surely in agreement that our community should not be a new bloc but an exemplary system, which should serve as an important part of a balanced European Peace system. It is in this sense that the Federal Republic of Germany seeks understanding towards the East with the co-operation and agreement of her Western allies.

The notion of a European peace system, with its all-European[47] focus, was almost bound to be in tension with the development of a too strongly supranational EEC. In practice, however, the tension usually remained implicit since Brandt's earlier support for European integration, while it was modified by these ideas (in essence those of Egon Bahr), was not completely displaced by them. Moreover, support in the SPD for further European integration remained high, particularly in the *Bundestagsfraktion*. In his first term as Chancellor, European integration was definitely accorded less priority than *Ostpolitik*. The Hague Summit of 1969 represents only a partial exception, since it is clear from Brandt's speech to the Summit conference that he was more interested in the extension of the Community (with its attendant advantages for *Ostpolitik*) than in its inner development.[48]

By the time of the formulation of the second Brandt/Scheel Government, the major treaties with the East had been concluded (though the negotiations with Czechoslovakia remained to be completed), and it looked unlikely that any further dramatic progress would be achieved in that area. In this situation Brandt concentrated much more than hitherto on Western European integration. In his second Governmental Declaration on 18 January 1973, Brandt stated that European Union was to be the foremost goal of the federal government.[49] While the declaration made some reference to political union, it was merely in terms of greater inter-governmental co-operation. The main emphasis in Brandt's declaration was laid on economic union. The conception of this was a loose one, involving much more consultation and co-ordination than at present prevails between the various governments but stopping far short of the federal model. This emphasis on economic union was associated with the rising influence of Helmut Schmidt, then Finance Minister, and his belief that some financial discipline would have to be imposed on West Germany's fellow members.

The final objectives of Brandt's European policy remained vague and ambiguous since he never really made clear how the tensions between *Ost-* and *West politik,* between a 'closer union' and the continued existence of national governments, between extension and a 'deepening' of the Community were to be resolved. Moreover, Brandt's style of describing the European future in very evocative terms, while not in practice being really able to make financial sacrifices for the attainment of these goals, helped to weaken the attraction of the European ideal both in the SPD and in the West German population in general.

The European Policy of Helmut Schmidt

SPD governmental policy on European integration has been changed more in emphasis than substance by the Chancellorship of Helmut Schmidt. Schmidt had already played a major role in the formulation of European policy while he was still Finance Minister. Hans Apel, the man responsible for day-to-day execution of European policy, was close to Schmidt in temperament and background (a fellow Hamburger). He is now Finance Minister and has continued to play a very active role in policy-making on Europe.

The visionary strain in Brandt's policy in which Western European integration was a minor theme in the creation of some vast 'European Peace Order' has been rendered irrelevant by the seriousness of the crisis in Western Europe. In relation to West European integration in its narrower sense, Schmidt does not have the same visionary evocative quality of Brandt, though of course Brandt can be criticised for his rhetorical espousal of vague goals like that of a 'European Social Union'. Schmidt's tone is very different: 'It is always dangerous to set one's goals too high . . . and I think this is what all of our governments have in the meantime understood'.[50]

Schmidt accords a very important role to relations with France. But both as Defence and as Finance Minister he had been acutely aware of and had given the highest priority to close relations with the United States, even at the price of exacerbating Franco-German relations as during the Washington Energy Conference. Schmidt had also a long record of supporting British entry to the EEC. In line with his general values he would not, however, be prepared to pay a high financial price simply to keep Britain in the community.

Schmidt's most profound impact on European policy as Chancellor has been a continuation of his earlier role of counting the cost and encouraging budgetary stability. In this connection he has made some specific suggestions, i.e. that one of the Commissioners be appointed a sort of European Finance Minister and that a European *Rechnungshof* be created. More significantly, West German financial resources would not be committed to an EEC undertaking without being sure that tangible policy benefits would be realised. 'We must therefore insist that a general intra-European transfer of financial resources, of which regional policy is of course a part, should be linked with further progress in policy as a whole.'[51] Similarly in a study prepared for the SPD Präsidium shortly before he became Chancellor, Schmidt rejected any major West German financial sacrifice such as making West German currency resources available on an EC-wide basis or higher West German contributions to the Community budget, in the hope that it would impel other governments to move forward.[52] Chancellor Schmidt and Hans Apel are very critical of the EC Commission and it is clear that they regard intergovernmental consultation and co-operation as the way towards European Integration.[53] Katherina Focke, the most European member of the SPD ministerial team, resigned as expected after the Federal Election of 3 October 1976.[54]

Further consideration of the SPD's attitude to Europe really needs to be subdivided into the internal party debate about the goals of European integration and the position of the party in relation to other Social Democratic parties in this process.

Internal Party Debate

After a period of intense internal party debate about European integration in the 1950s the issue became less important for Party members.[55] They were content to leave the formulation of Party policy to Willy Brandt and a few expert members of the *Bundestagsfraktion* and the European Parliament. The Party leadership was, in other words, able to operate within a 'permissive consensus' as far as European questions were concerned.

This consensus was challenged by the Young Socialists. In their conference at Munich in December 1969 they passed resolutions which, while applauding the concept of European integration, sought to give it a different content.[56] They wished to alter the direction of the Community's efforts towards co-ordinating the European labour movement and controlling multinational companies. Their attacks on multinational companies found some support in the Party at large but their views on co-ordinating the labour movement and involving Left-Socialist parties and groups and Communist parties were anathema to most party members. The minority position of the Young Socialists in the Party was one in which they needed support from other groups to get their views accepted as Party policy. This was not forthcoming and even if it had been it is difficult to see how it would have constrained the party leadership, since even the Young Socialist critics were in favour of the maintenance of the present structures so that they could be given a different content later. In recent years there has been a continual though not very intense debate about European integration in the Party. There was some discussion at the party conference in Hanover in April 1973 when the so-called *Orientierungsrahmen 85* was discussed. Despite attempts by the Young Socialists to engage in a discussion of the Party's European strategy the sections on Europe are loose and anodyne. At a special party conference on foreign policy in January 1975, Schmidt rejected the feasibility of a 'social democratic' foreign policy since the SPD in government must necessarily represent the national interest and also the interests of her Community partners.[57]

The party conference in Hanover referred to above had agreed to set up an *Europakommission der SPD*. This duly reported in

September 1975. This report was intended both to integrate the internal party discussion about Europe and to represent an SPD contribution to a common platform on the transnational level. The report endorses the long-term goal of a European Federation and more importantly accepts the corollary that this necessarily means a transfer of resources to reduce the economic disparities between the member states of the Community. Institutionally, the report has a number of recommendations to make. It asks that the European Parliament be directly elected and vested with greater powers (especially election of the executive, the power of law-making and of the purse). The Council of Ministers, it is suggested, should become a Second Parliamentary Chamber and the European Commission should become the future government of Europe.[58]

Tension Between Governmental and Party Level

It is clear that there is some considerable discrepancy between the views of the governmental members of the SPD and the views expressed in party debate. Yet in practice the governmental members of the SPD can safely ignore reports like that of the *Europakommission* because its status is unclear and they can always point to 'objective realities'.

This situation would alter somewhat if Brandt, in his role as Party Chairman and integrator of party factions, closely identified himself with these views, particularly as he intends to compete for a directly elected seat in the European Parliament. There are already some signs that Brandt is less prepared than Schmidt to see the EC used to discourage Communism both outside (Spain and Portugal) and inside the EC (Italy).[59] There are differences of emphasis in relation to institutional innovation with Brandt more than ever predisposed to think in the long-term now he is out of office, while Schmidt remains a convinced pragmatist immersed in day-to-day governmental realities.

Transnational Party Co-operation

In 1974 the Confederation of Social Democratic Parties of the EC was created. This Confederation can best be seen as a compromise between different points of view about the future of transnational co-operation among Social Democratic and Socialist parties. The Dutch were in favour of the immediate creation of a European socialist party. The SPD, on the contrary, favoured 'a cautious approach via a gradual harmonisation of programmes'; this approach would mean maintenance of full autonomy of the single party organisation. It is generally true that the SPD has been unwilling to countenance very significant progress in this field — an area in which, in default of the British Labour Party, it alone could take a lead. Instead it has shown itself more eager to keep in touch with the Gaullists than the French Left because of the dangers of being identified with Communism.[60] The SPD has, of course, played an active role in the recent creation of the Confederation of Social Democratic Parties and its related bureau, but at the level of practical policy rather than programmatic utterances this is likely to be little better than its predecessors, despite having an SPD Party Executive member, Wilhelm Dröscher, as its President.

Conclusion

It is clear from the historical evolution of the SPD that the cohesion of the Party can never be taken for granted. Traditionally, the Party has been subject to fission. Paradoxically the post-war division of Germany, which in one sense cut the SPD off from a great deal of its traditional support, has acted as a great unifying element by identifying Communism, and by extension extreme Left-wing policies, with a hated and rival system. The force of this factor had abated by the early seventies and it was possible both to pursue *Ostpolitik* and have a wide-ranging programmatic debate in the Party. The left alternative, for the reasons outlined above, no longer offers the challenge to the cohesion of the Party it once did.[61] And yet one can identify four possible threats to the cohesion of the Party. There is the external threat posed by the possible leftward changes in France and Italy and the difficulties this would pose for Party attitudes. The narrowness of the present coalition's majority means too that it is quite possible that the SPD will have to relinquish office before the present term (1980) is up. Governmental office has been an important element since 1969 in unifying the Party by directing its attention to external threats. Again the electoral reverse of 1976 dealt a severe blow to the notion of an automatic trend towards the SPD (*Genosse Trend*) and to the belief that youth would inevitably vote for the Party. If this pattern is repeated then the party leadership will be unable sooner or later to avoid making choices with the resultant risks to cohesion. Finally, much depends on the attitude of trade unions and more especially of trade unionists. Were they to take a less active role in the SPD then it is likely that the cohesion of the Party would suffer. These threats to the cohesion of the Party are mainly hypothetical however and the forces of inertia involved in the electoral system and in the organisation of the SPD are very great. This will probably be enough to ensure no very dramatic changes at least in the immediate future.

204 The German Social Democratic Party

Notes

1. See Peter Gay, *The Dilemma of Democratic Socialism, Eduard Bernstein's Challenge to Marx* (New York, Collier Books, 1962). See also Carl E. Schorske, *German Social Democracy 1905-1917, The Development of the Great Schism* (New York, John Wiley, 1965).
2. Viz. especially Schorske for a brilliant analysis of the development of this duality.
3. H. Grebing, *History of the German Labour Movement* (London, Oswald Wolff, 1969), p. 73.
4. See Peter Nettl, 'The German Social Democratic Party 1890-1914 as a Political Model', *Past and Present,* no. 30 (April 1965), pp. 65-95, especially pp. 83-5.
5. Roberto Michels, *Political Parties – a Sociological Study of the Oligarchical Tendencies in Modern Democracy* (Berlin, 1911).
6. See Julius Braunthal, *History of the International 1914-43,* (London, Nelson, 1967), vol. II, pp. 1-35.
7. Richard N. Hunt, *German Social Democracy 1918-33* (Yale University Press, London, 1964), pp. 63-98.
8. *Jahrbuch,* 1930, p.134.
9. Viz. Hunt, p. 104.
10. Ibid. p. 105.
11. Grebing, p. 149.
12. Viz. Albrecht Kaden, 'Die Wiedergründung der SPD, 1945-46', Ph.D. dissertation, Hamburg 1960, p. 247.
13. Arno Scholz, *Turmwachter der Demokratie,* vol. II, Reden und Schriften (Berlin, Irani Verlag, 1952), p.33.
14. Cited in H.K. Schellenger, 'The German Social Democratic Party after World War II: The Conservatism of Power', *Western Political Quarterly,* 1967, pp.251-65, cit. p.252.
15. Schellenger, p. 255.
16. Otto Kirchheimer, 'The Transformation of the Western European Party Systems', in Joseph La Palombara and Myron Weiner (eds.), *Political Parties and Political Development* (Princeton, New Jersey, Princeton University Press, 1966), pp. 184-200.
17. Wolf-Dieter Narr, Hermann Scheer and Dieter Spöri, *SPD – Staatspartei oder Reformpartei?* (Munich, R. Piper, 1976), p.91.
18. See especially Kurt Shell, 'Extraparliamentary Opposition in Post-War Germany', *Comparative Politics,* July 1970, pp.653-80.
19. All the membership figures are taken from *Jahrbücher der SPD,* 1968-9, 1970-2, and 1972-4.
20. JI Reihe Jugend, Heft I (Bonn, Hsg. vom Vorstand der SPD, 1970), p.9..
21. For a discussion of these concepts see N. Gansel, *Uberwindet den Kapitalismus oder was wollen die Jungsozialisten?* (Reinbek, Ro Ro, 1971). V. Häse and P. Müller, 'Die Jungsozialisten in der SPD', in J. Dittberner *et al.* (ed.), *Parteiensystem in der Legitimationskrise* (Cologne, Westdeutscher Verlag. and Opladen, 1973), pp. 277-306.
22. *Suddeutsche Zeitung,* 15 Oct. 1973.
23. *Die Zeit,* 5 Apr. 1974.
24. *FAZ,* 5 Apr. 1974.
25. *Die Zeit,* 12 and 26 Apr. 1974.
26. For details see Narr, Scheer, and Spöri, p. 132-3.
27. For a representative sample of anti-Juso views by DGB leaders see *Suddeutsche Zeitung,* 5 Sept. 1973.

28. For an analysis of Schumacher as party leader see Lewis J. Edinger, *Kurt Schumacher — A Study in Personality and Political Behaviour* OUP 1965), pp. 94-143. By far the best chapter in an uneven study.
29. See especially G.K. Braunthal, 'The West German Trade Unions and Disarmament', *Political Science Quarterly,* March 1958, pp. 82-99.
30. The union involved was the Public Service Union Ö.T.V.
31. Cf. Schorske, p. 108.
32. Cited in W.E. Paterson and Ian Campbell, *Social Democracy in Post-War Europe* (London, Macmillan, 1974), p.32.
33. See special issue of *Comparative Politics,* July 1970.
34. Under the West German electoral law each voter has two votes: one for a constituency candidate, the other for a party list (the parties draw up lists for each *Land*). One half of the Bundestag, i.e. 248 of its 496 members, are deputies representing constituencies; as in Britain, they are elected by simple relative majority. The other half is drawn up from the *Land* lists in such a way that the overall composition of the Bundestag reflects the national strength of the parties as shown by the second votes cast for them; i.e. proportional representation is the predominant element in the German electoral system. List seats are filled in the order in which candidates appear on the party lists in each *Land.* However, no party can be represented in the Bundestag unless it either wins three constituency seats or obtains at least 5 per cent of the national second votes. (The FDP, for example, has not returned a constituency candidate since 1957, although it has succeeded in negotiating the 5 per cent 'hurdle' at subsequent elections, and in consequence continues to be represented in the Bundestag.) For full details about the German electoral law, see Gerhard Löwenberg, *Parliament in the German Political System* (Cornell University Press, 1966), pp.63-7. For a Table of Election Results since 1949, see below, p.208.
35. *Der Spiegel,* 20 Sept. 1976.
36. R. Wildenmann, 'Warum sie so gewahlt haben', *Die Zeit,* 8 Oct. 1976.
37. Infas survey, 4 Oct. 1976.
38. Analysis by Professor Dieter Oberndörfer in *Die Welt,* 5 Oct. 1976.
39. Wildenmann, op. cit.
40. W. Kaltefleiter in *Der Spiegel,* No. 7, 1976.
41. The *Berufsverbot* is the term used to describe the measures designed to prevent the employment of radicals in the public service.
42. *Numerus clausus* refers to restricted entry in certain university subjects.
43. For the development of SPD attitudes see William E. Paterson, *The SPD and European Integration* (Farnborough, Saxon House, 1974).
44. Ibid. ch. V.
45. Ibid. ch. VI.
46. W. Brandt, *Aussenpolitik, Deutschlandpolitik, Europapolitik* (Berlin, 1968), p. 85.
47. W. Brandt, *Bundeskanzler Brandt — Reden und Interviews* (Bonn, 1969), p. 47.
48. Ibid. pp. 47-54.
49. *Das Parlament,* 27 Jan. 1973.
50. Interview with Keith Kyle broadcast on BBC-TV, 20 May 1974, transcript, p. 11.
51. Speech at Chatham House, 29 Jan. 1974.
52. *Die Zeit,* 17 May 1974.
53. *Die Zeit,* 25 Oct. 1974.
54. Whilst Frau Focke resigned because of disappointment expressed in her performance as Health and Social Security Minister her resignation did remove the most committed European from the Cabinet.

55. Paterson, ch. VI, pp. 152-3.
56. Viz. R. Hrbek, 'The SPD and European Integration in the EC and Atlantic Relations', unpublished paper, Stirling, 1976, p. 6.
57. *Aussenpolitische Bundeskonferenz der SPD*, 17-19 Jan. 1975, Bonn Dokumente, ed. SPD Executive.
58. *Sozialdemokratische Europapolitik. Bericht vorgelegt von der Europakommission der SPD*. Materialien, ed.: Vorstand der SPD., Bonn, 1975.
59. Contacts in SPD Executive.
60. In the last year a Bilateral Commission has been set up to improve relations with the PS.
61. The election of Klaus-Uwe Benneter in March 1977 to the chairmanship of the *Jusos* probably heralds a renewed period of conflict with the party leadership. In the author's opinion a challenge from the *Jusos* could at present be contained by the party executive.

Abbreviations

Parties and Party Components

ADF   Aktion Demokratischer Fortschritt (Action for Democratic Progress)
APO   Ausserparlamentarische Opposition (Extra-Parliamentary Opposition)
CDU   Christlich Demokratische Union (Christian Democratic Union)
DFU   Deutsche Friedensunion (German Peace Union)
DKP   Deutsche Kommunistische Partei (German Communist Party [1968])
FDP   Freie Demokratische Partei Deutschlands (Free Democrat Party of Germany)
ISK   Internationaler Sozialistischer Kampfbund (International Socialist Struggle League)
Jusos   Jungsozialisten (Young Socialists)
KPD   Kommunistische Partei Deutschlands (Communist Party of Germany)
LDP   Liberal-Demokratische Partei (Liberal Democratic Party)
NSDAP   Nationalsozialistische Deutsche Arbeiterpartei (National Socialist German Workers' Party)
NPD   Nationaldemokratische Partei Deutschlands (National Democratic Party of Germany)
NB   Neu Beginnen (New Beginnings Group)
SAP   Sozialistische Arbeiter Partei (Socialist Workers' Party)
SDS   Sozialistischer Deutscher Studentenbund (Socialist German Student Federation)
SED   Sozialistische Einheits Partei Deutschlands (Socialist Unity Party of Germany)

SPD   Sozialdemokratische Partei Deutschlands (Social Democratic Party of Germany)

SRP   Sozialistische Reichspartei (Socialist State Party)

USPD   Unabhängige Sozialdemokratische Partei Deutschlands (Independent Social Democratic Party of Germany, 1917-1922)

Other Abbreviations

ADGB   Allgemeiner Deutscher Gewerkschafts Bund (Free Trade Unions — Weimar)

BRD   Bundesrepublik Deutschlands (German Federal Republic)

DGB   Deutscher Gewerkschafts Bund (German Trade Union Federation)

GDR   Deutsche Demokratische Republik (German Democratic Republic)

GG   Grundgesetz (Basic Law)

Table 1. West German general elections, 1949-76

	1949			1953			1957			1961			1965			1969			1972			1976		
	votes	%	seats	votes	%	seats	votes	%	seats	votes	%	seats	votes	%	seats	votes	%	seats	votes	%	seats	votes	%	seats
Electorate[2]	31.2			33.2			35.4			37.4			38.5			38.6			40.6			41.6		
Turnout %	78.5			86.2			88.2			87.7			86.8			86.7			91.2			90.7		
CDU/CSU	7.4	31.0	139	12.4	45.2	243	15.0	50.2	270	14.3	45.4	242	15.5	47.6	245	15.2	46.1	242	16.8	44.8	225	18.4	48.6	243
SPD	6.9	29.7	131	7.9	28.8	151	9.5	31.8	169	11.4	36.2	190	12.8	39.3	202	14.1	42.7	224	17.2	45.9	230	16.1	42.6	214
FDP	2.8	11.9	52	2.6	9.5	48	2.3	7.7	41	4.0	12.8	67	3.1	9.5	49	1.9	5.8	30	3.2	8.4	41	3.0	7.9	39
Extreme Left	1.4	5.7	15	0.6	2.2	–	–	–	–	0.6	1.9	–	0.4	1.3	–	0.2	0.6	–	0.1	0.3	–	0.1	0.3	–
Extreme Right	0.4	1.8	5	0.3	1.1	–	0.3	1.0	–	0.3	0.8	–	0.7	2.0	–	1.4	4.3	–	0.2	0.6	–	0.1	0.3	–
Total Deputies		402			487			497			499			496			496			496			496	

N.B.
1. This Table refers to second votes, i.e. those which decide the final composition of the Bundestag.
2. The size of the electorate and the voting figures are in millions.
3. Minor parties, which were important in the early years of the Federal Republic (e.g. the Refugees), but which have not competed at recent elections, have been omitted. Hence the apparent discrepancy between party seats and total deputies up to 1957.
4. The Extreme Left have competed under a variety of names: KPD (*Kommunistische Partei Deutschlands*) in 1949 and 1953; DFU (*Deutsche Friedens Union*) in 1961 and 1965; ADF (*Aktion Demokratischer Fortschritt*) in 1969; DKP (*Deutsche Kommunistische Partei*) in 1972 and 1976. The Extreme Right competed as DRP (*Deutsche Reichspartei*) until 1961, and as NPD (*National-demokratische Partei Deutschlands*) since 1965.
5. This Table excludes the 22 deputies who represent West Berlin, as they do not have full voting rights in the Bundestag. After the 1976 Election party strength in the Bundestag was 11 CDU (previously 9), 10 SPD (12), 1 FDP (1).

Table 2. Membership in the SPD since 1931

1931	602,084	Deutsches Reich
1946	711,448	Westzones/Berlin
1947	875,479	Westzones/Berlin
1948	846,518	Westzones/Berlin
1949	736,218	BRD/West Berlin
1950	683,896	" "
1951	649,529	" "
1952	627,817	" "
1953	607,456	" "
1954	585,479	" "
1955	589,051	" "
1956	612,219	" "
1957	626,189	" "
1958	623,816	" "
1959	634,254	" "
1960	649,578	" "
1961	644,780	" "
1962	646,584	" "
1963	648,415	" "
1964	678,484	" "
1965	710,448	" "
1966	727,890	" "
1967	733,004	" "
1968	732,446	" "
1969	778,945	" "
1970	820,202	" "
1971	847,456	" "
1972	954,394	" "
1973	973,601	" "
1974	957,253	" "
1975	Over 1,000,000	

Source: *Jahrbücher der SPD*

Table 3. West Germany: SPD party membership, 1972-4 (as at 31 Dec), by district.

Bezirk	1972	%	1973	%	1974	%
Schleswig-Holstein	38,680	4.05	39,295	4.04	39,511	4.13
Hamburg	36,196	3.79	36,229	3.72	34,905	3.65
Bremen	16,346	1.71	16,254	1.70	16,015	1.67
Nord-Niedersachsen	8,791	0.92	9,087	0.93	9,223	0.96
Weser-Ems	22,426	2.35	23,968	2.46	24,117	2.52
Hannover	67,593	7.08	69,613	7.15	67,552	7.06
Braunschweig	18,036	1.89	18,499	1.90	20,344	2.13
Ostwestfalen-Lippe	28,536	2.99	28,887	2.96	28,279	2.95
Westliches Westfalen	135,522	14.20	136,098	13.98	134,213	14.02
Niederrhein	74,379	7.80	74,042	7.60	71,316	7.45
Mittelrhein	39,404	4.12	41,288	4.24	40,536	4.23
Hessen-Nord	39,911	4.18	41,757	4.29	42,123	4.40
Hessen-Süd	93,115	9.76	97,059	9.97	97,118	10.15
Baden-Württemberg	68,002	7.13	69,989	7.19	67,984	7.10
Franken	61,677	6.48	60,612	6.23	57,945	6.05
Niderbayern/Oberpfalz	23,972	2.51	23,756	2.44	22,817	2.38
Südbayern	50,138	5.25	50,322	5.17	47,585	4.97
Rheinland-Hessen-Nassau	28,945	3.03	30,140	3.10	29,568	3.09
Rheinhessen	10,188	1.07	10,763	1.10	10,879	1.14
Pfalz	29,563	3.09	30,848	3.16	30,247	3.16
Saar	24,491	2.57	25,572	2.62	26,140	2.73
Berlin	38,483	4.03	39,523	4.05	38,863	4.06
Whole party	954,394	100.00	973,601	100.00	957,253	100.00

Source: Jahrbuch der SPD, 1972-4, pp. 270-1.

Table 4. West Germany: analysis of new members of the SPD joining in 1974 and of social composition of all SPD members on 31 Dec. 1975

By age	New members 1974 Number	Percentage	All members 1975 Percentage
21 and under	7,772	14.13	
22-25	9,134	16.60	
26-30	8,169	14.84	
31-35	7,722	14.03	
36-40	6,403	11.63	
41-50	7,727	14.04	
51-60	3,734	6.78	
61-70	2,694	4.89	
71 and over	1,681	3.06	
Total	55,036	100%	
By social composition			
Independent	1,578	2.87	4.67
Non-established officials	12,130	22.04	23.69
Workers, skilled and unskilled	14,334	26.04	27.64
Established officials	4,273	7.76	9.53
Soldiers	521	0.95	
Housewives	6,438	11.70	9.85
Farmers	83	0.15	0.24
Apprentices	2,144	3.90	1.33
Pensioners	2,184	3.97	11.25
Students	7,946	14.43	6.64
No occupation given	3,405	6.19	4.61
Total	55,036	100%	99.45%

Source: Jahrbuch der SPD, 1972-4, pp.270-1 and SPD Jahresstatistik, Answertung des Mitgliederbestandes, 31 Dec. 1975.

Further Reading

For a comprehensive bibliography see the excellent reference work by
Klaus Günther and Kurt Schmitz, *SPD, KPD/DKP, DGB in den Westzonen
und in der BRD — Eine Bibliographie* (Bonn — Bad Godesberg, Verlag
Neue Gesellschaft, 1976).

Articles

Kirchheimer, O. 'Germany: the Vanishing Opposition', in R. Dahl (ed.),
  Political Oppositions in Western Democracies. New Haven, Yale
  U.P., 1966. Pp. 237-59.
Paterson, W.E. 'Social Democracy — the West German Example', in
  M. Kolinsky and W.E. Paterson, *Social and Political Movements in
  Western Europe.* London, Croom Helm, 1976. Pp. 211-42.

Books

Chalmers, D. *The Social Democratic Party of Germany: From Working
  Class Movement to Modern Political Party.* New Haven, Yale
  University Press, 1964.
Edinger, L. *Kurt Schumacher: A Study in Personality and Political
  Behaviour.* Stanford, Stanford University Press, 1965.
Gay, P. *The Dilemma of Democratic Socialism.* New York, Columbia
  University Press, 1952.
Graf, W.D. *The German Left since 1945.* Cambridge, Oleander Press,
  1976.
Nettl, P. *Rosa Luxemburg.* 2 vols. London, Oxford University Press,
  1966.
Paterson, W.E. *The SPD and European Integration.* Farnborough, Saxon
  House, 1974.
Schellenger, H.K. *The SPD in the Bonn Republic: A Socialist Party
  Modernizes.* The Hague, Nijhoff, 1968.
Schorske, C. *German Social Democracy 1905-1917.* New York, John
  Wiley, 1965.
Soell, Hartmut. *Fritz Erler, Eine politische Bibliographie.* 2 vols. Berlin,
  Bonn — Bad Godesberg, Verlag J.H.W. Dietz, 1976.
Based on extensive use of archival material, Soell's study is the most
  substantial piece on the SPD to appear in recent years and will prove
  invaluable for all students of the party.

8 THE SOCIALIST PARTY OF AUSTRIA*

Melanie A. Sully

The Socialist Party of Austria (SPÖ) is one of the most successful Social Democratic parties in Western Europe. The Party has, in two successive elections (in 1971 and 1975), won over 50 per cent of the total vote and gained an absolute majority of the seats in the National Assembly (*Nationalrat*). The SPÖ, under the leadership of Bruno Kreisky, has a clear mandate until the election in 1979; by then Austria will have had a Socialist government for almost a decade. The prospects for the Party, however, have not always been so propitious.

Historical Evolution

The present Socialist Party was founded in April 1945 but claims a longer history, regarding itself as the oldest of Austria's parties. Viktor Adler formed the original Social Democratic Workers' Party at the Hainfeld Congress in 1889. The SPÖ is a descendant of this earlier party which was dissolved by Dollfuss, after a civil war, in 1934.

At the turn of the century the Party became synonymous with a school of thought later called Austro-Marxism; among its leading theoreticians were Karl Renner, Otto Bauer, Max Adler and Rudolf Hilferding. After the collapse of the multinational Habsburg Empire in 1918, party unity was threatened by the growth of Communism. The Austrian Social Democrats avoided a split by incorporating under their aegis both a Left wing (associated with Max Adler and Otto Bauer) and a Right wing under Karl Renner. For Bauer Austro-Marxism 'had always striven to adopt a middle course between reformism and Bolshevism';[1] the attempt to contain this dualism led to serious contradictions and ambiguity in Party policy.

The political structure of Austria is often associated with three *Lager* (encampments): the Christian-Social Conservative, the Socialist, and the Nationalist.[2] In the First Republic (1918-34) the Social Democrats were in a potentially powerful position and, for a brief period, were the strongest partners in a coalition government. The

*I should like to thank Peter Pulzer for his helpful comments on the draft for this chapter. Acknowledgement is also due to Richard Klucsarits of the SPÖ in Vienna for providing material and arranging interviews.

213

Party, under the guidance of Otto Bauer, subsequently chose the more 'natural' role (for a workers' party) of opposition, but still represented a formidable antagonist for the governing *Bürgerblock,* an uneasy alliance of Christian Socialists and anti-clerical Nationalists.

One of the chief pillars of Social Democratic support was 'red Vienna', a separate province, totally dominated by the Party. By 1930 the Social Democrats were the largest party in parliament with over 40 per cent of the vote but they lacked an absolute majority and preferred to remain in opposition. The Party also possessed its own paramilitary organisation, the Republican Defence League, but a strong pacifist conscience made it reluctant to mobilise effectively its physical and moral force. In 1934 the Party was defeated by Fascism and its most prominent leaders went into exile. An illegal cadre party continued under the name 'Revolutionary Socialists' (RS) which was critical of the old Party for its lack of militancy and dilatory policies. After the Second World War an attempt was made to fuse both precursors of Austrian Socialism and the cumbersome title of 'the Socialist Party of Austria (Social Democrats and Revolutionary Socialists)' was adopted. With an increase in anti-Communism, the RS was unable to influence significantly the post-war Party and it was not long before the shorter form 'the Socialist Party of Austria' came into general use.

The Second Republic

The first election after the war, in November 1945, was fought in an atmosphere of uncertainty and conducted under Allied scrutiny. A new Christian Conservative party, the People's Party (ÖVP), gained an absolute majority of parliamentary seats; no pan-German or other Rightist party was allowed to contest the election. The Communists (KPÖ), who had never been represented in parliament before the war, won four of the 165 seats which was a severe disappointment for them. The SPÖ emerged as the predominant force on the Left, accumulating over 44 per cent of the vote (see Table 1), an encouraging reassertion of pre-war strength.

Exile and political oppression had changed the Socialists and those who survived possessed sober and less radical philosophies. Many of the middle-class intellectuals, so prominent in the Party before the war, had either died or remained in exile. The impetus to create the new party came from those who, in the First Republic, had been on the Right-wing such as Adolf Schärf (Chairman of the SPÖ 1945-57) and Karl Renner, a constant critic of Bauer's 'all or nothing' opposition policy. Otto Bauer had died in Paris in 1938 and the new SPÖ was influenced more by the values of Renner who, at the age of seventy-five, assumed the initiative in reviving political life.[3] The traumatic experience of the inter-war period and the shock of defeat in 1934 had led to a desire to avoid open confrontation among the *Lager*. Thus in 1945 the SPÖ entered a coalition with the People's Party which was to last until 1966. For the Socialists the coalition meant not only access to Government ministries but also the possession of key posts in the nationalised banks and nationalised industries. The identification of the Party with the new political system was an important stabilising factor and a consensus developed on major issues which moderated the former antipathy between the two *Lager*. A by-product of the coalition was the establishment in 1957 of the Parity Commission for Wages and Prices consisting of representatives from the unions, employers and the Government. It has survived the break-up of the coalition and exists as an informal institution of consensus.[4]

The coalition ended after the Conservatives won an absolute majority in the 1966 election. For the SPÖ this was a serious setback and reluctantly the Party faced the harsh reality of opposition. In the following year Bruno Kreisky was elected as Party Chairman, although he was regarded with scepticsm by the Viennese organisation and some trade union leaders. Today Kreisky dominates Austrian politics and enjoys widespread support in his Party and throughout the country. Much of his popularity in the SPÖ is due to his reversal of the 1966 debacle. After 1967, Kreisky initiated a type of programmatic rearmament which was designed to present the Party as a viable alternative to the Conservatives.[5] In 1970 the SPÖ was able to form a minority government and in 1971, for the first time in their history, the Socialists won an absolute majority and formed a government independent of coalition partners; this was repeated in the 1975 election.

Ideology

The new style of politics which developed after 1945 was marked by the emergence of the political administrator; theoretical arguments have played a minor role. The SPÖ attempted, in this climate, to resolve the tension between reformism and Marxism which had plagued the old Social Democratic Party. The experience of coalition and the need to win the support of an increasingly diversified electorate prompted a move to reformism.

A major reformulation of principles came with the 'New Programme' of 1958 adopted unanimously after lengthy discussion at a special Party conference in Vienna. The previous basic programme had been the controversial Linz Programme of 1926 which had alluded to the possibility of a working-class dictatorship to forestall a bourgeois counter-revolution.[6] This had reinforced allegations by the Right that the Socialists were about to stage a Bolshevik-style coup d'état. The 1958 Programme categorically rejected Communism and any system based on dictatorship, stressing the concept of democracy — 'Socialism is unrestricted political, economic and social democracy; Socialism is democracy fulfilled'.[7] Less emphasis was placed on the working class and the SPÖ proclaimed itself as 'the party of all working people', which was understood to include intellectuals, agricultural workers, the self-employed and wage and salary earners.

In the First Republic, the Catholic Church was an intransigent opponent of the anti-clericalist Social Democrats. After 1945 a *modus vivendi* developed which was reflected in the 1958 Programme: Socialists and Christians were regarded as sharing common ethical aims and could thus co-exist. Some friction still occurs between the SPÖ and the Church on issues such as abortion and religious education in schools, but relationships between the two are reasonably harmonious.[8]

The main objective of the SPÖ in recent election campaigns has been to create a 'modern' and 'humane' Austria. Nationalisation is considered desirable only in the 'public interest'. The party in government has sought to maintain full employment and strengthen the welfare state. In its 1975 manifesto the SPÖ stressed 'security', a theme which could easily have been promoted by Conservatives and, since 1945, there has been a tendency for the policies of the two main *Lager* to converge.[9] Policies were given a low profile by the SPÖ in 1975 and the Party preferred to rely on the charisma of Kreisky to attract voters. Most revisions in Socialist orthodoxy have been tamely accepted by the Left which has little impact on the post-war Party. The 1958 Programme recognised that changes had taken place in society since Marx and that the workers had more to lose than their chains. Nevertheless the Programme mentioned the need to abolish class and triumph over Capitalism. It concluded that Democratic Socialism could come to terms neither with Communism nor Capitalism. Discussions are currently taking place on a new basic programme and this will be one of the main items on the agenda for the 1978 Party Conference.

Compared with the First Republic, the political atmosphere in Austria since 1945 has been less ideologically charged. Despite the formal break-up of the Great Coalition in 1966, a dialogue has continued between the top élites in both major parties and the bulk of parliamentary legislation is passed unanimously. The People's Party has found some Socialist reforms unacceptable, particularly in broadcasting, education, the liberalisation of the abortion law and defence. There is some support in the ÖVP for an open confrontation with the 'Marxists' in the SPÖ although the indications are that such a conflict would take place within the confines of parliamentary etiquette. An ideological 'great debate' is not, in any case, considered to be the basis for electoral victory.

Electoral Support

The last election of 1975 reinforced the *Machtwechsel* and the trend to the Socialists.[10] Since 1966 electoral fluctuation has been on the increase, making speculation on the future prospects of the SPÖ hazardous. In the landslide election of 1966 just under 10 per cent of voters changed party allegiance, a dramatic shift by Austrian standards. In 1970 slightly more than 10 per cent switched parties, this time in favour of the Socialists; electoral mobility in 1975 was, by comparison, modest. Research on the 1975 election has shown that the People's Party did better than average among those voting for the first time — here there was no absolute majority for the Socialists.[11] The SPÖ was more popular with the 23-30 age group and especially with women; these votes were not gained from the opposition camp but were drawn from previous non-voters. In 1975 women, representing 54 per cent of the total electorate, were mainly responsible for the SPÖ's absolute majority. The Party won the votes of elderly women who had previously turned out for the ÖVP, an unusual source of support for a Socialist party.

The SPÖ has broken through its 'ghetto' vote based on the urban working class and has won the confidence of voters not considered to be specifically attached to either major party — such as academics, civil servants and salaried employees. These are mostly 'Kreisky'-voters, attracted to the Party by the non-doctrinaire, 'liberal' image of its leader.

The Socialist Party is no longer restricted to Vienna and its environs but is gradually making inroads in rural, predominantly Catholic areas and proudly calls itself a 'national' party. The percentage of the Party's total votes from the capital has declined from 34.8 in 1949 to 26.8 in 1975. At the last election the SPÖ won over 50 per cent of the vote in the provinces of Burgenland, Styria and Carinthia. The SPÖ also consolidated its position with its traditional clientele and in Vienna won almost 60 per cent of the vote. The KPÖ has presented no real challenge to the SPÖ and has not been represented in parliament since 1959. The 1975 election meant that the ÖVP is stronger than the SPÖ only in Lower Austria, Tyrol and Vorarlberg. In the First Republic the Social Democrats were in control of only one province – Vienna. Now the SPÖ provides the governor (*Landeshauptmann*) in Burgenland and Carinthia as well as in Vienna. In regional elections between 1971 and 1975 the Socialists lost votes and seats. To some extent this was a protest vote against the governing party and also local issues and personalities play a more important role than in federal elections.

Industrialisation and an increase in the geographical mobility of the population have benefited the Socialists; these changes have contributed to a decrease in party identification. At the last election, 25 per cent of the electorate had not decided how to vote before the election campaign. Party identification tends to be greater among SPÖ supporters (see Table 2).

The SPÖ has, throughout the Second Republic, provided successful candidates for the Federal Presidency. With the exception of Karl Renner (President 1945-50), this office has been directly elected and voting is compulsory. The Party proposed prominent Socialists until 1974 when Dr. Kirschläger, a non-Socialist and practising Catholic, was the SPÖ's choice and won with 51.7 per cent of the vote. This again demonstrates that the Party is not limited to one section of the population for support and that the former rigidity of the *Lager* is loosening.

Party Membership

The SPÖ is a 'mass membership party'; only direct and individual membership is recognised. The SPÖ has 687,650 members (9.22 per cent of the total population) and dues are a vital source of financial support. Membership reached a peak in 1960 (see Table 3) although a new drive, which aims to win 2 per cent more voters as members in every electoral district, is proving successful. The latest unofficial figures indicate that membership now exceeds 700,000 and in Upper Austria and Carinthia the Party claims to have more members than at any other time in its history.[12]

The Party has a high ratio of members to voters but this is not so impressive as formerly: in 1950, 37.4 per cent of Socialist voters were also party members; by 1975 this had dropped to 29.6 per cent. In Vienna 40.9 per cent of the Party's voters are also members as opposed to 9.5 per cent in the westernmost province of Vorarlberg. Vienna however is not so important for the party as in the past: in 1932 61.8 per cent of the Party's members lived in the capital; today this is only 37.2 per cent.[13] The Party is slowly improving its strength in other parts of the country (see Table 4).

Only 7 per cent of members joined before 1934, so that links with the pre-war party are fading; a significant 43 per cent joined the Party after 1961 and 27 per cent have become members since 1966. This does not imply a youthful party − indeed the SPÖ is occasionally referred to as the 'red pensioners' party'. There is some evidence to support this − 65.2 per cent of the Party's membership is over 40 and 28.1 per cent over 60[14] (according to the 1971 census 41.7 per cent of the population is over 40 and 19 per cent over 60). The class nature of the Party is changing although the bulk of its membership is still drawn from the manual working class. The Party has been most successful in winning public service employees as members. Over-aging in the Party is clear from the dramatic rise in the percentage of pensioners compared with the 1929 figures (see Table 5).

Just over 10 per cent of members (69,405) are unpaid, committed Party workers. These are the *Vertrauenspersonen,* officially regarded as the 'vanguard' of the Party, who receive special instruction and are required to be model Socialists. The *Vertrauenspersonen* are engaged in arduous routine work and are responsible for the monthly collection of dues. One of the most important of their functions is to act as a channel of communication between the higher echelons of the Party and the ordinary member and the electorate; probably only one-third of the *Vertrauenspersonen* are regularly active in this capacity.[15] Public service employees constitute 20.7 per cent of the *Vertrauenspersonen* and 36.8 per cent are classified as workers.[16]

Of the Party's deputies in the National Assembly of 1971, 21.5 per cent were described as workers; the largest single group (40.9 per cent) was composed of salaried employees (*Angestellte*). This was a significant change from the 1956 parliament when 60.8 per cent of SPÖ deputies were classified as workers and only 17.6 per cent as salaried employees.[17] Socialist deputies tend to be much older than the average party member − in 1971, 92.5 per cent were over 40.

Party Organisation

The structure of the Socialist Party resembles a pyramid − at the base are 3,334 small, local units (*Ortsorganisationen*).[18] Combinations of these form the 113 district organisations (*Bezirksorganisationen*), mostly corresponding to political administrative areas; these are, in

turn, grouped into 9 *Land* organisations. At the apex is the federal
party *(Bundesparteiorganisation)*.

At federal level the biennial Party Conference *(Parteitag)*, in theory,
wields supreme authority and its decisions are binding on all party
institutions. Over 500 delegates are sent to Conference which severely
handicaps efficient decision-making. Delegates to Conference are
usually older than the average member — in 1974, over 80 per cent
were over 45. Salaried employees comprised 53 per cent of delegates,
public service employees 24 per cent and workers only 11 per cent.[19]
The district and *Land* organisations, and affiliated associations are
among those entitled to send delegates. Conference provides a forum
for Party workers to air views on a variety of topics, although
moments of drama are rare and intra-Party disputes are played down.
Speeches are delivered by the Party's leading politicians culminating
with a speech from the Party Chairman. The financial state of the
Party is presented and progress reports from the *Land* organisations are
dutifully given. Organs of the federal party address Conference
including the Women's Committee (on which all *Land* organisations are
represented), the Central Education Office (SBZ), and the Young
Generation *(Junge Generation, JG)*. The JG was not conceived as a
youth organisation of the Party and is aimed at the 25-35 age group. It
includes parliamentary deputies and Party functionaries and is
preoccupied with winning young members and voters for the Party.

One of the chief tasks of the Party Conference is to elect the 54
members of the Party Executive *(Bundesparteivorstand)*. A list of
proposed candidates is prepared for Conference by an Election
Committee. Before 1967 half of the seats on the Party Executive went
to the *Land* organisations;[20] now 40 of the 54 seats are assigned to
them. Distribution of these seats among the *Land* organisations is based
on membership strength and calculated according to the d'Hondt
system. Each *Land* must have at least one seat; if possessing only one,
after this electoral process, a *Land* is entitled to a further seat from the
14 remaining. For any seats still left over, the Election Committee can
propose party members, irrespective of origin, who will best serve the
interests of the party.[21] The Party Executive carries out decisions of
Conference, is entrusted with the management of Party finance and
decides on the bias of the Party press; it takes the main political
decisions of the Party. It proposes from its ranks the Party Chairman
and Vice-Chairmen, who together constitute the Party Presidium.
Confirmation by Conference is required but this is a formality. The
Party Executive also appoints the Party Treasurer and Central Party

Secretaries. In November 1975 the Party Executive appointed two Central Party Secretaries — one concerned with organisation and finance and the other with responsibilities for publicity, education, youth and the dissemination of internal information.

The Party Presidium, currently composed of the Party Chairman and five Vice-Chairmen, implements the decisions of the Party Executive. An Enlarged Party Presidium has existed since 1967, at present numbering fifteen, including members of the Presidium, Chairmen of the *Land* organisations, one representative from the federal Women's Committee and two from the Socialist trade unions (FSG). The Enlarged Presidium is engaged on preparatory work for the Party Executive and is empowered to take decisions on its behalf if it cannot meet in time.

Power in the Party is, *de facto,* concentrated in these smaller units and is not exercised by the Party Conference. The SPÖ insists nevertheless that the second highest authority in the Party is the Party Council (*Parteirat*) often referred to as 'the little party conference'. The Party Council can be invoked by the Party Executive in specified circumstances. One of these is to participate in the nomination of candidates for the National Assembly. Proposals for candidates on the Party list come from the Party Executive by way of recommendations from the *Land* organisations. The Party Council cannot ignore these entirely and so independent action is restricted. The Party Council can also nominate the Socialists' candidate for the Federal Presidency, but this again is based on suggestions from the Party Executive. Delegates to the Party Council come from the Party Executive, the *Land* organisations, the federal Women's Committee, the Socialist trade unions and other organisations entitled to send delegates to Conference.

The Affiliated Associations

There are twenty-eight affiliated socialist organisations and 'factions' (*Fraktionen*). Before 1934 these satellite organisations fulfilled a spiritual as well as political need for the working class, in an attempt to counter the omnipresence of the Catholic Church. Today they are less ideologically orientated but still play an important part in the mobilisation of Party supporters. Their existence is valued by the SPÖ which likes to think of itself as a large family where all may pursue recreational or political interests.

Many of these organisations first developed under the old Social Democratic Party, among them the famous 'Workers' Stamp Collecting Association' still in existence with over 4,000 members.[22] The

'Friends of Nature' is over eighty years old and, at present, has a membership of 126,484; it is concerned that the leisure time of working people should be enjoyed and arranges outdoor activities such as mountaineering and skiing. Some of these older societies still bear the ethos of the pre-war party, although modifications are apparent. The 'Workers' Temperance League', for instance, changed its name in 1975 to the *Aktion für O,O Promille,* i.e. it now campaigns to reduce the permitted level of alcohol in the blood for drivers to zero, a specific attack on drinking and driving.

Austrian Socialists have always stressed the importance of correctly educating the young and have been particularly concerned to negate the influence of the Church. The Party's parents' association, 'The Children's Friends', began in 1908 and today has a large membership of 295,811 and sends six delegates to the Party Conference. It aims to help parents bring up children in a Socialist environment before and during school days. Among the youth organisations affiliated to the SPÖ are the 'Association of Socialist Students' (VSStÖ) and the 'Socialist Youth of Austria' (SJÖ). The students' organisation opposes the SPÖ's willingness to co-operate with Industry as a 'social partner'. Considerable friction periodically breaks out between the student youth and the Party leadership, suspicious of the slightest 'Communist' infiltration or collaboration;[23] only about 50 per cent of the VSStÖ are members of the Party. The SJÖ caters for those in the 14-20 age group and aims to create a politically conscious youth with a knowledge of Marxism; it too is critical of the reformist tendencies of the adult party. The SJÖ would like to see the introduction of more nationalisation, particularly in the insurance and pharmaceutical industries. The quantitative strength of the SJÖ is not considered satisfactory and in 1970 it had a membership of 25,800 compared with 34,632 in 1923.[24] The SJÖ sends six delegates to Conference, but is frequently outmanoeuvred by the party's *Junge Generation* for contact with top politicians – a cause for discontent in the SJÖ.

One of the most popular organisations is the sports association (ASKÖ) founded in 1925; it now has a membership of 724,678 and sends six delegates to Conference. The pensioners' association (*Verband der österreichischen Rentner und Pensionisten*) also has a high membership of 345,000 and sends eight delegates to Conference.[25]

Some organisations have declared 'unpolitical' aims such as the social welfare society, *Die Volkshilfe,* which provides a home-help service, 'meals on wheels', and looks after the handicapped. It has a membership of over 35,000. One of the smallest organisations is the Esperanto

Society with 120 members.

Among the organisations that have developed since World War II is the 'League of Socialist Academics' (BSA) which began in 1946 and has enjoyed a rapid increase in membership, now totalling 13,467. It includes doctors and engineers and was quite successful in the immediate post-war period in enrolling former Nazis. Membership of the SPÖ is not obligatory for those belonging to the affiliated organisations (except for elected functionaries and delegates to Conference) but generally between 80 and 90 per cent of the BSA are party members. Many in the BSA hold important positions in the nationalised industries, nationalised banks and in parliament. In 1976, 12 of the 18 members of the Socialist Government were BSA members; 37 of the 93 Socialist deputies in the National Assembly and 8 of the 29 Socialists in the Federal Council (*Bundesrat*) belonged to the BSA.[26] Membership of the BSA can, in some cases, be helpful in promoting careers in public office, especially during a period when the Socialists are in government. This form of patronage has attracted intellectuals to the Party. Other organisations aimed at winning new members have been less successful, such as the 'League of Working Farmers' (*Arbeitsbauernbund*) and the 'Free Business League' (*Freier Wirtschaftsbund*), an intended rallying point for small businessmen and the self-employed.

One of the most important of the affiliated organisations is the Socialist trade union group — *Fraktion der Sozialistischen Gewerkschafter im ÖGB* (FSG). The FSG sends fifty delegates to the Party Conference and nineteen to the Party Council. It plays an important role for the party on the shop floor and at election times.

The Party and the Trade Unions

Although the Austrian Trade Union Federation (ÖGB) was founded as a suprapartisan (*überparteilich*) institution in 1945, there are strong links between the SPÖ and the Trade Unions. The ÖGB consists of *Fraktionen* of which the Socialist FSG is by far the largest; a member of the FSG must also belong to the SPÖ.[27] Ties are not so close as before the war when the 'Free' Trade Unions and the Social Democratic Party were regarded as 'Siamese' twins. The ÖGB has over 1½ million members, almost two-thirds of the labour force, and is extremely wealthy. It cannot directly finance political parties although 1 per cent of its income is distributed every year among the *Fraktionen*. In 1975 this amounted to 8,550,000 Schilling, of which 5,500,000 Schilling went to the FSG. The political neutralisation of the trade unions has meant a loss for the SPÖ which can now receive only modest financial help from this quarter. The ÖGB values its independence of parties and under the ÖVP Government of 1966-70 it was able to retain influence and a post in the Cabinet. From 1966-70 the Minister for Social Affairs was a member of the Christian fraction in the ÖGB. Since 1945 the ÖGB has monopolised this post which, apart from this interlude, has been occupied by members from the FSG.

Considerable overlapping of membership is apparent at top level between the FSG and the SPÖ. The President of the ÖGB, Anton Benya, is a member of both the Socialists' Party Executive and its Enlarged Presidium; he is also First President of the National Assembly. One of the Vice-Presidents of the ÖGB, Hans Böck, has a seat on the Party Executive and is a Socialist deputy in the Federal Council (*Bundesrat*). Alfred Dallinger, also (since 1975) Vice-President of the ÖGB, is a Socialist deputy in the National Assembly and Chairman of the Party's Control Commission. He occupies a powerful position as Chairman of the largest union in the ÖGB, the Salaried Clerical, Commercial and Technical Employees (*Privatangestellte*). Rudolf Häuser was Vice-President of the ÖGB before Herr Dallinger and, at the same time, was Vice-Chancellor and Minister of Social Affairs in Kreisky's Government. The FSG has altogether 7 of the 54 seats on the SPÖ Party Executive. In the present National Assembly a total of 34 of the 93 Socialist deputies are members of the FSG; in the Federal Council 6 of the 29 SPÖ deputies are Socialist trade unionists. The FSG is currently represented in the Cabinet by the Minister of Trade (who is also a member of the SPÖ's Executive), the Minister of Agriculture, and the Minister of Social Affairs.

The constituent parts of the ÖGB comprise sixteen individual unions; of these fourteen have Socialist Chairmen. The Public Service Employees' Union is chaired by a member from the Christian fraction and the Chairman of the Art and Professional Employees' Union is non-partisan. The FSG also dominates the ÖGB Executive (*Bundesvorstand*) possessing thirty-five of the forty-eight seats. Although Socialists figure prominently in the ÖGB, the unions have attempted to steer clear of intra-Party feuds. The ÖGB chiefly concentrates its energies on wage and social policies, and safeguarding jobs. So far the Socialist Government has been relatively successful in weathering the world recession and unemployment fell to only 1.5 per cent in 1974.[28] The ÖGB is one of the most powerful interest groups in Austria and as such cannot be ignored by the Socialist Party. The Trade Union Federation is represented on the Parity Commission for Wages and Prices along with the Chambers of Commerce, Labour and Agriculture,[29] and in this capacity influences Government policy.

The FSG is the link between the SPÖ and the Socialist-dominated Chamber of Labour. There is some duplication of work by the ÖGB and the Chamber of Labour but the latter, unlike the ÖGB, is a statutory body and membership is compulsory for manual and salaried employees. The Chamber of Labour has a well-equipped, specialised staff and is consulted by the Government on relevant legislation. It has access to Government departments and is empowered to draft legislation; collective bargaining is left to the ÖGB. The Chambers of Labour exist in each of the nine *Bundesländer* and, with the exception of Vorarlberg, all have Socialist Presidents. The FSG submits a list for the election of 'councillors' to the Chambers of Labour once every five years and usually polls well over two-thirds of all votes. At the last election, in 1974, the FSG won 63.4 per cent of the vote.[30] The Chambers of Commerce and Agriculture have similar advisory and administrative functions; they provide legal representation for their members and undertake research. These two Chambers are dominated by the OVP. In 1970, SPÖ representation in the Chamber of Commerce amounted to 10.7 per cent, and in the Chamber of Agriculture to 10 per cent.

The SPÖ and Europe

The Party's 'New Programme' of 1958 welcomed economic union in Europe as a 'step towards the establishment of a democratic United States of Europe'. Initially the Party was more sympathetic to EFTA than the Common Market, which was opposed on ideological grounds. Under Kreisky the Party became less suspicious of the EEC and interested in closer links.[31] Finally, in 1972, Kreisky signed an industrial free trade agreement with the European Community. Austria's policy of permanent neutrality means that further integration with the EEC would be difficult to negotiate.

Karl Czernetz, one of the Party's leading spokesmen on Europe, regards the Common Market as a fine weather community which has succeeded as a customs union but is stagnating on most other issues. He believes that national traditions are likely to persist and that a 'European' consciousness will be difficult to create.[32] Czernetz is apprehensive of the EEC (regarding it as a possible instrument of French *Machtpolitik*)[33] and believes that the pace of further integration should be cautious. Austria has been a member of the Council of Europe since 1956 and the SPÖ sends three delegates to Strasbourg.

Czernetz, currently President of the Council of Europe, considers this institution to be important in linking members of the Common Market with other European states, thereby providing the greatest parliamentary forum in Europe. Kreisky (who was Foreign Minister in the Great Coalition 1959-66) sees an opportunity for Social Democracy to shake integration in Europe from its torpor. In this context, he regards the development of a common social policy and closer co-operation with the Third World as important. Kreisky envisages the creation of a loosely united Europe of 300 million people as a feasible proposition.[34]

Austria is a member of the United Nations and the Socialist Government is keen to develop Vienna as an international conference centre; work is going ahead to make Vienna the third 'UNO-city'. The SPÖ has strong links with the Socialist International and provided its last General Secretary, Hans Janitschek; Dr. Pittermann (Chairman of the SPÖ 1957-67) was President of the SI from 1964-76.

Party Reform

Reform of the Party was the main theme of the last Conference in 1976. Although the SPÖ enjoys a high ratio of members to voters, the Party is dissatisfied that of 2.3 million voters 'only' 700,000 are members. Under the slogan of 'the open Party', the SPÖ aims to democratise the Party structure and improve its image with potential members. The Party intends to mobilise fellow-travellers by giving them a say in policy formation. Meetings of the Party are, in future, to be open to non-members to encourage participation. The object is to ensure that the 'liberal' voters, (estimated at around 6 per cent), who are crucial in providing the Party with its absolute majority, do not drift away at the next election. Kreisky has attempted to win the sympathy of 'progressive liberals' by including non-Socialists in his Cabinet such as the Minister of Defence, who is unpopular with the Left wing, and the new Foreign Minister, until recently a member of the People's Party. Socialism is portrayed by the Party's Central Secretary, Karl Blecha, as a logical extension of liberalism since both value the freedom of the individual.[35] There are some grumbles on the Left that such an ideologically 'open' party will produce too much dilution of Party policy.

Despite electoral success, there is evidence of some ossification in the Party organisation. The new reforms are designed to regenerate the enthusiasm of existing members, many of whom faithfully pay their dues and vote but play no active role in the Party.[36] The SPÖ is attempting to overcome this passivity by involving the ordinary member more in decision-making. Accordingly the 1976 Party Conference agreed that all members should have the right to put questions to the Party Executive directly and receive a reply within eight weeks; this has been written into the new Party statute.[37] In addition, an SPÖ deputy must be available for questions at a public meeting in his constituency at least once a year.[38] This movement to increase inner-Party democracy has been received with scepticism by those who believe that the existing, highly centralised power structure cannot be easily changed.[39] The 1976 Party Conference also attempted to tackle the inveterate problem of the 'accumulation of offices' (*Ämterkumulierung*), which has led to the concentration of power in the hands of a few. Leading politicians are now required to submit in writing every year the number of offices they hold, and the *Vertrauenspersonen* are limited to only one paid Party post.[40] Exceptions are possible and some regard this as an important loophole.

With the new emphasis on the SPÖ as an 'open' party, a definite break has been made with the inflexible *Lagermentalität*. The Party now regards itself as part of society and not as an enclosed fortress pitted against it. New members are not expected to undergo stringent ideological conversion; the political socialisation, which was so important for the pre-war party, is less conspicuous. Although its election victories are impressive, the absence of ideological lustre could be a problem for the Party in the future. There are limits to the number of voters and members a party can mobilise and the SPÖ must be close to exhausting its share. Without a more determined sense of direction such an accumulation of support could, in any case, appear a fruitless exercise.

Notes

1. Cited in Norbert Leser, 'Austro-Marxism: A Reappraisal', *Journal of Contemporary History*, vol. XI (1976), p. 137. For detail on the theories of the early Social Democrats see N. Leser, *Zwischen Reformismus und Bolschewismus* (Vienna, Europa Verlag, 1968).
2. See Adam Wandruszka, *Geschichte der Republik Österreich* (Vienna, 1954), pp. 289-485 and A. Diamant, 'The Group Basis of Austrain Politics', *Journal of Central European Affairs*, vol. XVIII (1958), pp. 134-55.
3. See E. Weinzierl and K. Skalnik (eds.) *Das Neue Österreich* (Styria, 1975), pp. 31ff.
4. For a lucid explanation of this controversial 'economic and social partnership' system see Thomas Lachs, *Wirtschaftspartnerschaft in Österreich* (Vienna, ÖGB, 1976).
5. For the programmatic discussion in the Party see F. Kreissler, 'Vom Austro-Marxismus zum Austro-Sozialismus', *Revue D'Allemagne*, vol. V (1973), pp. 1-39.

6. See Ernst Winkler, *Die österreichische Sozialdemokratie im Spiegel ihrer Programme* (Vienna, Verlag der Wiener Volksbuchhandlung, 1971), p. 56.

7. *The New Programme of Austrian Socialism* (Vienna, 1958), p.6.

8. See Heinz Fischer, 'Kirche und Staat in Österreich', *Die Zukunft*, Jan. 1976.

9. See A. Pelinka and M. Welan, *Demokratie und Verfassung in Österreich*, (Vienna, Europa Verlag, 1971), pp. 275-86.

10. For further information on this election see Melanie Sully, 'The Austrian Parliamentary Election of 1975', *Parliamentary Affairs*, vol. XXIX (1976), pp. 293-309.

11. See Karl Blecha, 'Die Grossen Trends', *Die Zukunft*, Nov. 1975.

12. Cited in *Politik und Dokumentation*, 27. Aug. 1976.

13. See F. Kreissler, op. cit., p. 28 and *Bericht an den Bundesparteitag 1976* (SPÖ).

14. The figures here are from the *Bericht an den Bundesparteitag 1972* (SPÖ).

15. See A. Pelinka in Heinz Fischer (ed.), *Das Politische System Österreichs* (Vienna, Europa Verlag, 1974), p. 39.

16. *Bericht an den Bundesparteitag 1972.*

17. See Heinz Fischer, *Das Politische System Österreichs*, pp. 126-9.

18. *Bericht an den Bundesparteitag 1976.*

19. H. Fischer, 'Parteitag 1974', *Die Zukunft*, Mar. 1974.

20. Kurt Shell, *The Transformation of Austrian Socialism* (New York, State University of New York, 1962), p. 78.

21. *Organisationsstatut* (Vienna, SPÖ, 1976), p. 32.

22. Figures relating to membership, unless otherwise stated, from *Bericht an den Bundesparteitag 1976.*

23. See *Profil*, no. 23, 1976.

24. Figures from W. Oberleitner, *Politisches Handbuch Österreichs 1945-1972* (Vienna, Österreichischer Bundesverlag, 1972) and K. Shell, op.cit., p.53.

25. For the number of delegates each organisation can send to Conference see *Organisationsstatut*, 1976, pp. 24-8.

26. See a three-part series on the BSA, 'Die Karrierehelfer', *Stern*, Apr. 1976 (Austrian edition only).

27. For the following information I am greatly indebted to Alfred Ströer, Executive Secretary of the ÖGB and member of the SPÖ Party Executive.

28. Details of prices, wages and employment can be found in *Wirtschafts-und-Sozial-Statistisches Taschenbuch* (Vienna, Arbeiterkammer, 1976).

29. An account of the historical development and functions of the Chambers can be found in K. Ucakar, *Das Politische System Österreichs*, pp. 397-428.

30. Detailed results of this election are in O. Scheer, *Arbeit und Wirtschaft*, Dec. 1974.

31. For a discussion of the intra-party conflicts on this question see P.J. Katzenstein, 'Trends and Oscillations in Austrian Integration Policy since 1955: Alternative Explanations', *Journal of Common Market Studies*, Dec. 1975, pp. 171-97.

32. K. Czernetz, 'Europarat und Europäische Union', *Die Zukunft*, Feb. 1976.

33. K. Czernetz, 'Europa – wohin?', *Die Zukunft*, Apr. 1974.

34. B. Kreisky, *Aspekte des demokratischen Sozialismus* (Munich, List Verlag, 1974), pp. 165-77.

35. *Protokoll des 23. Ordentlichen Bundesparteitages* (SPÖ, 1976), p. 32.

36. In Autumn 1972 the Party sent to all members a letter asking them to give opinions on the general policies of the Party – only 10 per cent were returned. Cited in H. Brantl, 'Wie modernisiert man eine Partei?', *Die Zukunft*, Feb. 1974.

37. *Organisationsstatut*, 1976, p. 12.
38. Ibid. p. 45.
39. See J. Benda and P. Pelinka, 'Für eine sozialistische Parteireform', *Die Zukunft*, Feb. 1976.
40. *Organisationsstatut*, 1976, pp. 47-8.

Table 1. Parliamentary election results in the Second Republic (1945-75)

Year of Election	SPÖ % of votes	SPÖ No. of seats	ÖVP % of votes	ÖVP No. of seats	FPÖ % of votes	FPÖ No. of seats	KPÖ % of votes	KPÖ No.of seats	Others % of votes	No. of seats
1945	44.60	76	49.80	85	–	–	5.42	4	0.19	–
1949	38.71	67	44.03	77	11.67	16*	5.08	5	0.51	–
1953	42.11	73	41.26	74	10.95	14*	5.28	4	0.40	–
1956	43.05	74	45.96	82	6.52	6	4.42	3	0.06	–
1959	44.79	78	44.19	79	7.70	8	3.27	–	0.05	–
1962	44.00	76	45.43	81	7.04	8	3.04	–	0.48	–
1966	42.56	74	48.35	85	5.35	6	0.41	–	3.32	–
1970	48.42	81	44.69	78	5.52	6	0.98	–	0.39	–
1971†	50.04	93	43.11	80	5.45	10	1.36	–	0.04	–
1975	50.42	93	42.95	80	5.41	10	1.19	–	0.03	–

* In 1949 and 1953 the WdU (*Wahlpartei der Unabhängigen*) was the third main party. This was the forerunner of the Freedom Party (FPÖ) which was formed in 1956.
† The electoral reform of 1970 increased the number of seats from 165 to 183.
Source: Figures compiled from *Die Nationalratswahl vom 5. Oktober 1975* and Wolfgang Oberleitner, *Politisches Handbuch Österreichs 1945-1972* (Vienna, Österreichischer Bundesverlag, 1972).

Table 2. Party supporters making voting decision before start of election campaign, 1975 (in %)

SPÖ	ÖVP	FPÖ	KPÖ	Non-partisan
87 (87)	81 (84)	61 (67)	86 (87)	41 (47)

(Figures for the 1971 election are in brackets.)

Source: *Sozialwissenschaftliche Studiengesellschaft, Fragebogen Nr. 157,* Dec. 1975.

Table 3. Party membership (1945-74)

Year (ending December 31)	Men Number	% of total	Women Number	% of total	Total Membership
1945	230,794	64.50	127,024	35.50	357,818
1950	397,446	65.45	209,837	34.55	607,283
1955	447,721	64.78	243,429	35.22	691,150
1960	471,659	64.85	255,606	35.15	727,265
1965	462,517	65.33	245,455	34.67	707,972
1970	472,495	65.68	246,894	34.32	719,389
1973	454,637	66.14	232,738	33.86	687,375
1974	454,634	66.11	233,016	33.89	687,650

Source: From *Bericht an den Bundesparteitag 1976* (SPÖ).

Table 4. Party support in the provinces

Province	Party membership in province as % of national membership 1975	1951	Party votes in province as % of total Party vote, 1975	Party members as % of population in province, 1975
Burgenland	3.90	3.14	3.86	9.84
Carinthia	6.27	5.36	7.34	8.20
Lower Austria	18.74	19.90	18.47	9.11
Upper Austria	12.81	9.43	15.45	7.20
Salzburg	3.71	3.21	4.60	6.35
Styria	14.49	13.41	16.00	8.36
Tyrol	2.18	1.68	5.10	2.77
Vorarlberg	0.75	0.66	2.35	1.91
Vienna	37.16	43.22	26.83	15.82

Source: Figures compiled from *Bericht an den Bundesparteitag 1976* (SPÖ); *Die Nationalratswahl vom 5. Oktober 1975,* and 1971 Census figures.

Table 5. Occupational stratification of Party membership (in %)

	1929	1972
Industrial workers	51.2	37.3
Agricultural and forestry workers	–	1.0
Salaried employees in private employment	11.8	13.4
Employees in public service	8.6	13.8
Professions	1.5	1.1
Self-employed in industry and trade	4.3	2.1
Farmers	–	0.7
Pensioners	2.2	16.4
Housewives	16.1	12.2
Students	–	0.6
Unknown or no occupation	1.6	1.4

Source: Figures for 1929 are estimates only and are cited in Kurt Shell, *The Transformation of Austrian Socialism* (New York, 1962), p. 50. Figures for 1972 are from *Bericht an den Bundesparteitag 1972* (SPÖ).

Further Reading

Books

Blecha, K. et al. *Rote Markierungen.* Vienna, Europa Verlag, 1972.
Fischer, H. (ed.). *Das Politische System Österreichs.* Vienna, Europa Verlag, 1974.
Pelinka, A. and Welan, M. *Demokratie und Verfassung in Österreich.* Vienna, Europa Verlag, 1971.
Leser, N. *Zwischen Reformismus und Bolschewismus.* Vienna, Europa Verlag, 1968.
Shell, K. *The Transformation of Austrian Socialism.* New York, State University of New York, 1962.
Steiner, K. *Politics in Austria.* Boston, Little, Brown and Company, 1972.

Articles

Kreissler, F. 'Vom Austro-Marxismus zum Austro-Sozialismus'. *Revue D'Allemagne.* Vol. V. 1973. Pp. 1-39.
Leser, N. 'Gesellschaftsreform ohne Parteireform?' *Festschrift für Eduard März,* Vienna, 1973.

Introduction

Social Democracy in Denmark began in 1871, but it was only with the establishment of the parliamentary principle in 1901 that the stage was set for the Party's growth. It became the largest of the four main parties in the Danish political system in 1913 and has retained this position since 1924. The Party's golden age was probably the 1930s when it was in power as the senior partner in a majority coalition with the Radical Liberals. Its leader, Thorvald Stauning, became a father figure around whom the nation gathered in the looming chaos.[1] And his Government was able to enact extensive reforms which influenced the shape of Danish social relationships for a generation.

After the war the Party regained its leading role in 1947-50 and was in power continuously from 1953-68, gaining its largest-ever number of voters in 1964. But now it faced a decline in the proportion of the electorate which it could attract into membership, increasing competition from the Left, and the realisation that it was unlikely to achieve the dominant position which the progress of its Swedish sister party had encouraged it to expect.[2]

In 1960 the Socialist People's Party established its claim to be counted with the four main parties which had dominated Danish politics since the 'freezing of the party system' in the early years of the century. From then on the Social Democrats were constantly aware of the need to compete for support on their left.

The 1973 and 1975 elections presented a starker challenge: could the Party ever retain the support of an increasingly well-educated, mobile, radical, affluent and heavily taxed population which showed itself sharply mistrustful of the established parties and susceptible to the wilder claims of populism?

The following pages will examine how the Party has responded to the challenges facing it, consider changes in the basis of Party support and membership, the Party's relationship to the party system and to the other parties of the Left, and trace the development of the Party's ideology.

Origins and Organisation

The Danish Social Democratic Party traces its origins to a weekly paper,

Socialisten, first published in July 1871. A Danish branch of the First International was formed the following October from which the trade union movement and Social Democracy as a political party originate. Its three founders were Louis Pio, who started the paper, his cousin Harald Brix,[3] its editor and main contributor, and Paul Geleff, who carried the new ideas out into the country and so laid the foundation of a national movement.

In the spring of 1872 *Socialisten* actively supported a bricklayers' strike and called a public meeting. This and all other meetings of the International were banned by the police and the three leaders were sentenced to three to five years in prison. The paper continued under the name *Social-Demokraten*[4] and in 1876 the Party held its first Congress, chaired by Pio, newly released from prison. But his oratorical abilities were outweighed by criticisms of his undemocratic leadership and his lack of interest in the trade union movement. A year later he resigned and emigrated to the USA with Geleff, paid to do so by the police.

The Party was restructured in 1878, separating trade union and political activity.[5] In depressed economic conditions it was hard to persuade people to stay in a union which could not protect them, and hard to justify paying dues to an organisation the Socialist ideas of which they perhaps did not sympathise with or understand. The organisational structure of the Party was not based on theoretical considerations, but was strictly practical. There was no thought whether a Socialist organisation should differ from others and no attempt to use foreign models: the German party, for example, was seen to be facing very different circumstances, internally and externally.

Despite formal separation, the Party and the trade union movement· have co-operated closely and the national trade union organisation (*Landsorganisationen De samvirkende Fagforbund,* or LO) is represented by its Chairman and one other Party member on the Party's fourteen-member Executive Committee. LO took its present name in 1959 but originated in 1898 as a joint forum and spokesman for the unions. The following year it played a decisive part in three months of industrial conflict and lockout which culminated in the September Agreement. This laid down rules for negotiations between unions and employers on rights, recognition and procedures. The Agreement remained in force, with revisions in 1960, until 1969 and a new Agreement came into force in 1973. It was this Agreement which ensured industrial peace for most of the century. It required a three-quarters majority in a competent meeting to take strike or lockout

decisions, with fourteen days notice to be given to the opposing party.
Wage agreements required three months notice of termination. There
was provision for arbitration and the organisations on each side promised
to work for peaceful, stable and good labour relations. Initially the
Agreement favoured decentralised wage bargaining but during and since
the 1950s there has been a tendency towards central negotiation of
general demands, with industry or plant-specific issues negotiated at
those levels.[6]

Parliamentary seats were more than just another indication of the
Party's progress: they were seen as the key to Socialism, since the
Party's strategy was clearly parliamentary, with a Folketing majority as
the only way to social and economic reform. Since 1888 the Party's
Congress has been the Party's supreme authority, but the Executive
Committee remained the main source of co-ordination and continuity,
deciding tactics, negotiating with other parties and directing the
activities of the party group in the Folketing. An extensive branch
structure was soon developed, but each branch has substantial freedom
of action within the broad policy lines determined by the National
Executive.

The Party's long traditions made a powerful impact on the young
Jens Otto Krag, attending his first Party Congress in 1945.[7] He saw it
more as a movement than as a party, with its own history, symbols and
flag, its own ways of thinking and expression (the familiar *du* rather
than the formal *De*), its special connections with work-places and the
trade unions, its own newspapers and publishing house, its string of
towns with their burly mayors, its international connections: many such
factors, strengthening the Party in difficult times,as well as perhaps
isolating it from some sources of support such as the increasing body of
salaried employees. The subsequent decline of this exceptionalism,
common to other Social Democratic parties, has encouraged the
parties to take on a more 'catch-all' character, but has at the same time
reduced one important source of their social cohesion.

Party Membership

In the 1880s the Party faced the difficulties of organisation and personal
relationships common to the establishment of an anti-élitist movement.
In Denmark these were compounded by the country's economic
difficulties, which bore especially heavily on the Party's potential
supporters. But by the 1890s pressure from the opposition parties,
including SD and the Liberals (*Venstre*) at last made constitutional
change a real possibility. Industry began to develop and this increased

the number of potential and actual Social Democrats. Although the Party was organised separately from the trade unions from 1878 there has been a general rule[8] that people who work in an organised trade must be members of their union to be members of a Party association.

Initially the Party could rely on very few voters apart from its members, but as local Party newspapers were set up throughout the country during the 1890s both categories of supporters increased steadily and rapidly.

In 1901 the parliamentary principle of government accountability to the majority in the Folketing (the *lower* house) was established. At the same time open voting at elections gave way to the secret ballot, although proportionality did not replace the plurality principle until 1915 when women gained the vote and universal suffrage was achieved.[9] Secrecy, as Stein Rokkan points out, could cut the voter off from his peers as well as his superiors, making it possible to keep his decision private and avoid sanctions, but also making it impossible to prove how he voted.[10] Coinciding with this change, there was a fall in membership numbers in both relative and absolute terms and there was also a fall in the number of Party associations.[11] It was soon followed by the formation in 1905 of the Radical Liberal Party. Although this restricted one source of SD support — smallholders and the rural poor — the two parties were able to form electoral alliances to reduce the adverse effects of the electoral system. They went on to co-operate closely over the next sixty years. Figure 1 juxtaposes Party membership as a percentage of the electorate, 1890-1974; party votes as a percentage of total votes cast, 1884-1975; and the relationship between these two, Party membership as a percentage of Party votes.[12] It can be seen that membership trends improved again in 1909, while voting support continued to rise steadily as an increasing proportion of the population was mobilised into political activity: electoral turnout in 1901 was 49.8 per cent but by 1910 it was up to 74.8 per cent, remaining at about that level for the next decade.

During 1909-18 the Party stagnated and lost its radical image, supporting legislation for a permanent system of arbitration of industrial disputes in 1910 and agreeing to support the Radical Liberal Government of 1913-20. The Party's reformism was confirmed when its leader Thorvald Stauning accepted a position in the cabinet from 1916 onwards.[13] At the same time syndicalist activities at home and the revolutions in Germany and Russia offered counter-attractions for many of the more ideologically inclined workers.

New electoral laws in 1915 introduced proportional representation

and constituencies were reapportioned in 1920. These changes ended
the need for electoral alliances with the Radical Liberals to counter
Liberal overrepresentation in Jutland: Social Democrats had not
contested rural districts and Radicals had not opposed them in urban
areas.

In March 1920 wage negotiations collapsed and there was a major
strike and lockout. There had just been a Government crisis[14] when
the King had dismissed the Radical Liberal Prime Minister despite his
claim to a majority in the Folketing for his policies on the German
border issue. Stauning as SD Chairman was able to use the threat of a
general strike against both the King and the Employers' Association. In
this he also gained the reluctant support of the syndicalists, despite their
willingness to be linked with the Social Democrats. The employers
emphasised the political rather than economic aspect of the crisis and
accepted a compromise wage agreement, under some pressure from the
King and in the hope of strengthening anti-Socialist parties at the
forthcoming general election. The syndicalists felt betrayed as they had
gained nothing except an amnesty for political crimes. They continued
the strike, mainly among seamen, but went bankrupt in June. This
defeat of Left-wing opposition significantly strengthened the SD in the
trade union movement.[15]

From 1920 to 1945 Party membership grew but remained within
about 9-10 per cent of the electorate, while Party voting increased
steadily. The Party became the largest in the Folketing in 1924,
gaining mainly from the Liberals and continuing to do so during the
1930s. The following year it also achieved a majority for the first time
in the Landsting (upper house) with the Radicals. Over the 1930s the
Party was clearly successful in renewing the strength of its membership
and in using this resource to improve its electoral position. After 1945
it retained its momentum in terms of the total of votes cast for it,
achieving over 1.1 million votes in 1964, but as Figure 1 shows, its
party membership base was in overall decline from 1945 and its
membership ratio fell seriously from 1964 onwards. The strong
membership position during the 1930s allowed the Party to meet
quite successfully the challenges to it from the Communists, the youth
organisations of the Conservatives, and later, small emergent groups
of Fascists. While Party strategy in the 1920s was directed mainly at
extending membership support, in the 1930s it shifted towards
intensified Party activity, particularly by establishing an information
and propaganda service jointly with the trade unions in 1935, by
forming active élite groups available for instant action, and by raising

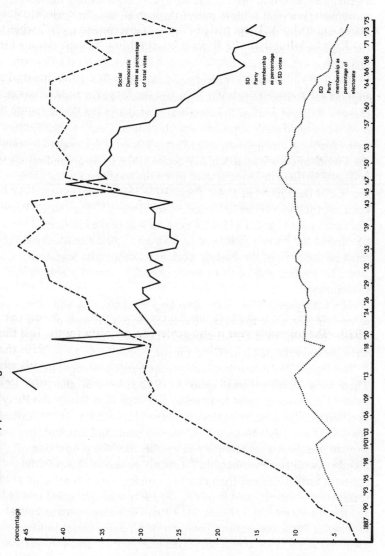

Figure 1. Social Democratic Party in Denmark: share of votes, Party membership and membership ratio, 1884-1975, percentages.[12]

Social Democratic votes as percentage of total votes

SD Party membership as percentage of SD votes

SD Party membership as percentage of electorate

percentage

45

40

35

30

25

20

15

10

5

1887 '90 '93 '95 '98 1901 '03 '06 '09 '13 '18 '20 '24 '26 '29 '32 '35 '39 '43 '45 '47 '50 '53 '57 '60 '64 '66 '68 '71 '73 75

the subscription.[16]

In the inter-war period there was growing support for a party that demanded decisive changes in established values and sought these changes by reformist and pragmatic means. Within the Party there was a general expectation that, as the sole party representing the labour movement, it would achieve power through an absolute majority of the electorate. Until then the Party could afford to moderate its demands, for example by working with the Radical Liberals in a majority coalition.

The 1943 election was an extraordinary demonstration of national support for legitimate popular representatives against the occupying powers. 89.5 per cent of the electorate voted and the Social Democrats probably gained some support from those who would normally have voted for the banned Communist Party. But over the next two years the Communists were particularly active in the underground resistance and, as elsewhere in Europe, they made substantial electoral gains from the Social Democrats in 1945. From 1943 there were negotiations between the two parties for a unified movement,[17] but the SD Party Conference in August 1945, two months before the election, confirmed the Party's insistence on two principles: Danish democracy must be the basis of the Party's work and Democratic Socialism its aim. The implications of these were, of course, unacceptable to the Communists.

The SD losses in 1945 proved to be only temporary and recruitment of new members improved rapidly, reaching a maximum of 296,175 in 1948. The 1947 election substantially restored the Party's voting strength and returned it to Government.

But from 1948 onwards effective membership strength declined. There were occasional small gains in 1952-3, 1959-60 and 1964. But Figure 1 shows that these were seldom enough to maintain the Party's position in relation to the growing electorate, even briefly.[18] Further analysis of the 1940-64 period shows that gains and losses of men and women members were generally in parallel. But the proportion of members with free membership[19] (mainly pensioners) was fairly constant until 1950 and then climbed rapidly from 5.6 per cent of all members to 19.6 per cent in 1963: the Party was ageing and was failing to attract new members. From 1954 there was also a decline in the number of Party associations (branches). A further major loss of members came in 1966 and coincided with SPP advances. Arguably the Socialist majority, achieved in 1966 for the first time, was based on increasingly Socialist attitudes among the core of SD supporters.[20] But by 1968 both membership and votes had declined so far that the non-Socialist bloc was able to form its first majority coalition.

In 1971 there was a partial SD recovery but the 1973 election brought disastrous losses: the Party held a smaller proportion of the electorate than at any time since 1906. In 1975 Party votes and membership figures were more encouraging but it remains to be seen whether the Party can stabilise this recovery in an era of economic retrenchment and against the competing claims of populist self-interest.

Social Compostion of Party Support

Analysis of the social basis of the Party's support has shown important changes in recent years. In 1954[21] 84 per cent of support for the Social Democrats came from social groups which included people in skilled but not supervisory positions, unskilled and agricultural workers and smallholders. A 1968 Gallup survey[22] showed a broadly similar pattern, with the Party slightly more reliant on the lower strata than in 1954. But another analysis of the Gallup data using the same strata finds the party to be much more reliant on middle-strata support, with only 68 per cent of its electorate drawn from the lower strata.[23]

Table 1 shows the distribution of party support in 1974 by occupation, age and education.[24] By comparison with the other categories the Social Democrats still have a very high proportion of pensioners among their supporters and they have clearly been much less successful than parties further to their Left in recruiting supporters under thirty. Their supporters are very much less educated, over 80 per cent having had no more than the legal minimum education,[25] and the Left wing has been more successful than the other groups in recruiting support from those with a higher education. This is borne out also in the analysis of party preference by occupational group: the Left wing has more support than the Social Democrats among salaried employees, skilled workers and students. It is still true that the Party increases in relative popularity with decreasing social status[26] and the typical pensioner or worker, skilled or unskilled, is still most likely to vote SD. The Left-wing parties rely far more than others on students and other non-employed people, have made significant inroads into the skilled workers' group and also have an important share of the lower salaried employees. The minor Centre and Right parties also rely on the latter group and on the urban middle classes generally. The main strength of the Liberals is among self-employed farmers and the Progress Party is strongest among the self-employed in urban occupations.

After relative stability in Danish politics from 1920-70, the elections of the 1970s imposed sweeping changes. 1971 brought some return of votes to the Social Democrats after their 1968 losses to the Radical Liberals, but the Socialist People's Party (SPP) gained mainly from SD and to some extent from the Radicals. The general swing to the Left was only just enough to create a Socialist majority and confrontation between the Socialist and non-Socialist blocs sharpened, especially on housing legislation: this issue eventually gave rise to the break-away Centre Democrats. When the December 1973 election came, however, it was the Progress Party led by Mogens Glistrup which made the most devastating impact on all the established parties. Analysis of the movement of electors between parties from 1971 to 1973[27] shows that the Social Democrats lost most to the Centre Democrats (indeed this was the predominant source of CD support) with significant losses also to the Progress Party and the SPP. The new parties were the only ones to make net gains and the Progress Party won support from all parties from Left to Right. The extent of the 1973 changes is evident when it is noted that only 47 per cent of respondents voted for the same party over the elections of 1968, 1971 and 1973, whereas the 'four old parties' had attracted an average of over 90 per cent of the vote over the fifty years to 1970. It seems that in 1973 SD relied almost exclusively on a core of regular supporters and, unlike the previous election, attracted almost no floating voters. Reasons for the Party's long-term decline are obviously complex. One is that the two large social groups, farmers and workers, which previously supported the Liberals and SD respectively, are in decline. But, more importantly, the significance of belonging to these groups is diminishing as their closed social systems,[28] their special cultures, their group consciousness, their specific opinion formation and communication processes, their conceptual worlds, become submerged in the mass culture disseminated by national mass communications media, particularly television. As a result, links are broken, ideological differences become less intense, relationships with the political system are less secure. All these factors allow a new idea, a new political leader, a movement such as the Progress Party to make an unprecedentedly great impact on the established parties and organisations. But at the same time such mushroom growths will probably not withstand further short-term changes in the way that the more solidly based parties have done in the past.[29]

The impact of the Progress Party seems to have been due to its ability to capitalise on pre-existing attitudes of discontent and predispositions to authoritarian solutions, both characteristic of Progress Party supporters.[30]

SD losses in 1973 might have been even greater but for the major organisational changes made only four years earlier, transferring as many decisions as possible to the basic level of the party associations. Candidates may be put up for election by twenty-five members of an association and MFs have to be renominated annually, when they may be challenged by counter-candidates. The party list was replaced by a personal vote system which reduced the safe-seat factor and encouraged candidates to fight for every vote. And important issues were put out for discussion to the associations as a way of politicising Party members, as was the new Party programme in the interval between the 1973 and 1977 Party Congresses.[31] These moves may have contributed to the Party's partial recovery at the 1975 election. While the Party again lost some support equally to each of the five large parties (SPP, Radicals, Liberals, Conservatives and Progress Party each took 0.5 per cent of the 1973 SD voters), it also made gains from the Progress Party and the Centre Democrats (1.1 per cent each) with smaller net gains from each of the others except the Liberals and the Conservatives.[32]

There was evidence that, while the Party still relied heavily on the support of manual workers, it was attracting more salaried employees than in either 1971 or 1973.[33] The pressure from the other parties of the Left has also meant that the main SD strength now comes from the country towns rather than the capital, formerly its main stronghold. It is still the party preferred by people with low incomes, by the elderly, and by those who left school early.

Social Democracy in the Danish Party System

By the early 1920s, in Denmark as elsewhere in Europe, the major party alternatives had frozen in the wake of extensions to the suffrage and mobilisation of major sections of potential supporters. For the next fifty years the party system reflected, with few exceptions, the cleavage structures of the 1920s.[34] In Denmark the party system during this period comprised, in addition to the Social Democrats, the Radical Liberals, the Liberals (*Venstre,* literally 'the Left', sometimes referred to as 'agrarian liberals' in contrast to the Conservative 'Right') and the Conservative People's Party, a 'social conservative' party reconstructed from the remains of more reactionary groups of the nineteenth century. These four 'old parties' were joined after 1932 by the Communists. In 1960 the Socialist People's Party (SPP) replaced the Communists in the Folketing, the first new party since 1920 to compete seriously with the four 'old parties'.

Figure 2: Parties' percentage share of Folketing seats and Cabinet representation, Denmark, 1920-75

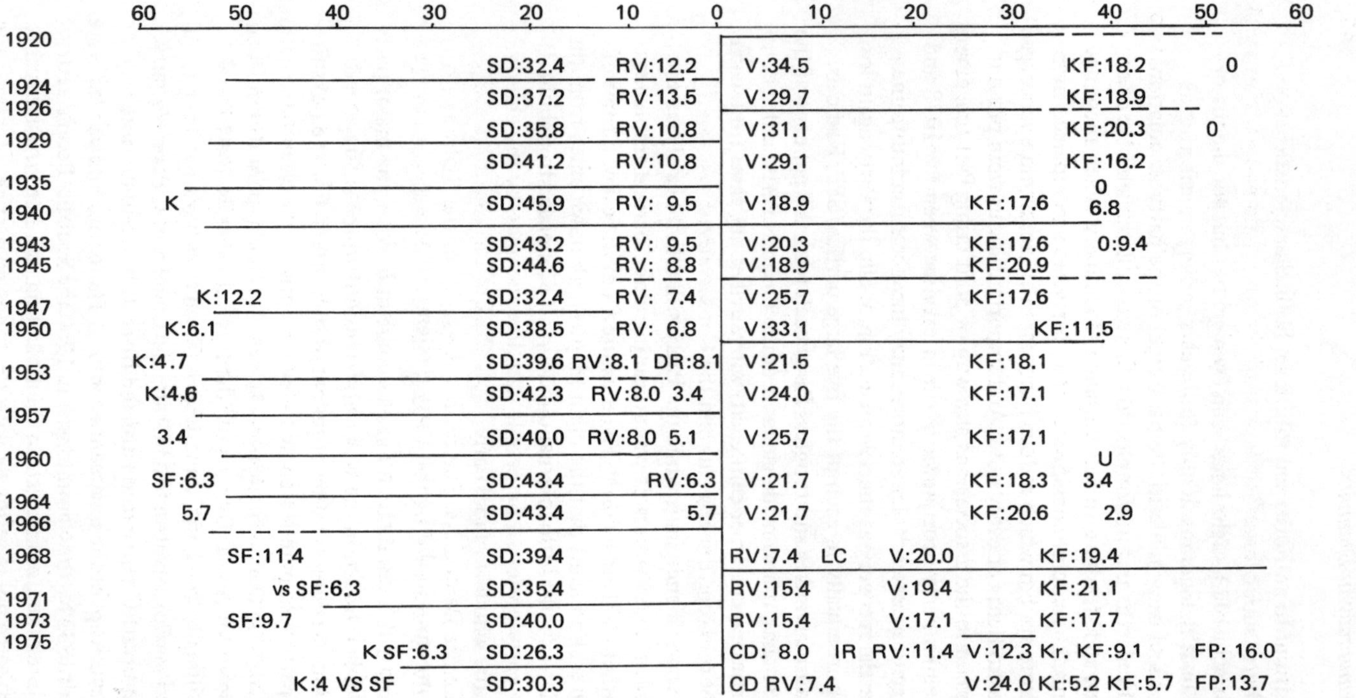

1920	SD:32.4	RV:12.2	V:34.5	KF:18.2 0
1924	SD:37.2	RV:13.5	V:29.7	KF:18.9 — —
1926	SD:35.8	RV:10.8	V:31.1	KF:20.3 0
1929	SD:41.2	RV:10.8	V:29.1	KF:16.2
1935	SD:45.9	RV: 9.5	V:18.9	K KF:17.6 0
1940				KF:17.6 6.8
1943	SD:43.2	RV: 9.5	V:20.3	KF:17.6 0:9.4
1945	SD:44.6	RV: 8.8	V:18.9	KF:20.9 — —
1947	SD:32.4	RV: 7.4	V:25.7	KF:17.6
1950	SD:38.5	RV: 6.8	V:33.1	KF:11.5
1953	SD:39.6	RV:8.1 DR:8.1	V:21.5	KF:18.1
1957	SD:42.3	RV:8.0 3.4	V:24.0	KF:17.1
1960	SD:40.0	RV:8.0 5.1	V:25.7	KF:17.1
1964	SD:43.4	RV:6.3	V:21.7	KF:18.3 3.4 U
1966	SD:43.4	5.7	V:21.7	KF:20.6 2.9
1968	SD:39.4	RV:7.4 LC	V:20.0	KF:19.4
1971	SD:35.4	RV:15.4	V:19.4	KF:21.1
1973	SD:40.0	RV:15.4	V:17.1	KF:17.7
1975	SD:30.3	CD RV:7.4	CD: 8.0 IR RV:11.4 Kr:12.3 Kr. KF:9.1 FP: 16.0	V:24.0 Kr:5.2 KF:5.7 FP:13.7

Left side values:
1935 K 3.4
1940 K:12.2
1943 K:6.1
1947 K:4.7
1950 K:4.6
1957 3.4
1960 SF:6.3
1964 5.7
1966 SF:11.4 vs SF:6.3
1968 SF:9.7 K:4 VS SF
1971 K SF:6.3
1973 K:4 VS SF

Parties:

K:	Communists	SD:	Social Democrats
VS:	Left Socialists	RV:	Radical Liberals
SF:	Socialist People's Party	DR:	Justice Party
CD:	Centre Democrats	Kr:	Christian People's Party
LC:	Liberal Centre	KF:	Conservative People's Party
V:	Liberals (Venstre)	FP:	Progress Party
O:	Others	U:	Independents' Party

Key: A solid line above a party indicates that it held Cabinet portfolios
A broken line above a party indicates that it gave the government popular majority support and/or minister solicitor opinions but

Thus from the 1920s to the 1960s the Danish party system was remarkably stable. SD was the largest of the four main parties from 1924 but never achieved a majority and always had to seek parliamentary support, usually from the Radical Liberals.

The task of carrying legislation through the Folketing is aided by two factors. First, the individual and collective responsibility of Ministers takes a negative form in the Constitution,[35] so that a government need not submit to a vote of confidence on its formation and has to resign only if there is a Folketing majority *against* it. Secondly, the majority of bills is passed by the Folketing unanimously or at least with the broad agreement of the major parties (until 1973 this meant the 'four old parties'). Bills are put forward only if they have a real chance of obtaining a majority or they are amended during the legislative process: controversial bills are dropped or amended usually at the committee stage.[36] In this way minority governments are able to act effectively and, because representation is highly proportional,[37] bills are guaranteed the support of an electoral majority and usually a large one. Small parties can gain Folketing seats fairly easily, the threshold being 2 per cent of the poll giving four seats in the 179-seat Folketing.[38]

Fifty years of stability was shaken drastically at the 1973 election, which added five new or previously unrepresented parties, backed by over one-third of the electorate, to the 'four old parties' plus the SPP. The Progress Party was particularly disruptive; with 28 seats second in size to SD; showing little internal cohesion; and opposed to taxation, defence expenditure and the 'paper-shuffling' activities of all bureaucrats. The other new parties were the Christian People's Party and the Centre Democrats. The former is a party of the Right and is particularly opposed to the 'permissive' aspects of Danish society. The latter is a group formed around Erhard Jakobsen, the well-known Mayor of Gladsaxe (a well-heeled suburb of Copenhagen) who broke with SD on the argument that house ownership was too heavily taxed. The Justice Party[39] and the Communists had their first electoral success for thirteen years and were represented in the Folketing with five and six seats respectively. A liberal government was formed with the backing of only 22 MFs, but it had the close support of the Christian People's Party and the Centre Democrats, the relatively close allegiance of the Conservatives and the Radical Liberals and some intermittent help from the Progress Party on its right (although this was not always welcomed) and from the Social Democrats on its left. Hopes of improving his party's parliamentary position led the Liberal Prime Minister Poul Hartling to the polls in January 1975. The outcome of that election indicated some polarisation around the Social Democrats and the Liberals. The Progress Party retained most of its support despite prior opinion polls indicating the contrary.[40] The main parties to suffer losses were the Radicals, the Conservatives and the Centre Democrats, partly as the price of their support for the Hartling Government: such a role is often risky, as the Justice Party had found in 1960 and again in 1975. The Conservatives were deeply divided about the party leadership and this added to their losses. The Centre Democrats could not maintain the salience of the house ownership issue to which they owed their origin and no longer presented a serious threat to SD. There were extensive but unsuccessful negotiations to form a government with majority or broad-based support and SD returned to office under Anker Jørgensen with the assurance that they would not be opposed by the Radical Liberals. The Government was later able to reach firm agreement on a programme of economic legislation supported by four other parties of the Centre-Right.[41]

The 1975 'September Agreement' brought some stability to economic policy, mainly on the basis of co-operation between the Social Democrats and the Liberals, the two largest parties in the Folketing. But this co-operation proved to be short-lived and the following August the Government preferred to rely on the smaller Centre-Right parties only. This support was put to the test in December 1976 when strikes of oil-delivery drivers brought the Government to the brink of a forced election. Liberal pressure for legal enforcement of wage agreements was resisted by the trade unions (LO) and support for the Government from the Conservatives achieved a bare majority for an interim freeze of prices, wages and rents until the expiry in March 1977 of the current agreement on these matters: the terms of the ensuing wage and price negotiations would be covered by the 1976 August Agreement. Negotiations on defence, housing, an energy tax and a job creation programme failed to gain parliamentary support for the government's policies and Anker Jørgensen called an election for February 1977. This restored SD to its pre-1973 position, once again supported by over one million voters. The Centre Democrats, Justice Party and Conservatives also gained while both the Liberals and the Radicals lost half their strength. This left the Progress Party second only to SD in size on a one per cent gain in votes. Anker Jørgensen's minority SD government continued in office, significantly strengthened and supported as before by the Centre Right parties.[42]

From the 1920s the 'four old parties' maintained fluid relationships, but generally the Radicals grouped with SD and, at least in opposition, the Liberals with the Conservatives. This constellation lasted until the mid-1960s when a two-bloc system emerged,[43] grouping SD with the SPP in a Socialist bloc and Radicals, Liberals and Conservatives in a 'bourgeois' bloc. This implied a breach with the long tradition that parliamentary support was sought from the Centre and it contributed to the far-reaching changes of the 1973 election. The nascent party system which began to coalesce in 1975 had a four-bloc structure: a Left-wing with 10 per cent of the 1977 votes included Communists, Left Socialists and the SPP; the Social Democrats were a force of their own with 37 per cent of the vote; a Centre-Right group was dominated by the Liberals and included the Radicals, the Conservatives, the Christian People's Party and the Centre Democrats, totalling 37.2 per cent of the votes; and the Progress Party occupied its own distinct position with 14.6 per cent of the poll. The allegiance of the Conservatives to the *Centre-Right* may be open to some question following rejection by most of the Party of a move towards bourgeois unity by a former Party leader.[44]

SD had been used to maintaining flexible relations with the other parties since the turn of the century and the new circumstances after 1973, although demanding imaginative tactics, were also not without precedents. The Party had worked with the Liberals in united opposition to the reactionary Right in the closing years of the century but were soon disappointed with the early Liberal Governments' favouring the landowning farmers over those of more humble means. There was common ground here with the Radicals: SD support of the Radical Government of 1913-20 gave SD first influence then a seat in the Cabinet. The first SD Government under Stauning relied on Radical support. This relationship continued until 1964. It was the basis of a major set of reforms in the 1930s covering social legislation, reform of the criminal law and disarmament. The SD-Radical coalition of the 1930s, led by Stauning and with a Radical Foreign Minister, proved to be long and fruitful: indeed, the golden age of Social-Liberal reform. The centrepiece was K.K. Steincke's Social Reform, which replaced all existing social legislation by four new Acts: the Social Security Act covering sickness, disablement and old age, the Unemployment Insurance Act, the Accident Insurance Act and the Public Care Act. Their implementation rested largely on the Kanslergade Agreement of 1933 between the two Government parties and the Liberals, one of the most extensive settlements in Danish politics. The two main points were a 10 per cent devaluation of the *krone* to strengthen agricultural exports and the continuation unchanged of wage agreements, as a concession to workers faced by a lockout of 100,000 or a reduction of wages by 20 per cent. The Agreement opened the way to broad acceptance of the social reforms. SD conceded state interference in industrial bargaining but gained a long period of industrial peace. The Agreement vindicated Stauning's efforts to reach broad agreement with other parties.

But there were limits to the extent of possible compromise. During the war-time occupation of the country in all-party government continued in office,[45] supplemented by Communists and others for six months during 1945, but this 'coalition of all' was split by internal differences on almost every issue.

The pattern of Radical support for SD Governments continued with reservations until Hans Hedtoft's premiership, 1947-50, but then the Party had to look elsewhere for support to reverse its traditional foreign policies of neutrality and disarmament. Although a Scandinavian defence agreement would have been preferable, this proved impossible to negotiate and the Government took the country into NATO with Norway, but with important reservations against the stationing of long-range rockets or nuclear weapons on Danish soil. The Radicals would not support such a move and the Government looked to the Liberals and its traditional enemy, the Conservatives, for support. This was readily given, in line with the long-standing Conservative interest in strong defence measures. The Hedtoft Government was followed by a Liberal-Conservative coalition from 1950-3, but SD gave limited co-operation in exchange for the new Government's willingness to carry through reform of the constitution. SD thus gained many of the changes which it had long worked for, including abolition of the *Landsting,* the upper house.

Although SD normally thought of the Conservatives (and often the Liberals, except on agricultural policy) as 'the opposition', co-operation with these 'bourgeois' parties was possible on several issues, and with the Radicals it remained close until 1966.

Co-operation and Factionalism on the Left

While co-operation with the 'bourgeois' parties was a tactical parliamentary necessity, relationships with parties of the Left had important strategic and ideological implications.

Until 1945 SD successfully asserted the claim to be the sole significant representatives of the labour movement. Their dominance and tactical flexibility in 1920 prevented the syndicalists from splitting the labour movement. But elements involved with the

unsuccessful 1919 general strike, including the 'Socialist Labour Party'
and some members of the SD Youth Association, formed the Left
Socialist Party of Denmark, changing its name to The Danish Communist
Party the following year. In 1923 most of the remaining syndicalists
also merged with the Communists. During their early years the
Communists were weakened by factionalism and made little impression,
some of their Right wing joining SD in 1930.[46] From 1932 the
Communist Chairman was Aksel Larsen, one of the first two
Communist MFs elected that year, and he remained a leading member
until breaking from the Party in 1958. He was a constant and vigorous
critic of any discrepancy he saw between Marxist theory and Social
Democratic practice. During the war-time occupation the Communists
were outlawed but they played a significant part in the resistance
movement and reaped the benefits of this in the 1945 election. From
1943 they had worked for a popular front with SD, but SD suspicion
remained strong: their response was that the Communists could always
join the Party provided they also accepted the principles of democracy
without reservation, a condition they were unwilling to meet.[47]

As can be seen from Figure 3, the Communists made substantial
gains in the 1945 election, partly for reasons already discussed and
partly as a result of popular confusion over the implications of the
amalgamation discussions. But SD was able to regain much of this
ground two years later helped by events in Central Europe. The
Communist vote dwindled further over the ensuing decade.
De-Stalinisation had an important effect in Denmark, however: Aksel
Larsen was among the leading revisionists, arguing for a middle way
between a slavishly pro-Soviet line and a Social Democracy which had
lost sight of Socialism.[48] As a result he was expelled from the
Communist Party and formed the Socialist People's Party. The Social
Democrats hoped that this fission on the Left would reduce their
problems of boundary maintainance. But the 1960 election saw a swing
to the Left, with some SD gains but also with the new party firmly
established in the Folketing with eleven seats, more than the
Communists had ever had except in 1945. The SPP had clearly
succeeded where the Communists had failed as a real alternative to SD
on the left.

Recent analysis of the parties' voting records in the Folketing over
the period 1953-73[49] shows that, taking all issues together, the parties
can be ranged on a spectrum with the Communists and the SPP at one
extreme and the Conservatives at the other, with the Liberals (Venstre)
quite close to them. Until 1966 SD occupied the centre ground, with

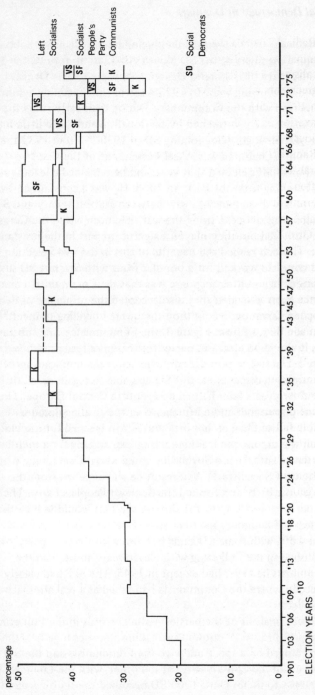

Figure 3. The Danish Social Democratic Party and the left: shares of votes of socialist parties at Folketing elections, 1901-75

the Radical Liberals taking a marginally more radical position. Examination of policy areas indicates that the main source of this radicalism was the Radical Liberals' refusal to accept NATO and their disagreements with SD over foreign policy, especially during 1953-7.[50]

In 1966-8 SD and SPP moved much closer to each other especially on taxation and labour market policy. On these issues there had previously been a three-bloc cleavage dominated by centre-orientated SD/Radical/Justice Party governments, while the SPP joined the Liberals and Conservatives in opposing Governmental intentions to raise taxation. A similar bourgeois/Communist alliance in 1953-7 opposed Government wage policies. The 1966 election brought the first ever Socialist majority and, despite past tensions between the two parties, Jens Otto Krag, as SD Prime Minister, opened negotiations between them. These did not reach a common basis for a Government programme, however, partly because of differences over tax and housing policies but mainly because SD would not agree to changes in defence and foreign policy including the relationships with EFTA and the European Communities. In the subsequent Folketing debate the claim was made that, while the Socialist majority in the Folketing would be used, it would be used to put through SD policy and not one jot more. more.[51] The two parties did agree on the introduction of value-added tax and the taxation of incomes at source. They also agreed to work more closely on other matters and set up a contact committee which became popularly known as 'the red cabinet'. Threatened with the possible fall of the Government, the SPP also voted for the budget with its military expenditure, having previously abstained on such votes in accordance with their neutral and anti-military ideology.

There were two consequences of the SD/SPP co-operation: the 'bourgeois' parties were encouraged in their efforts to form the 1968-71 Radical/Liberal/Conservative Government; and the SPP was split between a Right wing in favour of co-operation (with its main strength in the parliamentary group) and a predominantly Left wing based in the Party organisation.[52] The conflict deepened, the Government found itself in a minority in December 1967 on legislation consequential to the devaluation of the *krone,* and there followed a general election at which the newly formed Left Socialists won four seats, having broken away from the SPP immediately after the fateful Folketing vote.

The 'bourgeois' government which followed lasted almost a full four-year term. The 1971 election again brought a very narrow majority for SD and SPP together. But this time the latter were wary of direct co-operation and insisted on changes in the minority SD Government's economic policy as the price of assistance. Jens Otto Krag now had Danish membership of the European Communities as a primary objective, however, and he could rely on support from the 'bourgeois' parties to keep him in office until this was achieved: the Liberals and the Conservatives were especially keen on membership (for agricultural and industrial reasons respectively) and the 1968-71 Baunsgaard Government had reopened negotiations with the Six together with Britain.

The legislation to affiliate to the Communities was passed on 8 September 1971 by 141 votes to 34, with two abstentions and two absentees. Apart from all 17 SPP members, the opposition came from 12 Social Democrats, four Radicals and one Greenlander. The abstainers were the two Færø representatives, one a Social Democrat and the other a member of the Færø People's Party.

The parliamentary vote for Denmark's joining the EC was over four to one in favour but the constitution requires a five-sixths majority,[53] failing which the proposal goes to a referendum. The Danish referendum was thus mandatory, in contrast to the merely consultative Norwegian vote. The Norwegian vote against entry rather strengthened Danish opposition, which rested mainly on fears for the loss of national and cultural identity and for the future of the Danish form of Social Democracy and the welfare state. On the other hand, the economic arguments pointed strongly towards entry: the terms of entry were almost ideal for Denmark, since at last her two largest trading partners, West Germany and Britain, would be within the same economic grouping. On 1970 figures the enlarged Common Market would account for 47 per cent of her imports and 42.1 per cent of exports. Exports to these trading partners had been growing at about 5 per cent annually over the previous eight years, but imports had been growing faster, resulting in an increasingly serious balance of payments deficit. An economic counter-argument lay in the rapidly growing trade with Norway and Sweden: indeed, Sweden had replaced Britain as Denmark's largest export customer, with West Germany as her largest supplier.

The referendum was held on 2 October 1972 and 90.1 per cent of the electorate voted, 63.3 per cent of voters voting Yes and 36.7 per cent voting No, a decisive majority in favour of joining. Almost as soon as the result was released, Jens Otto Krag made the surprise announcement of his retirement from public life, and he was replaced by Anker Jørgensen.

The trade union movement as a whole had favoured joining the EC, voting 525 for, 406 against, with 38 abstentions, in April 1972, but the

General and Semi-skilled Workers Union (DASF)[54] had been prominent in opposing entry. The new Prime Minister had voted with the trade union majority but against most members of his own union in supporting the Government's European policy. Beyond this, his views on international affairs were little known when he came to office.

On domestic economic policy Jørgensen's position was towards the left of the Party, but the SPP, on whose support he relied on economic issues, was suspicious of his position on Europe. At the same time his views on capital gains tax, redistribution of wealth and economic democracy risked antagonising the pro-EC parties in the 'bourgeois' bloc. The new Government had to steer a difficult course between these two limitations. But ultimately its fall was due to a split within the Party. Led by Erhard Jakobsen, some members of the parliamentary party were increasingly convinced that Anker Jørgensen's leadership was taking the Party too far to the Left, that it was excessively dependent on the SPP, and that the Government's policies of high taxation would bring electoral disaster. On 6 November 1973 Jakobsen resigned from the Party over the proposal to increase the taxation paid by house owners. Although promising continued conditional support for the Government, he was not in the Folketing two days later for a crucial division on income tax changes: as a result there was a tied vote and the proposals failed, and the government called the 1973 election.

As a new Prime Minister Anker Jørgensen faced a variety of difficulties. His relatively brief parliamentary experience of only eight years and his complete lack of cabinet experience encouraged him sometimes to comment publicly with more forthrightness than forethought. It was also suggested that he was too ready to consult former trade union colleagues before he consulted the cabinet. But his stand on the EC showed that he could hold to his opinions against opposition. His election as leader was not opposed either in the parliamentary group or at the Party Congress:[55] criticisms all came from the press and from the lower levels of the party. In fact he did much to reunite the party after its divisions over the EC. He deserves much credit for his leadership and for generating an appearance of stability after the turmoil following the 1973 election. When the Party returned to Government in February 1975, agreements to pass legislation were reached with other parties, the Folketing worked, and labour market disputes were settled. The election of a trade unionist (Jørgensen) in succession to an academic (Krag) did not at once change the Party's relationship with the unions, but the usual good relationships were maintained despite the Government's need to rely on the 'bourgeois' parties for parliamentary support, and despite the increased tendency of Communist, Left Socialist and SPP trade unionists to pursue a much harder line against the Government's policies, in the Seamen's Union for example. In this situation Anker Jørgensen encouraged the SD trade unionists to emphasise views which might perhaps have been taken for granted before. He was helped in these efforts to return his party to its roots through his childhood in working-class Copenhagen and his trade union career.

Ideology

Danish social democracy is the intellectual descendant of Ferdinand Lassalle and Eduard Bernstein. The Party followed the German debate at the turn of the century with interest but its influence on the party's ideology was tempered by the long Danish tradition of peaceful change: the reformation in 1536, constitutionalism in 1849 and parliamentarism in 1901 were all achieved without bloodshed. Although the movement was considered in its early days to be revolutionary by its opponents, Pio and others argued that workers could gain much from universal suffrage, from an active labour party which could exert influence in parliament and from practical reforms. The early emphasis was not on Marxist collectivism but on mutualism: workers should establish producers' associations which would outcompete Capitalism, especially when universal suffrage gave workers the power to use state credits for their finance. The impact of such ideas is reflected in the limited extent of nationalisation in Denmark. The depression of the 1930s brought less hardship to Denmark than to other countries and economic decisions were made on the basis of a pragmatic rather than an ideological approach to current problems.[56]

Although the Social Democratic Party is based firmly on the working class, it has never seen itself as a narrow class party but has always sought to represent the disadvantaged throughout society. Its concept of Socialism has therefore been a society which itself controlled the means of production and in which the state acted in the interests of the whole society. A parliamentary majority would allow real social reforms and an end to the worst consequences of capitalism, including unemployment and economic crises, to the benefit not only of labour but of smallholders, small tradesmen and the poor generally.

Pio made contact with Marx[57] but the moderate statist Socialism of Lassalle remained strong for the first ten or fifteen years and the trade union movement took on a role subsidiary to the Party's parliamentary activities. Only during the last years of the century did the Party find an interpreter for Marx's ideas. Gustav Bang[58] joined *'Social-Demokraten'* in 1896 and contributed weekly articles setting out Kautsky's presentation of Marxism. While Kautsky's views were adopted as a theoretical basis, the Party in practice took a pragmatic line and was more often in agreement with Bernstein. Bang's contribution was taken up mainly by Left-wing opponents of the Party and his influence within the Party did not last.[59]

In an extensive analysis of the importance of revisionism for the ideological development of SD from the 1890s to the 1930s,[60] Lise Togeby considers that Bernstein's most important contribution was to have formed the theoretical background for a tactical alternative to orthodox Marxism. She concludes that in a narrow sense, revisionism had practically no relevance to the Danish party.[61] But if a broader definition is taken, giving less weight to the specific influence of the *German* revisionist movement and to Bernstein himself and instead emphasising reformism, willingness to redefine goals in the light of developing circumstances as perceived from a Danish viewpoint, and rejection of dialectical class struggle leading to revolution, then it is clear that Danish Social Democracy has been revisionist from its origins. The Party's reactions in periods of crisis repeatedly illustrated its view that industrial peace rather than confrontation with Capitalism would best serve the interests of workers and of society as a whole.[62]

Party Programmes

The Party's first programme of 1876 is known as the 'Gimle Programme'[63] and is substantially derived from the 1875 Gotha Programme of the newly amalgamated Socialist Workers' Party of Germany. This was superseded by a 'Declaration of Principles' in 1913 incorporating the extensive ideological developments of the intervening years. These were symbolised by the 1910 Copenhagen Congress of the Second International, attended by Jaurès, Keir Hardie, Lenin and Trotsky. The Danish party now had 43,000 members and close on 100,000 voters and could claim to be the sole party of the proletariat in Denmark.

The 1913 Principles were not rewritten until 1961 but were reinterpreted in 1945 when the young future Prime Minister and party leader Jens Otto Krag was charged with producing a programme suitable for the post-war years entitled 'Denmark of the Future'.[64] Building on a radical Marxist analysis of the failure of monopoly Capitalism to solve the problems of the inter-war years, the programme pointed to recurrent crises resulting from unequal distribution of income and wealth and the consequent inability of consumption to keep pace with production. The immediate priority was therefore to modernise production methods, including a system of works councils, industrial councils and a national socio-economic council as the basis of economic democracy and the Socialisation of industry. There would be greater state control of finance, banking and insurance through a few state and co-operative units. Speculation would be removed from housebuilding and larger pieces of agricultural land would be divided up when offered for sale. A land tax would bring all land into social ownership within sixty years. Several medium-term demands included constitutional reform, with the abolition of the upper house (the *landsting*) and the voting age reduced from twenty-five to twenty-one; improvements in arbitration of industrial disputes; improved pensions for the elderly, invalids, accidents and illness; and possibly a free health service.

The Party's preoccupation with Socialisation of industry after the First World War was seen in 1944 as no longer central, and *'Denmark of the Future'* set out to achieve three main aims: full employment, social security and effective, democratic industry. Underlying the whole programme was fear of a post-war depression and realisation that labour shortages in the belligerent countries might produce a rationalised industrial structure with which Denmark would have to compete, relying only on its people's initiative and ability: hence the need for workers to have greater influence on the conduct of their workplace. Much of the inspiration for the programme derived from the writings of Keynes, the Swedes Gunnar Myrdal and Per Albin Hansson, and Beveridge's Social Liberalism. The programme played an important part in the 1945 election. It was well received by the Party Congress but was too detailed (and perhaps too radical) for Party activists in the country, and was overinfluenced by the controls necessary in a war-time economy. It gave hostages which opponents were not slow to use, and the Party lost votes heavily. Nevertheless many of its aims were achieved in the 1950s and 1960s. Writing in 1954, Anker Jørgensen considered that the post-war losses were mainly attributable to the Party's participation in the war-time Government.[65]

In 1961 the Declaration of Principles was re-written in more moderate language.[66] Nationalisation, for example, was given a lower priority and was seen as only one means for the defence of community interests, and then not the only one or necessarily the best. The main emphasis was on achievements gained or in prospect, and the goals were stated in concrete, short-run terms.

Not surprisingly, then, within fifteen years there was a call for a new programme of principles: *'Solidarity, Equality and Human Welfare'*[67] was a significant change in emphasis from the more traditional slogan 'liberty, equality and fraternity'. Concerned at the Party's severe loss of popular support,[68] the 1973 Party Congress resolved on a new manifesto to be drafted for the 1977 Congress, to reinterpret the Party's principles and their application to the new problems and the rapid social changes of the 1970s and 1980s. The procedure chosen was novel: the draft was put out to public debate in the hope that such openness would provide a unique opportunity to discuss basic social problems and attract contributions from the many people, including Social Democrats, who saw the need for change. In his introduction to the draft programme Anker Jørgensen justifies this approach with the view that 'Socialism is in fact democracy carried to its logical conclusion'.[69] In other words the Party's aims remained unchanged but the means it would employ to achieve them must be adapted to the new conditions (the programme itself lists nineteen of these) which no longer make it possible to believe, as the Party did in its earlier days, in 'capitalism with a human face'.[70]

In launching the draft programme it was emphasised that there was no intention to introduce nationalisation or to direct industry in detail, and businesses would have to operate in the market economy. But there must be broad overall control. Any attempts at co-ordination with other SD parties were directed more to fraternal parties elsewhere in Scandinavia than southward to Germany. The emphasis on equality in the programme derived especially from the work of the Party's Commission on Equality (inspired directly by the Swedish precedent) which reported shortly before the 1973 Congress, for example.[71]

Some critics of the draft pointed to internal inconsistencies.[72] There was a greater emphasis than before on common ownership of the means of production and on a class analysis of social problems, illustrated by the omission in 1975 of the two italicised words from the following section of the 1961 programme: 'The capitalist society's inequality and *the* uncontrolled exercise of economic power is the real danger threatening a *free* society.' But it was also argued that there was a lack of clarity between ultimate goals, transitional means and current demands. The opening statement that the ultimate goal is the common ownership of the means of production is unqualified, but the text concludes with a demand for the right of collective part-ownership for all wage-earners: was this to be jointly with Capitalists? This seemed to be the intention, since collective ownership appeared only to mean that a 'joint fund should secure investment capital and support democratic control of the application of investment'. Could this be reconciled with demands for public control of 'national energy sources, energy supply and development of new forms of energy; use of land; credit and insurance and other private economic power concentrations, including the activities of multi-national companies'? All of these points had long been included in Party manifestos, but they presupposed arrangements very different from the right of collective part-ownership for all wage-earners.

Again, 'differences in wages and capital should be levelled out to ensure that market forces are a socially just reflection of the requirements of all consumers'. But it is hard to envisage a Marxist view of 'socially just market forces'. If a full development of economic democracy, in the sense of the common ownership of the means of production, means that all production and distribution takes place by democratic decision, there will no longer be a market and so no longer market forces to be subjected to social justice.

Industry would consist of jointly owned and locally administered concerns, but direct state ownership might be necessary where there were strong concentrations of private economic power as in banking and insurance. It was not clear, however, how private economic power might exist in a society without private ownership of the means of production, except (in this instance) through an unlikely dictatorship of bank clerks and insurance agents.

It was both logical and in conformity with Marxist theory to argue that interim measures, including economic democracy, participation in decisions at work, and later joint ownership in a form of market economy were no more than instruments against the power of Capitalism and a means of guiding the direction of social investment. But if the ultimate goal was obscured, the only viable alternative to subjugation by market forces or bureaucracy was also lost.

In reply to such criticisms it was said[73] that no fully explained model of the democratic socialist society existed, nor was there an unambiguous form for a problem-free social economy. The Party's aim was a society which could lay down firm lines, by democratic decision, for its industrial development, with the rights of ownership of the means of production held in common. Democratisation of the economy would be achieved partly by limiting the rights accompanying ownership of capital, and in the long run by winding up the independent powers of capital as a power factor by spreading rights of ownership to all. The introduction of this economic democracy would, however, be a gradual transfer of rights of ownership in the great industries to the collectivity of wage-earners: once a majority shareholding was achieved the influence of the private shareholder would be reduced to that of a bond-holder or a depositor in a bank. Capital for investment would be obtained primarily from collective savings and allocated through a banking system under direct social control. But there was no reason to believe that the detailed distribution of consumer goods could be better ordered than through the consumer's genuinely free choice between goods of various price and quality.

The programme recognised that the 'post-war era' characterised by growth expectations and a consumer orientation had ended. The extent and form of the social services and education, for example, could not any longer be determined by market forces. The tendency of society to respond passively to increasing demands in these fields faced obvious limits, not the least of these being public reaction against collective consumption and high taxation. But the underlying problem was seen as an inability in the past to prevent the social and health costs which arose from Capitalist production methods, so that society had to resort to expensive patchwork repairs. The solution was not to make panic cuts in public services but to demand production methods which reduced the need for social intervention.

As a whole the programme was revolutionary in comparison with its 1961 predecessor, and at some points it conformed more closely to Marxist thought than even the Gimle Programme of 1876. It certainly made serious attempts to come to grips with a post-industrial society and with a world of scarce resources unevenly distributed between individuals, regions and continents. But the test must be whether its ideas and its relevance attract sufficient voters to the Party to give it the opportunities in the last quarter of the twentieth century which it has had in the past to put its ideas into practice.

Power Within the Party

The Party's many years in Government have ensured that leadership is exercised predominantly from the top, a tradition firmly established by Stauning in the inter-war period. Of all the parties, SD had the reputation of maintaining the tightest discipline, and the Party's Folketing group had a notable record of cohesion.[74] But the deliberate decision in 1969 to open the Party to initiatives from associations (*foreninger* or branches) did much to lower the centre of gravity of the Party. For example, Folketing candidates are nominated annually in each constituency. The candidate at the previous election is normally deemed to be standing, but another candidate may be nominated by any twenty-five members of the association.[75] One result has been that factionalism has become more evident than before Anker Jørgensen's accession to the leadership. For example, in the parliamentary group Jørgensen himself stands rather to the Left[76] and with a small group of about six colleagues forms the centre of gravity of the Party. From there he can rely on support from the middle (the position occupied by Krag) and the Left wing, whose strength tends to lie in its ability to veto a proposed compromise or agreement with another party if it should wish to do so. The Right wing, with Per Hækkerup as a leading figure, cannot always be relied on to carry the rest of the party with it in negotiations,[77] and has clearly been weakened by losses to the Centre Democrats as well as by the change of leadership. But despite the renewed emphasis on links with trade unionism, the Party has not succeeded in carrying through its policy of economic democracy, put forward in a group of Bills in January 1973 which had three main aims:

1. to ensure employees a reasonable share of the future capital growth of the Danish economy;
2. to strengthen the right of co-determination exercised by employees in the management of the concern to which they are attached;
3. to contribute to future capital formation and so establish a better basis for full employment, a rising standard of living and social progress.

These aims were to be achieved through an 'Employees' Investment and Dividend Fund', to which all employers, whether public or private, would contribute a percentage of their total bill for wages and salaries, from 0.5 per cent in 1974 rising by 0.5 per cent annually to 5.0 per cent in 1983. This proposal was extensively debated in the Folketing and outside,[78] but its implication of further deductions from heavily taxed incomes probably contributed to the Party's electoral losses in 1973. By 1976 a modified proposal, that wage-earners should have an obligatory share in the surplus of a business, was included in a package of measures to limit inflation, reduce taxation and public expenditure and increase employment, with the promise of broadly based co-operation on industrial policy. It may be noted, however, that the term used was 'right of joint-ownership' rather than 'economic democracy' as such.[79]

The Danish Social Democratic Party has always had to live with parliamentary limitations and has had to rely on co-operation and compromise, usually with parties of the Centre, to carry through its measures. Yet its influence in forming the social-liberal character of Danish society as it developed from the 1920s to the 1970s has been decisive. Its electoral strength reached a peak in the late 1930s and its membership has declined (in common with that of other Danish parties) since 1949. But it has responded with organisational and programmatic renewal to the social differentiation of the post-industrial era. It has retained its position as the leading political expression of the working-class, but has had to compete increasingly with growing Socialist diversity to its left. And it has recently been able to act as an element of stability in a party system which has had to accommodate a confusion of populist currents. It is still true to say that in Denmark one can not govern without Social Democracy.

Notes

1. The 1935 election was fought by the Social Democrats under the slogan 'Stauning or chaos' and they won by an unsurpassed plurality.
2. In 1964, 1,103,667 votes were cast for the Party, more than ever before or since. But as a proportion of the votes cast, the peak was reached in 1935 at 46.1 per cent, compared to 41.9 per cent in 1964. From 1929 until the 1945 election the Party's proportion of votes was never less than 41.8 per cent, whereas it subsequently only exceeded 40 per cent in 1960 and 1964. It was the 1935 result in particular which encouraged the hope of an absolute parliamentary majority, when 46.1 per cent of Folketing seats were gained, but this was never bettered. The following year the Social Democrats also became the largest party in the Landsting (the upper house) with 32 seats out of 76, and with its Radical Liberal partners the Government had a majority there for the first time. See Figure 1 for the Social Democratic votes as a percentage of all votes cast, 1884-1975.
3. Brix's work is assessed by Jens Engberg in *'Harald Brix. Revolutionen og Reformen'* (København, SFAH, 1975).
4. The new name took effect in 1874. From its origins as a near-sectarian paper for Party members the paper was transformed to present a broad appeal by Emil Wiinblad when he took over as editor in 1881. By the 1950s the Party's press was making increasing losses and *'Social-Demokraten'* was renamed *'Aktuelt'* in 1959.
5. Originally the Party had been called the Social Democratic Labour Party but in 1878 it became the Social Democratic Association, *Det socialdemokratiske Forbund*. In 1965 the name was changed again to Social Democracy in Denmark, *Socialdemokratiet i Danmark*. The Party's organisational development in its 'breakthrough' years is extensively analysed by Jesper Jarmbæk, *'Reorganisering af SD. Socialdemokratisk forbund, 1878-1890'* (København, 1972, dissertation).
6. Anthony Carew, 'Democracy and Government in European Trade Unions' (London, Allen and Unwin, 1976) provides a comparative account of European bargaining arrangements.

262   *Social Democracy in Denmark*

7. *Travl tid, god tid* (København, Gyldendal, 1974), p. 23.
8. See, for example, para.2 s.3 of the Party's rules, *Love for socialdemokratiet vedtaget på partiets kongres september 1973.*
9. Since the 1849 Constitution the Folketing has been directly elected in single-member constituencies by all men of thirty and over without a criminal record, except paupers and servants without their own household. Candidates had to be over twenty-five. While the introduction of universal manhood suffrage was fairly general in Europe in about 1849, Denmark maintained an open public vote much longer than elsewhere. In France, for example, secret voting came in 1875, although not strictly enforced until 1913. By European standards the Danish suffrage was one of the most liberal, enfranchising about 73 per cent of men over thirty, a proportion which increased until in practice all men had the vote from 1901 and all women from 1918. Povl Engelstoft and Franz Wilhelm Wendt, *Haandbog i Danmarks Politiske Historie 1814-1933* (København, Gyldendal, 1964), p. 96. For interesting comparisons with other Scandinavian countries see Stein Kuhnle, *Patterns of Social and Political Mobilisation: a Historical Analysis of the Nordic Countries* (Sage, 1975).
10. 'Mass suffrage, secret voting and political participation', *European Journal of Sociology*, vol. II (1961), pp. 132-52.
11. These associations are the basic units of party organisation.
    There were 109 in 1890, with about 14,000 members

239	"	1896	"	"	23,000	"
210	"	1901	"	"	30,000	"
110	"	1903	"	"	22,000	"
361	"	1915				
869	"	1919	"	"	110,000	"

    Source: O. Bertolt, E. Christiansen and P. Hansen, *En bygning vi rejser. Den politiske arbejderbevægelses historie i Danmark* (København, Fremad, 1954-55), vols. I and II, *passim.*
12. Sources: party membership, 1890-1920 – Bertolt *et al., loc. cit.;* 1924-43 – *Socialdemokratiet, Årsberetninger* for each year; 1944-74 – personal communication from SD Party headquarters, *'Medlemsudviklingen* 1944-74'. Votes – T.T. Mackie and R. Rose, *The International Almanac of Electoral History* (London, Macmillan, 1974) and *Statistiske Meddelelser 1975:7, 'Folketingsvalget den 9. januar 1975'* (København, Danmarks Statistik, 1975), pp. 62-3. Table 2 (following these notes) shows the Party's membership figures, 1924-74.
13. The Party's youth wing (*Socialdemokratisk Ungdoms Forbund,* SUF, started in 1906), normally more radical than the main party, supported this decision with the view that 'We think that even this sacrifice, a Minister in a bourgeois government, can be fully defensible if it means sparing the lives of thousands of young Danish men'. (*Fremad,* 14 Oct. 1916.)
14. An extensive account of the 1920 Easter government crisis is given by Tage Kaarsted, *Påskekrisen 1920* (Aarhus, Universitetsforlaget, for *Jysk Selskab for Historie,* 1968).
15. An account sympathetic to the syndicalist movement is in Lisa Bang *et al., Fagoppositionens sammenslutning (1910-21): de danske syndikalister* (Aarhus, Modtryk, 1975).
16. Party membership is illustrated in Figure 1. Figures for each year from 1924-64 are published in the Party's annual report (*årsberetning*) and are available in *Arbejderbevægelsens Bibliotek og Arkiv* in Copenhagen. The figures are directly related to audited membership income and appear to be substantially reliable, with only very few Party associations neglecting to

submit figures in any year and no incentive to inflate the number of members since this would also require payment. Trade unions are organised separately and so the notoriously inflated figures of the British Labour Party are avoided. Palle Svensson's analysis in Eastonian terms of 'Support for the Danish Social Democratic Party 1924-39 – Growth and Response', *Scandinavian Political Studies,* 9 (1974), pp. 127-46, is largely based on these figures and offers useful comment.
17. Mogens Nielsen, *Enhed i arbejderbevægelsen. Kilder til belysning af forhandlinger mellem Danmarks kommunistiske Parti og Socialdemokratiet 1945* (København, Fremad, 1973) offers readings to illustrate these negotiations.
18. By way of comparison, figures for Party membership of the Liberal Party (*Venstre*) show that both they and SD rely on well-defined social groups (farmers and proletariat) for support. With wider fluctuations in electoral support but a fairly clear downward trend over the twentieth century, Liberal Party membership declined from 9.33 per cent of the electorate in 1931 to 5.96 per cent in 1940, rising after 1945 to 8.18 per cent in 1949. From there it has fallen steadily but more slowly than in the SD case to 3.26 per cent in 1974. (Cf. SD: 1931, 9.7 per cent; 1940, 9.6 per cent; 1949, 12.1 per cent; 1974, 3.5 per cent.) The Liberals declined seriously in the 1930s and recovered less after 1945, but the two parties had very similar numbers of members in 1974. The proportion of voters who were party members was similar. In the Liberal Party it was 40 per cent ±6 per cent from 1930 to 1957, falling from 38 per cent in 1960 to 15.9 per cent in 1974. The SD figure was between 25 per cent and 30 per cent during 1930-44, rose to 39.9 per cent in 1946 and then fell steadily to 14.1 per cent in 1972 before picking up again slightly in 1973-4. Thus the Liberals had a consistently higher ratio in the 1930s, but in both cases the decline in membership ratios began in the early 1950s and reached similar low points of 14-15 per cent in 1974. Sources: Social Democrats – *Medlemsudvikling,* op cit. Liberals – *Organisations-meddelelser* and *Medlemsopgørelser* for 1930-75, kindly supplied by the Party's headquarters office.
19. Listed in *Årsberetninger* as *'frikort'* until 1949 and then as *rentemodtagere.*
20. Full accounts of the 1966 election and its aftermath are given by K.S. Pedersen, 'The first socialist majority: Denmark's 1966 election', *Parliamentary Affairs,* vol. 20, no. 2 (1967), pp. 144-57; Jan Stehouwer and Ole Borre, 'Four general elections in Denmark, 1960-68', *Scandinavian Political Studies* vol. 4 (1969), pp. 133-50; Curt Sørensen, 'Denmark: politics since 1964', *Scandinavian Political Studies* vol. 2 (1967), pp. 263-5; Lars Bille, *S-SF: kilder til belysning af forholdet mellem Socialdemokratiet og Socialistisk Folkeparti 1959-73* (København, Gyldendal, 1974); and Vagn Oluf Nielsen, *Danmarks første arbejderflertal: kilder til belysning af det parlamentariske samarbejde mellem Socialdemokratiet og Socialistisk Folkeparti 1966-67* (København, Fremad, 1974).
21. Kaare Svalastoga, *Prestige, Class and Mobility* (København, Gyldendal, 1959), p. 265. (Figures recalculated to show sources of support for each party.)
22. Conducted by Gallup Markedsanalyse A/S in February 1968 and published in Alastair H. Thomas, *Parliamentary Parties in Denmark 1945-1972* (Glasgow, University of Strathclyde Survey Research Centre Occasional Paper No. 13, 1973), p. 62. This groups replies in Svalastoga's stratum I as Social Group III, strata II and III as Social Group II and strata IV and V as Social Group I, so that direct comparisons are not possible. But the 1968 figure for strata IV and V is 85.1 per cent compared with 83.7 per cent in 1954; for strata II and III, 14.3 per cent compared with 15.9 per cent in 1954; and in stratum I,

0.6 per cent compared with 0.3 per cent.

23. Jørgen Albæk Jensen, *En undersøgelse af danske partiers sociale struktur,* (unpublished thesis, København, Institut for Samtidshistorie og Statskundskab, 1972) finds the party's electoral support to be drawn 13.6 per cent from strata I and II, 18.5 per cent from stratum III, 29.6 per cent from stratum IV and 38.3 per cent from stratum V.

24. Based on data from *Vælgernes veje* (København, Børsen, 1974) and Ole Borre, *Recent Trends in Danish Voting Behaviour* (Århus, Institute for Political Science, May 1975, draft). 'Left-wing parties' here are the Socialist People's Party, the Communists and the Left Socialists. 'Minor Centre/Right parties' are the Radical Liberals, the Justice Party, the Centre Democrats, the Christian People's Party and the Conservative People's Party.

25. The current Danish education system provided for a nine-year general school with a voluntary tenth year. The starting age has long been seven.

26. Svalastoga, *Prestige, Class and Mobility.* Thus the party has retained its social structure over the twenty years since Svalastoga's surveys.

27. Torben Worre, 'Partistabilitet og vælgervandring ved valgene i 1971 og 1973' in Ole Borre, Hans Jørgen Nielsen, Steen Sauerberg and Torben Worre, *Vælgerskreddet 1971-73: arbejdspapirer fra en interviewundersøgelse* (København, n.d.) pp. 7-8.

28. That this applies to all the parties is confirmed by the fact that only about 7 per cent of the Danish population belongs to political associations, the ratio of men to women who are prepared to join being about 2:3. *Levevilkår i Danmark* (København, *Danmarks Statistik* and Socialforskningsinstituttet) 1976.

29. Torben Worre, 'Partistabilitet og vælgervandringer' in Ole Borre, Hans Jørgen Nielsen, Steen Sauerberg and Torben Worre, *Vælgere i 70'erne: resultater fra interviewundersøgelser ved folketingsvalgene i 1971, 1973 og 1975* (København, Akademisk Forlag, 1976) puts forward much evidence in support of these hypotheses, showing (pp.31-3) for example that farmers and workers have high proportions of 'core-voters' by comparison with other social groups:

Voting stability of occupational groups. 1971. Percentages vertically.

	Farmers	Workers	Higher salaried employees	Lower salaried employees	Economically independent
Core voters	83	74	75	66	64
Party changers	11	15	20	21	26
Non-voters	6	11	5	13	10
Reasons for party choice					
long-term	39	47	18	24	23
short-term	25	34	45	45	43
Strength of party attitude					
Strong attachment	33	30	21	19	20
Weak attachment	36	29	26	25	31
Has party preference	28	30	41	43	34
No party preference	3	11	12	13	15

30. Hans Jørgen Nielsen, *The Un-civic Culture: Attitudes Towards the Political System and Vote for the Danish Progress Party 1973-75* (University of Copenhagen, Institute for Political Studies, Forskningsrapport 1976/2).

31. Søren Hansen, organisation secretary of the SD party, interviewed 13 Apr. 1976.

32. Borre *et al.*, (1976) op.cit. p.23.
33. *loc. cit.* p. 83.
34. S.M. Lipset and Stein Rokkan, *Party Systems and Voter Alignments: Cross-National Perspectives* (International Yearbook of Political Behaviour Research No. 7, New York, Free Press, 1967).
35. *Danmarks Riges Grundlov af 5. juni 1953*, para. 15. For commentary see Max Sørensen, *'Statsforfatningsret'* (København, Juristforbundets Forlag, 1969) pp. 116-21. The practice originated in 1901 with the adoption of the parliamentary principle. It was recognised in the King's statement on 4 Mar. 1919 that 'As a result of my deliberations I declare that I shall not appoint a government not acceptable to the majority of the Folketing.' See Tage Kaarsted, *Paskekrisen 1920* (Århus, Universitetsforlaget, 1969), ch.1.
36. Mogens N. Pedersen, 'Consensus and conflict in the Danish Folketing 1945-65', *Scandinavian Political Studies* vol. 2 (1967), pp. 143-66, found that in 2,600 divisions over the twenty-year period, 58.4 per cent were passed unanimously (i.e. *all* the parties voted for the bill) and 26.3 per cent were passed with the 'broad agreement' of the 'four old parties'; only 15.3 per cent of bills had less widespread support.
37. Douglas W. Rae, *The Political Consequences of Electoral Laws* revised edition (Yale University Press, 1971), p. 30, found that Denmark (with Israel, Iceland and the Netherlands) approaches the limit of theoretical proportionality more closely than any other system, but still falls short of it to some extent.
38. This point is well illustrated by the Left Socialists at the 1968 election. They gained 57,184 votes in a total poll of 2,864,805 votes, only 2,854,647 of which were valid. After discussion in the Folketing Committee for the Proof of Elections, turning on whether blank and other invalid votes were to be included in the calculation, it was decided that they should not be. The party gained four mandates as its share of the seats allocated on the basis of votes cast in each of the three main regions of the country. *(Folketings-årbog 1967-68* (København, J.H. Schultz, 1968), pp. 636-8.)
39. The Justice Party advocates the single-tax and social-credit ideas of Henry George. It took part in the 'triangular' coalition of 1957-60 with SD and the Radicals but failed to gain much for its supporters and was demolished at the polls. For further information see A.H. Thomas, *Parliamentary Parties in Denmark 1945-1972* (Glasgow, 1973), pp. 27-30.
40. See Ole Borre, 'The General Election in Denmark, January 1975: toward a new structure of the party system', *Scandinavian Political Studies,* vol.10 (1975), pp.211-16.
41. The 'September Compromise' (*septemberforliget*) had the support of SD (53 seats), Liberals (42), Radicals (13), Christian People's Party (9) and Centre Democrats (4) for a series of initiatives enacted over the ensuing period, involving a temporary reduction of VAT; an end to the compulsory savings scheme; expenditure on job creation; dampening down of price increases, incomes and overhead costs over the following three years; and agreement on reductions in public expenditure of 4.5 milliard kroner (about £409 million) over the same period. (*Nordisk Kontakt,* 1975:12, pp. 782-9.)
42. The 1976 'August Agreement' was concluded between the Social Democrats, Centre Democrats, Christian People's Party and Radical Liberals, with additional Conservative support for the incomes policy measures. After the 1977 election these parties supported the measures which the Government was seeking and the Liberals added their support on defence. The strengths of the five blocs after the 1975 and 1977 elections were:

	1975 Election		1977 Election	
	% Votes	Seats	% Votes	Seats
Left-wing parties	11.3	20	10.3	19
Social Democrats	29.9	53	37.0	65
Small Centre Right parties	21.9	36	25.2	44
Liberals (Venstre)	23.3	42	12.0	21
Progress Party	13.6	24	14.6	26

43. Forecast by Erik Rasmussen, *'Parlamentarismens typologi i svensk teori og dansk politik: nogle hovedpunkter'*, *Statens almindelige videnskabsfond årsberetning*, 1956/7. (København 1958) pp.18-27.
44. 'Erik Ninn-Hansen: om fem år har vi det store borgerlige parti, jeg taler om,' *Morgenposten*, 27 July 1975 and subsequent discussion in *Berlingske Tidende*.
45. The war-time Ministry submitted its resignation to the King on 29 August 1943 and then ceased to act, in face of increasing pressures from the occupying power. For the remainder of the period until 5 May 1945 the country was administered by Heads of Departments on a caretaker basis.
46. These included Sigvard Hellberg, who had been a leading member of the SD Youth Association (SUF) until 1919, had run the Left Socialist Newspaper for two years and was Chairman of the Communist Party in 1926-7, sponsoring a resolution that the whole party should amalgamate with SD. Ernst Christiansen was Chairman of SUF 1913-19 and Communist Chairman until 1926; after 1930 he wrote for the SD newspaper, presided over the *Landsting* 1947-53, and as a member of the Radio Council in the 1940s and 1950s did much to ensure a fair hearing for the SD point of view.
47. Aksel Larsen in his memoirs gives the following statement of the conditions made by Hans Hedtoft on behalf of SD for the organisational union of SD and the Communists: the two parties would amalgamate before the (1945) election. SD Party rules would govern the united party until a Congress could be held, probably in 1947. The Communists would have reasonable representation in the united party's leading organs. The departments and branch associations would be amalgamated. The Communist daily *Land and People* and weekly papers would cease publication. The Communists would immediately cease collecting money for a press and would repay a state loan intended as (war-time) compensation and for the purchase of premises and printing machinery etc. The Communists would be assured a reasonable number (e.g. eight) of candidates in safe seats.

   The Communist reply was that their party had acted strictly democratically both before and during the war, unlike other parties. Then, that the 'dictatorship of the proletariat' as defined by Marx is the right of the great majority of the people to decide on social affairs. And finally, that statements should not be made so soon after the liberation of the country, made possible by the war effort of the Soviet Union among others, which could be understood as a dissociation from the political system of the Soviet Union. (*Aksel Larsen ser tilbage* (København, Rhodos, 1970), pp. 79-81.
48. Aksel Larsen, *Valget* (København, Hans Reitzel, 1964) gives the arguments for this decision.
49. Erik Damgaard and Jerrold G. Rusk, 'Cleavage structures and representational linkages: a longitudinal analysis of Danish legislative behaviour', *American Journal of Political Science*, vol. 20, no. 2 (1976), pp. 179-205.
50. Danish defence and foreign policy since 1945 is examined by Eric S. Einhorn, *National Security and Domestic Politics in Post-War Denmark: Some Principal Issues, 1945-71'* (Odense University Press, 1975), and by Bertel Heurlin (comp.), *Danmarks udenrigspolitik efter 1945. Kilder til belysning af Danmarks*

udenrigspolitiske mål 1945-70 (København, Gyldendal, 1971).
51. Per Hækkerup, *'Folketingstidende'* 1966/67, 2. samling, sp. 148ff.
52. See Ejvind Riisgård, *Aksel Larsens spil. Konflikten i SF* (København, Gerhard Eriksen Forlag, 1967) for the Left-wing view and Lars Bille, *S-SF. Kilder til belysning af forholdet mellem Socialdemokratiet og Socialistisk Folkeparti 1959-73* (København, Gyldendal, 1974) for a more impartial collection of sources.
53. Para.20, s.1 of the Constitution of 1953 states that 'Powers vested in the authorities of the Realm under this Constitution Act may, to such extent as shall be provided by Statute, be delegated to International authorities set up by mutual agreement with other states for the promotion of international rules of law and co-operation'.
      Section 2 lays down the procedure as follows: 'For the passing of a Bill dealing with the above a majority of five-sixths of the Members of the Folketing shall be required. If this majority is not obtained, whereas the majority for the passing of ordinary Bills is obtained, and if the Government maintains it, the Bill shall be submitted to the electorate for approval or rejection in accordance with the rules for Referenda laid down in section 42.'
54. *Dansk Arbejdsmands- og Specialarbejder Forbund.* Anker Jørgensen had been manager and then Chairman of DASF. With 249,867 members out of a total fully paid membership of LO (the Danish 'TUC') of 862,440 as at 31 December 1973, DASF is much the largest Danish trade union.
55. Poul-Ove Kühnel, 'Han vil ikke vælte Anker: Erling Jensen siger nej til at konkurrere om posten som Socialdemokratiets leder', *Ekstra Bladet,* 14 Aug. 1974, p. 6.
56. Hans Enghave Jensen, 'Foreign Trade, Institutional Change and Economic Development in Denmark' (Ph.D. thesis, University of Texas, 1961).
57. With optimistic expectations for the advent of Socialism in Denmark 'thanks largely to the enlightened and politically developed peasantry', whom Pio was convinced were essential allies. Børge Schmidt, *80 Louis Pio breve* (København, 1950), p. 35.
58. Apart from his newspaper articles, Gustav Bang's most important works are *Kapitalismens Gennembrud* (1902), *Den socialistiske Fremtidsstat* (1903) and *Den kapitalistiske Samfundsholdning* (1912).
59. Ernst Christiansen, 'The ideological development of democratic socialism in Denmark', *Socialist International Information,* vol. 8, no. 1 (1958).
60. *Revisionismens betydning for socialdemokratiets ideudvikling fra 1890erne til 1930erne* (Århus, Institut for Statskundskab, 1964, reprinted 1974, pp. 283), pp. 1-3.
61. Ibid. p. 248.
62. The conflict between revisionism and radical syndicalism is discussed by Lisa Bang *et al., Fagoppositionens sammenslutning (1910-21): De danske syndikalister* (Århus, Modtryk, 1975), pp.18-21. See also Christian Breinholt, *Krisen i 1930erne og Socialdemokratiet: overvejelser til en belysning af den socialdemokratiske revisionisme, med krise- og arbejdsmarkedslovsgivningen 1931-34 som historisk-konkret eksempel. (*Århus, Institut for Statskundskab, 1975, dissertation.)
63. Named after a restaurant in Fredriksberg, just west of Copenhagen. The text is reprinted in *Solidaritet, lighed og trivsel, en samfundsdebat* (København, Fremad, 1975), the draft Programme of Principles, and in Henry Karlsson, *Dansk arbejderbevægelse 1871-1939* (København, Gyldendal, 1975), pp. 48-50.
64. *'Fremtidens Danmark'.*
65. Anker Jørgensen, 'Bort fra vanetænkning', *Verdens Gang,* Sept. 1954, reprinted

in his *Til venstre for midten* (København, Fremad, 1975), p. 59.
66. 'Vejen frem, Socialdemokratiets principprogram, vedtaget i 1961' reprinted in *Solidaritet, lighed og trivsel.* An English version, 'The Road Ahead, the programme of the Danish Social Democratic Party, 1961' was distributed by the Party. The background and content are summarised in J.O. Krag and K.B. Andersen, *Kamp og Fornyelse: Socialdemokratiets indsats i dansk politik 1955-1971* (København, Fremad, 1971), pp.189-92.
67. *Solidaritet, lighed og trivsel.*
68. Predicted by the Gallup polls which showed the meteoric rise of Mogens Glistrup's Progress Party, and confirmed by the results of the December 1973 election.
69. *Loc. cit.,* p. 6.
70. The debate within the Party on policy responses to Danish membership of the European Community, is discussed in Alastair H. Thomas, 'Danish Social Democracy and the European Community', *Journal of Common Market Studies,* vol. 13, no. 4 (1975), pp. 454-68.
71. *Kravet om lighed: en redegørelse for ulighed i vort samfund og forslag til en politisk strategi, der kan skabe større lighed* (København, Fremad, 1973).
72. Ejvind Larsen, 'Socialdemokratiets Falkonér-program: to skridt frem og et tilbage', *Information,* 5 Sept. 1975, p. 4.
73. Mogens Lykketoft, 'Ingen fuldt afklaret model for det demokratiske, socialistiske samfund', *Information,* 11 Sept. 1975.
74. Mogens N. Pedersen, 'Consensus and conflict in the Danish Folketing, 1945-65', *Scandinavian Political Studies,* vol. 2 (1967), p. 147.
75. *'Love for socialdemokratiet',* para. 10.
76. Anker Jørgensen, *Til venstre for midten. Taler, artikler og interviews ved Bent Hansen* (København, Fremad, 1975), 'Left of centre' is the title of an autobiographical selection of speeches, articles and interviews setting out his ideology and his views on man at work, on being Prime Minister and on Denmark in the world.
77. Ove Sundberg, 'Magtkampen i Socialdemokratiet. Den socialdemokratiske folketingsgruppe er præget af splittelse både om de kortsigtede og de langsigtede politiske løsninger op til partiets landsmøde i denne weekend', *Berlingske Tidende,* 8 Sept. 1974.
78. *Forslag til lov om lønmodtagernes medejendomsret.* It received its first reading on 13 February 1973 but did not complete its committee stage; reintroduced 3 October 1973 and again referred to committee, but lost when the election was called for December 1973 and not reintroduced during the 1974/75 Folketing session.
79. *medejendomsret* rather than *økonomisk demokrati.* Report, *Weekendavisen Berlingske Aften,* 30 July 1976, p. 13.

Table 1. Party preferences by occupational group, percentages, 1974[24]

	Left wing	Soc. Dem.	Minor Centre /Right	Libs. (Venstre)	Progress Party
Self-employed in urban industry	4.0	3.0	13.2	12.9	23.0
Self-employed farmers	0.5	0.4	5.1	20.6	5.9
Higher salaried employees	8.9	4.6	14.5	13.7	10.3
Lower salaried employees	22.0	17.8	23.8	13.8	18.4
Skilled workers	24.0	19.9	11.0	6.5	17.4
Unskilled workers	15.6	21.4	6.2	3.8	13.2
Pensioners (old or disabled)	7.2	30.2	22.1	25.0	9.5
Students, non-employed	17.8	3.0	4.3	3.7	2.3
(N : 100%)	648	1,732	1,417	884	611

Party preferences by age, percentages, 1974

Age group :	Left wing	Soc. Dem.	Minor Centre /Right	Libs. (Venstre)	Progress Party
20-24	33.1	6.1	9.3	6.0	13.6
25-29	22.3	9.0	12.4	7.3	16.9
30-39	16.9	15.7	17.8	20.1	19.8
40-49	12.0	17.6	17.3	15.8	17.0
50-64	11.6	28.3	24.6	26.3	23.2
64 +	4.4	23.6	18.6	24.3	9.6
(N : 100%)	658	1,713	1,397	872	605

Party preference by length of school attendance, percentages, 1974[25]

Educational attendance for	Left wing	Soc. Dem.	Minor Centre /Right	Libs. (Venstre)	Progress Party
7-9 years (elementary)	46	81	55	62	60
9-10 years (secondary)	26	14	32	23	31
12+ years (higher)	28	5	13	15	9

Table 2. Denmark: Social Democratic Party membership figures

Year	Number of Members	Members as % of SD voters	Members as % of electorate	Year	Number of Members	Members as % of SD voters	Members as % of electorate
				1941	212,106	29.0	9.8
				1942	223,098	30.5	10.3
1903	22,061	47.3	5.3	1943	233,417	26.0	10.2
				1944	249,317	27.8	10.2
				1945	260,566	38.8	10.2
1906	29,651	38.6	6.8	1946	285,634	42.6	11.3
				1947	305,606	36.7	11.8
1908	34,078	44.5	7.8	1948	316,027	37.9	12.2
				1949	294,969	35.4	12.1
				1950	283,907	34.9	11.3
				1951	275,994	34.0	11.0
				1952	277,658	34.2	11.1
1913	48,985	45.5	10.0	1953	283,525	33.9	10.5
1914	57,115	53.4	11.6	1954	283,221	33.8	10.5
1915	60,072	56.5	12.2	1955	278,299	33.2	10.3
1916	67,724	63.1	13.8	1956	275,363	32.8	10.2
1917	78,320	72.9	15.9	1957	265,174	29.1	9.6
1918	91,791	34.9	7.5	1958	256,759	28.2	9.3
1919	115,900	44.0	9.5	1959	257,219	28.2	9.3
1920	126,603	32.4	8.0	1960	259,459	25.3	9.1
1921	129,756	33.2	8.2	1961	252,667	24.7	8.9
1922	124,549	31.9	7.9	1962	237,671	23.2	8.4
1923	130,371	34.1	8.5	1963	228,137	22.2	8.0
1924	143,203	30.5	8.7	1964	229,275	20.8	7.4
1925	146,258	31.1	8.9	1965	223,977	20.3	7.3
1926	144,346	29.0	8.3	1966	188,859	17.8	6.0
1927	148,138	29.8	8.5	1967	177,997	16.8	5.6
1928	148,786	29.9	8.5	1968	176,729	18.1	5.5
1929	162,859	27.5	9.1	1969	179,609	18.4	5.6
1930	171,073	28.8	9.6	1970	177,507	18.2	5.6
1931	173,890	29.3	9.7	1971	165,645	15.4	5.0
1932	179,579	27.2	9.4	1972	152,174	14.1	4.6
1933	190,070	28.8	10.0	1973	130,476	16.7	3.8
1934	191,995	29.1	10.1	1974	120,474	15.4	3.5
1935	195,142	25.7	9.5				
1936	191,424	25.2	9.4				
1937	199,283	26.3	9.7				
1938	198,836	26.2	9.7				
1939	206,995	28.4	9.6				
1940	207,052	28.4	9.6				

Sources: O. Bertolt, E. Christiansen and P. Hansen, *En bygning vi rejser. Den politiske arbejderbevægelses historie i Danmark* (København, Fremad, 1954-55) vols. I and II, *passim; Socialdemokratiet, årsberetninger* 1924-43; personal communications from SD Party headquarters, *Medlemsudviklingen 1944-74;* T.T. Mackie and R. Rose, *The International Almanac of Electoral History* (London, Macmillan, 1974); *Statistiske Meddelelser 1975:7, Folketingsvalget den 9. januar 1975* (København, Danmarks Statistik, 1975).

Further Reading

Bertolt, O., Christiansen, E. and Hansen, P. *En bygning vi rejser. Den politiske arbejderbevægelses historie i Danmark.* 3 vols. København, Forlaget Fremad, 1954-55: the official party history.

Bille, Lars. *S-SF: kilder til belysning af forholdet mellem Socialdemokratiet og Socialistisk Folkeparti 1959-73.* København, Gyldendal, 1974.

Borre, Ole, Nielsen, Hans Jørgen, Sauerberg, Steen and Worre, Torben. *Vælgere i 70'erne. Resultater fra interviewundersøgelser ved folketingsvalgene i 1971, 1973 og 1975.* København, Akademisk Forlag, 1976.

Dybedahl, Vagn, (ed.). *Arbejderbevægelsens hvem-hvad-hvor.* København, Politikens Forlag, 1974: a concise encyclopædia of facts on the Danish labour movement.

Jones, W. Glyn. *Denmark.* London, Ernest Benn, Nations of the Modern World series, 1970: an excellent modern history of Denmark.

Karlsson, Henry. *Dansk arbejderbevægelse 1871-1939.* København, Gyldendal, 1975.

Krag, Jens Otto. *Travl tid, god tid.* København, Gyldendal, 1974.

Krag, Jens Otto and Andersen, K.B. *Kamp og fornyelse. Socialdemokratiets indsats i dansk politik 1955-71.* København, Fremad, 1971: continues the official party history from Bertolt *et al.*

Krag, Jens Otto. *Ung mand fra trediverne.* København, Gyldendal, 1962.

Miller, Kenneth E. *Government and Politics in Denmark.* Boston, Houghton Mifflin Co., 1968: a well-informed introduction, and the only recent one in English, to the Danish political system.

Nielsen, Mogens (ed.). *Enhed i arbejderbevægelsen. Kilder til belysning af forhandlingerne mellem DKP og SD 1945.* København, Fremad, 1973.

Solidaritet, Lighed og Trivsel – en samfundsdebat. København, Fremad, 1975: the most recent draft party programme.

Togeby, Lise. *Var de sa røde? Tekster og dokumenter til belysning af Socialdemokratiets gennembrudsår.* København, Fremad, 1968.

THE FINNISH SOCIAL DEMOCRATIC PARTY

Ralf Helenius

The size of the Finnish Social Democratic Party is modest compared with corresponding parties in Scandinavia and Central Europe. This is explained by the relative strength of the Communists, who have taken part in general elections after World War II through the Finnish People's Democratic League. The predecessor of this Communist electoral alliance got between 10 and 15 per cent of the votes in the general elections of the 1920s. Communist organisations were, however, outlawed in 1930 until 1944. Since the war Social Democrats, Communists and casual Leftist parties have usually gained somewhat less than half of the votes cast in general elections (Table 1). Bourgeois parties, however, have had a majority for most of the period since 1906 when Finland obtained direct and proportional suffrage. The Left has won a majority only three times, in 1915, 1958 and 1966. These facts tell us two interesting things about Finnish politics: first, that the Communists have been almost as strong as in Italy and France; and second, that voters in Finland seem to prefer non-socialist parties. The last fact fits a pattern that has been typical for most political systems of the Western world.

The Finnish Political System

Some basic facts ought to be kept in mind for our analysis of SDP, the Finnish Social Democratic Party.

Finland has, first of all, a strong Presidential power. The constitution fits more to the model of separation of powers as worked out by Montesquieu than in many other comparable nations. The executive is, according to the Constitution of 1919, basically led by a President whose powers are comparable with those of the Presidents of the United States and France. Although there is a Prime Minister in Finland, as in France, there is no doubt about the President's strong position within the executive as well as within the state system as a whole. Foreign affairs are, for instance, sovereignly conducted by the President. He may determine matters in the Council of the State even if all ministers hold a different view. The President has used his powers to appoint and dismiss ministers, to bring governments into being, to dissolve parliament and to order new elections. The President of Finland in recent practice has gone beyond the formal powers allocated to him by the Constitution.

Observers generally agree on the existence of a more or less permanent crisis of parliamentarism in Finland.[1] Not only do governments have an average life of only one year: in 1976 Finland had been a sovereign nation for 59 years (from 1917) and the number of governments over that period is exactly 59. Governments tend to change after general elections, which are held every fourth year. But there have also been new governments after local elections. It is rare that a Finnish Government falls because of a vote of confidence. Two problems seem to have overshadowed others in recent years. One is that irrespective of which party gained most in an election, governments have been majority coalitions with four or five parties, caretaker governments or, exceptionally, minority cabinets. The last two types of government are formed because of the second main threat to parliamentarism: the difficulty of forming governments.[2]

Any Socialist movement aiming at fundamental changes of the existing order in Finland faces severe constitutional obstacles. A Bill which proposes nationalisation and similar changes of ownership or amendments to the Constitution is subject to procedures different from ordinary legislation. It may be postponed for decision until after the next general election and then must be adopted without amendment by two-thirds of the votes cast in the first ordinary session of the new parliament. Alternatively it can be declared to be of an urgent nature by a resolution passed by at least a five-sixths majority, and then requires adoption by two-thirds of the votes cast at the same session of parliament (e.g. the Third Reading). Of 200 members of parliament there need only be 34 to prevent a Constitutional Bill from being declared to be of an urgent nature. Since the 1970 election the Conservatives alone have had at least this number of Members, for example. In theory the President may intervene by dissolving parliament in order to further the aims of a two-thirds parliamentary majority. There has not, however, been a Socialist president in Finland yet.

Place in the Party System

Under normal circumstances one in four votes goes to the Social Democrats in general elections (see Table 1). Since the election of 1945 there have been only three exceptions, and these can be easily explained. In the general election of 1958 three MPs were elected from independent Social Democratic lists. This was one of the consequences of the party split which began three years earlier (see below). In the general election of 1962 the Social Democrats were also competing with the Social Democratic League of Workers and Smallholders, founded in 1959 by many who had formed the opposition at the 1957 Party Conference, who got more than 4 per cent of the votes and two seats in the parliament. The 1962 general election was the worst for the Left in Finland since the Second World War: all the socialist parties suffered losses for a variety of reasons, above all in the Presidential campaign and election of 1962, and the 'Note Crisis' with the Soviet Union in 1961. The third occasion when the Social Democrats obtained less than 25 per cent of the votes was in the general election of 1970. This time political stability in Finland was shaken by a protest from the voters. The Finnish Rural Party made a successful populist appeal and gained somewhat over 10 per cent of the votes. This gain came from Socialist as well as bourgeois parties.

Finland has proportional representation on the d'Hondt system. The bigger electors' associations gain from this and small associations are disfavoured. In order to get a seat in parliament from the constituency of Helsinki about 7,000 votes are necessary. In spite of this an increasing number of small parties has gained seats in parliament in recent years. At the general election of 1966 there were seven parties in parliament. In 1976 there are not less than ten groups in parliament. All the new parliamentary parties in this decade have been non-socialist.

This growth of small parties is partly due to splits within the Centre Party (agrarians), the Conservatives and the Swedish People's Party. Without electoral alliances the new party units might not have survived on the political scene. All the bourgeois parties have generally and increasingly used the constitutional possibilities of allying with each other, but on the left alliances are rare. The Communists co-operated like this with the Socialist opposition party in the 1960s. But in general Social Democrats and Communists are strong enough to compete electorally without partners and are too cautious to co-operate on other grounds than those determining electoral alliances.

In recent years the setting of a threshold to minor parties has been discussed. All big parties might be interested in such a measure but the bourgeois parties seem likely to gain most from the proposed 4 or 5 per cent threshold than the Socialist parties. The electoral system has been an object of frequent, if small, amendments. For instance, parties of the left would probably prefer so called long lists to short lists. The former method, which is used in Sweden, gives the Party the right to rank the candidates. The short lists method, which has been used since 1953, makes it too easy for popular personalities to get into parliament. Many ski-ing and other sports champions as well as stars from popular culture (television, broadcasting, entertainment) have been elected to parliament recently.

Political parties are legally recognised in the sense that they get State aid according to their number of seats in parliament. Political parties, but not civil organisations, would be mentioned in a proposed new Constitution. The question of reforming the Constitution, which was taken up at the end of the sixties, is still under discussion; it has been a constant item on the Government programme during this decade.

Finland resembles the Netherlands and Switzerland in having a multi-party system where no single party dominates the others.[3] The formation of coalitions of the Left has been generally opposed by the voters. A Socialist party is thus bound to form alliances with non-Socialist parties if it aims at a majority in parliament. And a parliamentary majority is widely accepted as the most natural way of carrying through more systematic and far-reaching government policies. This holds true even though parliamentarism mainly works negatively (votes of confidence need not be explicitly cast)[4] or bears the appearance of being in a state of permanent crisis.

Participation in Government

The Finnish Social Democratic Party entered government for the first time in 1916-17 when the Party had a clear majority in parliament. Such an occasion is unlikely to recur for the reasons discussed above. The first experience of office did not, however, mean that the Party had made a definite decision for government socialism. There was, in fact, hard opposition in the 1920s to a party strategy according to which socialism would be implemented by accepting the rules set by the bourgeois state. Nevertheless a door was left open at the Party Conference of 1922 to ministerial socialism. Those who argued for this referred to the positive experiences of the first Social Democratic cabinet: the Government of 1916-17 had brought about peace with the Soviet Union, communal suffrage, primary legislation on labour protection, tax legislation, compulsory education, a prohibition law and initiated legislation for religious freedom.[5]

The Party was prepared to govern in a coalition of socialists and non-socialists in 1926. The negotiations failed and led to the forming of the first minority Social Democrat cabinet. This experience did not as such lead to a permanently favourable attitude to government participation. The crisis of capitalism and the growing hostilities between Soviet socialism and Western imperialism brought sharpened measures towards left-wing radicalism. The Communists were forced to leave socialist policies in the hands of the Social Democrats, and the relations between the Party and the Communist Party of the Soviet Union deteriorated.[6]

Social Democrats have thus been ready to govern in Finland from the 1930s onwards. The first experience of coalition with the predecessor of the Centre Party came at the end of the 1930s and most Government experience since then has been with the Centre Party. These two parties have been the most influential in Finnish politics during the post-war period. The Social Democrats were, however, in opposition between 1959 and 1966. This is mainly said to be due to two factors: the party split (see below) and a difficult foreign policy position. The party, together with the Conservatives, had nominated a non-socialist for the presidency in 1961 but their candidate had to retire, partly because of his implication in events surrounding the Note Crisis and apparently partly because of more or less explicit Soviet suspicion. There were also indications that certain people within the party were not fully acceptable in Moscow. Such events threw a shadow over the whole Social Democratic Party, although the appropriateness of its foreign policy as such was never in doubt. The most frequent government party in the post-war period has thus been the Centre Party, which has been in opposition only very occasionally during the period. The Centre Party has sometimes but not always been number two among the parties in parliament (see Table 1): to be the foremost government party does not in Finland relate to size so much as to ideological or tactical position.[7] As government policies seem to be handled by those who are in the middle of the party scale, two other parties of the Centre have often been in the government. These are the Liberal People's Party and the Swedish People's Party which together have had about 10 per cent in most of the general elections of the post-war period.

It is well known that Mr Urho Kekkonen, who has been President of Finland since 1956, favours broad government coalitions. It has almost become a matter of prestige to try to form such coalitions in Finland. It is, for instance, regarded as quite reasonable for leaders of the Social Democrats and the Centre Party to suggest a multi-party government immediately after a minority cabinet of the Centre Party and the two People's Parties was formed, as was the case in October 1976.

Figure 1. SDP in post-war government coalitions 1945-1976

1945-50		1950-60		1960-70		1970-76	
No.	ABCDE	No.	ABCDE	No.	ABCDE	No.	ABCDE
29.	XXXX	33.		45.		52.	(X XX)
30.	XXXX	34.	X XX	46.		53.	XXXX
31.	XXXX	35.	X XX	47.		54.	(X XX)
32.	X	36.		48.	(X)	55.	X
		37.		49.		56.	X XX
		38.	X XX(X)	50.	XXX	57.	(X XXX)
		39.	X X	51.	XXXX	58.	XXXX
		40.	X XX			59.	
		41.	X XX				
		42.	(X X)				
		43.	(X XX)				
		44.	X XXX				

KEY

No. refers to the serial number of the Government during the period since independence

A SDP in Government

B SDP in Government with Socialists

C SDP in Government with the Centre Party

D SDP in Government with the non-Socialist Liberal and Swedish People's Parties

E SDP in Government with the Conservatives

( ) special cases when the parties were not officially represented

Source: Guy Ahonen, The Swedish School of Economics, Helsinki.

To form governments with the Centre Party, the Social Democrats and the Communists as a base, with the support of the small parties of the centre, has become an officially declared policy. Negotiations on forming such coalitions seem to take place consistently whenever the country has a minority cabinet or a caretaker government (Figure 1). A five-party government is expected to have a sufficient base — at least two-thirds of the seats in parliament — to take the kind of economic and social measures that are needed in current conditions. The incomes policies of the eight years to 1976 seemed to presuppose far-reaching and widely based consensus. There is, of course, a price for this. The

Conservatives had been out of office for ten years in 1976 and gained much popularity during the 1970s. The parties in office have to make compromises and expect more or less formally expressed opposition from the rank and file. When we try to explain the Social Democrats' problem of governing we must also point to a feature that seems general to the typical Government parties of the Finnish political system: an apparently growing discrepancy between fundamental and operative ideology.[8] Any party that aspires to office in Finland has to renounce its principles for practical reasons. Communists seem to meet the situation with more resistance than the Socialists. They have been quite formally split into two factions since the party conferences at the end of the sixties. The majority is much more favourable to government participation than is the Moscow-orientated minority. The factions differ in their application of Communist ideology to the present stage of capitalist society.

The Social Democrats also hold divergent views on the Party's engagement in Government. These views are, however, much less ideologically than tactically based. Most members of the Party would apparently favour co-operation with the Communists in joint governments. Both parties have also discussed common aims in more or less regular bilateral talks in recent years. Government policies have been the central theme of talks which are not as a rule conducted as formalised negotiations.

Multiparty governments are likely to have a bourgeois majority and the changes of bringing through pure socialist aims will always be restricted. In such a state a coalition of both left parties (Socialists and Communists) and the Centre Party is regarded by some Party members as the best alternative. The second-best coalition would comprise Social Democrats and all the parties of the centre (the Centre Party, the Liberal People's Party and the Swedish People's Party). This 'static solution' of the government question is apt to be the most common in Finnish politics today. A still worse alternative would be a majority government of the three parties of the centre and the Conservatives.[9] Such a coalition seems, however, to be quite unrealistic; leaders of the Centre Party have time after time declared their unwillingness to rule with the Right.

Party Structure and Cohesion

The Finnish Social Democratic Party had rather over 100,000 members in 1976. This is not so many in comparison with other parties in the Socialist International or even in Finland. But all member parties of the

Socialist International are not comparable with each other. Some
parties, like those in Sweden and Great Britain have collective
membership whereas others have only individual membership. The
Norwegian Labour Party had over 200,000 individual members and
somewhat over 46 per cent of the votes in 1975.[10] This may show that
Social Democrats in Finland have a relatively modest organisational
basis as compared with corresponding parties. There are two Finnish
parties which get fewer votes but claim more members than the
Socialists.[11]

The membership of the Party dropped constantly between the end
of the 1940s and the beginning of the 1960s. The Party Conference of
1963 seems to have been a turning-point in this respect as well as in
many others: membership has increased steadily since then.

The Finnish Social Democratic Party makes its appeal to all strata
of the population as do most Socialist and other parties which pursue a
parliamentary strategy. There will, of course, be far fewer people in
agriculture or in leading positions who vote for a Socialist party in a
system where the Centre Party gets at least 80 per cent of the agrarian
votes and many bourgeois parties compete for the votes of the better
off. Eighty per cent of the Party's voters are union members within the
Confederation of Finnish Trade Unions (*Suomen Ammatti yhdistysten
Keskusliitto*, SAK). One-third of the Party's members is occupied in
industry and transport, 14 per cent in technology, 13 per cent in trade
and services and 22 per cent in other professions. This distribution of
members shows that the Party represents a cross-section of the Finnish
people.[12] But men predominate over women: 65 per cent of the
members are men.[13]

Some features of the membership composition have raised comment.
The average age of Party members is regarded as too high, although
there are no less than 45 per cent of members between 30 and 49 and
most of the new members are between 25 and 29. There is, however,
some evidence that young people do not seem to be so attracted by
the Social Democratic appeal as by appeals from some other parties in
Finland.[14] The Conservatives are usually more popular among school
children and students than they are within the electorate as a whole.
This has also been the case with the Communists in recent years. The
Socialists' situation is quite the reverse. This undeniable fact can also
be noted at the organisational level.

The youth and students' organisations of the Social Democrats seem
to be fairly weak, but a lot of work has been done in recent years to
improve the situation. The Central League of Social Democratic Youth

(with some 32,000 members in 1976) has a much more Socialist profile in the 1970s than it had in the 1960s. There is apparently lack of neither debate nor will to do something. But a tendency to favour extreme movements seems to have been quite strong among young people in the decade since 1966. There was a great Social Democratic victory in the general election of 1966 and later there were the student troubles around the world. The election and the return to government brought educated people particularly to the Social Democratic Party as well as to the Communists, and the students' movement made young people more aware of socialism. Around 1970 there was, for a year or two, a fairly radical group outside the formal organisations of the Social Democratic Party, the so-called *'Pälkäne läiset'*. These young people, workers and intellectuals alike, held to the line of the Party programme, but they wanted more distinct action in some fields of politics, particularly foreign policy. They were also in favour of co-operation with the Communists and they disliked the 'anti-Communism' of the Socialist International.[15] Some of these people went to the Communists; many of them, perhaps most, stayed in the Party and more or less disappeared from the scene. There is no doubt, however, that the ideas of this rather informally organised group have wide support in the Party as a whole, and have expressed a change of attitude and views among the rank and file. This was perhaps best noticed at the Party Conference of 1975 (see below) which apparently sharpened the Socialist profile of the Party.

The organisation of the Finnish Social Democratic Party has remained unchanged for many years. The formal structure[16] seems to work adequately but suggestions designed to raise the level of activity are continuously presented in the Finnish as in other Socialist parties. Most local associations are related either to geographic area or work place. There are also associations — one could even call them 'clubs' — for members of specific educational or professional groups, however. These organisations ought to be treated separately from ordinary associations, not for ideological but for technical reasons.[17]

The Party has split twice since its foundation in 1899. The first split was, in Finland as in many other countries, around 1918 when the Marxist-Lenninists left the Social Democrats and formed their own organisation — the Finnish Communist Party was founded in Moscow in 1919.

The second split was in the years between 1953 and 1969. This time not only the Party but most of the labour movement was involved. It started with a conflict about the policies of the Workers' Sports

Confederation in 1953. The Party split at an Extraordinary Conference in 1957 when those who had opposed the Party line for some years gained a majority of the delegates. The losers subsequently formed their own organisations, first within and then outside the Party. In the 1958 general election three Socialist candidates won parliamentary seats with their own election alliances and eleven members of the Social Democratic group in parliament joined the opposition soon after the election. In early 1959 a new party was formed: the Social Democratic League of Workers and Smallholders.[18] This socialist party was represented in parliament for three periods between 1958 and 1970. It ceased to exist in the early 1970s when the conflict was settled and many of its leading representatives returned to their old party.

The split also involved the Confederation of Finnish Trade Unions (SAK), which was divided into two different and partly competing central organisations for a whole decade. Those unions which had left their former Confederation, and either stayed in the competing one or outside any central organisation, returned in 1969. From that year on Finnish workers have had a common central organisation that has gained considerable power and respect in recent years. SAK had almost 1 million members in 1976. More than 75 per cent of manual labour is organised in the unions of the Confederation.[19] This is much more than in most European countries outside Scandinavia.

The party split was due apparently much less to ideological and strategic factors than to personal reasons and group interests. Most of the differences of view were on foreign policy, the attitude towards the Communists, perhaps also the place of agriculture in modern society. The majority (and thus the Party) was critical in these matters while the Opposition took a more favourable position. The conflict persisted within the Party and there were critical minorities at the 1957 and 1960 Conferences. The dispute was finally settled at the 1963 Conference when a new Chairman and a fairly balanced Party Committee were elected. The cohesion of the Party has not been severely threatened since then although the ideological cleavages seem to have been more articulated than before.

The Finnish Social Democratic Party cannot claim undisputed leadership of the labour movement as can its sister party in Sweden. The Communists are strong enough to have an extensive influence on the Unions and the Co-operative movement. They have one Chairman out of three and about one-third of the Committee seats in the Confederation. They control three of its over twenty unions. They have also some say in the Sports Confederation of Workers. But the Social

Democrats have a majority in most of the labour movement branches and are not severely challenged by the Communists. They also exert a great influence on the Confederation of Salaried Employees and Civil Servants (*Toimihenkilö- ja Virkamiesjärjestöjen Keskusliitto,* TVK) with its almost 300,000 members. The co-operation between the Party and the Unions need not be close in all respects and it is not always easy to say who commands whom. Sometimes, as in incomes policies, the Unions seem to have had much more to say in recent years. But the people who make decisions within the different branches of the labour movement are for the most part more or less loyal members of the Socialist and Communist parties.

Towards Socialism

The Social Democrats in Finland are apparently more socialist than many similar parties. This Socialism seems, however, to be more evident on the level of fundamental ideology than in operative ideology.

When the first Party Programme was approved in 1903 its principles were more Marxist than reformist. This reflected the influence of Austro-Marxism and the writings of Karl Kautsky. There was some revisionist influence from Sweden.[20] In the period between 1918, when the Communists left the Party, and 1952, when the Party drew up a new programme, there were constantly differing lines on strategy and tactics. Those who preferred a reformist analysis of the situation and step-by-step measures towards Socialism were numerous, but those who had a deep respect for the Marxist traditions had apparently more analytical skill. So the Party Programme of 1952, even seen from the perspective of the 1970s, seems to be more radical than many corresponding labour party programmes in Europe. It is certainly more socialist than, for instance, the Godesberg Programme of the German Social Democratic Party but also more radical than the corresponding document of the Swedish party of 1960.

The programme of the Finnish Social Democrats does not, however, suggest 'common ownership of the means of production, distribution and exchange' as does Clause Four for the British Labour Party Constitution.[21] Nationalisation will be carried out as far as such measures are meaningful. The Programme is perhaps most radical in its severe criticism of the present stage of capitalism. This part resembles very much the criticism of capitalism in the 1970s which had been included in recent action programmes. Furthermore, the Party's fundamental ideology was less Socialist in the 1950s and 1960s but today the Party Programme has become more up to date than it was ten or fifteen years ago.

On the other hand we should keep in mind the constitutional and political obstacles to socialist measures on the operational level: the blocking vote rules of parliament; the likelihood of a bourgeois President and majority in parliament; as well as majority coalitions with the Centre Party. So many thorough reforms cannot, therefore, be expected in Finland as, for instance, in Sweden. There is much less hope for such reforms as the nationalisation of pharmacies, the founding of a State Investment Bank or perhaps the proposed scheme of wage-earners' funds. On the whole Sweden is five to ten years ahead in most social reforms. This may be as much due to the above-mentioned operational factors as to differences of material resources.

Few would doubt the statement that the Finnish Socialists are more ideologically orientated today than perhaps ever before. From the Party Conference of 1969 onwards action programmes have been systematically developed in all fields of policy. There is no doubting the Party's intentions to try to carry the proposed measures into practice. And the Party became much more radical at the last Conference of 1975 than previously in the post-war period. There are very frank analyses of the present state of things in Finland and in the capitalist world in current party documents. The Party also makes more sophisticated claims for socialist reforms than for years. The proposed measures may often relate more to extending public control and planning than ownership as such. The common intention is to handle matters from a comprehensive point of view. 'All-embracingness' seems to be the strategy for reforming society in a socialist direction.

Future Goals

Let us, finally, point to some primary goals of the Finnish Social Democratic Party of today.

Constitutional reform has been proposed for a decade now. Socialists want, first of all, to remove the blocking vote clause in parliament. Within the executive they would give more power to the Prime Minister; for instance, the right to choose members of the cabinet. And they would prefer, as would some other parties also, to decrease the President's powers in the Council of the State. There seems to be a majority in the responsible organs of the Party that would prefer the President to be chosen by parliament and not by a 300-member electoral college as now. The reform of presidential power has been separated from other constitutional claims for the near future. The Party has nominated Mr Kekkonen (a non-Socialist) as its candidate for the Presidency in the election of 1978. It seems highly unlikely that any measures will be taken concerning the Presidency before the election.

Like many other socialist parties SDP would like to push forward suggested measures for industrial democracy. On regional democracy Finnish Socialists are in favour of balanced development in the whole country and oppose the Centrist policy of giving benefits without controls to companies in the under-developed areas.

The field of foreign policy and defence is influenced by basically geopolitical factors. Finland follows a policy of neutrality and is not a member of any military bloc. It has, however, made a Treaty of Friendship, Co-operation and Mutual Assistance with the Soviet Union. To have good relations with the Soviet Union in particular, with Nordic countries by tradition, and with other countries in general, is the basic orientation of Finnish foreign policy. Most parties from the Communists to the Conservatives have declared their desire to follow the Paasikivi-Kekkonen line of foreign policy which has been developed by these two Presidents in the post-war period. Accordingly Finland has supported the United Nations' measures for disarmament and strengthening international security. To plan and act as host for the Helsinki Conference on Security and Co-operation in Europe is a logical outcome of these aspects of Finnish foreign policy. The distinctive socialist aims on defence and foreign affairs are fairly similar in many countries. The Finnish Social Democrats are in favour of a defence force suited to the needs of Finland's strategic situation without putting excessive strains on the economy.

The Party's view in the field of trade policy is based on the country's official foreign policy: it aims to stay outside the blocs and to maintain friendly relations with the Soviet Union and other trade partners in Eastern Europe. SDP was sceptical of the free trade agreement formed with the Common Market in 1972 for foreign policy as well as Socialist considerations. The Party put forward 'protection bills' to be enacted to protect the Finnish economy from the negative effects of an agreement with the Common Market. The agreement was accepted but the Party follows its effects with a critical eye. The energy crisis some years ago, currency fluctuation, rising inflation and the deterioration of the balance of payments are evils that have followed the closer co-operation of the Western trade markets. Trade with the Common Market countries has tended to increase imports as compared with exports (see Table 2). Finland formed a Treaty with the Council for Mutual Economic Assistance organisation similar to its agreement with the Market. This was, in fact, one of the conditions for entering into the Western trade co-operation agreement. Finland has taken active measures to enlarge trade with CMEA countries, and this trade has grown in absolute terms but has diminished relative to trade with the West.

One question should be particularly mentioned in connection with economic and social policy: since 1968 so called 'incomes policies' agreements have been made, most of them for one year and one for two years. Twice in 1973 and 1977, there was no such agreement on the labour market. In those years wages and salaries were determined on the basis of collective agreements only. These incomes policies agreements differ from ordinary central income agreements in being tripartite between labour, management and the State. Incomes policies agreements include also legislation on welfare, labour, environment, education, price control, prices of agricultural products, taxes; in theory, whatever will be included in legislation.[22]

The Social Democrats have played their role in this new game of politics through their dominance of the unions. There has been much to criticise in incomes policies, not least the tendency to transfer political power from the legislature and the executive to the interest organisations. But it is also one way of gaining control over the economy as a whole. The Party is apparently much more in favour of incomes policies agreements than the Communists who have often opposed such measures. Real wages developed, however, most favourably during the period of the first centralised agreements.

One sign of this is the Party Chairman's proposal to prolong the agreements from the normal one year to longer periods, and two years were suggested. The Social Democratic Secretary of the Finnish Confederation of Labour has also very recently made a similar proposal.

Finnish socialists have in recent years suggested consumer legislation in a rather more extended form than in Sweden. Responsibility for products sold to the consumer is a specific objective of Finnish socialists which has caused much resistance. This claim was in fact rejected and taken out of the proposal. In the field of social welfare it is proposed to handle employment pensions and other pensions as one comprehensive system. The extension of children's day care might be mentioned as one example of such social reforms that have been put forward by the left in Finland.

In the field of education policy, the comprehensive school system is almost completed. This will be linked with the development of professional and university education. Examinations and forms of

286   The Finnish Social Democratic Party

administration in advanced education have been debated for years in Finland. Few areas of public policy are so divided into two sectors as this. The Socialist threat is perhaps more intuitively experienced in cultural than in other matters. Education remains, however, an area of primary concern to the party.

Notes

1. Harto Hakovirta, 'Suomalaisen parlamentarismin kriisi: Oireita – analyysiongelmia – taustatekijöitä', in Harto Hakovirta, and Tapio Koskiaho (eds.), *Suomen hallitukset ja hallitusohjelmat 1945-1973* (Oy Gaudeamus Ab, 1973), p. 93, ch. 4.2.
2. Ibid. ch. 4.6.
3. Ibid. ch. 4.5.
4. See, for instance, Jaakko Nousiainen, *Suomen poliittinen järjestelmä*, 3rd edition (Helsinki, WSOY, 1966), p.313. Jaako Nousiainen, *The Finnish Political System* (Cambridge, Mass., Harvard University Press, 1971), pp. 270-1.
5. Hannu Soikkanen, 'Suomen Sosialidemokraattisen Puolueen ideologinen kehitys kansalaissodan jälkeen', in Pentti Holappa (ed.), *Käytännön sosialidemokratia* (Helsinki, Tammi, 1973), p. 20.
6. Ibid. pp.26-8.
7. Hakovirta, op. cit. ch. 4.5-4.6.
8. The terms 'fundamental' and 'operative' ideology have been used very convincingly in a recently published book: Martin Seliger, *Ideology and Politics* (London, Allen & Unwin, 1976).
9. Bo Ahlfors and Seppo Lindblom, 'Vasemmiston Poliittinen voima täysitehoiseksi', *Sosialistinen Aikakauslehti*, 2/76, pp. 16-21.
10. *Uuden jäsenen kirja* information brochure published by the Finnish Social Democratic Party, Vaasa, 1976, p. 79. But these figures are more optimistic than the ones given by Heidar, pp.311-12 below.
11. The Finnish People's Democratic League had about 175,000 members in 1976 if the members of affiliated organisations for youth and students are also counted. This party has about 60,000 individually affiliated members. The Centre Party reports about 297,000 members in 1975. The criteria for counting members are known to be much less rigid among bourgeois parties generally than among Socialist parties. For details see the 1975 year books of the parties mentioned.
12. *Uuden jäsenen kirja*, p.8.
13. Ibid.
14. Ibid.
15. Erkki Uitto, 'SDP – nuorisoliike – pälkäneläisyys', *Sosialistinen Aikakauslehti*, 3/70, pp. 28-30.
16. 'The Party's highest decision-making body is the Party Congress (held every three years), the representatives to which are elected by district members from the candidates nominated by the Party's branch offices. The number of candidates from each district depends on the number of members in the district.
   'Between the Party Congresses the highest power is vested in the Party Council elected by the Party Congress. To the Council belong 51 representatives nominated by district organisations.
   'The executive body of the Party is the Party Committee.
   'In addition to the Chairman and the Party Secretary (in October 1976 these were respectively, Kalevi Sorsa, and Ulf Sundqvist) there are 10 other

members . . . The Party bureau works under the Party Committee.
'In the whole country there are 16 district organisations one of which, the Swedish-speaking Social Democrats' organisation, operates in many districts. The Party's branch offices in each district belong to the district organisation, whose activities are decided upon in the annual District Conferences and in the District Committee then elected.

'If there are three party local clubs in a community they form together a Local Party that has its own decision-making bodies and determines the Social Democratic policy in the community. The local clubs have only individual members.' (Quoted from a brochure presenting the SDP, publ. by the Finnish Social Democratic Party, p. 5.)

17. Unto Niemi, 'Uudistusten umpisolmut', *Sosialistinen Aikakauslehti*, 1/71 pp. 3-4. Paavo Lipponen: 'Sosialidemokratia 1970-luvun vaaleissa', *Socialistinen Aikakauslehti*, 1/71, pp.10-15.
18. Soikkanen, op. cit. pp. 46-7.
19. Information from SAK to the author, Oct. 1976.
20. Soikkanen, op. cit. pp. 11-12. The principles of the Forssa Program of 1903 were, in fact, directly translated from the programme of the Austrian Social Democratic Party. See Olavi Borg, *Suomen puloueideologiat* (Vammala, WSOY, 1964), p. 63.
21. See e.g. Ralf Helenius, *The Profile of Party Ideologies* (doctoral dissertation, Helsinki, 1969), p. 89-93.
22. Ralf Helenius, 'Incomes Policies and the Separation of Power in a Liberal Democracy' (paper for the ECPR Conference in Louvain-La-Neuve, 8-14 Apr. 1976).

Table 1. Socialist seats in parliament 1945-75

Year	45	48	51	54	58	62	66	70	72	75
1. SDP	50	54	53	54	48	38	55	52	55	54
2. SKDL	49	38	43	43	50	47	41	36	37	40
3. TPSL					3	2	7			
Socialists	99	92	96	97	101	87	103	88	92	94
Others	101	108	104	103	99	113	97	112	108	106

1. Suomen Sosialidemokraattinen Puolue — Finnish Social Democratic Party;
2. Suomen Kansan Demokraattinen Liitto — Finnish People's Democratic League;
3. Työväen ja Pienviljelujäin Sosialidemokraattinen Liitto — Social Democratic League of Workers and Smallholders.

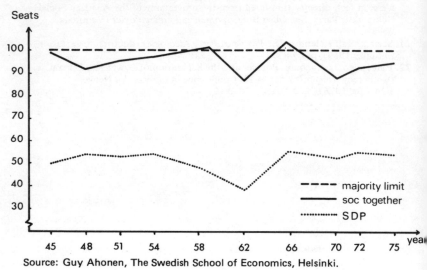

Source: Guy Ahonen, The Swedish School of Economics, Helsinki.

Table 2. Figures on Finnish foreign trade 1958-75
(% of total foreign trade)

	1958		1972		1975	
	Imp.	Exp.	Imp.	Exp.	Imp.	Exp.
EFTA-countries	31.3	30.3	44.7	47.4	25.8	25.7
EEC-countries	29.8	26.9	29.0	21.3	38.6	36.4
East-European countries	25.7	24.9	15.4	15.7	21.1	23.6

Source: Guy Ahonen, The Swedish School of Economics, Helsinki.

Table 3. Finland: general election results, 1972 and 1975

Party	1972			1975		
	Number of votes	Percentage of votes	Number of seats	Number of votes	Percentage of votes	Number of seats
1. SDP	664,724	25.8	55	695,394	24.9	54
2. SKDL	438,767	17.0	37	528,026	18.9	40
3. TPSL	25,527	1.0	—	9,675	0.3	—
Socialist total	1,129,018	43.8	92	1,233,095	44.1	94
4. SMP	236,206	9.2	18	100,771	3.6	2
5. KESK	423,041	16.4	35	488,930	17.7	39
6. LKP	132,955	5.2	7	121,722	4.4	9
7. RKP	138,079	5.3	10	141,381	4.8	10
8. SKL	65,228	2.5	4	32,108	3.3	9
9. KOK	453,434	17.6	34	513,213	18.4	35
Others	—	—	—	103,918	3.7	2
Bourgeois total	1,448,943	56.2	108	1,562,043	55.9	106
Total	2,577,961	100	200	2,795,138	100	200

PARTY NAMES

1. SDP *Suomen Sosialidemokraattinen Puolue*
Finnish Social Democratic Party
2. SKDL *Suomen Kansan Demokraattinen Liitto*
Finnish People's Democratic League
3. TPSL *Työväen ja Pienviljeliujäin Sosialidemokraattinen Liitto*
Social Democratic League of Workers and Smallholders
4. SMP *Suomen Maaseudun Puolue*
Finnish Rural Party
5. KESK *Keskustapuolue*
The Centre Party
6. LKP *Liberaalinen Kansanpuolue*
Liberal People's Party
7. RKP *Svenska Folkpartiet/ Ruotsalainen Kansanpuolue*
Swedish People's Party
8. SKL *Suomen Kristillinen Liitto*
Finnish Christian League
9. KOK *Kansallinen Kokoomuspuolue*
National Coalition Party (Conservatives)

Further Reading

In Finnish

Borg, Olavi. *Suomen puolueideologiat.* Vammala, WSOY, 1964.
Hakovirta, Harto and Koskiaho, Tapio (eds.). *Suomen hallitukset ja hallitusohjelmat.* Oy Gaudeamus Ab, place of print not mentioned, 1973.
Helenius, Ralf. *Suuret ismit 1970-luvun politiikassa.* Helsinki, Kyriiri Oy, 1972.
Holappa, Pentti (ed.). *Käytännön sosialidemokratiaa.* Helsinki, Tammi, 1973.
Koivisto, Mauno. *Linjan vetoa.* Helsinki, Kirjayhtymä, 1968.
Sorsa, Kalevi. *Kansanvallan kysymyksiä.* Helsinki, Tammi, 1974.

In English

De Swaan, Abram. *Coalition Theories and Cabinet Formations.* Amsterdam, Elsevier Scientific Publishing Co., 1973, pp. 237-53.
Nousiainen, Jaakko. *The Finnish Political System.* Cambridge, Mass., Harvard University Press, 1971.
Törnudd, Klaus. *The Electoral System of Finland.* London, Hugh Evelyn, 1968.
Uotila, Jaakko (ed.). *The Finnish Legal System.* Helsinki, The Union of Finnish Lawyers Publishing Company Ltd, 1966.
See also various issues of *Scandinavian Political Studies,* published annually by the Scandinavian Political Science Associations.

11

THE NORWEGIAN LABOUR PARTY: SOCIAL
DEMOCRACY IN A PERIPHERY OF EUROPE

Knut Heidar

The peripheral position of Norway in relation to the dominant powers
of Europe has in important respects defined the parameters of
Norwegian politics in general[1] and, arguably, of its labour movement in
particular. The organisational structure of the movement is to this day
marked by its German legacy.[2] Its theoretical debates have almost
exclusively been fought with arguments borrowed from the great
debates of European socialism − often as they sifted through the
Danish and Swedish debates.[3] The party splits in the 1920s were
occasioned by the Russian revolution and the subsequent schism in
international labour organisations. The party split in 1961 had its
background in opposition to the party line on foreign policy issues, and
the largest electoral setback in Arbeiderpartiet's history in 1973 can
only be explained by the Common Market issue in Norwegian politics.
It has *not* primarily been endogenous change or 'the tradition of all
the dead generations' which has weighed like a nightmare on Social
Democrats[4] in Norway, but rather the developments in European
politics in general and European working-class politics in particular.[5]

Apart from presenting the basic features of Arbeiderpartiet's growth
to dominance in Norwegian politics, its recent past and present
challenges, two main lines of argument are presented. The first is that
we are witnessing the end of Arbeiderpartiet's exceptionalism among
Norwegian parties in the sense of being qualitatively different as an
organisation and as a political collectivity. The second is that the
periods of opposition (1965-71, 1972-3) and electoral disappointment
(1971, 1972, 1973) have been a refreshing experience for the party −
modifying its tight-knit ruling élite system and giving the alternative
élite in the loyal left-wing more influence than before.

Lineages: Electoral Development and Political Context

Arbeiderpartiet was founded in 1887 with the aim of giving the
scattered trade unions and political associations of the working class
an overarching, national structure. For a long time, however, the local
level continued to be the decisive base of a rather shaky national
organisation.[6] The new alternative in Norwegian politics − leading a

life in political obscurity well outside the spotlight circling the major parties *Venstre* (the Liberals) and *Høyre* (the Conservatives) — was of course hindered in its growth by the restricted suffrage, but not by that alone.[7] The dominant political issue — dissolution of the union with Sweden — ensured in addition that the national question took priority over the social.

Both these restrictive features of the Norwegian setting disappeared at the turn of the century and at the same time Norway experienced a major industrial surge from which the contours of a modern working-class emerged.[8] Arbeiderpartiet had an explosive growth in its electoral base during the first fifteen years of this century (Table 1). The change to proportional representation in 1921 transformed a loss of votes into a gain in Storting representatives. This decline of votes in the early twenties was the triple brother of the general industrial crises following World War I — prolonged in Norway due to a misguided fiscal policy — and the political split in the labour movement in the wake of the Russian revolution.

A partial reunion in 1927 brought an electoral victory to the party and Arbeiderpartiet formed a minority government which only lasted eighteen days but was a prelude to the *Nygaardsvold* Government formed in 1935. This was a pure party government but included the agrarian *Bondepartiet* in its parliamentary base, and it was formed to implement a Keynesian policy of deficit budgeting as a remedy against the industrial and rural crises. The 'crisis compromise' of 1935 introduced twenty-five years of labour government, only interrupted by five years of war. In 1945 DNA* returned with a parliamentary majority and the period ended with the victory of the *'borgerlige partier'*, the bourgeois parties at the 1965 election.[9]

Arbeiderpartiet and the Labour Movement

Arbeiderpartiet emerged as the political section of a movement with a simple structure and a diffuse division of labour. In 1899 the national co-ordination of trade union matters was transferred to *Arbeidernes Faglige Landsorganisasjon* (LO) — established at a common Scandinavian initiative.[10] The organisational differentiation continued in 1901 with the founding of the women's association, while the youth organisation elected its first leaders in 1903.

The relationship between the two most important sections of the labour movement — party and trade unions — has for most of the time been 'one body, two arms': the separation was much clearer in terms of organisational structure than organisational practice.[11] At the local

* See pp.311 and 314 for party names and abbreviations.

level many party members have always been affiliated collectively through their trade union branch. In 1922 the share of collective members was estimated at about two-thirds and forty years later to slightly below 60 per cent[12], and the institution has been a permanent guarantee of union influence in the Party.[13] At the top level the same influence was secured through a mutual representation in the central committees.[14] This particular arrangement broke down, however, in 1925 but an equivalent re-emerged in 1927 in the form of a co-operation committee which formalised the exclusive contract between the four most influential men within the entire movement. LO was also the purse of the entire movement which still benefits the party – particularly at election times.[15]

The proper relationship between trade unions and party has been a controversial issue in theory as well as practice in labour movement history. In Norway the twenties was a turning-point in this relationship. Before the years of exhausting infighting and economic crises, the party claimed and held primacy in the political field – the decisive policy-making process took place within the party. This relative autonomy, however, eroded gradually under the impact of a growing reliance on economic and organisational support from the trade union movement. The party splits revealed – for LO – an intolerable political weakness and brought an organisational and financial crisis to DNA. In initiating the reunion process and providing the necessary financial backing, LO established itself as the dominant partner and was particularly instrumental in the speedy deradicalisation of the party.[16] It is today unthinkable that the two may part on a major political issue as they did just after World War I. [17]

While the first spurt in working-class organisation took place around the turn of the century and covered the 'basic' sphere of production, politics and consumption,[18] the second spurt in the twenties saw the rise of a set of 'alternative' organisations providing for the broader needs and aspirations in the working-class sub-culture. These covered the spheres of education, culture, leisure and housing.[19] Their blooming was, however, short – they either died in the post-World War II era, were swallowed by comparable bourgeois organisations or redefined their purpose. The trade unions are the only dynamic institution still claiming 'organisational totality' within its field. The rest are either considered sectional interest agencies or just one organisation among many in a pluralist system.

The organisational growth of Arbeiderpartiet itself follows the general lines of the entire movement: from insignificance around 1890 the membership reached 100,000 in 1919 (Table 2): a peak followed by massive desertion, arrested in 1923 by a steady growth which doubled the membership twice before 1940. The culmination comes around 1950 when the trend turns downwards. An elaborate organisational structure was created on this basis — a structure not free from the oligarchic tendencies of which Michels speaks so eloquently in his discussion of the German party as a necessary consequence of organisational dynamics.[20] The interesting feature of the Norwegian situation in this respect is that, even if present before 1920,[21] it was the *political* factors of party splits in the twenties and the fight against Communists in the thirties which crystallised the oligarchic tendencies. Before 1920 the internal debates had generated formally organised opposition groups which were tolerated by the entrenched leadership — a practice unthinkable and prohibited later.[22] The organisational complexities are of course the major conditional factor but the releasing forces seem to have been of a political nature. The oligarchic tendencies may later have been softened by another political factor — the Common Market issue — this time operational on the background of declining organisational strength.[23]

Social Composition

The social composition of the electorate and the leadership of the Party has varied considerably and the discrepancies between the levels have been more or less pronounced.[24] Before 1900 it was predominantly based on urban workers and crafsmen. From around 1902 with the adoption of a new agrarian programme the party also widened its support in the countryside. But these are primarily the years when DNA gained the confidence and votes of the emerging industrial working class. The thirties was the time for a major breakthrough in the countryside, completing the particular alliance of Norwegian social democracy which has given it its comparatively strong position: Arbeiderpartiet became the party of the industrial workers, the small-scale farmers, agrarian and forestry workers and fishermen. In the post-war period the lower and particularly public white-collar personnel has increased its share of the Party vote.

The changing composition of the élite underlines the structural isolation of the labour movement in Norway (Table 3). The liberal professions and the craftsmen were the midwives of the Party, but very soon the professionals of the movement took over: journalists, parliamentarians, the employees of the Party and the trade unions. None of the dominant social groups at the voter level have any significant representation in the élite, with the exception of the craftsmen in the first period. When looking at the social background of the élite in terms of father's occupation and own initial occupation, however, the discrepancies are considerably smaller.[25] But the best mirror of élite recruitment and its changes is not the electoral base, but is provided by the social composition of the trade union movement.[26]

Politics as Superstructure

In looking at the ideological development of DNA one is very much reminded of Bernstein's dictum that 'the final goal is nothing, the movement everything'. The twists and turns of ideology above the level of daily interest articulation, with the exception of the twenties, have not been a major challenge to the cohesiveness of the party.

Arbeiderpartiet started as a fairly moderate party — a party not exceeding the limits of 'trade union consciousness'. It was not, of course, moderate in the context of Norwegian politics at the time, but as measured against the standards of contemporary socialist debate in Europe. Around 1912 the organised opposition in the 'New Direction' and the youth movement gained momentum, basing its critique on arguments from the 'revisionist' debate inside the international movement and the practice of American syndicalism. The Left opposition won power in the party in 1918 and brought the party into Comintern a year later. As an indicator of radicalism, however, this is not entirely reliable either for the party itself or the Norwegian working class.[27] Its essential motive was loyalty to the Russian revolution as an historical act — not to its international expression. DNA never accepted the '21 theses' adopted by Comintern in 1920 and membership was retrospectively described as a mutual misunderstanding.[28] But the party was so radical that the moderate opposition left in 1921 to form *Norges Sosialdemokratiske Arbeiderparti* (NSA). At the break with Comintern two years later, the Communists left to create *Norges Kommunistiske Parti* (NKP). The period is in ideological terms one of official adherence to the doctrine of centralism, but in practice a fight for self-determination. After the flirtation with international Communism DNA quickly returned to practical reform-orientated work. They reunited with NSA in 1927 and the process of deradicalisation continued well into the 1960s — accelerated by three major developments: the world economic crisis in the thirties, the emergent threat of Fascism and the war experience 1940-5.

The development of Labour policy in Norway has taken place in relative isolation from theoretical debate. The spread and intensity of these debates have in general been low (again excepting 1921-3 and possibly 1970-3) and very little original theoretical activity on a socialist basis has materialised. Within Arbeiderpartiet there has always been a strong scepticism towards intellectuals and intellectualism.[29] The practical emphasis of DNA's politics also comes out in that the times of intense ideological discussion did have *international* issues in the forefront.[30] Indeed, the *unity* of the movement is everything — the necessary programmatic elements of ideology are left to a party committee every now and then as a 'superstructural' element with the function of legitimising *party politics.*

The Recent Past

The social and economic change occuring after 1945 has transformed virtually every aspect of Norwegian society, but until 1971 this change was not followed by any political changes of a similar magnitude — either in the balance between the different parties or their basic politics. It was a system-bolstering growth and the first twenty years was the golden age for its major party. The Communists emerged just after the war with a substantial following, but were soon declining in the wake of the 1948 coup in Czechoslovakia and local outbreaks of McCarthyism. The next rival to DNA for working-class support appeared in 1961 with the Socialist Peoples Party (SF). Its leadership had a common background in opposition to the foreign policy adopted by Arbeiderpartiet and the formation of SF was sparked off by the expulsion of some key figures from the Party.[31] SF emerged as an electorally minor, but parliamentarily important, party, holding the balancing vote from 1961 to 1965.

EC: a Socialist Commonwealth or a Capitalist Demon?

Significant political change was first set off by the purely political issue of whether to join the European Community (EC) or not.[32] Negotiations between EC and the four applicant states started in the spring of 1970 and they soon revealed sharp disagreement within the Norwegian Government.[33] This internal disagreement brought it down in February 1971 and the task of carrying the negotiations to an end was left to a Labour Government.

At this point DNA had its all-time peak in the polls, with 50 per cent of the electorate. Three years later this was down to 32 per cent — while four years after the EC referendum it was up again to 44 per cent.[34] Nothing but the rise and fall of the EC issue in the public debate can explain these changes.

From the start there were strong disagreements within the labour movement. SF and the small but active Communist Party were violently opposed to membership. According to the polls very few DNA voters wanted it in early 1971.[35] Those who did were predominantly to be found in the party leadership, among its parliamentarians and the top officials in LO. The internal oppostion to the leadership's pro-EC policy organised themselves in January 1972 at the initiative of DNA's own youth movement, AUF, the General Workers Union and the Graphical Union in an 'Information Committee Against Membership' (AIK). This group worked closely with SF and NKP within the umbrella organisation 'The People's Movement Against EC' (*Folkebevegelsen*).

The debate inside the labour movement, centred around the question of whether to join the EC, was an advance for socialism. Protagonists argued that the institutions of EC were neither capitalist nor socialist at present and that Norway with its strong labour movement and egalitarian tradition might contribute to push it in the right direction. But it was primarily an arrangement beneficial to the Norwegian economy which in addition would integrate the economies of previous enemies and prevent war.[36] It was also argued that EC was the only institution which effectively could curb the power of the multinational companies. Among the counter arguments, the capitalist freedom of the Rome Treaty was emphasised, also that joining the EC would rule out a possible future socialist development in Norway and tie the country even closer to the 'haves' against the 'have-nots' in the international community.[37]

But in spite of considerable pressure on party voters, not to speak of the active members and the higher echelons of the party,[38] the official 'yes' to EC — adopted by a 3 to 1 majority at a special conference — did not convince more than 54 per cent of the DNA supporters.[39] This was not enough to offset the strong no-vote among the supporters of the agrarian Centre Party, the Christian People's Party, SF, and generally in the districts tied to the primary sector of the economy. Membership was rejected in September 1972 by a 53.5 per cent majority.

Shortly afterwards what remained of AIK left the Party and with SF and NKP formed a 'Socialist Election Party' (SV) which at the 1973 Storting election managed to attract 11.2 per cent of the votes, while SF and NKP only had 4.5 per cent in the 1969 election. For Arbeiderpartiet the election was a disaster, a 'political earthquake' its vice-chairman labelled it.[40] The party vote fell from 46.5 to 35.2 per cent. (Table 4.)

Back to 'Normal'?

This did not last, however, and the turning-point came during 1975. A downward trend started for SV in January bringing the Party to 5-6 per cent before the end of the year. DNA started to climb in June. An explanation of this turn must start with the disintegration of SV. The negotiations to form a proper party were troubled by the Communist Party. Their long tradition as an independent party, their special relationship with the Soviet Union and tight-knit ideology put heavy strains on the party building process, and the public quarrels between the élite factions — not exclusively involving NKP — were eagerly reported in the mass media.[41] In addition one must include a tactical blunder of its parliamentarians[42] and their generally unsuccessful attempts at finding a distinct political profile.

But the return towards previous levels of support also took place at a time when the international economic recession hit Norway and possibly channelled the voters back to safe, well-tried alternatives. Supporting this thesis is the credit given to the governing party for doing comparatively well in a European perspective.

Internal changes in Arbeiderpartiet itself also took place in this period. A new leadership, less tied to the pro-EC image, was elected in April. In January 1976 the previous Chairman also had to resign as Prime Minister after polite but decisive action by leaders in the Party and LO.[43] All the changes discussed so far, however, are either only contributing factors or symptoms of the underlying causal agent: the entrance and exit of the Common Market issue in Norwegian politics. As this issue is on its way out, Norwegian politics — at least *formally* — 'return to normal'.[44] In the great debate over endogenous *v.* exogenous forces in the explanation of political development it is ammunition for both groups in this account: politics did matter because change was forced onto a remarkably stable situation, and did not because no fundamental and lasting change came out of it.

DNA: Just an Ordinary Party?

Another more general observation emerging from the Norwegian scene concerns the validity of the Duverger distinction between cadre and mass parties or Neumann's between parties of individual representation and social integration, both of which are basically distinctions between bourgeois and working-class parties.[45] The concepts of mass party and of social integration delineate parties where the members have a special status, parties which are qualitatively different from bourgeois élite parties as organised political collectives. They are parties of a distinct and inclusive social community as well as of political agency. This was a useful distinction in pre-1940 Norway, but has become less so in the post-war period.[46]

It is not only the sudden interest in DNA in ending its self-imposed celibacy and if necessary entering a coalition government after the 1977 election which makes the party less exceptional.[47] More importantly, Arbeiderpartiet's organisational strength has undoubtedly deteriorated in the post-war era and the party:member relationship has declined in inclusiveness and intensity. Party membership as well as the number of branches has fallen.[48] The internal discussions about the growing 'organisational problem' started as early as the late 1940s, and the severity of the problem was clearly recognised by three successive committees established to look into the matter in 1958, 1963 and 1972.[49] The leadership is in other words desperately aware of the drying out of its grass roots, but the fact that 'organisational engineering' does not help suggests the changes in the working-class rather than the party to be pivotal. On the other hand, the negative organisational experiences in connection with the EC debate — when, for example, AUF had their financial support cut and some of those most actively against the EC had their membership suspended during the continued fight after the referendum — obviously contributed to a further weakening of the party organisation.[50] The sharp fluctuations in DNA's electoral support over the last six years are in themselves a sign of a declining core of stable party supporters.[51]

Another sector of convergence between Arbeiderpartiet and the bourgeois parties is that of élite composition. The sources of recruitment are of course still very different — as they are between the bourgeois parties themselves — but the explosion in educational opportunities has made the Labour élite much more similar to the other élites in this respect.[52] And it is probable that the educational revolution will further weaken the social dependence of both the élite and the rank and file on the labour movement which made Arbeiderpartiet so characteristically different in the past.[53]

There are, however, still strong counterforces to this process of breakdown in the 'organic' link between party and class. In the forefront here is the trade union movement which is still a potent force in resisting the trend towards a purer political market for the working-class vote.[54] The development means nevertheless that Arbeiderpartiet cannot any longer take electoral mass support for granted. It must fight a continuous *political* struggle to renew and win contracts with individual voters, and the fluctuations in level of support may be just as sharp in the future as they have been in the past six years, if any new critical issue appears.

At a Crossroads?

Over the last forty years the characteristic electoral alliance of DNA between industrial workers, small farmers, agricultural workers and fishermen has been gradually undermined as a basis for parliamentary majorities by structural changes in the economy. In the census of 1930 the primary and secondary sectors accounted for 62 per cent of the 'economically active' population, while 37 per cent had their main occupation within the tertiary sector. In 1973 this sector had increased its share to 55 per cent, the manufacturing sector had grown from 27 to 34 and agriculture, forestry and fisheries had declined quite dramatically from 36 to 11 per cent.[55]

From the late 1950s the consequences to be drawn from these changes — organisational and political — have been debated within the labour movement. To DNA's right wing the growth in the tertiary sector has been a forceful argument in favour of a moderate policy. The left has pointed to the fact that the traditional groups are still the dominant base of the Party. While the former wants to adopt an 'activist strategy' towards the new groups in searching for new issues and programmes with a multi-group appeal embracing all 'wage-earners', the latter represent a 'passive approach' by either leaving the enlarged bougeois groups in peace as before or simply defining them as new sections of the working-class posing no qualitatively new questions.[56]

The activist strategy which would propel change from a class-based to an ideologically founded party is strongly supported by younger, well-educated middle-level leaders,[57] but also by many others. At the 1975 Congress the party leader, Mr Bratteli, discussed the issue in detail. He identified two main trends: a decline in the traditional electoral base of the party, and the transformation of industrial work which gradually removes the worker/functionary distinction, concluding that a large party like DNA in the future had to win broad support from the electorate of the tertiary sector.[58] The outgoing Party Secretary was more direct in making it a precondition for future electoral success to win support from these groups.[59] And the way to achieve this was to sacrific a few 'sacred cows' and adopt a more moderate, centre policy in certain areas.[60] The activist strategy is probably dominant within the party today.

What is undecided, however, is the lesson to draw from this. Does a

multi-group appeal necessarily imply a deceleration of state ownership
in the productive field, an end to the expansion of welfare services and
income redistribution through taxation and a general downgrading of
'equality' and 'societal interests' by throwing bureaucrats out and
getting the market in? Or what is the *political* connection between a
changing social terrain and increased voter support for Arbeiderpartiet?
The question is crucial to the party at present, but here two points of
caution will be noted.

The growth in the tertiary sector is usually seen indiscriminately as a
growth of the white-collar groups. The pitfalls to this assertion are that
the 'work active' population is not the whole electorate and that a large
portion of those classified within the tertiary sector are not white-collar
workers.[61] On the other hand they do not include the functionaries of
the manufacturing industries. The surveys, however, covering people
actually using their vote — which is really what we are interested in —
shows the white-collar groups to be just above 40 per cent — which is
far from the 55 per cent usually quoted.[62]

Still, this group is obviously increasing, and clearly no party aspiring
to electoral majority can ignore it. The tendency to call for a moderate
policy to attract it is inspired by the 'clerk-image' of the white-collar
worker: when the traditional patriarchy of the employers retreated from
'my workers' to 'my functionaries', the 'clerk-image' emerged of a loyal
employee, closely tied to his employer and supporting his politics. It is
high time to challenge this stereotype, and the best way of doing it is to
propose another — namely the 'social-worker-image': publicly employed
and radicalised through education and the impossible task of remedying
the symptoms of the malaise — of caring for the victims of a merciless
capitalist system. But stereotypes aside — the public/private
dichotomy is obviously crucial.[63] Even more important is the distinction
between higher and lower functionaries.[64] But in total, in the general
elections from 1957 to 1969 DNA *already had support* from close to
50 per cent of the white-collar workers.[65] This share declined drastically
to 34 per cent in the election following the referendum, a development
which is not neatly explained by the equation: more moderation equals
more white-collar voters.[66] In addition, these occupational groups have
been the basis for the fastest-growing sections of the trade union
movement since the late 1950s.[67] All this make it dubious whether a
turn to the right will increase DNA's support from the white-collar
voters. It rather suggests — which of course is the fear of the 'activists' —
that it will make better room to the left for a more radical version of
social democracy like SV.

The Unending Struggle

The denial of a left-wing/right-wing continuum within the Party is a favourite theme for its leadership in public statements, and this 'fiction of the bourgeois press' is as old as the Party and the internal struggle itself. The basic denominators defining the left-right dimension in Arbeiderpartiet today are the role of the market in the Norwegian economy and the position of Norway in the international arena. Arising from these core positions is the public struggle about the issues of the day and for positions of power instrumental in deciding party policy.

The white-collar debate is part of this dimension, but recently two issues have taken priority: the selection of a new leadership in 1975 and the question of extending oil exploration to the waters outside northern Norway. Both can be seen as test cases for the balance between left and right at present.[68]

The leadership debate started when Mr Bratteli in June 1974 announced that he would retire as Chairman at the Congress a year later. Soon it was also clear that the important position as Secretary became vacant as well, at least if the Vice-Chairman, Mr Steen, became the successor. Steen had his main support in the party organisation and sections of the press and trade union movement. The other contender, Mr Nordli, was parliamentary leader of the party and had strong support there, in the Government and, although passively, from Bratteli. Steen was the candidate of the left-centre group, Nordli of the right-centre. To handle the selection process a small committee was set up, headed by Bratteli, which invited everybody in the movement to address them. This could not, however, keep the factions from organising clandestine campaigns, discover each other and causing quite a stir in and around the party.

When the Congress opened the question was still not decided — an opinion poll had just shown the expected lead for Nordli among DNA *voters* and those of the bourgeois parties, and for Steen among SV's supporters.[69] At the Congress the pressure on undecided and 'weak' delegates was considerable from both sides, but eventually it turned out to be a small majority for Steen (unofficially of course), and the Conference unanimously decided that he should be the new Chairman while Nordli should succeed Bratteli when he retired as Prime Minister.[70] The outcome was a compromise, although clearly a victory for the left, where the factions were entrenched in different institutional frameworks[71] from where the struggle could continue.

It did so some months later over the Government proposal to start oil exploration north of latitude 62° in 1977. This was and is an explosive issue in Norwegian politics: are the safety conditions satisfactory for drilling in these rough waters, what are the consequences for fishing and the many small communities dependent on it, and, on the other hand, how will it affect the manufacturing industries of the region not to start? In March 1975 a leading Left-wing member of the Party criticised the Government proposal publicly in an SV publication.[72] In turn the Secretary for Environmental Protection, Mrs Harlem Brundtland, who was also the Party Vice-Chairman, argued in favour of postponing drilling for one year, for 'safety reasons', and was strongly backed by Steen. This move gained the support of many parliamentarians, forcing the centre-right to concede an important symbolic victory to the left wing. The Prime Minister received a public reprimand from his Party Chairman. At the same time, however, it demonstrated where the real power lay: in the parliamentary group and in the Government, where the moderates are dominant.

From this point of view it was not at all surprising when Steen a few weeks later announced his intention to enter the Storting and the parliamentary group at the 1977 election. And at the time of writing (October 1976) the contest continues more quietly in the nomination process for this election. So whether the offensive of the left over the last 2-3 years will have any lasting effects on the party in organs which count can only be seen in the composition and work of Arbeiderpartiet's Storting group when it meets in October 1977. A crucial determinant of this struggle is, however, outside the immediate control of both groups: whether or not there will be a Labour Government. A Labour Government will very much leave the initiative where it is now, with the moderates. In opposition the Party organisation, dominated by the left, will again be an important and perhaps decisive platform.[73]

The successes of the internal Left have clearly weakened the external socialist opposition centred around SV. The fundamental dilemma for the left wing since 1945 has been whether to work inside or outside the party. The question was acute for AIK just after the referendum. Was the Common Market issue an exception to the favourable trend which started with the period of party opposition in 1965? When the Party was relieved of the constraints of twenty years' continuous rule, there was a considerable turnover in élite as well as organisational activists, and Party policy changed favourably.[74] Or was it the ultimate proof of its hopeless conservatism? The ensuing years have pointed more to the former than the latter. But an additional reason for this shake-up of the Party may have been the emergence of a dangerous alternative to DNA hegemony in the working class. The decline of SV can therefore also *diminish* the chances of continued success for Arbeiderpartiet's left wing.

The 1977 Election

Since so much depends on the outcome of the 1977 election what are the prospects? According to the polls Arbeiderpartiet will certainly do much better than in 1973 and might even win a majority in the Storting alone.[75] What the conservative newspaper *Aftenposten* calls the 'Janus-face' of DNA,[76] the broad electoral appeal of a moderate Nordli and a radical Steen has undoubtedly been a vote catching success. A more likely outcome, however, will be that DNA and SV (which is expected to be at least halved) together will provide the parliamentary base for a continued minority DNA government. Arbeiderpartiet will probably not enter a coalition either with SV or one of the centre parties. The latter *might* happen if a bourgeois majority failed to form a government or this broke down – the former only by a highly unlikely left-wing dominance in DNA's parliamentary group.

But very much will of course depend on the campaign – which issues will predominate, will any new foreign policy issues suddenly break into the re-established Norwegian tranquillity, what effects will a possible accident in the North Sea have and will the left-right struggle remain silent till after the election?

In a longer perspective, what will the social base of Arbeiderpartiet look like in the years to come? That of course depends on the future changes in social structure and the political fortunes of the Party leadership. There is reason to expect a continued decline of the fishery and agricultural communites and a rise in urbanisation and the white-collar sector. The pressure on the economy due to the expanding petro-chemical industries will most likely override the political measures to counter this trend. To remain an aspiring single majority party DNA will obviously turn to the expanding white-collar groups. The test then is whether they will succeed in doing this at the same time as they keep up the traditional alliance with the countryside. It is clear, however, that the dominant element of this base will remain the working-class – one can only guess as to whether it will be broadened or purified.

But this social development coupled with a higher level of education and the decline of working-class communities and the integrative capacity of the labour movement are likely to nourish a greater voter independence and increased electoral volatility. A consequence of this may be that political skills and campaigns rather than allegiance will determine the shape of Norwegian labour politics in the future.[77]

Notes

1. Henry Valen and Stein Rokkan, 'Norway: Conflict Structure and Mass Politics in an European Periphery', in Rose (ed.), *Electoral Behaviour. A Comparative Handbook* (London, Collier Macmillan Publishers, 1974), pp. 315-70.
2. See the general historical accounts given in Aksel Zachariassen, *Fra Marcus Thrane til Martin Tranmæl* (Oslo, AOF, 1962); Edvard Bull, *Norsk Fagbevegelse* (Oslo, Tiden, 1968) and Einhart Lorenz, *Arbeiderbevegelsens Historie I & II* (Oslo, Pax, 1972 and 73). For a personal experience of this legacy, see Konrad Nordahl, *Gode arbeidsar* (Oslo, Tiden, 1973), p. 174.
3. Consider for example the role played by the Swedish youth organisation and syndicalists in the build-up of Radicalism 1909-18. See W.M. Lafferty, *Economic Development and the Response of Labour in Scandinavia* (Oslo, Universitetsforlaget, 1971), and *Tidsskrift for Arbeiderbevegelsens Historie,* vol. 1, 1976.
4. It is of course historically incorrect to label Arbeiderpartiet 'Social Democratic' in all its phases as will soon become evident. But for convenience the present takes precedence over the past.
5. Major political changes explained by endogenous developments are however prominent in the radicalisation of DNA around WWI. See Lafferty, op. cit.
6. Halvard Lange, *Fra sekt til parti* (Oslo, Universitetsforlaget, 1962).
7. For a discussion of the development of the Norwegian party system, see Valen and Rokkan, op. cit. and the references given there. The effects of the institutional structure on the labour movement are taken up in Lafferty, op. cit. ch. 4.
8. Lafferty, op. cit. ch. 2.
9. These were Høyre (Conservatives), Kristelig Folkeparti (Christian People's Party), Senterpartiet (The Agrarians, formerly Bondepartiet) and Venstre (Liberals).
10. At the 5th Workers Congress in Stockholm in 1897.
11. This account is based on Knut Heidar, 'Institusjonalisering i DNA 1887-1940' (unpublished thesis, Institute for Social Research, Oslo, 1974), part I.
12. The 1963 figures are found in Aksel Zachariassen, *Det kollektive medlemskap* (Oslo, Tiden, 1966).
13. See also the debate on the relationship with LO at the 1975 Congress, DNA, *Protokollforhandlingene fra DNA's ordinære Landsmøte 20-23 april 1975 i Oslo,* (Oslo, DNA, 1966), p. 199-217.
14. This has not, however, primarily been the influence of the top union officials as in the British case. The collective affiliation has always been by the *local* trade union branch through the *local* party branch. See Kjell Eliassen, *'Fagbevegelsen og de sosialdemokratiske partier'* (unpublished Master Thesis, University of Bergen, 1971).
15. See Heidar, op. cit. section 1.2.
16. Ulf Torgersen's 'The Trend Towards Political Consensus: The Case of Norway', *Acta Sociologica,* vol. V (1962), pp.159-72, poses this deradicalisation as a problem not easily explained by social variables, p. 170.
17. One of the conditioning factors when the Prime Minister, Einar Gerhardsen, temporarily stepped back in 1951, was disagreements with LO over prices and incomes policy.
18. *Norges Kooperative Landsforening,* the national consumer co-operative, was started in 1906.

19. See Lorenz, op. cit. II, p. 33-8.
20. R. Michels, *Political Parties* (New York, The Free Press, 1962).
21. See e.g. Bull, op. cit. p. 63 on the party press.
22. The possibility of an organised internal opposition is the criterion of 'non-oligarchy' employed by Lipset, Trow and Coleman, *Union Democracy* (New York, The Free Press, 1956). For an account of the oligarchic tendencies in DNA, see Heidar, op. cit. pp.53-4; Jardar Seim, *Hvordan Hovedavtalen av 1935 ble til* (Oslo, Tiden, 1972) and Ottar Hellevik, 'Kan Bratteli gjøre som han vil?', in Kjeldstadli and Keul (eds.), *DNA – fra foklebevegelse til statsstøtte* (Oslo, Pax, 1973), pp. 207-32.
23. See the discussion later in this article.
24. Detailed studies on the changes in the electoral base of DNA have not been done so far, but the general trend is known.
25. Heidar, op. cit. part III and Knut Heidar. 'Partielite og Politikk', *Tidsskrift for Samfunnsforskning*, vol.15 (1974), pp.314-41.
26. See Heidar, *'Institusjonalisering'*, pp.134-9.
27. See Lafferty, op. cit. pp.182-98, and Odd-Bjørn Fure, *'Synspunkter og historie–teoretiske tendenser i forskningen om den norske arbeiderklasse og – bevegelse i den radikale fase 1918-1933'*, in *Tidsskrift for arbeiderbevegelsens historie*, vol. 1 (1976).
28. See the accounts in Knut Langfeldt, *Moskvatesene i norsk politikk* (Oslo, Universitetsforlaget, 1961) and Per Maurseth, *Fra Moskvateser til Kristiania-forslag* (Oslo, Pax, 1972).
29. See Trygve Bull, *Mot Dag og Erling Falk* (Oslo, Cappelen, 1955).
30. This does not only come out in the struggle over Comintern 1921-3 and the Common Market issue 1971-3, but also with the debates over the Franco regime in Spain, the NATO issue and the question of West German rearmament.
31. A detailed account is found in Ragnar Kvam jun., *DNA mot splittelse. Da venstrefløyen ble ekskludert og SF stiftet* (Oslo, Cappelen, 1973).
32. A prelude to this struggle occurred during the winter 1962-3 which was stopped by de Gaulle's No to Britain. Without this No there is reason to believe that Norway would have been an EC member now due to the weakness of the Left opposition at the time.
33. Its partners had been on opposite sides in 1962-3 and were shortly after the break on different sides again.
34. These figures are taken from the Norwegian Gallup Institute which has proved fairly reliable at most elections.
35. Lorenz, op. cit. II, p. 189.
36. Strongly emphasised by the Prime Minister, Bratteli, himself a concentration camp prisoner in Germany during the war.
37. This summary of the arguments is based upon the proceedings and the extraordinary Party Congress in 1972. DNA, *Protokoll over forhandlingene på det ekstraordinære Landsmøte 21-22 april 1972* (Oslo, DNA, 1972).
38. See Ottar Hellevik and Nils Petter Gleditsch, 'The Common Market Decision in Norway: A Clash between Direct and Indirect Democracy', *Scandinavian Political Studies*, vol. 8 (1973), pp. 227-35.
39. Ibid. p. 232.
40. See *Sosialistisk Perspektiv*, no. 4, 1973.
41. In addition to this most visible and damaging struggle, the other SV sections as well had difficulties forgetting their organisational ties. The ideological spectrum represented was also stretching fairly wide, from various shades of reformism to the revolutionaries and a substantial populist grouping. The common denominators were the opposition to Arbeiderpartiet and the victorious struggle against EC membership.

42. Its resistance to the buying out of the foreign owner of an alumina plant on the west coast of Norway put a heavy strain on SV's relations with the trade union movement.
43. See Per Bratland's article in *Sosialistisk Perspektiv,* no.1, 1976, p.12.
44. Jens A. Christophersen, 'Valget 1975. Tilbake til det normale?', *Samtiden,* vol. 85 (1976), no. 1, pp. 1-12, and an editorial in the national newspaper of DNA, *Arbeiderbladet,* 14 Sept. 1976, labour the point that Norwegian politics now are on their way to 'normal'. This is true only in a formal sense, however. The content of politics was decisively altered with the EC debate 1971-3.
45. Maurice Duverger, *Political Parties,* 2nd edition (London, Methuen, 1959), and Sigmund Neumann, *Modern Political Parties* (Chicago, The University of Chicago Press, 1956). In this generalisation I deliberately overlook the troublesome case of Fascism.
46. When a Party Secretary at a Party Conference suggested that the truism of Arbeiderpartiet's organisational superiority was a myth, he was met with sceptical disbelief. Today his views would probably get a more affirmative response. See Magne Nedregard, '1. etappe av partiets langtidsplan – "Partiundersøkelsen 1970" ' (mimeo, Oct. 1969). After the 1973 election, Reiulf Steen admitted that DNA had 'lost its traditionally good contact with the grass roots'. Lorenz, op. cit. II, p. 200.
47. DNA has never under normal circumstances entered a coalition government. After the election defeat of 1973, the Chairman suggested that this tradition ought to be discussed in the Party.
48. The measure, although precarious, adequately indicates long-time trends.
49. In the report of the first, the decline in members, absolute and relative (as proportion of voters), and the deterioration of organisational work in general is characterised as a real 'challenge to all of us'. The Party's existence depended on the Party worker which 'must give impulses to the leadership, and bring party policy to the people. This contact is the life-nerve of the party'. And what follows is a detailed programme for improving organisational vitality. Unsuccessful it seems, for five years later the Party set up another committee to examine the same problems and what to do about them. They sent a questionnaire to the local branches, and the picture which emerged from this inquiry was a bleak one: Among the 23 per cent of the branches which answered at all, many hold only the one meeting a year necessary to elect leaders and keep it officially alive. When asked about the causes for this miserable state of affairs they mentioned the 'well-known ones' – according to the committee – of people having it too good to care, a feeling that things were straightened out without 'their' participation, that the members were too old, the competition with television and alternative leisure activities, etc. The third of the committees was appointed in 1972 and concentrated on measures to streamline the organisational apparatus and played down the importance of the social movement aspect: 'The organisational forms in the local communities must be framed so as to give *everybody who wishes to participate* satisfactory possibilities' (my *emphasis).* The reports can be found at th at the *Arbeiderbevegelsens Arkiv,* Oslo.
50. This is not only because some of the activists later left with AIK, but also because many, both pro- and anti-, found the political and social atmosphere unpleasant and opted for 'political retirement'. See Lorenz, op. cit. II, pp. 188-97, and Lise Winther, *Da partipisken smalt i Asker* (Oslo, Pax, 1973).
51. In the Norwegian programme for electoral research (see references in Valen and Rokkan, op. cit.) unpublished data show a clear decline in the proportion of the sample considering themselves a 'party man or woman', from 1965 over 1969 to 1973.

52. See Heidar, *'Partielite'*, p. 324.
53. In the connection, see Stein Rokkan, *'Utdanningseksplosjonen og Partisystemene'* (Lecture at University of Bergen, 1969, mimeo). It is indicative of the whole trend that one of the main problems during the 1976 First of May celebrations was the televising of the British football cup final (*Tillitsmannen,* no. 3, 1976).
54. Among workers organised in LO 84 per cent voted with DNA in 1961 while 57 per cent among the non-members did. Among male functionaries the figures are 77 per cent *v.* 42 per cent. The member/non-member difference was just as marked among women. See Sverre Lysgaard, *Arbeidernes syn på faglige og politiske spørsmål* (Oslo, Universitetsforlaget, 1965), pp. 58-9.
55. Rogoff Ramsøand Vaa (eds.), *Det norske samfunn I* (Oslo, Universitetsforlaget, 1975), p. 112.
56. See Penny Gill Martin, 'Party Strategies and Social Change: The Norwegian Labour Party' (unpublished Ph.D. thesis, Yale University, 1972), pp. 177-8.
57. Martin, op. cit. pp. 201 and 209. On the other hand, a recently retired district secretary who had started as forestry worker and later been twenty-nine years in service of the Party expressed his feelings thus: 'To me it would be a great disappointment if a better society will create more middle-class.' (*Tillitsmannen,* no. 1, 1976.)
58. DNA, op. cit. 1976, p. 32. See also Trygve Bratteli, 'Filosofien bak velferdsstaten', *Sosialistisk Perspektiv,* no. 1, 1974.
59. DNA, op. cit. p. 224.
60. Outlined in Ronald Bye, *Synspunkter og vurderinger* (Oslo, Tiden, 1975).
61. In 1970 18.3 per cent of 'resident population' had pensions, social security, funds, etc. as main source of livelihood. Norges Offisielle Statistikk, *Statistisk Årbok 1975* (Oslo, 1975), Table 16, p. 15.
62. Henry Valen and Willy Martinussen (eds.), *Velgerne og politiske frontlinjer* (Oslo, Gyldendal, 1972), table 9.2, p. 290.
63. Henry Valen, 'Partiforskyvningene ved stortingsvalget i 1965', *Tidsskrift for Samfunnsforskning,* vol. 8 (1967), p. 115. Teachers have always been radical in Norwegian politics and public employees have for a long time been among the activists within DNA itself.
64. Ibid.
65. Henry Valen, 'The Local Elections of September 1975', *Scandinavian Political Studies,* vol. II (1976), p. 181.
66. Ibid. The equation was in fact argued, see Per Bratland in *Sosialistisk Perspektiv,* no. 1, 1973.
67. The Union of Trade and Office Workers will soon be the third largest in LO.
68. In order not to exaggerate, however, it is important to note that the *common* perspective of these groups (which are not that homogeneous and exclusive either), their outer boundary for permissible debate and decisions, place both within the species called West European Social Democracy where the call for gradual reforms is the banner.
69. See *Dagbladet,* 19 Apr. 1975.
70. Which he did in January 1976. See also note 43.
71. While the top positions in DNA's Central Committee before had been manned with people with independent power bases in the movement, Steen now emerged as dominant. See Nils Ørvik, *Aftenposten,* 26 May 1976. The Left has also won a series of organisational positions, among them the important position as Chairman of the Oslo Party.
72. *Ny Tid,* March 1976.
73. The party organisation was probably the dominant organ in the Party well into the 1950s.

74. See the account of DNA's 'bourgeois phase' by Guttorm Hansen in 'Arbeiderpartiet og sosialdemokratiet', in E. Fromm (ed.), *Demokratisk sosialisme* (Oslo, Dreyer, 1975), pp. 192-8. An indication of a changing state of affairs came when Steen after the 1973 election asked all Party workers to express freely their 'true viewpoints'. See *Arbeiderbladet,* 25 Oct. 1973.

75. The Party Secretary expressed that belief at a National Conference meeting 5 Oct. 1976. See *Arbeiderbladet,* 6 Oct. 1976.

76. Editorial in *Aftenposten,* 14 June 1976.

77. In its political expression we may therefore speak about a growing 'americanisation' of the class struggle in Norway.

The Norwegian Labour Party

Table 1. The labour movement at Storting elections

Party:	DNA		NSA		NKP		SF		SV		Total Storting
Year	%	Repr.	%	Repr.	%	Repr.	%	Repr.	%	Repr.	Repr.
1894	—										
1897	—										
1900	2.9										
1903	10.4	4									117
1906	16.0	10									123
1909	20.4	11									123
1912	26.5	23									123
1915	32.1	19									123
1918	30.9	18									126
1921	21.3	29	9.2	8							150
1924	18.4	24	8.8	8	6.1	6					150
1927	36.8	59			4.0	3					150
1930	31.4	47			1.7	—					150
1933	40.1	69			1.8	—					150
1936	42.5	70			0.3	—					150
1945	41.0	76			11.9	11					150
1949	45.7	85			5.8	—					150
1953	46.7	77			5.0	3					150
1957	48.3	78			3.4	1					150
1961	46.8	74			2.9	—	2.4	2			150
1965	43.2	68			1.4	—	6.0	2			150
1969	46.5	74			1.0	—	3.5	—			150
1973	35.3	62							11.2	16	155

DNA Det Norske Arbeiderparti (The Norwegian Labour Party)
NSA Norges Sosialdemokratiske Arbeiderparti (The Norwegian Social Democratic Labour Party)
NKP Norges Kommunistiske parti (The Norwegian Communist Party)
SF Sosialistisk Folkeparti (Socialist People's Party)
SV Sosialistisk Valgallianse (Socialist Election alliance)

Table 2. Membership in DNA at selected years

Year	Membership
1890	1,633
1895	6,000
1900	10,655
1905	16,500
1910	32,926
1915	62,952
1919	105,348
1923	40,260
1930	80,177
1935	122,007
1938	170,889
1945	191,045
1949	204,055
1955	174,080
1960	165,096
1965	150,262
1970	155,254
1974	130,489

Table 3. Social composition of DNA's organisational leadership
1887-1971. Percentages

Period	Occupational category:												Sum	(N)
	0	1	2	3	4	5	6	7	8	9	10	11		
1887-1903	0	0	2	6	34	0	1	11	24	11	12	0	101	(140)
1904-17	9	1	9	24	10	3	3	4	9	4	25	1	102	(106)
1918-26	4	6	4	19	4	4	9	6	8	6	28	2	100	(191)
1927-39	15	4	4	8	2	8	5	7	3	3	38	4	101	(184)
1945-49	23	11	2	8	5	6	4	2	0	0	35	3	99	(97)
1950-59	21	19	2	13	3	2	2	1	0	0	38	1	102	(167)
1960-65	22	17	5	9	2	0	3	2	0	1	35	5	101	(130)
1966-71	12	19	9	3	4	2	0	2	1	2	44	2	100	(129)
1887-1971	13	10	4	11	8	3	4	4	6	4	32	2	101	(1144)

Occupational code:

0 — Storting representatives/Government Ministers
1 — Higher official employees
2 — Lower official employees
3 — Journalists/editors
4 — Liberal professions — higher private employees
5 — Lower private (functionaries)
6 — Farmers, fishermen
7 — Industrial workers
8 — Crafts
9 — Manual non-industry workers
10 — Employee of party or trade union
11 — Housewives

Sources: Knut Heidar, 'Institusjonalisering i DNA 1887-1940' (unpublished thesis,
Institute for Social Research, Oslo, 1974), p. 173 and *idem,* 'Partielite
og Politikk', *Tidsskrift for Samfuansforskning,* vol. 15 (1974), p. 323.

Table 4. Votes and Seats in the Storting Elections of 1969 and 1973

Party			Votes		Seats	
1969	1969 & 1973	1973	1969	1973	1969	1073
		Marxists-Leninists	—	0.43	—	—
NKP			1.04	—	—	—
SF			3.50	—	—	—
		SV	—	11.23	—	16
	DNA		46.53	35.29	74	62
V			9.38		13	
		V	—	3.49	—	2
		DNF	—	3.43	—	1
	KRF		9.40	12.24	14	20
	S		10.53	11.03	20	21
	H		19.57	17.38	29	29
		ALP	—	5.01	—	4
		Other	0.05	0.47	—	—
Total votes			2162.596	2152.204		
Turnout			83.8%	80.2%		
Seats					150	155

Parties: NKP, SF, SV, DNA, see Table 1.

V   Venstre (Liberals)
DNF   Det Nye Folkepartiet (Split off Liberals)
KRF   Kristelig Folkeparti (Christian People's Party)
S   Senterpartiet (Agrarians)
H   Høyre (Conservatives)
ALP   Anders Langes Parti (Right-wing Conservatives)

Source: Valen and Rokkan, 'Norway: The Election to the Storting in
September 1973', *Scandinavian Political Studies,* vol. 9 (1974), p. 207.

Further Reading

Bull, Edvard d.y. *The Norwegian Trade Union Movement.* Brussels,
International Confederation of Free Trade Unions, 1956.

Fivelsdal, Egil and Higley, John. 'The Labour Union Elite in Norway'.
Scandinavian Political Studies, vol. 5 (1970).

Galeson, Walter. 'Scandinavia,' In Galeson (ed.), *Comparative Labor
Movements.* New York, Prentice Hall, 1952.

Lafferty, William M. *Economic Development and the Response of
Labour in Norway.* Oslo, Universitetsforlaget, 1971.

Rokkan, Stein and Valen, Henry. 'The mobilisation of the periphery.'
In Rokkan (ed.), *Approaches to the study of political participation.*
Bergen, Chr. Michelsens Institutt, 1962.

Valen, Henry and Katz, Daniel. *Political Parties in Norway.* Oslo,
Universitetsforlaget, 1964.

12 SOCIAL DEMOCRACY IN SWEDEN[1]

Richard Scase

Sweden, in popular discussion, is often regarded as a synthesis of the more desirable features of both capitalist and state socialist countries. Thus, it is often considered to have discarded the unacceptable faces of both capitalism and socialism. Such an image stems largely from the fact that until October 1976 it had experienced forty-four years of Social Democratic Governments. These administrations, so it is often asserted, have 'domesticated' capital to the extent that its benefits are equitably enjoyed by all sectors of society. Consequently, Sweden is frequently seen to be the prototype of the modern welfare state within which the more acute dimensions of poverty, deprivation and economic exploitation have been eliminated.

Despite these claims, however, Sweden has one of the most developed forms of monopoly capital in the world; in no other Western country is there such a high concentration of privately owned economic resources. In the 1960s, the hundred largest companies employed 43 per cent of all workers in manufacturing industry and accounted for 46 per cent of the total product.[2] A Swedish Government enquiry reported in 1968 that the level of industrial and commercial concentration had increased during the post-war era and that it was now a higher level than in either the United States or Western Germany. This trend has been reflected in the ownership of Swedish companies so that, again in the mid-1960s, one-quarter of the share capital was held by 0.1 per cent of shareholders and about three-quarters by 10 per cent.[3] Social Democratic Governments, then, have not destroyed the dynamics of capital accumulation. Indeed, they have encouraged industrial and commercial amalgamation on the ground that it strengthens the competitiveness of Swedish manufactured goods in world markets. Thus, for many Marxist writers, Sweden is a 'write off'; it is an outstanding example of a country in which parliamentary socialism has failed to further the interests of industrial workers. Such a view, however, tends to be an oversimplification since it fails to take into account the influence of the Swedish working-class movement and the tensions and contradictions which this has created in the structure of a capitalist society. Unlike in many other countries the Social Democratic Party and the Labour unions are ideologically and organisationally

316

interconnected so that their industrial and political objectives can only be properly understood by reference to their interdependence within the working-class movement. Thus, in order to investigate the nature of Social Democracy in Sweden it is necessary to trace the historical development of (1) the trade unions and (2) the Social Democratic Party.

1. Trade Unions

Because of its late industrialisation, the origins of trade unionism in Sweden are fairly recent. It was not until the 1880s that they were first established, although workers' associations existed before that time; it is often claimed that the oldest dates from 1846, when the Union of Typographers was formed in Stockholm. But this was not a trade union in the contemporary sense: it was a 'club' which provided educational facilities for its members.[4] Similarly, during the 1860s and 1870s there were many comparable organisations but few of these provided the bases for 'genuine' trade unions, established to pursue the economic objectives of their members. Trade unions only began to flourish during the 1880s among printers, machinists and other skilled craftsmen in the larger urban areas.[5] By contrast, the smaller industrial towns with traditions derived from the *bruks* were of little consequence for the development of trade unionism because their 'paternalistic' social structure reduced the degree to which workers could organise themselves for the purposes of bargaining, and also because the strains of industrialisation were less severely experienced by these workers than by those who had migrated to the growing industrial communities.[6] Consequently, it was among the craftsmen of the larger urban areas that the bases of Swedish trade unionism were established. Often these workers had travelled abroad, especially to England and Germany, in order to obtain craft skills and this had brought them into contact with trade union organisations.[7] This, coupled with the deprivations which they experienced in Swedish industrial communities, together with the absence of 'welfare benefits' available to workers in *bruks,* led to the rapid acceptance of trade union ideas. Thus, during the 1880s a number of local trade unions developed, particularly in Stockholm and the growing industrial communities in southern Sweden. But it was not until the end of the decade that national federations emerged; the first was established in 1886 and in the 1890s this became the dominant form of union structure among both unskilled and skilled workers.[8] At this time, however, Swedish trade unions were numerically weak. Bäckström claims that at the beginning of the 1880s there were only 9,000 members and by the end of the century this had only increased to 66,000; a figure equivalent to about 25 per cent of all industrial workers.[9]

In 1898 Swedish trade unions formed their own central organisation – the Confederation of Trade Unions (*Landsorganisation,* LO); until then, the activities of the national unions had been co-ordinated by the Social Democratic Party.[10] But in its early years LO had only limited influence and its major function was to provide advisory services and information to the various affiliated unions. It was not until the formation of the Confederation of Swedish Employers (*Svenska Arbetsgivareföreningen,* SAF) in 1902 that LO began to operate as an effective centralised negotiating body for the trade union movement. As a result, collective agreements were negotiated between SAF and LO. The first of these was in 1905 and possibly because of this, there was an increase in union membership; by 1909 the number had reached 231,000 – equivalent to approximately two-thirds of the industrial labour force.[11] But then SAF organised a lockout; LO lost more than one-half of its membership and it was not until 1917 that the 1909 figures were again achieved.[12] From 1911, however, trade union membership continued to grow so that, despite temporary setbacks, it had reached a figure of more than 1,600,000 by 1967.[13] The growth of LO membership during the twentieth century is shown in Table 1.

Table 1. The Growth of Membership among Trade Unions Affiliated to LO

Date	Nos. of Unions Affiliated to LO	Nos. of Members
1899	16	37,523
1907	28	186,226
1911	26	79,926
1920	31	280,029
1929	36	508,107
1939	45	961,216
1949	44	1,255,987
1959	44	1,467,117
1967	37	1,607,007

Source: T. Karlbom, *Arbetarnas Fackföreningar* (Workers' Trade Unions), Helsinki, 1969, p. 72.

During the 1920s the labour movement had several policies for changing the structure of society and for improving the economic, political and social conditions of workers, but little was achieved because of its weak bargaining position. The decade was characterised by high unemployment, political instability and a labour movement divided by a wide range of ideological issues.[14] Nevertheless, membership of LO continued to grow and this, coupled with an increase in the number of working days lost through strikes, led to pressure from Conservative groups for the Government to introduce laws to 'regularise' the labour market. Consequently, in 1928 laws were passed which made strikes illegal while collective agreements between LO and SAF were in force. Although the trade union movement protested, these laws continue to constitute one of the bases for industrial relations in present-day Sweden.

In the 1930s the position of trade unions in Sweden was fundamentally altered by the general election of 1932; this produced the first Social Democratic Government to have an effective majority in parliament. It meant that trade unions were now in partnership with the Government rather than in opposition to it and for the first time LO was actively involved in the formulation of economic and social policies. This, of course, strengthened the position of trade unions in Sweden, but it also led to the development of internal strains within the labour movement, since Social Democratic governments formulated policies in collaboration with LO which were often contrary to the economic interests of specified affiliated unions. The priority given to economic growth by LO and Social Democratic governments, for example, led to attempts to develop a 'rational' economy and this often produced unemployment among workers of specific unions within particular industries. Since the 1940s, furthermore, LO's policy of 'wage solidarity', backed by government support, has meant that unions in powerful bargaining situations have often been forced to moderate their wage claims.[15]

The 1932 general election was not the only factor which strengthened the influence of trade unions in Sweden; an important event was the 1938 'Saltsjöbaden Agreement' which reinforced the 'centralised' features of Swedish industrial relations which had existed since 1905. As a result of this agreement, LO and SAF established a code of practice for regulating industrial relations at the plant, company, and industrial levels.[16] One of the major consequences of the agreement was that it confirmed the superordinate authority of LO over the member unions. Thus, power within the labour movement became more concentrated in the full-time officials of LO with the result that member unions became highly constrained in terms of the policies which they could independently pursue. Whether or not this has been to the advantage of rank-and-file members is problematic but because LO has been the central negotiating body for manual unions, it has been able to pursue egalitarian policies in two directions. The first, in attempting to narrow wage differentials between various groups of manual workers by its policy of 'wage solidarity', and the second in trying to reduce differences in the earnings and employment conditions of manual workers and other occupational groups in society.[17] It is possible that with a less centralised structure, Swedish trade unions would have been less concerned about narrowing such differentials and that various manual unions would have been in greater competition with each other over wage increases. Furthermore the centralised system of collective bargaining in Sweden has enabled LO, together with the Social Democratic Party, to present itself as the institutional representative of the organised working class. With a more fragmented union structure it is doubtful whether it could perform this function as effectively. Consequently, it can be argued that the highly centralised Swedish working-class movement has, potentially, been in a better position to impose 'constraints' upon the prerogatives of capitalism than labour organisations in other countries where they have been more divided and fragmented. But the strength of LO is not determined solely by its centralised structure; it is also a product of the high allegiance which it commands from the industrial manual workers. This is shown in Table 2 which gives the percentage of workers who, in 1968, were members of LO-affiliated Unions.

From Table 2 it is evident that the level of LO penetration among manual workers is very high; approximately 70 per cent. Indeed, among men it is as high as 80 per cent, while for women it is 52 per cent.[18] Clearly, LO is a very influential movement within the social structure of contemporary Sweden if only because it is the largest organisation of any kind measured in terms of its membership.[19] But it is the structure of trade unionism which is conducive to a greater articulation of industrial working-class interests in Sweden than in most other Western capitalist countries.

In the first place, LO has superordinate authority over its affiliated organisations to the extent that Swedish trade unionism is characterised by a far greater degree of centralisation than its counterpart in, for example, Britain. Although the British Trades Union Congress (TUC) often operates as a centralised negotiating body, agreements do not

Table 2. Percentage of LO Membership among Manual Workers in Different Sectors of the Swedish Economy in 1968

Sector	Nos. of Employees (000's)	% of Employees who are Members of LO-Affiliated Unions
Wood and paper products	103	88.8
Fabricated metal goods, machinery and equipment	340	87.9
Building and construction	233	87.3
Textile and leather	77	83.5
Engineering goods	94	76.1
Food, beverages, tobacco	96	71.0
Public utilities	414	67.5
Transport and services	69	61.3
Retail trades	217	54.3
Forestry and farming	110	38.1
Other sectors	154	50.8
Unemployed	104	13.3
Total	2,012	69.7

Source: C.V. Otter, 'Arbetarnas Fackliga Organisationsgrad' [The Strength of Trade Unions], *Arkiv för Studier i Arbetarrörelsens Historia* [Journal for the Study of the History of Labour Movements], no. 4 (1973).

have the same binding consequences for its member unions as in Sweden. They are only recommendations which may be generally accepted as, for example, the pay policy in 1975 but they may also be the basis for acute cleavages within the trade union movement. By contrast, the centralised structure of Swedish unionism has had important consequences for the economy since LO has been able to formulate policies of 'wage solidarity', intended to reduce differentials in the earnings of different categories of manual and non-manual workers. Structurally, therefore, the Swedish labour movement is in a better position to bargain for a more egalitarian pattern of incomes than the TUC. Indeed, one of the major features of wage bargaining in Britain has been the efforts of particular unions, especially those of craft workers, to preserve, if not increase, differentials as they exist between themselves and other categories of workers. In Sweden, the structural supports for an ideological commitment to egalitarianism have helped to maintain a united working-class movement and to reduce wage differentials *among* manual workers in different industrial sectors.[20]

Furthermore, they have encouraged the development of an adaptive and mobile labour force since within the context of reduced wage inequalities *among* industrial manual workers, comprehensive occupational retraining schemes, and the planned provision of housing, workers have been prepared to change jobs between different industrial sectors. At the same time, a reduction in differentials between various categories of skilled and semi-skilled workers has reduced the degree to which the former have resisted large-scale technological innovations that tend to 'de-skill' jobs. In Britain, by contrast, the organisational structure of trade unionism, together with inadequate occupational retraining and housing policies, has not been conducive to the development of an occupationally and geographically mobile labour force.

Secondly, LO is a powerful articulation of working-class interests because white-collar and professional and managerial workers belong to unions which are affiliated to separate Confederations. Thus, unlike in many other countries, there is a direct relationship between the major divisions within the occupational structure and the composition of the separate union confederations.[21] The National Federation of Civil Servants (*Statsjänstemännens Riksförbund,* SR) represents the interests of higher civil servants, the Swedish Confederation of Professional Associations (*Sveriges Akademikers Centralorganisation,* SACO) those of professional and managerial workers, the Central Organisation of Salaried Employees (*Tjänstemännens Centralorganisation,* TCO) those of lower-grade white-collar employees, and LO those of manual workers. Admittedly the 'fit' is not so clear-cut as this because of the small proportion of lower-grade white-collar workers affiliated to LO, and the rather ambiguous division between 'professional' and 'non-professional' workers which constitutes the basis for some conflict between TCO and SACO about the eligibility of some occupational groups for membership. Despite this, however, the occupational structure is linked to the various trade union confederations in the following manner:

Table 3. The Relationship between Occupational Categories and Trade Union Confederations

Occupational Category	Trade Union Confederation
Professional, managerial and administrative workers	SACO and SR
Semi-professional, lower-administrative and routine white-collar workers	TCO
Skilled, semi-skilled and unskilled manual workers	LO

A consequence of these interrelationships is that LO can represent the interests of industrial manual workers as a *class* in society by emphasising the differences between manual, white-collar and managerial groups in terms of their earnings, fringe benefits and conditions of employment. This, in turn, is likely to generate a heightened awareness of the social and economic rewards of different occupational groups. When there are national wage negotiations it is evident that SACO, SR, TCO and LO are pursuing the interests of clearly delineated socio-economic groups. Fulcher, in fact, has argued that the structure of trade unionism in Sweden is such that it constitutes an institutionalised form of class conflict.[22] If this is so, it can be suggested that it is conducive to resentment among manual and lower-grade white-collar workers, if only because they are aware of the higher rewards accruing to other occupational groups. Indeed, such attitudes are likely to be more pronounced among manual workers in Sweden than among those in other countries where patterns of trade unionism are less consistent with occupational divisions. In such countries it might be expected that there will be less awareness of *class* inequalities and limited resentment over economic rewards.

If the structure of Swedish trade unionism contributes to the expression of class interests, then LO is in a better position to do this than any of the other confederations. The high level of LO density among industrial manual workers strengthens its bargaining position but also, unlike the other confederations, it acts as a political pressure group. Whereas they explicitly stress their political non-allegiance, LO, at all organisational levels, is closely connected to the Social Democratic Party. Consequently, it performs a number of 'political' functions in addition to those of an 'industrial' or 'economic' kind; taken with the fact that the Social Democratic Party has been in office since 1932, it means that the institutional basis for the expression of working-class interests is extensive.

2. The Social Democratic Party

The Social Democratic Workers Party (*Socialdemoratiska Arbetartpartiet,* SAP) was founded in 1889. Before the foundation of LO in 1898, it was the central organisation of the working class.[23] With the formation of LO, strong links were established so that LO and the Social Democratic Party became closely interrelated wings of the same movement. As Branting, the first leader of the Social Democratic Party, stated in 1898, 'the Labour movement is a single entity, working in a trade-union direction and in a political direction, neither stifling the other, but supporting each other and working hand in hand for social emancipation'.[24] Indeed, until the present, the Social Democratic Party and LO have continued to be ideologically and organisationally connected. At general elections, for example, LO explicity urges its members to support the Party and it finances large-scale publicity campaigns to this effect. At the same time they are united in an ideological commitment to egalitarianism which has been reflected in their ongoing co-operation in the formulation of LO wage policies and the determination of Social Democratic fiscal and budgetary measures. This ideological interdependence has been reinforced by close relationships between the structures of the two organisations. Thus, for instance, all LO members are collectively affiliated to the Party and the trade union movement has traditionally provided avenues of upward mobility for those aspiring to a political career.

The origins of the Social Democratic Party were among skilled workers who had been introduced to Socialist ideas in different European countries: for example, in Germany, Denmark and, to a lesser extent, Britain.[25] The ideological basis of the Party was Marxist and within the context of Swedish politics in the latter part of the nineteenth century, it emphasised the need for universal suffrage. During the 1890s only one-quarter of men over the age of twenty-one were entitled to vote. This meant that the two-chamber parliament was dominated by the land-owning class in the upper house and by farmers and urban traders in the lower house; in the latter, farmers generally held a majority. In 1890 a Universal Franchise Union was formed in order to press for electoral reform. This consisted mainly of 'radical' intellectuals and the more liberal representatives of the urban lower middle classes; in 1902 they organised themselves into a national political group, the Folk Party.[26] The Social Democratic Party, although committed to universal suffrage, had no representatives in parliament until 1897 when Branting was elected. Consequently, the Folk and the Social Democratic parties co-operated against the vested interests of the upper classes. In order to protect these interests, the Conservatives organised themselves into a national party — the Högern Party — in 1904.

Universal suffrage was gradually introduced in 1907 but by then Membership of the Social Democratic Party had grown rapidly. Tomasson has suggested that between 1895 and 1907 it had increased from 10,000 to 133,000.[27] In the elections which were held in 1911 — the first after the franchise reforms — the Social Democrats won 64 of the 230 seats in the Lower Chamber, with the Folk Party gaining 101 and the Högern Party, 65.[28] The franchise reforms, therefore, had increased Social Democratic representation in the lower chamber but the upper chamber continued to be dominated by wealthy businessmen and land-owners. This was because representatives to this chamber were elected by municipal and county councils. The electoral reforms had not been applied to municipal and county elections so that in the 150-seat upper chamber there were only 12 Social Democrats but as many as 87 representatives of the Högern Party.[29] However, after the 1917 elections a coalition Government consisting of the Folk and Social Democratic Parties was formed which introduced further electoral changes so that the domination of the Högern Party in the upper chamber was broken.

The coalition Government, formed as a result of the 1917 elections, was the first to include representatives of the Social Democratic Party. But in 1920 the coalition collapsed and the Social Democrats continued in office as a minority Government; this only lasted for six months. A major reason for the breakdown in co-operation between the Social Democratic and Folk Parties was that their joint programme for constitutional reform had been completed by 1920 and there was little else to keep them together. They had very different socio-economic policies; whereas the Social Democrats were in favour of nationalisation and increased state intervention in the economy, the Folk Party only wanted to reform the existing system. Public ownership of the means of production became the major source of cleavage between the political parties with the Folk, Högern and the newly established *Bonderförbundet* (agrarian) parties opposed to further state intervention, and the Social Democratic and Communist Parties in favour.[30]

The period 1920-32 has often been called the era of 'minority parliamentarism'. During the 1920s the electoral support of the Folk Party declined, the *Bondeförbundet* became an influential national political organisation and since 1917 the left wing of the Social Democratic Party had formed its own separate organisation, the Communist Party. None of the political parties was able to establish majority Governments and it was almost impossible to form coalitions; the Social Democrats failed to reach agreement with any of the 'non-socialist' parties and these, in turn, were unable to collaborate with each other. Consequently, there were frequent changes of administration but with the election of a Social Democratic Government in 1932 political instability in Sweden came to an end. From then until October 1976, except for a brief period of three months in 1936, Sweden was governed by either a majority Social Democratic Government or by a coalition, with the Social Democratic Party as the dominant partner.

The history of Swedish Governments since 1905 is shown in Table 4:

Table 4. The Composition of Swedish Governments 1905-1977

Dates				Government
July	1905	— October	1905	National Coalition (no Social Democrats)
October	1905	— May	1906	Folk
May	1906	— October	1911	Högern*
October	1911	— February	1914	Folk
February	1914	— March	1917	Högern
March	1917	— October	1917	Högern (caretaker government)
October	1917	— March	1920	Folk/Social Democratic
March	1920	— Autumn	1920	Social Democratic
Autumn	1920	— Autumn	1921	Non-party government
Autumn	1921	— April	1923	Social Democratic
April	1923	— October	1924	Högern
October	1924	— June	1926	Social Democratic
June	1926	— October	1928	Folk
October	1928	— June	1930	Högern
June	1930	— September	1932	Folk
September	1932	— June	1936	Social Democratic
June	1936	— September	1936	Bondeförbundet*
September	1936	— December	1939	Social Democratic/Bondeförbundet
December	1939	— July	1945	Social Democratic/Folk/Högern/ Bondeförbundet
July	1945	— October	1951	Social Democratic
October	1951	— October	1957	Social Democratic/Bondeförbundet
October	1957	— October	1976	Social Democratic
October	1976			Centre/Folk/Conservative

*The 'Högern' Party is now known as the 'Moderata Samlingspartiet' (The Conservative Party) and the 'Bondeförbundet' as the 'Centerpartiet' (Centre Party).

Source: K. Samuelsson, *From Great Power to Welfare State* (London, 1968), Appendix 3.

It is clear from Table 4 that 1932 is an important watershed in Swedish politics; indeed, the dominance of the Social Democratic Party since then has led Tomasson to remark that 'probably no democratic party anywhere has been able to maintain for such a long period the overall legislative and popular support enjoyed by the Swedish Social Democrats . . . '[31] Thus, he claims that the Swedish Social Democrats are the pre-eminent example of Maurice Duverger's 'dominant party'. Similarly, in a speculative account of contemporary Sweden, Huntford has argued that the success of the Social Democratic Party has led to 'new totalitarianism', characteristic of Aldous Huxley's *Brave New World*.[32] Clearly, the political ascendancy of the Swedish Social Democrats has been impressive, certainly by comparison with similar parties in other countries.[33]

Although the Social Democrats were in government for brief periods during the 1920s, they achieved little; there was no nationalisation of the economy and few other Socialist measures were introduced. When they came to power in the 1930s, they pursued policies which established the basis for the welfare state and the 'mixed economy'. There were no attempts to transfer the means of production to state ownership since it was argued that Socialist ideals could be attained by 'gradual' and 'indirect' means.[34] This, in fact, has been the major characteristic of successive Social Democratic policies; they have tended to concentrate upon measures intended to regulate the distribution of income and personal wealth *after* it has been created. But these policies have not, as yet, altered the essential generic features of any Capitalist society; the means of production remain privately owned. This is justified by some sectors of the Social Democratic Party on the grounds that successive Governments have been able to develop sufficient controls over economic production. There is no injustice in the private ownership of wealth, therefore, since economic rewards can be redistributed by Government action. Consequently, it is claimed that it is unnecessary to *own* in order to *control* the means of production and that socialist ideals, particularly those relating to economic and social equality, can be as easily achieved in a society where property is privately owned as in one in which all the resources are owned by the state.[35] Although this view has been challenged by the Swedish 'New Left' in recent years, there is little doubt that the policies of the Social Democratic Party have enabled it to retain a high degree of electoral support among the more disadvantaged groups in society, particularly industrial manual workers. This is illustrated in Table 5, which shows the electoral support for the Social Democratic Party among voters of different occupational groups in general elections between 1956 and 1973.

Table 5 suggests that since 1956 the Social Democratic Party has never failed to obtain at least 69 per cent of the votes of industrial manual workers. Indeed, in elections during the 1960s the level of support among this occupational group was around 80 per cent. At the

Table 5. Electoral Support for the Social Democratic Party among
Voters of Different Occupational Groups, 1956-1973 (percentages)

Occupational Group	Percentage supporting the Social Democratic Party in General Elections held in:					
	1956	1960	1964	1968	1970	1973
Employers, company directors, managers and professional workers	4	10	8	14	15	16
Small business owners	21	19	26	32	28	21
Lower-grade white-collar workers	37	42	46	47	41	37
Shop assistants and service workers	72	68	64	67	60	61
Industrial manual workers	77	83	78	79	71	69
Farmers	14	7	7	6	5	9
Agricultural workers	58	57	53	57	51	64

Source: O. Petersson and B. Särlvik, 'The 1973 Election', *General Elections 1973*,
vol. 3 (Central Bureau of Statistics, Stockholm, 1975), pp. 88-9.

same time, it has been able to command the voting allegiance of
two-thirds of all shop assistants, service workers and agricultural
employees, and about 40 per cent of the electoral support of lower-grade
white-collar workers. It is, then, the dominant party in Swedish politics;
it always gets a greater degree of electoral support than any of the
other parties and, as a result, until 1976 it had been in Government for
forty-four years. It is the party which is overwhelmingly supported by
agricultural, industrial and service workers and, to a lesser extent, by
lower-grade white-collar workers. In essence, it is a working-class
party.[36] Thus, in view of its long period in Government, it can be argued
that the interests of industrial workers in Sweden have been better
represented in the formal political structure than in other capitalist
countries where similar parties have commanded less electoral support.

If Sweden is distinctive among Western capitalist countries in having
a powerful and coherent working-class movement, how has this affected
the dynamics of monopoly capital? One of the major results has been
the development of a system of checks and balances in relation to the
prerogatives of capital which operate at every level in the economy.
Within privately owned companies, for example, the consequences of
Social Democratic legislation and the influence of labour unions is
reflected in complex rules and regulations in relation to employment
contracts, employment conditions and the quality of the working
environment for industrial manual workers.[37] In each of these, the

position of Swedish manual workers is more favourable than those of employees in any other capitalist country. All companies with more than a hundred employees must have at least two trade union representatives on their main boards and since 1976, LO has adopted as policy the objective that unions should buy shares in companies so that during the 1980s they will have majority holdings.[38] If this policy is achieved – and this will depend to a large extent upon whether a Social Democratic Government is returned to office – it will constitute a fundamental change in the nature of the Swedish economy.

At the level of the national economy, the power of the labour movement has not only been reflected through policies implemented by successive Social Democratic Governments but also by its role in the National Labour Market Board. This is probably the most influential of all Swedish economic institutions and is a good example of the degree to which Sweden has become a corporatist state. It also represents the limits to which an economy can be planned without abolishing the relations of private ownership and control. The governing body of the National Labour Board consists of a Director General, a Deputy Director General, three representatives of the Confederation of Swedish Employers, three from LO, two from the white-collar workers' Confederation, and one from the Confederation of Professional and Managerial Employees. There are two further members, to represent women and agricultural interests. This institution is central to the operation of the Swedish economy since it is directly involved in all aspects of manpower planning, occupational training, employment services, unemployment benefits, industrial location, long-term economic planning, and the manipulation of fiscal and economic resources in order to guarantee sustained economic growth. It is because of its success in these terms that Sweden has been regarded by many commentators as having a very 'rational' economy. Indeed, the management of the economy through the National Labour Market Board has enabled Sweden to avoid many of the economic recessions experienced by Britain and to keep the level of unemployment almost consistently below one per cent. If, as Winkler has suggested, 'unity', 'order', 'nationalism' and 'success' are the essential principles around which a corporatist economy is organised, the institutional basis for the expression of these ideals is more evident in Sweden than in Britain and most other Western societies.[39] This is because the National Labour Market Board tries to integrate the interests of the State, organised labour and monopoly capital according to such principles. However, although the National Labour Market Board represents the extent to which the Swedish Labour movement has become 'incorporated' within the institutional framework of Swedish capitalism this should not detract from the tensions which have emerged directly as a consequence of these same developments. These are particularly reflected in the socio-political perspectives of industrial manual workers.

This has been confirmed in a number of studies including a social survey of English and Swedish manual workers.[40] This found that the Swedes were more aware of economic inequalities as they existed between various categories of manual, white-collar and managerial workers. At the same time they expressed greater resentment about these and held coherent views about the need for the creation of a more egalitarian society. Among the English workers, on the other hand, the awareness of economic inequalities tended to be linked to comparisons among various manual occupations, resentment was limited and there was little to suggest that respondents supported the need for fundamental social reforms. It can be suggested that the attitudes of the Swedish workers were shaped, at least to some extent, by the ideological appeals and the institutional structure of the Swedish labour movement. Thus, there has been the development of attitudes among industrial manual workers over recent years which has increasingly 'forced' the leadership of the labour movement to adopt a more radical stance towards capital. Social Democratic proposals to 'democratise' the control functions of capital and LO's policy to take over majority shareholdings are but two examples of the leadership responding to rank-and-file pressures.[41] Thus, the ideological commitment to egalitarianism by the Party appears to have been conducive to the generation of attitudes which could have important implications for the long-term development of the Swedish working-class movement, particularly in generating feelings of relative deprivation and resentment. These attitudes could — if they are indicative of wider patterns in Sweden — lead to an increased recognition among workers of the inherent contradictions between the movement's goals and the existing socio-economic structure. So far, these contradictions have been successfully accommodated by the Social Democratic Party, by adopting a number of tactics for the purposes of legitimation, of which the following are but two of the more important.

In the first place, the Party claims to be equalising opportunities for workers' children by reforming the educational system, and to be pursuing policies which will ultimately break down existing economic inequalities.[42] But at the same time, it has legitimated its relationship with industrial manual workers by emphasising the improvements in the standard of living which have occurred since the 1930s. This argument has been strengthened by the adoption of the two sets of comparisons which are frequently used in Social Democratic debate — one historical, the other cross-national. In terms of the first, the Party has always presented itself as an instrument of progress and change. Thus, for the purposes of political rhetoric, history has often been categorised in terms of two eras — the 'old' and the 'new' Sweden.[43] 'Old' Sweden is described as consisting of widespread and acute inequalities, injustices and deprivations which have only been removed as a result of the achievements of the working-class movement. According to many of the arguments, the Social Democratic Party and the Labour movement have contributed to the development of a 'new' society in which remaining inequalities and social injustices are finally being abolished. The second set of comparisons emphasises the advantages of industrial manual workers in Sweden over those of workers in other countries.[44] For these purposes, Britain and the United States are the two countries which are most frequently chosen. Britain is used in order to demonstrate the relative equality of Swedish society and the socio-economic advantages of Swedish manual workers. Journalists in newspapers, radio and television emphasise the inequalities of British society and the poor living conditions of the industrial working class. At the same time, the United States is often used to emphasise the high standard of the Swedish urban environment, the 'progressive' attitude of Sweden towards developing countries and the lack of 'corruption' in Swedish political life. If, then, to put the matter crudely, Britain, the United States and other Western countries are characterised by glaring social, political and economic injustices and if, at the same time, East European state socialist countries fail to protect individual and civil liberties then, according to the arguments, Swedish workers must live in one of the most egalitarian and democratic countries in the world; an achievement, so it is claimed, which has been brought about by the policies pursued by the leadership of the working-class movement.

These are but two examples of the rhetoric used by the Social Democratic Party in order to maintain its legitimacy with rank-and-file supporters. In these ways it has been possible for leaders of the Swedish Labour movement to conceal — if not completely successfully — some of the inherent contradictions between an ideological commitment to egalitarianism and a capitalist productive system. By the use of cross-national comparisons, the attempt has been made to demonstrate that the labour movement has, indeed, achieved a considerable degree of equality. If there are persisting inequalities in Sweden these will be removed, according to the appeals of the leadership, provided that continued support of the movement by rank-and-file supporters is forthcoming. But such appeals tend to reinforce the tensions that exist between ideology and material infrastructure. If efforts by the leadership to accommodate these strains become less successful in the future, then the Social Democratic Party may either lose its broadly based support among industrial workers or be increasingly forced to adopt more radical policies towards existing patterns of ownership and control.

Although the Social Democratic Party is no longer in Government it still has almost twice as many seats as the next largest party in the new parliament. In the 1976 election it lost less than 1 per cent of its share of the vote compared with the previous elections held in 1973. Progressive reforms in the structure of Swedish society have been largely the result of the ideological and institutional influences of the organised working-class movement. This has led to transformations in the administration of the economy which suggest that social changes of the sort which have given Sweden a high international reputation have been heavily dependent upon the existence of Social Democratic Governments. Thus, in view of the influence of the labour movement it is difficult to envisage how a coalition of non-Social Democratic Parties can stay in office for any significant length of time. Certainly, Sweden constitutes a unique case for studying the effects of Social Democracy in a Capitalist society.

Notes

1. This chapter is reprinted from sections of 'Social Models Revisited – Sweden', *New Society*, 23 December 1976; and *Social Democracy in Capitalist Society: Working-Class Politics in Britain and Sweden* (London, 1977). Only minor amendments have been made.
2. Commission on Industrial and Economic Concentration, 'Ownership and Influence in the Economy', in R. Scase (ed.), *Readings in the Swedish Class Structure* (Oxford, 1976).
3. Commission on Industrial and Economic Concentration, in R. Scase, op. cit.
4. T. Karlbom, *Arbetarnas Fackföreningar* [Workers' Trade Unions], (Helsinki, 1969), p. 12.
5. For discussions of the development of trade unionism in Sweden, see K. Bäckström, *Arbetarrörelsen i Sverige*, vols. I and II [The Labour Movement in Sweden] (Stockholm 1971); B. Carlson, *Trade Unions in Sweden* (Stockholm, 1969) ch. 3; and Karlbom, op. cit., ch. 1.
6. *Bruks* were essentially mining villages which had developed within the context of the rural economy. They were usually controlled by a single family, who

owned the mines, the land and the employees' houses. They were structured in a very hierarchical manner, so that social relationships between employer and employee were often paternalistic, with the owners providing not only employment but also rudimentary forms of 'social welfare' such as care of the sick, the old and the widowed.

7. Carlson, op. cit.
8. Ibid.
9. Bäckström, op. cit., vol. I, p. 231.
10. D. Blake, 'Swedish Trade Unions and the Social Democratic Party: The Formative Years', *Scandinavian Economic History Review,* vol. 8 (1960).
11. K. Samuelsson, *From Great Power to Welfare State* (London, 1968), p. 208.
12. N. Elvander, *Intresseorganisationerna i Dagens Sverige* [Interest Groups in Contemporary Sweden] (Lund, 1969), p. 27.
13. Karlbom, op. cit., p. 72.
14. For a detailed discussion of economic and political developments in Sweden during this period, see H. Tingsten, *The Swedish Social Democrats* (New Jersey, 1973).
15. For a discussion of these and other strains within the labour movement see J. Fulcher, 'Class Conflict: Joint Regulation and its Decline', in Scase op. cit., 1976.
16. The details of this agreement are discussed by T. Johnston, *Collective Bargaining in Sweden,* London, 1962.
17. LO's policy of wage solidarity has been evaluated by R. Meidner, 'Samordning och Solidarisk Lönepolitik under tre Decennier' ['Co-ordination and the Policy of Wage Solidarity'], in Landsorganisation (LO), *Tvarsnitt* [Cross-Section] (Stockholm, 1973). See also J. Ullenhag, *Den Solidariska Lönepolitiken i Sverige* [The Policy of Wage Solidarity in Sweden] (Stockholm, 1971).
18. Otter, op. cit., table 2.
19. Elvander, op. cit., ch. 1.
20. But LO's attempt to reduce wage differentials between manual workers and other occupational groups seems to have had little effect. For a discussion of this, see Scase, op. cit., 1977, ch. 2.
21. For an account of this, see Elvander, op. cit.; and Scase, op. cit., 1977, ch. 1.
22. Fulcher, op. cit.
23. For a detailed discussion of the development of the Social Democratic Party during the last decades of the nineteenth century, see Tingsten, op. cit.
24. Quoted by Blake, op. cit., p. 21.
25. This point is made by Tingsten, op. cit.
26. *'Folkpartiet'* is often translated as 'Liberal Party'. It has traditionally represented the interests of the more 'progressive' sectors of the Swedish middle class.
27. R. Tomasson, *Sweden: Prototype of Modern Society* (New York, 1970), p. 30.
28. Central Bureau of Statistics, *Historical Statistics of Sweden* [Statistical Survey] (Stockholm, 1960), table 276.
29. Central Bureau of Statistics, op. cit., table 274.
30. See Tingsten, op. cit.
31. R. Tomasson, 'The Extraordinary Success of the Swedish Social Democrats', *Journal of Politics,* vol. 31 (1969), p. 772.
32. R. Huntford, *The New Totalitarians* (London, 1971).
33. For a comparative account of the development of Social Democratic parties in different European countries, see C. Landauer, *European Socialism,* vols. I and II (Berkeley, 1959).
34. The central thesis of Tingsten, op. cit., is that the development of the Social

334   *Social Democracy in Sweden*

Democratic Party, up until the late 1930s, was characterised by the increasing rejection of revolutionary ideals and the adoption of reformist-welfare ideologies.

35. For such a view see, for example, G. Adler-Karlsson, *Functional Socialism: A Swedish Theory for Democratic Socialism* (Stockholm, 1967).
36. This is emphasised by M.D. Hancock, *Sweden: The Politics of Post-Industrial Change* (Hinsdale, Ill.), 1972).
37. See, for example, Landsorganisation (LO), *Demokrati i Företagen* [Democracy in Companies] (Stockholm, 1971).
38. Landsorganisation (LO), *Kollektiv Kapital Bildning Genom Löntagarefonder* [Capital Formation Through the Wage Earners' Fund] (Lund, 1976).
39. J. Winkler, 'Corporatism', in R. Scase (ed.), *Industrial Society: Class Cleavage and Control* (London, 1977).
40. The results of this survey are discussed in detail in Scase, op. cit. (1977), chs. 3-6.
41. In 1975 a Government Commission put forward proposals for 'company democracy'. See, Statens Offentliga Utredningar (SOU), *Demokrati pa Arbetsplatsen* [Democracy at the Workplace] (Stockholm, 1975). LO's proposals for taking over majority shareholdings are discussed in Landsorganisation (LO), op. cit., 1976.
42. These policies are discussed in Scase, op. cit. (1977), chs. 4 and 5.
43. Often expressed in terms of *Förr i Tiden* and *Nuförtiden*. Although these terms have a general meaning and refer to 'past' and 'present', they have acquired the more specific interpretation in political debate.
44. This and the following comments are derived from the author's personal experience of the interpretation of news and current affairs by Party spokesmen in the Swedish mass media over the past ten years; particularly in the radio, television and the press as reflected in *Dagens Nyheter, Expressen* and *Aftonbladet* – the largest selling daily newspapers in Sweden. Although there was no attempt to undertake a systematic content analysis, such an investigation would almost certainly confirm the present observations.

The Editors are grateful to the Swedish Institute, Stockholm, and the Swedish Social Democratic Party for help in compiling the following statistical and bibliographical information to supplement the foregoing chapter.

Appendix 1: Sweden: parliamentary election results, 1948-1976, percentages of votes and seats

Year	Social Democrats	Communists (Left Party)	Centre Party	People's Party	Conservatives (Moderate Unity Party)	Others
1948						
votes	46.1	6.3	12.4	22.7	12.3	
seats	48.7	3.5	13.0	24.8	10.0	
1952						
votes	46.0	4.3	10.7	24.4	14.4	
seats	47.8	2.2	11.3	25.2	13.5	
1956						
votes	44.6	5.0	9.5	23.8	17.1	
seats	45.9	2.6	8.2	25.1	18.2	
1958						
votes	46.2	3.4	12.7	18.2	19.5	
seats	48.1	2.2	13.9	16.5	19.5	
1960						
votes	47.8	4.5	13.6	17.5	16.6	
seats	49.1	2.2	14.7	17.2	16.8	
1964						
votes	47.3	5.2	13.2	17.0	13.7	3.6
seats	48.5	3.4	14.2	18.0	13.7	2.2
1968						
votes	50.1	3.0	15.7	14.3	12.9	4.1
seats	53.6	1.3	15.9	13.7	12.4	3.0
1970						
votes	45.3	4.8	19.9	16.2	11.5	1.8
seats	46.6	4.9	20.3	16.6	11.7	0.0
1973						
votes	43.6	5.3	25.1	9.4	14.3	2.3
seats	44.6	5.4	25.7	9.7	14.6	0.0
1976						
votes	42.7	4.8	24.1	11.1	15.6	1.7
seats	43.6	4.9	24.6	11.2	15.8	0.0

Appendix 2: Social Democracy in Sweden

Year	Number of Party members	Social Democratic votes in Riksdag elections		Members as percentage of voters
1886				
1887			241	
1888				
1889	3,194			
1890	6,922		749	924.2
1891	7,534			
1892	5,630			
1893	6,571		1,207	544.4
1894	7,625			
1895	10,250			
1896	15,646		1,250	1251.7
1897	27,136			
1898	39,476			
1899	44,489		3,006	1480.0
1900	44,100			
1901	48,241			
1902	49,190		8,751	562.1
1903	54,552			
1904	64,835			
1905	67,325		26,083	258.1
1906	101,929			
1907	133,388			
1908	112,693		54,044	208.5
1909	60,813			
1910	55,248			
1911	57,721		172,196	33.5
1912	61,000			
1913	75,444			
1914	84,410	April	228,662	36.9
		Sept.	265,428	31.8
1915	85,937			
1916	105,275			
1917	114,450		288,777	38.6
1918	129,432			
1919	151,364			

Appendix 2 continued

Year	Number of Party members	Social Democratic votes in Riksdag elections	Members as percentage of voters
1920	143,090	195,121	73.3
1921	134,753	630,855	21.2
1922	133,042		
1923	138,510		
1924	153,187	725,407	21.1
1925	167,823		
1926	189,122		
1927	203,338		
1928	221,419	873,931	25.3
1929	234,962		
1930	277,017		
1931	296,507		
1932	312,934	1,040,689	30.0
1933	326,734		
1934	330,350		
1935	346,786		
1936	368,158	1,338,120	27.5
1937	398,625		
1938	437,239		
1939	458,831		
1940	487,257	1,546,804	31.5
1941	498,209		
1942	519,322		
1943	538,747		
1944	553,724	1,432,571	38.7
1945	563,981		
1946	558,584		
1947	588,044		
1948	635,658	1,789,459	35.5
1949	668,817		
1950	722,073		
1951	739,474		
1952	746,004	1,742,284	42.8
1953	753,785		
1954	757,426		

Appendix 2 continued

Year	Number of Party members	Social Democratic votes in Riksdag elections	Members as percentage of voters
1955	770,140		
1956	777,860	1,729,463	45.0
1957	774,866		
1958	780,686	1,776,667	43.9
1959	796,106		
1960	801,068	2,033,016	39.4
1961	808,817		
1962	836,012		
1963	867,086		
1964	881,035	2,066,923	42.6
1965	873,024		
1966	885,832		
1967	891,450		
1968	888,294	2,420,277	36.7
1969	907,502		
1970	890,070	2,256,369	39.5
1971	909,140		
1972	938,315		
1973	952,519	2,247,727	42.4
1974	1,001,406		
1975			
1976		2,324,603	

Further Reading

In English

Adler-Karlsson, G. *Functional Socialism: A Swedish Theory for Democratic Socialism.* Stockholm, Bokförlaget Prisma, 1967.

Blake, D. 'Swedish Trade Unions and the Social Democratic Party: the formative years.' *Scandinavian Economic History Review.* Vol. 8, 1960.

Board, Joseph P. *The Government and Politics of Sweden.* Boston, Houghton Mifflin Co. 1970.

Castles, Francis G. 'Swedish Social Democracy: the conditions of success'. *Political Quarterly.* Vol. 46, no. 2. 1975. Pp. 171-85.

Castles, Francis G. 'Policy innovation and institutional stability in Sweden.' *British Journal of Political Science.* Vol. 6. 1976. Pp. 203-16.

Elder, Neil. *Government in Sweden: the executive at work.* Oxford, Pergamon Press, 1970.

Elvander, Nils. 'In search of new relationships: parties, unions and salaried employees' associations in Sweden.' *Industrial and Labour Relations Reivew.* Vol. 28, no. 1. 1974. Pp. 60-74.

Hancock, M. Donald. *Sweden: the Politics of Postindustrial Change.* The Dryden Press, Inc., Hinsdale, Illinois, 1972.

Huntford, Roland. *The New Totalitarians.* Allen Lane The Penguin Press, London, 1971.

Lansbury, Russell. *Swedish Social Democracy: into the seventies.* Fabian Society, London, Young Fabian Pamphlet 29, 1972.

Petersson, Olof. 'The 1973 General Election in Sweden.' *Scandinavian Political Studies.* Vol. 9. 1974. Pp. 219-28.

Rustow, Dankwart A. *The Politics of Compromise: a study of parties and cabinet government in Sweden.* Princeton, Princeton University Press, 1955.

Samuelsson, K. *From Great Power to Welfare State.* London, 1968.

Stjernqvist, Nils. 'Sweden: stability or deadlock?' In Robert A. Dahl (ed.), *Political Oppostions in Western Democracies.* Yale University Press, New Haven and London, 1966.

Tilton, Timothy A. 'The Social Origins of Liberal Democracy: the Swedish case.' *American Political Science Review.* Vol. 68. 1974. Pp. 561-71.

340   *Social Democracy in Sweden*

Tingsten, H. *The Swedish Social Democrats.* New Jersey, 1973.

Tomasson, R.F. 'The extraordinary success of the Swedish Social Democrats.' *Journal of Politics.* Vol. 31, no. 3. 1969. Pp. 772-98.

Tomasson, R.F. *Sweden: Prototype of Modern Society.* New York, 1970.

In Swedish

Arvidsson, Håkan (red). *Revolutionen i Sverige 1917-1924.* Kristianstad, 1972.

Branting, Hjalmar. *Socialdemokratiens århundrade. Frankrike – England.* Stockholm, 1904.

Branting, Hjalmar. *Socialdemokratiens århundrade. Tyskland. Sverige, Danmark, Norge.* Stockholm, 1906.

Bäckström, Knut. *Arbetarrörelsen i Sverige 1.* Stockholm, 1971.

Bäckström, Knut. *Arbetarrörelsen i Sverige 2.* Stockholm, 1971.

Carlesson, C.N. *Svenska socialdemokratins ursprung.* Stockholm, 1927.

Casparsson, Ragnar. *LO under fem årtionden I. 1898-1923.* Stockholm, 1951.

Casparsson, Ragnar. *LO under fem årtionden II. 1924-1947.* Stockholm, 1951.

Dahlkvist, Mats. *Staten, socialdemokratin och socialismen.* Lund, 1975.

Flood, Hulda. *Den socialdemokratiska kvinnorörelsen i Sverige.* Stockholm, 1960.

Föreningen Socialistisk Debatt. *Från Palm till Palme. Den svenska socialdemokratins program 1882-1960.* Stockholm. 1972.

Gunnarsson, Gunnar. *Arbetarrörelsens genombrottsår i dokument.* Falköping, 1965.

Gunnarsson, Gunnar. *Arbetarrörelsens historia 1881-1938.* Stockholm, 1970.

Gunnarsson, Gunnar. *Arbetarrörelsens historia 1939-1970.* Stockholm, 1970.

Gunnarsson, Gunnar. *Socialdemokratisk idéarv.* Malmö, 1971.

Hansson, Sigfrid. *Arbetarrörelsen i Sverige.* Stockholm, 1935.

Hansson, Sigfrid. *Bidrag till den svenska fackföreningsrörelsens historia. Svenska sko- och läderindustriarbetareförbundet.* Stockholm, 1920.

Hansson, Sigfrid. *Den svenska fackföreningsrörelsen.* Stockholm, 1923.

Hansson, Sigfrid. *Minneskrift. Landsorganisationens första kvartsekel 1898-1923.* Stockholm, 1923.

Hansson, Sigfrid. *Svenskt fackföreningsliv under fem decennier.* Stockholm, 1932.

Heffler, Hugo. *Arbetarnas Bildningsförbund. Krönika vid halvsekelgränsen.*

1912-1962. Stockholm, 1962.

Kennerström, Bernt. *Mellan två internationaler. Socialistiska Partiet 1929-1937.*

Kjellvard, Henry. *Arbetarrörelsen i Sverige.* Stockholm, 1962.

Klockare, Sigurd. *Svenska revolutionen 1917-1918.* Halmstad, 1967.

Lindbom, Tage. *Den svenska fackföreningens uppkomst och tidigare historia, 1872-1900.* Stockholm, 1938.

Lindbom, Tage. *Den socialdemokratiska ungdomsrörelsen i Sverige.* Stockholm, 1952.

Lindgren, John. *Det socialdemokratiska arbetarepartiets uppkomst.* Stockholm, 1927.

Lindhagen, Jan. *Socialdemokratins program. Första delen. I rörelsens tid 1890-1930.* Karlskrona, 1972.

Lindhagen, Jan. *Socialdemokratins program. Andra delen. Boljevikstriden.* Karlskrona, 1974.

Magnusson, Gerhard. *Socialdemokratin i Sverige. Första delen.* Stockholm, 1920.

Magnusson, Gerhard. *Socialdemokratin i Sverige. Andra delen.* Stockholm, 1921.

Magnusson, Gerhard. *Socialdemokratin i Sverige. Tredje delen.* Stockholm, 1924.

Nerman, Ture (red). *Svensk arbetarörelse i ord och bild. 1881-1955.* Stockholm, 1956.

Nordström, Hilding. *Sveriges socialdemokratiska arbetareparti 1889-1894.* Stockholm, 1938.

Nyman, Olle. *Krisuppgörelsen mellan socialdemokraterna och bondeförbundet 1933.* Uppsala, 1944.

Peterson, Carl-Gunnar. *Sveriges socialdemokratiska ungdomsförbund 1917-1967.* Stockholm, 1970.

Steg för steg. 1945-1973. En krönika om den svenska fackföreningsrörelsens utveckling under efterkrigstiden. Stockholm, 1973.

Ruin, Olof. *Kooperativa förbundet 1899-1929.* Lund, 1960.

Ström, Fredrik (red). *Arbetets söner. Pionärtiden.* Stockholm, 1944.

Ström, Fredrik (red). *Arbetets söner. Samlingens tid.* Stockholm, 1946.

Ström, Fredrik (red). *Arbetets söner. Segrarnas tid.* Stockholm, 1946.

Sunesson, Sune. *Politik och organisation.* Kristianstad, 1974.

Svenning, Olle. *Socialdemokratin och näringslivet.* Borås, 1972.

Tingsten, Herbert. *Den svenska socialdemokratins utveckling. I.* Stockholm, 1941.

Tingsten, Herbert. *Den svenska socialdemokratins utveckling. II.* Stockholm, 1941.

13 THE DUTCH LABOUR PARTY: A SOCIAL DEMOCRATIC PARTY IN TRANSITION*

Steven B. Wolinetz

1. Introduction

The stereotype image of a Social Democratic party resembles a portrait of a former revolutionary in middle age. Mention Social Democracy and one immediately gets a picture of a party which has abandoned revolutionary goals in favour of incremental reforms in the context of a mixed economy. Ten years ago, the Dutch Labour Party (PvdA) conformed to this stereotype: although descended from an orthodox Marxist party, the PvdA had settled in and become a moderate party devoted to the interests of the lower classes and anxious to improve social welfare systems, but barely concerned with class struggle or revolution. Today, however, red flags and other Socialist symbols have been removed and the PvdA characterises itself as an agent of change, advocates greater redistribution of incomes, and insists on the democratisation of political, economic, and social institutions. At the same time, the PvdA has assumed a more radical posture in foreign affairs and has become less willing to compromise with other parties.

2. Historical Development

Recent changes in the Dutch Labour Party cannot be understood without examining the position of Social Democrats in the Dutch party system. One factor has overriding importance: despite a long-standing

*Material for this study is drawn from interviews and conversations with members and officials of the Dutch Socialist Party (PvdA) conducted during visits to the Netherlands in 1968-9, the summer of 1972, 1974 and 1976. The earlier research was part of a larger study on changes in the Dutch party alignment. This essay draws heavily on my doctoral dissertation, *Party Re-alignment in the Netherlands* (Yale University, 1973) and a subsequent paper, 'New Left and the Transformation of the Dutch Socialist Party' (paper presented to the Annual Convention of the American Political Science Association, San Francisco, 1975). The earlier research was funded by a Fulbright fellowship and a grant from the Yale Council on Comparative and Western European Studies. Subsequent research has been funded by Memorial University of Newfoundland, a Fulbright Grant, and a Canada Council Post-Doctoral Fellowship. I am indebted to Rudy B. Andeweg and Karl Dittrich of the Institute of Political Science, University of Leiden, for their critiques of this article.

commitment to the establishment of a Socialist society by parliamentary means, Dutch Social Democrats have never been able to secure the support of more than one-third of the electorate. Instead, the strength of Dutch Social Democracy has been sapped by the presence of Catholic and Protestant parties able to organise a part of the working-class and, to a lesser degree, by competition from smaller parties to the left of the Socialists.

The situation has deep historical roots. The Protestant Reformation left the Netherlands a religiously plural society and the Socialists were only one of three social movements to emerge in the nineteenth century. They were preceded by Calvinists demanding state support for separate denominational schools, and parallelled by Catholics seeking state aid for religious schools and trying to promote the advancement of a Catholic population relegated to second-class status by the Reformation. Both Calvinists and Catholics organised their followers into distinctive pillars or subcultures: cradle-to-grave networks of religiously based organisations. Although the schools question was resolved in 1917 as party of the Pacification settlements (an all-party compromise which provided for state support for denominational schools, universal suffrage, and proportional representation) 'pillarisation' persisted and became more extensive. Separate schools, newspapers, trade unions, broadcasting organisations and social clubs proved to be ideal mechanisms for perpetuating the confessional parties.[1] Until recently, the Catholic Party (KVP) and the two Protestant parties, the Anti-Revolutionary Party (ARP) and the Christian Historical Union (CHU) could command half of the popular vote and seats in parliament.[2] As a result, Socialists have been unable to come to power except with the assent of at least one of the three confessional parties. In addition, because of the parliamentary arithmetic and a desire by Dutch party élites to overcome and avoid the dangers of fragmentation, cabinets have tended to be broad, overarching and nearly inclusive.[3] Consociational practices and a desire to include and accommodate as many groups as possible have reduced Socialists' influence when they are in the cabinet.

At the same time, Socialists have invariably had competition from the Left. In the interwar years, Communists drew 2-3 per cent of the vote. Since 1946, Communist strength has ranged from a high of 10.6 per cent in 1946 to a low of 2.4 per cent in 1959. The PvdA has also faced competition from the Pacifist Socialist Party (PSP), founded after a split on NATO policy in 1956, and, more recently, from the Radical Political Party (PPR), established by a dissident group in the Catholic Party (KVP) and since evolved into a distinctly Left-wing party, and

from a Right-wing Socialist party, Democratic Socialists '70. The PvdA
and its predecessor, the SDAP, have generally eschewed coalitions or
alliances with the Communists.

The first Socialist party in the Netherlands was the Social Democratic
League (SDB), founded in 1881. Although initially committed to the
establishment of a classless society by parliamentary means, the SDB
and its leader, F. Domela Nieuwenhuis, rapidly became frustrated by
the limitations of the electoral process and the parliamentary arena and
veered toward Anarchism.[4] In 1891, another party, the Social
Democratic Workers Party (SDAP) was established. Supported
financially and theoretically by the SPD (its programmes were copied
from the SPD's Erfurt Programme of 1891), the SDAP was an orthodox
Marxist party devoted to advancing the cause of the proletariat via the
ballot box and parliamentary means.[5]

After the schism, the SDB declined in strength and dissolved itself
in 1900. The younger SDAP grew steadily and built an organisational
structure similar to the SPD's and began to develop a network or 'pillar'
of related organisations. By 1908, the Party had established a
secretariat and sprouted women's organisations, youth clubs, study
groups, a magazine and a newspaper. Close ties developed between the
party and the newly formed Dutch Federation of Trade Unions (NVV).
Although there were no blocs of trade unionists enrolled *en masse* in
the party, SDAP and NVV memberships were intertwined. Party and
trade union co-operated in campaigns for universal suffrage and in the
sponsorship of other Socialist organisations. During and after the 1920s,
joint meetings of their overlapping directorates were common.[6]

For most of its career, the SDAP was firmly lodged in the reformist
camp of Social Democracy. Violent and Anarchistic tactics were
eschewed. Left-wing militants were expelled in 1909 (they eventually
formed a Communist party) and others left in the 1930s.[7] Only in
1918, when the Party's leader and founder, Pieter Jelles Troelstra,
mistakenly dreamed that revolution would spread beyond Germany's
borders did the SDAP make any attempt to seize power. Troelstra's
vague revolutionary gestures provoked immediate opposition. Party
élites quelled the would-be uprising by raising a volunteer army and
mounted a massive demonstration. The SDAP quickly backed off and
returned to its parliamentary commitments. However, the abortive
revolutionary attempt — for which the SDAP was totally unprepared —
isolated the Socialists from the bourgeois parties. Although the SDAP
had been asked to join a Liberal cabinet in 1913 (the offer was declined
by a special Party congress), the SDAP did not join a coalition until

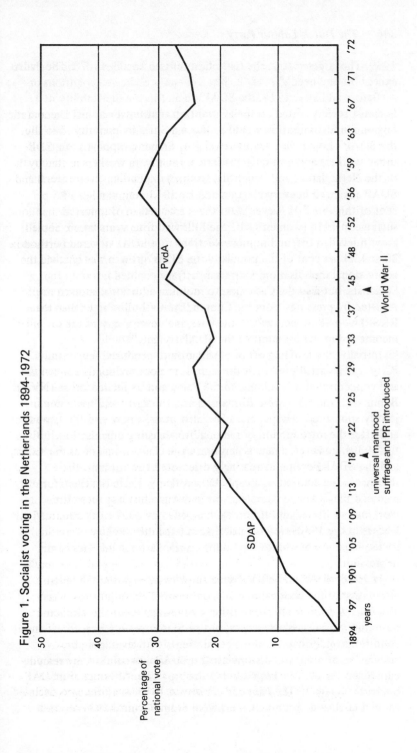

Figure 1. Socialist voting in the Netherlands 1894-1972

1939. The largest party, the Catholics, refused to ally with the Socialists except 'in dire need'.[8]

Before and after 1918, the SDAP's belief in the inevitability of a Socialist society rested on the assumption that universal suffrage and ongoing industrialisation would produce a Socialist majority. Initially, the SDAP's hopes were amply rewarded: drawing support both from urban workers and non-religious farmers and farm workers in the north of the Netherlands, and benefiting from an expanding electorate, the SDAP advanced in every election and by 1913 commanded 18.5 per cent of the vote.[9] However, after the introduction of universal manhood suffrage in 1918 (women's suffrage followed four years later), SDAP growth levelled off, and in most elections, the SDAP hovered between 20 and 23 per cent of the popular vote. SDAP growth was blocked by confessional mobilisation. Universal suffrage enabled not only the Socialists, but also the Catholics, to mobilise additional support. Assisted by pressures from the Church, the Catholic Party (then the RKSP) won 28-30 per cent of the vote, including many of the lower income groups whose support the SDAP sought.[10]

Initially, the levelling off of SDAP growth produced few changes. Party leaders attributed their difficulties to poor economic conditions and concentrated on building up the Party and its related organisations.[11] Bonds with the NVV were formalised and the Party and trade union jointly sponsored newspapers, a Socialist press, a new youth organisation, and after the introduction of radio, a broadcasting organisation.[12] By the 1930s, however, a new generation of Socialist leaders was in power and the SDAP became increasingly orientated toward immediate reforms in the context of a capitalist economy. Early Socialists had assumed that a Socialist society was inevitable but had spent little time working out the details of how such a society would come about. SDAP leaders in the 1930s were sceptical about the inevitability of a Socialist society and anxious to do something to alleviate the miseries of the depression.[13]

In 1935, SDAP and NVV issued the *Plan of Labour,* a detailed alternative to the classical liberal economics of the bourgeois parties. The *Plan of Labour* rejected neither class struggle nor the ultimate desirability of a classless society, but proposed nevertheless to ameliorate conditions under capitalism by regulating credit, increasing the circulation of money and stimulating industrial expansion. By rescuing capitalism the authors hoped to lay the groundwork for an eventual Socialist society.[14] The *Plan of Labour* was to serve as the basis of a cabinet coalition, but no partners were available until 1939. By this

Table 1. Parliamentary elections in the Netherlands, 1918-1937 in percentage of the popular vote

	1918	1922	1925	1929	1933	1937
Socialists (SDAP)	22.0	19.4	22.9	23.9	21.5	22.0
Other Left						
Communists (CPH)	2.3	1.8	1.2	2.0	3.2	3.3
Other Socialists	0.7	0.4	0.4	0.6	1.3	
Total	3.0	2.2	1.6	2.6	4.5	3.3
Confessionals*						
Anti-Revolutionaries (ARP)	13.4	13.7	12.2	11.6	13.4	16.4
Christian Historicals (CHU)	6.6	10.9	9.9	10.5	9.1	7.5
Catholics (RKSP)	30.0	29.9	28.6	29.6	27.9	28.8
Total	50.0	54.5	50.7	51.7	50.4	52.7
Liberals						
Liberal Party (LSP)**	15.1	9.3	9.7	7.4	7.0	4.0
Radical Democrats (VDB)†	5.3	4.6	6.1	6.2	5.1	5.9
Others						
Christian Democrats (CDU)†	0.8	0.7	0.5	0.4	1.0	2.1
Remaining Parties	4.2	9.1	8.0	5.9	9.0	10.2

* major parties only
**in 1918 diverse Liberal groupings
† in 1946 merged with the SDAP to form the PvdA

Source: Centraal Bureau voor de Statistiek, *Statistiek der Verkiezingen,* 1972 (The Hague, Staatsuitgeverij, 1973), p. 23. Mackie and Rose, *International Almanac of Electoral History* (London, Macmillan, 1974), p. 278.

time, SDAP leaders were more and more aware of the limitations of classical Marxism and several were deeply influenced by the religious Socialism of Hendrik de Man. Party leaders were increasingly anxious to broaden the base of the Socialist movement. Earlier objections to the monarchy and to defence expenditures had been scrapped in 1937, and the SDAP increasingly cast itself as the representative of all those disadvantaged by Capitalism.[15] Finally, in 1939. Two Socialist ministers entered the de Geer cabinet. Little time intervened before German troops swept across the Netherlands.

The PvdA

The SDAP was disbanded in 1946 and replaced by the present Labour Party (PvdA). Founded by the SDAP, two smaller pre-war parties, the Radical Democrats (VDB) and the Christian Democrats (CDU), along with members of some Resistance groups, the PvdA was a product both of the changes in the orientation of the SDAP in the 1930s and of the co-operative spirit which emerged from the Resistance movement and war-time detention camps. The party's founders hoped to 'break through' confessional lines of cleavage and rally a majority for a more moderate brand of Socialism.[16] PvdA leaders contended that confessional parties were no longer necessary because their principal objective (state support for religious schools) had been accomplished. The PvdA accepted the financial equality of public and denominational schools, acknowledged the relevance of Christian teachings, and created special communities in the Party for Catholics, Protestants, and Humanists.[17]

Party doctrines reflected the new mood. The orthodox Marxism of the SDAP was replaced by 'personal socialism' — a set of doctrines which could be derived from Marxist, religious or humanist perspectives. According to the Party's statement of principles, labour was the principal element in the productive process. The PvdA hoped to secure the rights of all men who laboured by establishing a Socialist society and 'a just order of labour'. This entailed a more equal distribution of income, greater public control of the economy, parliamentary democracy and greater chances for individual self-development. The Party's founders acknowledged the continuation of class struggle in a society based on profit and attempted to unify all groups opposed to Capitalism. However, nationalisation was considered a means and not an end in itself and the PvdA recognised the utility of the private sector — if it served the public interest.[18]

Moderation and pragmatism did not produce the electoral benefits that PvdA's founders had hoped for. Despite the contention that confessional parties were no longer necessary, the Catholic and Protestant parties were quickly re-established.[19] The first post-war elections in 1946 were a disappointment. Fresh from its role in the Resistance, the Communist Party surged to 10.6 per cent of the vote and siphoned off support on the Left. The PvdA won 28.3 per cent — more than the 22.0 per cent won by the SDAP in 1937, but slightly less than the combined totals of the SDAP, the Radical Democrats, and the Christian Democrats in the same year. In 1948, the PvdA dropped to

Table 2. Parliamentary elections in the Netherlands, 1946-1972 in percentage of the popular vote

	1946	1948	1952	1956	1959	1963	1967	1971	1972
Socialists (PvdA)	28.3	25.6	29.0	32.7	30.3	28.0	23.5	24.7	27.3
Other Left									
Communists (CPN)	10.6	7.7	6.2	4.8	2.4	2.8	3.6	2.9	4.5
Pacifist Soc. (PSP)					1.8	3.0	2.9	1.4	1.5
Radicals (PPR)								1.8	4.8
Total	10.6	7.7	6.2	4.8	4.2	5.8	6.5	7.1	10.8
Progressive/Centre									
Democrats '66 (D'66) (Centre-left)							4.5	6.8	4.2
Democratic Soc. '70 (DS'70) (Centre-right)								5.3	4.1
Confessionals									
Anti-Revolutionaries (ARP)	12.9	13.2	11.3	9.9	9.4	8.7	9.9	8.6	8.8
Christian Historicals (CHU)	7.9	9.2	8.9	8.4	8.1	8.6	8.1	6.3	4.8
Catholics (KVP)	30.8	31.0	28.7	31.7	31.6	31.9	26.5	21.9	17.7
Total	51.6	53.4	48.9	50.0	49.1	49.2	44.5	36.8	31.3
Liberals (VVD)*	6.4	8.0	8.8	8.8	12.2	10.3	10.7	10.4	14.4
Others									
Farmers (BP)					0.7	2.1	4.7	1.1	1.9
Remaining parties	3.1	5.3	7.1	3.7	3.5	4.6	5.6	7.8	6.0

* in 1946, the Party of Freedom

Source: Centraal Bureau voor de Statistiek, *Statistiek der Verkiezingen, 1972* (The Hague, Staatsuitgeverij, 1973), p. 23.

Table 3. Religion and party, 1956

a. *The religious composition of PvdA support*

	%
Catholic	4.9
Dutch Reformed	41.0
Orthodox Reformed	2.2
No religion	43.5
Other	8.9
	100 N = 322

b. *Religion and party preference*

	PvdA	VVD	KVP	ARP	CHU	Other	%	N
	%	%	%	%	%	%		
Catholic	5	1	90	1	0	3	100	326
Dutch Reformed	41	13	0	10	29	7	100	321
Orthodox Reformed	6	0	0	85	3	6	100	114
No religion	72	12	1	1	1	14	100	194
Other	69	10	8	5	5	3	100	39
Total	32	7	30	14	19	7	100	994

Source: Arend Lijphart, 'The Netherlands: Continuity and Change in Voting behaviour', in *R. Rose* (ed.), *Electoral Behaviour: A Comparative Handbook* (New York, Free Press, 1974), p. 246. Data are from a survey conducted in April and May, 1956 by the Netherlands Institute of Public Opinion (NIPO). The original N of the survey was 1,226. However, Lijphart eliminated respondents over 65 years of age in order to compare the data with a 1968 survey. Individuals without a party preference were excluded from the analysis. (Copyright. Cited by permission of the publisher).

25.6 per cent but it climbed to 29.0 per cent in 1952 and 32.7 per cent in 1956. However, this proved to be the zenith of the Party's strength. The PvdA slipped to 30.3 per cent in 1959, fell to 28.0 per cent in 1963, and plummeted to 23.5 per cent in the 1967 parliamentary elections (Table 2).

The limited impact of the breakthrough is apparent in the earliest survey data. Analysing data from 1956, Lijphart found that most of the PvdA's support came from voters who were either Dutch Reformed or without a religion, and among Dutch Reformed, the bulk of the PvdA's support was from irregular church attenders. Only 5 per cent of the Party's support was Catholic (Tables 3 and 4).

Table 4. Social Class and Party, 1956

a. The class composition of PvdA support*

	%	
A (High)	5.0	
B	16.0	
C	38.6	
D (low)	37.4	
	100	N = 321

b. Social class and party preference

	PvdA	VVD	KVP	ARP	CHU	Other	%	N
	%	%	%	%	%	%		
A (High)	24	18	39	7	6	6	100	67
B	22	15	30	14	15	4	100	278
C	35	4	31	13	10	6	100	356
D (Low)	41	1	27	14	6	10	100	293
Total	32	7	30	14	10	7	100	994

* Respondents' social class assigned by interviewers:
    A = highest, D = lowest

Source: Arend Lijphart, 'The Netherlands: Continuity and Change in Voting
    Behaviour', in R. Rose (ed.), *Electoral Behaviour: A Comparative Handbook*,
    p. 243. Data are from a survey conducted in April and May 1956 by the
    Netherlands Institute of Public Opinion (NIPO). The original N of the survey
    was 1,226. However Lijphart eliminated respondents over 65 years of age in
    order to compare the data with a 1968 survey. Individuals without a party
    preference were excluded from the analysis. (Copyright. The Free Press, 1974.
    Cited by permission of the publisher.)

As Table 3 shows, this was equivalent to 5 per cent of all Catholic
voters. Religious mobilisation weakens the relationship between social
class and party. While a substantial proportion of the PvdA's following
came from the two lowest social classes (interviewer-assigned social
class), the PvdA failed to win a majority of either of these categories
(Table 4).[20]

Although the breakthrough was not a quantitative success, it altered
the position of Dutch Social Democrats in the party system and
changed the character of the Socialist movement. After World War II,
Catholic — and later on other confessional party leaders — recognised
the need for more extensive social welfare measures and for a greater

government role in the economy and joined the Socialists in a series of 'Red-Roman' coalitions. From 1946 until 1948, Catholics and Socialists governed alone under the Catholic Beel. From 1948 until 1958, the Catholics and the Socialists allied with the Christian Historicals and (later) the Anti-Revolutionaries under the Socialist Drees. These cabinets supervised the reconstruction of the economy and built the post-war welfare state. After 1958, however, the three confessional parties broke with the PvdA and allied with the Liberals (VVD). The Socialists remained in opposition until 1965.

At the same time, the character of the Party changed. The SDAP was a party of mass integration perched atop a pillar of Socialist organisations. However, this network has been partially dismantled. The formal ties between the SDAP and the NVV were not renewed when the PvdA replaced the NVV. After the war, the PvdA and the SDAP were linked by informal contacts, and, until recently, by the presence of trade union leaders in the PvdA Executive and parliamentary fraction. However, while PvdA and NVV memberships continue to overlap, personal ties at the élite level have all but disappeared. Other organisations are either independent or defunct. The PvdA and the NVV retain seats on the directorate of the Socialist broadcasting organisation (VARA) but ties are looser than before. The Party's former newspaper, *Het Vrije Volk,* was until recently owned by the NVV, but because of financial difficulties, the paper is now part of a newspaper conglomerate and is only published in Rotterdam.[21]

By the 1960s, Dutch Social Democracy had moved a considerable distance from its origins. The SDAP began as an orthodox Marxist party, committed to an inevitable revolution. By the 1960s, however, the PvdA was committed to incremental reforms and improving the position of the working-class in the context of a mixed economy. In 1959, the Party's statement of principles was revised and all traces of Marxism were deleted.[22] Partially by choice and partially by the determination of others, the SDAP had been an 'opposition of principle' for most of its career. The PvdA, from its inception, was a governing party, and even in opposition, it remained ready and willing to join coalitions. The SDAP was also a party of mass integration. But, while the PvdA remained a mass party, enrolling a larger membership than the SDAP (some 140,000 members in the late 1950s and early 1960s), the PvdA was more of an election society than a political movement.[23] By the 1960s, the party's main skills were not agitation or extra-parliamentary activity, but rather governing, research and expertise, and a pragmatic — some would say technocratic — approach to the problems of the day.

Figure 2. PvdA membership, 1947-1976

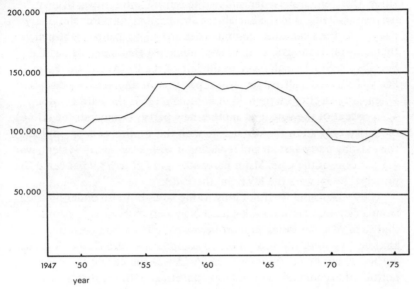

Source: Data supplied by the PvdA: centralised membership administration was established 1970, accounting in part for the sharp decline in members at this time.

3. Re-orientation in the late 1960s

The PvdA might have continued on this moderate course if changes in the Catholic subculture and the emergence of dissident groups and parties in the late 1960s had not undermined the consociational system and altered the shape of the party system. Until the 1960s, the five major parties regularly won 88-92 per cent of the popular vote. Secure in their bases of support, party élites engaged in the politics of compromise, forming broad, overarching, and nearly inclusive coalitions. Minor parties existed but had very little impact on political life.[24] By the 1960s however, major party positions had converged. The narrowing of party differences, coupled with a series of élite missteps, including the handling of royal marriages, responses to the Provo movement, and manoeuvres which brought the Socialists into the Government in 1965 and dumped them out again in 1966, eroded confidence in political élites. Dissident groups, demanding the reform and renewal of their parties, crystallised in the Socialist, Catholic, and Anti-Revolutionary parties. At the same time, minor parties articulating anti-establishment themes gained strength. In the 1966 municipal elections, the Pacifist Socialists (PSP), a small party to the left of the PvdA, and the Farmers Party (BP), a Poujadist-style protest party, won unprecedented support. When early elections were held in February 1967, the Farmers won 4.7 per cent of the vote, and another new party, Democrats '66 (D'66) organised only a few months before with the explicit goal of 'exploding' the existing party system and replacing it with a two-party system, won 4.5 per cent of the vote. Major party strength fell to 78.9 per cent. The principal losers were the KVP and the PvdA.[25]

The PvdA found itself not only losing votes but also under pressure from a dissident faction calling itself New Left.[26] New Left claimed that the PvdA was losing support because the Party had been too anxious to govern and too willing to compromise with the confessional parties. According to New Left, the PvdA was too caught up in the politics of accommodation and too concerned with the day-to-day business of governing to offer any critical vision of the future: the Party placed too much emphasis on short-run goals, such as wage and pension increases, and neglected the need for more fundamental reforms. New Left demanded a return to and a renewal of Socialist principles. This meant democratisation of the Party system, greater co-determination in industry, renewed commitments to social and economic equality, a more radical foreign policy, and a 'cultural policy' which would educate workers and allow them greater opportunities for mobility and individual self-development.[27]

New Left differed from previous dissident groups. The history of Dutch Socialism is replete with factional battles but these were either fought out in the party or resolved by dissidents leaving to establish their own church. In 1956, pacifists, opposed to the cold war stance of the PvdA, bolted from the Party, allied with other Socialists, and formed the Pacifist Socialist Party. Shortly afterwards, old-line Social Democrats, dismayed with the abandonment of Marx, tried to form a workgroup, the Social Democratic Centre, in the party. They were quickly rebuffed and told to cease their activities. They did.

New Left was different. Nor a formally organised group — lest they meet the same fate as the Social Democratic Centre — New Left consisted of a loose and somewhat fluid collection of individuals who met regularly, wrote books, and made public pronouncements.[28] Its adherents operated from diverse perspectives. The original group consisted of some individuals whose principal concerns were participatory democracy and greater well-being, some representatives of the youth culture, and a few neo-Marxists. At times they were joined by members of the 'old' Left (e.g. the Social Democratic Centre) within the Party.[29] What New Left had in common, though, was not ideology or beliefs but rather acquired social background. Almost all had secondary, if not university education, and many were involved in the 'soft', newer service sector — universities, research institutes, the media, social work, private or government bureaucracies.[30]

New Left took advantage of the positions and skills of its activists — several were employed in Socialist or Left-wing media — to launch an unprecedented public attack on the Party leadership. From 1966 until the group's dissolution in 1970, New Left activists issued a barrage of books, pamphlets and statements. Meetings were held throughout the Netherlands. New Left's attacks produced a sharp reaction. The leadership and a large proportion of the rank and file were appalled by the clear and overt violations of Party rules forbidding factions and by total disregard of Party traditions of solidarity.[31] By 1968, a Right-wing faction — Democratic Appeal — had crystallised and joined those demanding that New Left be curbed or ousted.

However, party leaders, convinced that New Left had to be kept within the Party, confined themselves to mild rebukes. Although they refused to sanction the formations of separate groups within the Party, PvdA leaders accepted the claim — part truth and part fiction — that New Left was not an organised faction (it was claimed that the only decision ever voted upon was a decision not to vote) but rather a group of party members interested in facilitating communication in the Party. For its part New Left narrowly skirted the injunctions of Party leaders, tried to avoid being thrown out, and ended up with unprecedented latitude in the PvdA.[32]

New Left took advantage of the latitude allowed it and used it to penetrate the Party. In part by being more active than other party members, in part by recruiting new members, and in part by articulating the concerns felt by a portion of the party membership (e.g. Old Left, former Social Democrats, individuals unhappy with the Party's abandonment of Marx), New Left gained influence in a number of party sections and sent large and vocal blocs of supporters to Party Congresses. By voting as a bloc at a time when the party leadership was unwilling to organise full-fledged resistance, New Left managed to elect seven of its number to the 21-member Party Executive in 1967. New Left repeated the feat in 1969, winning nine out of twenty-four places on the Executive. In the same year, the Party Congress endorsed New Left resolutions calling for the recognition of East Germany, and more important, forbidding the PvdA from joining cabinets with the catholic KVP.[33]

In 1970, the split in the PvdA came to a head. Angered by New Left influence and unwilling to accept the direction that the Party was taking, older and more conservative Socialists resigned from the PvdA and established a new party, Democratic Socialists '70.[34] In the same year (as part of a deal) New Left 'officially' dissolved itself. Ensconced in the PvdA apparatus, New Left adherents had little need of a separate organisation.[35]

By 1971, a semblance of peace had returned to the Party. Although New Left had formally disbanded the year before, New Left penetration was even more complete. From 1971 onward, New Left sympathisers constituted a majority of the Party Executive and included, for the first time, the Party Chairman. Nor was the New Left presence confined to the Party Executive. The 37-member parliamentary caucus which served from 1967 to 1971 contained one member of New Left. The caucus elected in 1971 contained five out of thirty-nine, and the caucus elected in 1972 contained ten out of forty-three. When a progressive cabinet was finally put together a few months later, the seven ministers and six state secretaries drawn from PvdA ranks included one minister and three junior ministers who had been active in New Left circles.[36] At the same time, younger individuals — sometimes former New Left activists and sometimes individuals whose thinking parallelled that of New Left — have moved into lower level Party offices and PvdA seats in municipal councils and provincial assemblies.

Why did New Left succeed? If we begin from our standard assumptions about parties — i.e. from Michels and the iron law of oligarchy — New Left's rapid penetration of the PvdA is inexplicable. However, neither the PvdA nor its leaders were in a particularly strong position in the 1960s. New Left penetration was facilitated by the open and direct structure of the Party, by the aloof posture of the Socialist trade unions, and by the conciliatory stance of the Party leadership. That posture was in turn dictated by the uncertain political climate of the late 1960s and the weak electoral position of the PvdA.

The position of the PvdA in the mid-1960s was precarious. Although the PvdA had climbed to 32.7 per cent of the vote in 1956 and had won

30.0 per cent in 1959 and 28.0 per cent in 1963, by the late 1960s the
PvdA was in a period of severe decline. In the March 1966 provincial
elections, the PvdA plummeted to 23.4 per cent of the vote. A few
months later, in the June 1966 municipal elections, the Party slipped
to 22.2 per cent of the vote. Party memberships were also declining:
while the PvdA had some 140,000 members in 1964, by 1968 this had
dropped to 116,000, and by 1969 to 107,000 (see Fig. 2). Nor were
the PvdA's fortunes in the politics of accommodation any better.
Although the PvdA had returned to the Government in 1965, the Cals
cabinet – intended to be the first in a series of progressive alliances –
fell a year and a half later, when the Right wing of the Catholic Party
withdrew its support. Early elections were held in February 1967. The
PvdA, already smarting from losses in the provincial and municipal
elections and from the fall of the cabinet, won only 23.5 per cent.
The formation of the confessional-liberal de Jong cabinet a few months
later confirmed the Party's return to the opposition.

The 1967 election results compounded the difficulties of the PvdA.
The Party's initial attempts to achieve a 'breakthrough' had been
thwarted by the re-emergence of the confessional parties and the
remobilisation of Catholic and Protestant workers. Now, however,
confessional strength was weakening. The Dutch Catholic Church,
which had previously mobilised support for the KVP, was caught up in
the ecumenical movement and had withdrawn from politics. The KVP,
which had previously won 30-32 per cent of the popular vote, slipped
to 26.5 per cent in 1967 and further decline appeared likely.[37] The
PvdA, however, was not the beneficiary. Minor, anti-establishment
parties – the Farmers and Democrats '66 – were gaining support. As we
have already noted, D'66 won 4.5 per cent of the vote in 1967. Opinion
polls showed D'66 doubling or even tripling its strength, winning
disproportionate support from the younger voters whom the PvdA
needed to bolster its sagging strength and get on with the business of
the 'breakthrough'.[38]

The weak electoral position of the PvdA and the danger that New
Left might bolt from the PvdA and form a separate party forced PvdA
leaders to adopt a conciliatory stance towards New Left. Under the best
of circumstances, the Dutch system of proportional representation is
extremely favourable to minor parties. Because the entire country is
treated as one national constituency, 1/150th of the national vote is
sufficient to win a seat in parliament. In the past the low threshold
(one hundredth before 1956) often encouraged dissidents to break
away and form new parties rather than attempt to change existing ones.

However, because major parties retained most of the vote, this provided dissidents with one or two seats in parliament but allowed them little power or influence.[39] The increased fluidity of the electorate in the late 1960s made the threat of exit more credible and more dangerous to the established parties. PvdA leaders believed that if the Party were to recover its strength, it would have to re-establish its credentials as a party of renewal and change. Although irksome, New Left represented a youthful and radical element in the Party. Its departure would have meant increased competition on the Left and would have made it more difficult for the PvdA to shed its stolid image and attract new support.[40]

New Left also benefited from the aloof position of the Socialist Trade Union Federation (NVV). Although there are no formal ties between the PvdA and the NVV, large numbers of PvdA members also belong to the NVV, and many local and regional Party officials were NVV members. Nevertheless, the NVV made no attempt to mobilise its troops within the Party to resist New Left's advances. The detached posture of the NVV reflects the divergent interests of the Party and the trade union federation. After the war, the PvdA was engaged in its breakthrough attempt and needed to distance itself somewhat from the NVV. For its part, the NVV had less need for the Party as a channel of access. With the advent of the managed economy and the elaboration of corporative structures like the Social and Economic Council (SER), the NVV became increasingly involved in deliberations with the Protestant and Catholic trade union federations, the Government, and employers' organisations. Participating in the SER and other accommodative bodies provided the NVV with direct access to the Government. The PvdA remained important − its support for NVV objectives might help − but the PvdA was not always in the Government. Even if it was, the NVV might still find it necessary to take an independent position. Aside from this, NVV leaders were reluctant to become too involved in PvdA affairs because they were interested in merging with the Protestant and Catholic Trade Union federations (the NVV and the NKV have recently joined in a loose organisation, the Federation of Dutch Trade Unions FNV). NVV leaders also feared that New Left activism might spread into the trade union movement if they became too involved in PvdA affairs. Because its interests and concerns were different the NVV adopted a hands-off attitude towards the conflict in the PvdA. NVV leaders felt that they could live with a PvdA penetrated by New Left, even if that meant that the Party would be in the opposition.[41]

The conciliatory attitude of the Party leadership and the aloof
posture of the NVV enabled the New Left to take advantage of the
openness of the PvdA's structure. The PvdA is a direct party with a
relatively simple structure and no formal trade union connections or
bloc memberships. Ultimate authority resides in the Congress, which
meets bi-annually, but *in interim,* the Party is governed by an Executive
Committee and by the Party Council. The latter may review decisions
of the Executive, but for the most part its *formal* responsibilities are
more administrative than political. The Party is organised into local
sections and regional federations. Local sections elect the greater portion
of the Congress and the Congress selects the Party Executive. Regional
Federations (elected by local sections) select the bulk of the Party
Council but have no formal control over the selection of the Party
Executive. Some areas also have subregional organisations, but on the
whole, the Party structure is simple and direct with few intervening
levels.[42]

To win influence on the Party Executive, all New Left had to do
was to gain control of, or influence within, local Party sections and then
elect sympathetic delegates to the Party Congress. Doing so was
facilitated by the integration and compactness of the Netherlands (no
part is more than a few hours drive from any other), the existence of a
nationally based but ideologically segmented media and the slack which
exists within any voluntary organisation. New Left was able to take
advantage of positions in the Socialist media and the ease of travel and
communication in the Netherlands to spread its ideas and enlist
followers. In addition, although the PvdA still had more than 100,000
members in the late 1960s most were not active participants. Slack
within the Party organisation enabled New Left to gain a foothold
at the base of the Party organisation and to send delegates to the
Congress as representatives of local sections. Operating as a bloc within
the Congress concentrated New Left strength, magnified it, and
permitted New Left to elect disproportionate numbers to the Party
Executive.

4. The Contemporary PvdA

What difference had New Left made? The conflict between New Left
and the PvdA leadership opened a deep rift in the PvdA, resolved in
part by the splintering off of Democratic Socialists '70 and in part by
the integration of New Left into the Party. This has produced a rapid
turnover in Party personnel. Previously Party officials, particularly at
the lower and intermediate levels, were likely to have a trade union

background. However, while the Party retains a working-class membership, its active cadres are younger, more educated, and more likely to be employed in the service sector of the economy.

While the Party's social and economic commitments remain substantially the same, a neo-democratic ethos has been grafted onto earlier commitments to a more equal and secure society. This manifests itself in a number of ways: anxious to promote change, the PvdA now characterises itself as a party in action and expresses its solidarity with the various social action groups which have sprung up in the late 1960s and early 1970s. Suspicious of expertise and fearful of bureaucratic machinations, the PvdA idealises the sentiments and goals of those at the bottom. Given a conflict, in the context of the Party's new populism, the PvdA view is that those who are at the bottom — those who are involved and affected — should govern.[43] This same ideal infuses internal party politics. PvdA politics have been democratised and Party cadres now attempt to bind leaders to specific programmatic commitments. At the same time, the Party now rejects the politics of accommodation and pursues a strategy of alliance and polarisation designed to give voters greater say and to prevent the desires of those at the bottom from being lost in compromises at the top.

Programmes and Policies

Party programmes reflect the new mood. PvdA foreign policy is more radical, domestic priorities have changed, and earlier commitments to a more equal society have been fused with demands for greater participation and greater popular control at all levels. This is evident in the PvdA's 1972 programme (jointly authored with Democrats '66 and the Radical Party). The PvdA of the 1950s and 1960s was concerned with promoting economic growth, the construction and elaboration of a welfare state, and establishing greater public control in a mixed economy, and the emphasis was on parliamentary and not participatory democracy. The PvdA of the 1970s is sceptical about economic growth, more concerned about the distribution of wealth, and anxious not only to guarantee material welfare but also to improve individual well-being and the quality of community life. The PvdA insists on priority for the needs of lower income groups and urges the redistribution of excess corporate profits and greater public control over private investment and financial institutions. This is to occur not only at the national but also at the European level. At the same time the PvdA contends that a new social and economic order cannot be built without extensive participation and extensive popular control over political, social, and economic institutions. The PvdA insists not only on greater political democracy (the direct election of mayors, provincial commissioners, and cabinet *formateurs*) but also on extensive co-determination in industry. According to the PvdA programme, workers are to have a voice in the selection of corporate directorates and workers' councils are to have a greater role in company decisions. Other institutions (schools, universities) are also to be subject to greater popular control. Educational programmes at all levels are to be revamped in order to provide greater opportunities for individual development and creativity and to prepare individuals for more extensive participation in community life.[44]

PvdA foreign policy is also different. The PvdA of the 1950s was pro-NATO and anti-Communist. The PvdA of the 1970s, however, is suspicious of American intentions and insists that Dutch membership in NATO be contingent on the extent to which the alliance can be used to promote world peace. Anti-NATO feeling is combined with a desire to reduce defence expenditures and increase aid to developing countries.[45] In general, the PvdA favours greater international solidarity, greater international equality, and greater control by international institutions. The PvdA advocates a united, democratically controlled (and preferably progressively orientated) Europe. Ideally the Party would like to see NATO and the Warsaw pact disbanded and replaced by a European security system. Before the overthrow of dictatorial regimes in Greece and Portugal, PvdA activists demanded that both countries be expelled from NATO unless they changed. The PvdA also expresses deep sympathy for anti-colonial (and often anti-American movements) such as the MPLA in Angola.[46]

Internal Politics

Internal politics are also changed. Prior to 1966, the PvdA was a democratically constituted organisation, but one in which leaders led and followers followed. The Party was dominated by its parliamentary leadership and the Party organisation was highly centralised. Largely because of New Left penetration and changes in the Party cadres, the Party became 'democratised' and power has become decentralised. The formal structure of the Party remains the same, yet the relations among leaders and followers are different. Party leaders are anything but authoritative. Imbued with a participatory ethos and suspicious of authority, PvdA members display an 'organised mistrust' of Party leaders, and engage in persistent attempts to control and influence them. Party activists demand extensive programmatic commitments and insist that elected representatives render account of their actions and explain any deviations from previous commitments. Meetings at all levels are now open to all Party members, and the Party Council – formally an administrative body elected by regional federations, now serves as interim Party Congress in which ministers, parliamentary leaders and the Party Executive are called to account. Both the Party Council and the Party Congress have turned into participatory events in which delegates vent their feelings and leaders attempt to explain themselves.[47]

The tone of Party Congresses is also different. Before 1967, a large proportion of the speaking time was taken up by Party leaders. Their proposals would generate some opposition, but once the discussion was over, the leadership invariably won out. In recent years, however, speaking time has been drastically reduced in order to allow more delegates to participate (if only for two-and-a-half minutes) and leaders do not necessarily get their way. The press of business is also much heavier. A rough comparison illustrates the difference. The agenda for the 1959 Congress contained a total of 224 resolutions – 194 from sections and 30 from the Party Executive. The agenda for the 1971 Congress contained 1,103 resolutions or suggestions.[48] Nor is the desire for greater participation and control confined to national politics. On the local level, Party sections suspiciously oversee the actions of municipal councillors and aldermen, and there have been discussions about instituting recall procedures to bring recalcitrant aldermen to heel.

The position of the Party Executive has also changed. Previously, the Party Executive was closely linked to the parliamentary caucus and the Executive co-ordinated the construction of parliamentary lists. Several members of the Executive were also members of the parliamentary group. In recent years, however, the number of legislators on the Executive has been reduced and the Executive now takes a more independent role, frequently criticising the caucus and the cabinet. At the same time, the Executive has less influence within the Party. Nominations for the parliaments are now handled by regional federations and the Executive has less control over recruitment. Party sections are more independent, and the Executive is subject to the same scrutiny from below at Party Congresses and Party Councils as is the parliamentary leadership.[49]

The Party as Action Group

The neo-democratic ethos which pervades the internal politics of the

PvdA spills over into the Party's external posture. The pre-1966 PvdA was a parliamentary party, *par excellence*, orientated toward legislation the politics of cabinet formation, and the tasks of governing. The present-day PvdA is a cross between a parliamentary party and a social action centre. Rather than regarding itself as the representative of certain classes, interests or principles, the PvdA characterises itself as a party in action. Members of parliament supplement legislative activities with visits to designated areas in which they assume the role of ombudsman, listening to and examining local grievances. At the same time, the PvdA is favourably disposed toward the various social action groups which have sprung up since the late 1960s. Anxious to maintain ties with those who are promoting change -- anxious to maintain ties with those at the bottom -- the Party supports, encourages, and occasionally organises action groups. These range from groups demanding changes in foreign policy to groups advocating specific issues -- liberalisation of abortion laws, improvement of the environment or demands about a specific neighbourhood or project.[50]

The Polarisation Strategy

Relationships with other parties have also changed. Since the adoption of the anti-KVP resolution in 1969, the PvdA has been committed to a strategy of alliance and polarisation. Rather than competing in elections and waiting to see what kind of cabinet can be formed on the basis of election results, the PvdA now demands that parties state with whom and on what basis they wish to govern before the elections are held. The term 'polarisation' reflects a desire to bring out existing differences rather than obscuring them. The strategy, as such, rejects the politics of accommodation and reflects an increasingly popular belief that voters, and not their elected representatives, should determine the composition and the policies of the cabinet. By insisting that parties form alliances and state their choices beforehand, voters are to be given a more clear-cut choice, and at the same time, politicians, because they are committed in advance, lose their freedom to negotiate with each other and form coalitions based on the parliamentary arithmetic.

Since 1970, the PvdA has entered pre-election alliances with other Left or progressive parties in successive municipal, provincial, and national elections. In the 1970 and 1974 municipal and provincial elections, formal and informal alliances (there were more formal agreements in 1970 than in 1974) were formed in many parts of the Netherlands. These usually involved Democrats '66 and the Radicals, but occasionally included the Pacifist Socialists as well. At the national level, the PvdA entered alliances with Democrats '66 and the Radicals for both the 1971 and 1972 parliamentary elections. In 1971, the three parties drew up a short common programme and formed a 'shadow cabinet' which was to take office if their parties won a majority. In 1972, the three parties rallied around a more extensive and detailed common programme, 'Turning Point' which was to be the basis of a governing coalition.[51] Since then, the polarisation strategy — or at least the desire for programmatic commitments — has been extended to municipal and provincial cabinets: Socialists and their allies have tried to replace broadly based or non-partisan cabinets (the norm in municipal and provincial politics) with either programmatic cabinets (broadly-based cabinets committed to a specific pre-agreed programme) or, if possible, progressive or left majority cabinets. This has occurred in several larger cities.

The polarisation strategy is a significant departure for the PvdA. Before 1969, the PvdA had been a willing partner in the politics of accommodation. However, by declaring itself unwilling to ally with the KVP in 1969 and by insisting that parties agree on coalitions before the elections, the PvdA has distanced itself from accommodative practices and widened the gulf between it and the other established parties.[52] Thus far, only Democrats '66 and the Radical Party have been willing to enter pre-election accords. The confessional parties have been unwilling to narrow their freedom of action by committing themselves beforehand, and the leftward shift of the PvdA has made alliance with the Liberals even more improbable than before.

5. Impact of the New Orientation

According to the conventional wisdom, when a party of the Left wants to win additional support, it moderates its views and moves toward the Centre. Confronted with declining electoral support, the PvdA has moved toward the Left. What difference has this made?

Electorally, the polarisation strategy has been neither highly successful nor as disastrous as some might have expected. In 1967, the PvdA won 23.5 per cent. In 1971, despite competition from Democratic Socialists '70 (which won 5.8 per cent and drew a third of its support from the PvdA)[53] the PvdA won 24.7 per cent of the vote. When early elections were held in November 1972 the PvdA won 27.3 per cent and emerged as the largest party in a fragmented party system. In addition, despite its oppositional posture, the PvdA returned to the Government in 1972. Nevertheless, the PvdA's base of support in the 1970s was not appreciably different than it had been in 1956. According to data from the 1971 Dutch Parliamentary Election Study (N=2495)[54] the PvdA remained not only a party which drew the bulk of its support from middle or lower income groups, but also a party whose weakness was its inability to draw a majority of these groups.

Respondents were asked whether they thought of themselves as belonging to a particular social class. Sixty-seven per cent of those intending to vote for the PvdA identified themselves as either working or lower working class, while 27 per cent thought of themselves as middle class and 7 per cent as upper middle or upper class. However, the PvdA won only 41 per cent of those respondents who identified themselves as working or lower working class and expressed a party preference.[55] (Table 5*) If we use respondents' income as an indicator, the picture remains the same: while a large proportion of the Party following comes from lower or middle income groups (those earning less than 15,600 guilders per year), the PvdA wins only 32-36 per cent of those indicating a party preference (Table 6).

Both religion and religious practice limit PvdA growth. In 1971, 17 per cent of the PvdA's support came from Catholics, 28 per cent came from Dutch Reformed and 49.6 per cent came from voters with no religion. This is an improvement over 1956, when only 5 per cent of the PvdA's support was Catholic, but nevertheless, the PvdA drew the support of only 13 per cent of those Catholics who expressed a party preference (Table 7).[56] The proportion of the PvdA vote from regular church attenders (Catholic or Protestant) also remains low. In 1971, only 13 per cent of the PvdA's support came from persons indicating that they attended church at least once a week.

Both religion and church attendance blunt the strength of the PvdA among lower classes.[57] As Tables 8 and 9 show, the proportion of working-class voters supporting the PvdA is greater among Dutch Reformed than among Catholics or Orthodox Reformed and greater among irregular church attenders and voters without a religion than among regular church attenders.

Other aspects of PvdA support are conditioned by the relationships among religion, class, and party preference. Reflecting its class background, the PvdA is somewhat stronger among voters with less education. Reflecting the religious composition of party support, the PvdA is weaker in the predominantly Catholic areas in the south of the Netherlands and stronger in the free-thinking Protestant and non-religious areas in the North (Groningen and Friesland).[58]

Age and Party Support

One of the purposes of the polarisation strategy was to restore the

*Tables 5-14 are on pp.379-87.

PvdA's credentials as a party of renewal and to attract the support of younger voters. Nevertheless, as Table 10 indicates, this has only been partially successful. The PvdA won 25 per cent of those indicating a party preference among the 21-30 age group (42 per cent of this group failed to give a preference), but the PvdA is strongest among the 41-50 age group and among voters over 65 years old. If we look at the composition of the PvdA's support, the PvdA emerges a party which is neither young nor old, but still weaker among younger voters than we might expect a party bidding for younger voters to be. The relative weakness of the PvdA becomes more apparent if we consider the fact that younger voters are much less likely to support confessional parties than their elders. As Table 11 indicates, only 29 per cent of voters in the 21-30 age group supported a confessional party. However, 15 per cent of the younger voters preferred D'66 while 25 per cent opted for other parties (Table 10).

Competition from minor parties continued to hurt the PvdA in 1972. According to a preliminary report of the 1972 national voting study, the PvdA drew 18 per cent of the votes of 18-20 year olds and 22 per cent of those aged 21-25. However, while D'66 strength declined, the Radicals (PPR) surged from 1.8 per cent to 4.8 per cent of the vote. The PPR drew 18 per cent of the 18-20 age group and 12 per cent of those aged 21-25. These two age groups accounted for 55 per cent of the PPR's support.[59]

To some extent, the PvdA's strategy of alliance and polarisation has compensated for the PvdA's narrow electoral base. By allying with parties such as D'66 and the PPR, the PvdA avoids direct frontal competition with these parties, and is able to benefit from the votes that they attract. This enlarges PvdA's base. However, polarisation strategy rejects coalitions unless agreements are worked out before the elections. If applied rigorously, neither the PvdA nor its allies can come to power unless they have won a majority of the electorate.

The PvdA between Government and Opposition

Initially, the polarisation strategy did little more than confirm the PvdA's return to the opposition. By declaring itself unwilling to ally with the KVP in 1969, the PvdA dealt itself out of the politics of cabinet formation. This ensured that the confessional-Liberal de Jong cabinet would survive a complete term. Because of the PvdA's posture, no alternative cabinet was possible and the fall of the cabinet would, under the changing rules of Dutch political life, have meant new elections for which no one was prepared. Alliance with the PPR and

D'66 in 1971 had much the same effect. Because of KVP losses, the three confessional parties and the Liberals had only 74 of the 150 seats in the Second Chamber. The PvdA, D'66 and the PPR won 33.3 per cent of the vote, but were not seriously involved in the cabinet formation Instead, the confessional-Liberal coalition was broadened by the addition of Democratic Socialists '70.

Only when the five-party Biesheuvel cabinet collapsed because of the withdrawal of Democratic Socialists '70 was the way opened for the PvdA's return to power. Because no alternate cabinet was available, new elections were called for November 1972. Both the election results and the polarisation strategy produced a prolonged cabinet crisis. Competing on the basis of an elaborate joint programme, the PvdA, the PPR and D'66 won 56 seats and 36.4 per cent of the vote, while the three confessional parties, competing in a loose alliance, slipped to 31.3 per cent — 48 instead of 58 seats. The Liberals jumped from 16 to 22 seats but these gains were insufficient to offset confessional losses: confessionals and Liberals commanded only 70 of the 150 seats. A new coalition with Democratic Socialists '70 was out of the question. As a result, no majority cabinet was possible without the PvdA.

Securing such a coalition was no easy matter. The PvdA and its allies were committed to govern on the basis of their programme and insisted on being allowed to form a minority government. The confessional parties rejected this and proposed a Centre-Left cabinet in which the three confessional and three progressive parties would be equal partners. However, the progressive parties insisted that their programme had received the support of their voters and refused to negotiate. Eventually — after five-and-a-half months — the deadlock was resolved by the formation of a progressively tinted cabinet with KVP and ARP support. The cabinet was headed by the former Socialist parliamentary leader den Uyl. The PvdA and its allies ended up with ten of sixteen portfolios and succeeded in splitting the CHU from the ARP and the KVP.[60] However, both the progressive and confessional programmes were to serve as joint sources of inspiration for the cabinet's policies.

If the polarisation strategy did not preclude the return of the PvdA to the Government, it has not made the life of the den Uyl cabinet or the PvdA ministers in it very comfortable. Aside from a nominal agreement that both the confessional and progressive programmes were to serve as joint sources of inspiration for the cabinet, there were no detailed agreements about just what the cabinet was to do. The progressive parties — and particularly the PvdA and the PPR — regard the cabinet as a progressive government charged with the task of carrying out the pledges in their joint programme. This has not been easy. The cabinet has found itself preoccupied with more basic problems: the energy crisis, inflation, recession, unemployment and more recently, trying to hold down the rate of increase in Government expenditures. This has restricted the opportunities for the introduction of new programmes. Moreover, while the KVP and the ARP support the cabinet, neither the confessional ministers nor their parties feel bound to the pledges in the progressives' programme. There are disagreements on the extent of co-determination to be introduced, on the nature and degree of redistribution, and on foreign policy and defence issues. On the latter, neither the confessional ministers nor their parties — nor for that matter, the PvdA ministers of foreign affairs or defence — have been willing to endorse the anti-NATO inclinations of PvdA militants.

Although it has been impossible to carry out many of the pledges in the progressive programme, the PvdA has lent the cabinet critical but nevertheless steady support. Reflecting increased decentralisation in the PvdA, there is a constant tug of war within and among levels of Party organisation. The parliamentary caucus assumes a critical posture *vis-à-vis* the cabinet, and the Party Executive attempts to influence both the caucus and the PvdA ministers. Because of the sense of organised mistrust which pervades the Party, ministers and Party leaders must constantly explain and account for their actions and sell compromises to their followers. So far this has worked. Although in some instances — e.g. the decision to adopt the F-16 bomber — there has been blunt criticism of PvdA ministers, until recently most PvdA members have found governing more satisfying than opposition, and few have wanted to be in the position of bringing down their own cabinet. Instead, PvdA frustrations have been displaced on to cabinet partners. The KVP, in particular, has been blamed for many of the shortcomings of the cabinet and regarded as a distrustful partner ready to bring down the cabinet rather than yield to PvdA demands.[61]

6. Conclusion

What is the future direction of the PvdA? Ten years ago, Otto Kirchheimer argued that parties of mass integration were abandoning ideological commitments and transforming themselves into bland catch-all parties bidding for support wherever it could be found.[62] The PvdA of the 1950s and 1960s fits Kirchheimer's descriptions, but largely because of electoral decline and New Left penetration, the PvdA has emerged as a radicalised and democratised party which flaunts rather than hides Socialist symbols. However, the present mixture is anything but stable. The PvdA is hindered by its limited electoral base, the necessity of joining coalitions, and the difficulties of carrying out its programmes once it is in Government. Any of these could produce frustrations, internal divisions and shifts in the direction of the Party.

On the surface, the PvdA's electoral prospects are improved. Previously, Socialist growth was held in check by pillarisation and confessional mobilisation. However, church attendance is declining and the impact of religion on politics is greatly diminished.[63] An increasingly large portion of the electorate consists of younger voters for whom confessional voting attachments have little meaning.[64] Barriers between subcultures are increasingly porous: the Socialist and Catholic trade union federations have recently banded together in the Federation of Dutch Trade Unions (FNV). At the same time, many of the smaller parties are in decline. Both Democrats '66 and Democratic Socialists '70 fared poorly in the 1974 provincial and municipal elections.[65]

Whether the PvdA can benefit from these developments remains to be seen. The decline of minor parties eliminates competition and reduces the need for alliances, but it also means that the PvdA must broaden its appeal and win the support of voters it has previously failed to attract. This is particularly important because Catholics, Anti-Revolutionaries, and Christian Historicals have recently decided to proceed with long-debated plans for the creation of an interconfessional Christian Democratic party.[66] The three parties will be submitting a joint list in the 1977 parliamentary elections. Although support for the traditional confessional parties has weakened, it is possible that the new formation, the Christian Democratic Appeal (CDA), will attract former confessional voters back to the fold. Whether this occurs or not will depend both on the ability of the CDA to present itself to the electorate as something more than a loose federation of three older parties and on the way in which the PvdA positions itself. The PvdA is committed to a wide range of programmes intended to create a more equal, more habitable and more democratic society. It is possible that these programmes could attract broader support, but, at the same time, different proposals could also repel voters. Demands for the levelling of incomes, restrictions on private property and investment, and restrictions on the use of cars could alienate both middle-class voters and better-paid workers, while too much emphasis on environmental goals – e.g. limited economic growth at the cost of employment – could cost the PvdA working-class support.

The PvdA's solution for its electoral problems has been to try to say what it wants and put its views to the voters. However, this may not be enough. Although there is some awareness of the danger of going too far and too fast, a party run by participatory democracy is not in a good position to select optimal electoral strategies. PvdA programmes are invariably hybrids, expressing activists' desire to push ahead on a variety of reforms, tempered to some extent by leaders' cautions that pressing too hard could alienate support. This may be adequate for a party whose support is loyal or for a party operating in a restricted electoral arena, but the Dutch electorate has been volatile in recent years and the PvdA is exposed to competition on all sides: the Radicals, Pacifist Socialists and Communists guard the left flank, while the newly formed Christian Democratic Appeal could hurt the party on the right.

Even if the PvdA does attract wider support, the Party is likely to remain hemmed in by the need to form coalitions with the confessional parties. In 1972, the PvdA won only 27.2 per cent of the vote. Although opinion polls in 1974 and 1975 have shown the Party winning up to one-third of those declaring a party preference (no mean achievement considering that the Party has been in Government in a time of inflation and recession), the PvdA is unlikely to command a majority in the near future. Unless the PvdA allies with the Liberals — improbable given the present distance between the two parties — the PvdA will be forced to share power with the confessionals or return to the opposition. In 1972, the PvdA used the polarisation strategy to wring concessions from the ARP and the KVP. This produced a divided cabinet in which political differences have been thrashed out in a series of mini-crises in which the cabinet appears ready to collapse but somehow does not. However, whether a coalition in which one partner insists on precedence for its goals can survive or be re-established is questionable. Although the Anti-Revolutionaries and at least part of the Catholic Party have favoured a continuation of the present cabinet after the 1977 election, the new Christian Democratic party will undoubtedly insist on an equal position in the cabinet. The PvdA has responded by resorting to a new version of the polarisation strategy: according to a resolution recently approved by the executive committees of the PvdA and the Radical Party (PPR), the two parties will govern after the next elections only if they (a) win more votes than they did in 1972 and (b) jointly form the largest bloc in the new parliament. If these stipulations do not automatically confine the PvdA to the opposition, they are likely to make it difficult to re-establish a confessional-left coalition after the election.

Finally, it is worth asking whether PvdA aims can be achieved and how the Party will react if they cannot. At the moment, the PvdA is committed to greater economic equality, greater public control over the economy, democratisation of political, social, and economic institutions, and a more livable society for all. In adopting these themes, the PvdA has demonstrated an awareness of many of the problems of an advanced industrial society. Whether it can solve them is another matter. In all but the most ideal situations, there is a sharp conflict between demands for greater control over the economy and greater decentralisation and the introduction of participatory democracy. Nor are demands for redistribution or limits on economic growth always compatible with commitments to re-establish and maintain full employment. Redistributive measures — e.g. profit sharing, extremely progressive systems of taxation — are likely to discourage investment and threaten jobs. The Government could ease the problem by using its resources to provide income for those displaced, but the Government is constrained by the need to reduce the rate of increase in Government expenditure in order to allow sufficient room for the private sector. Greater public control over investment — demanded by the PvdA — could solve some of these problems, but this would probably hasten the flow of capital elsewhere.

The PvdA could respond to these dilemmas either by advocating a much greater Government role in the economy, or by postponing some of its demands, selecting priorities, and implementing reforms where this is possible. The den Uyl cabinet has chosen the latter course. So far, it has retained the support of the Party, but whether this will continue to be true if cabinet partners or economic circumstances dictate further compromises is another matter. While many PvdA activists are satisfied with the cabinet's accomplishments in a difficult economic period, others — as the recent PvdA-PPR resolution indicates — are increasingly impatient with a politics of compromise. The problem of compromise — when to push and when to yield — could divide the Party in the future. So could the strains of participatory democracy (a draft, subsequently withdrawn, of the 1977 election programme under discussion in Party sections elicited some 5,000 amendments — many more than the Party could possibly handle) and a question implicit in our discussion: can the redistribution of income and power which the PvdA advocates be achieved in a capitalist economy?

372   *The Dutch Labour Party*

Notes

1. For descriptions of the Dutch party system and the pillarisation of Dutch society, see Hans Daalder, 'The Netherlands: Opposition in a Segmented Society' in Robert Dahl (ed.), *Political Oppositions in Western Democracy* (New Haven, Yale Press, 1966), pp. 188-236, Arend Lijphart, *The Politics of Accommodation,* 2nd edition (Berkeley, University of California Press, 1975), pp. 16-58, Peter Baehr, 'The Netherlands', in Stanley Henig and John Pinder (eds.), *European Political Parties* (London, Political and Economic Planning, 1969), pp. 256-81, and Arend Lijphart, 'The Netherlands: Continuity and Change in Voting Behaviour', in Richard Rose (ed.), *Electoral Behaviour: A Comparative Handbook* (New York, The Free Press, 1974), pp. 227-70. See also Steven B. Wolinetz, *Party Re-alignment in the Netherlands* (Ph.D. dissertation, Yale University, 1973), pp. 17-46.
2. Both the Anti-Revolutionary Party (ARP) and the Christian Historical Union (CHU) are Protestant parties. However, the ARP is a tightly organised mass party which draws most of its support from members of the Orthodox Reformed (Gereformeerd) churches. The CHU is a much more loosely organised election society which draws most of its support from members of the Dutch Reformed Churches. The ARP was founded in 1879. The CHU was established in 1908 after a split in the Anti-Revolutionary Party. See Daalder, pp. 202-3, 206.
3. On consociational practices in the Netherlands, see Lijphart, *The Politics of Accommodation,* pp. 103-38. See also Daalder, pp. 189-96, 216-20.
4. Daalder, pp. 209-11. J.J. de Jong, *Politieke Organizatie na 1800 in West Europa* (The Hague, Martinus Nijhoff, 1951), pp. 318-22. D.J. Wansink, *Het Socialisme op de Tweesprong: de Geboorte van de SDAP* (Haarlem, Tjeenk Willink, 1939), pp. 3-20, 30-3, 36-9, 107-10.
5. Daalder, pp. 209-11; J.J. de Jong, pp. 320-2; Wansink, pp. 171-4, 196, 200-4. See also H.F. Cohen, *Om de Vernieuwing van Het Socialisme: De Politieke Orientatie van de Nederlandse Sociaal-Democratie 1919-1930* (Leiden, Universitaire Pers Leiden, 1974), pp. 12-14.
6. J.J. de Jong, p. 323; John P. Windmuller, *Labor Relations in the Netherlands* (Ithaca, Cornell University Press, 1969), pp. 32ff. The NVV was established in 1906 after a split in the Dutch Labour Secretariat (NAS) and an unsuccessful general strike attempt in 1903. On the whole, it has favoured strong organisation and collective bargaining and rejected Anarchist or Syndicalist tactics. NVV faced competition from Catholic and Protestant unions. See Daalder, pp. 207-11.
7. H. von Hulst, A. Pleysier, and A. Scheffer, *Het Rode Vaandel Volgen Wij* (The Hague, Krusemans', 1963), pp. 211-12, 217. L. de Jong, *Het Koninkrijk der Nederlanden in de Tweede Wereld Oorlog, vol. 1. Voorspel* (The Hague, Martinus Nijhoff, 1969), pp. 54-5, 228-9.
8. L. de Jong, pp. 46-56, 73; Daalder, pp. 210-11. Troelstra's gestures seriously divided the Party. See H. Cohen, pp. 14-21ff.
9. In 1896, approximately 50 per cent of adult males could vote. By 1913, increasing prosperity had increased the proportion to 68 per cent. See Daalder, p. 205. On SDAP bases of support, see Daalder, pp. 207-8.
10. Universal manhood suffrage increased the size of the electorate from 960,595 in 1913 to 1,517,380 in 1918. The SDAP doubled its vote, increasing from 142,185 in 1913 to 296,145 in 1918. However, the Catholic Party nearly quadrupled its vote: 111,081 in 1913, 402,908 in 1918. Data from Thomas T. Mackie and Richard Rose, *International Almanac of Election Statistics* (London, Macmillan, 1974), pp. 272, 276. On Catholic political organisation

and the role of the Church see L. de Jong, pp. 74-6.

11. See Cohen, pp. 75-80. The SDAP also made overtures to Catholic workers and tried to lure the labour wing of the Catholic Party into a coalition. Both efforts were unsuccessful.
12. Until 1927, ties between the SDAP and NVV were informal. In 1924, NVV Chairman, Stenhuis, proposed fusing the SDAP and NVV into a British-style Labour party. Although this was rejected by both SDAP and NVV, Stenhuis' proposals opened up the question of the relationship between party and trade unions. A 1927 agreement created a General Council, consisting of the directorates of both organisations, plus five members of the SDAP caucus, which would consider questions of common interest, including nominations, programmes, cabinet participation and joint action. However, the agreement also reiterated the previous understanding that political matters were the competence of the Party, economic matters the competence of the trade unions. See Cohen, pp. 83-156, especially pp. 84-6, 91-3, 140-2. See also J.J. de Jong, pp. 384-5. On related organisations see Cohen, pp. 40-2, 229-30. The Party and many related organisations were dependent on NVV financial contributions.
13. See H. Cohen, pp. 231-44; Daalder, pp. 210-11, and H. Verwey-Jonker, 'Vijf en twintig jaar Socialistische Theorie', in J.W. Albarda, *Een Kwart Euwe Parlementaire Werkzaamheid in dienst van de bevrijding van de Nederlandse arbeidersklasse* (Amsterdam, Arbeiderspers, 1938), pp. 338-9, 342-7.
14. NVV and SDAP, *Het Plan van de Arbeid: Rapport van de Commissie uit NVV en SDAP* (1935), pp. 5-10, 11-12. See also Daalder, pp. 211-12, and L. de Jong, pp. 233-4.
15. See Cohen, pp. 237-44; L. de Jong, pp. 670-71; Daalder, p. 212; and Verwey-Jonker, pp. 335-8, 346-7.
16. Willem Verkade, *Democratic Parties in the Low Countries and Germany: Historical Origins and Development* (Leiden, Universitaire Pers Leiden, 1965), p. 54. A.F. Manning, 'Geen doorbraak van oude structuren: de confessionele partijen na 1945', in L.W.G. Scholten *et al., De Confessionelen* (Utrecht, Ambobockcn, 1968), pp. 61-5.
17. Daalder, p. 213. See W. Thomassen, *Opening van Zaken: Een en ander over de voorbereiding van de PvdA* (Amsterdam, Studie Commissie uit de SDAP, de VDB, de CDU, een deel van de Christofoor groep en de NVB, 1946), and G. Ruygers, 'Partij van de Arbeid: Een Nieuw Begin' (speech given in Amsterdam, 9 Feb. 1946), p. 3ff.
18. *Beginselprogram van de Partij van de Arbeid* (Amsterdam, PvdA, 1947). W. Banning, *Kompas: Een toelichting op het Beginselprogram van de Partijvan de Arbeid* (Amsterdam, PvdA, 1947), pp. 12, 20-3.
19. The Anti-Revolutionaries completely rejected the notion that anything had changed. The Catholic Church was instrumental in ensuring the re-establishment of a Catholic Party. The Catholic Peoples Party (KVP) succeeded the pre-war Roman Catholic State Party (RKSP). See Manning, pp. 69-78.
20. For further details and a comparison of voting behaviour in 1956 and 1968 see Lijphart, 'The Netherlands: Continuity and Change in Voting Behaviour', pp. 242-58. The 1956 data used by Lijphart is the earliest survey data available. There is however, an ecological analysis of PvdA support carried out by the PvdA's research bureau. See Dr Wiardi Beckman Stichting, *Verkiezingen in Nederland: De ontwikkeling en verspreiding van politieke voorkeuren en hun betekenis voor de PvdA* (Amsterdam, Wiardi Beckman Stichting, 1951).
21. See Windmuller, pp. 225-30, and 'De Verhouding tussen de PvdA en een aantal andere organizaties' (Amsterdam, PvdA, 1955), pp. 4-16. The Workers

Youth Central, the Party's youth organisation in the interwar years, was disbanded in the 1950s.

22. PvdA, *Beginselprogram,* 1959 (Amsterdam, PvdA, 1959). W. Banning, *Kompas: Toelichting op Het Beginselprogram, 1959* (Amsterdam, PvdA, 1959), pp. 30-6, 44-7ff.

23. SDAP membership ranged from 40,000-60,000 between 1918 and 1930. PvdA membership has ranged from 90,000-150,000. However, the PvdA had no central membership administration until 1970. Introduction of a computerised membership administration eliminated inaccuracies and reduced total enrolments. Before 1970, the party contained many 'paper' members. PvdA figures supplied by the PvdA. SDAP figures are from Cohen, pp. 40, 229-31.

24. On minor parties, see Daalder, 'The Netherlands', pp. 225-7, and Hans Daalder, 'De Kleine Partijen − Een voorlopige poging tot inventarisatie', *Acta Politica,* vol. 1 (1965-6), pp. 180ff. See also Lijphart, *The Politics of Accommodation,* 2nd edition, pp. 162-9.

25. On recent changes in the Dutch party system see Lijphart, *The Politics of Accommodation,* 2nd edition, pp. 196-214, Steven B. Wolinetz, *Party Re-alignment in the Netherlands* and Hans Daalder, *Politisering en Lijdelijkheid in de Nederlandse Politiek* (Assen, van Gorcum, 1974).

26. This section is drawn from my paper, 'New Left and the Transformation of the Dutch Socialist Party' (paper presented to the Annual Convention of the American Political Science Association, San Francisco, 1975). The name New Left distinguished the group from previous Left-wing groups in the PvdA. The faction bore little relation to the American New Left movement. For a comparison, see R. Kroes, 'New Left-Nieuw Links: De radicale jaren zestig in Amerika en Nederland', *Intermediair,* vol. 9, no. 37 (21 Sept. 1973), pp. 15-21 and R. Kroes 'Nieuw Links in de PvdA', *Intermediair,* vol. 9, no. 38 (28 Sept. 1973), pp. 1-13. These can also be found in R. Kroes, *New Left, Nieuw Links New Left: Verzet, beweging, verandering in Amerika, Nederland, Engeland* (Alphen aan den Rijn, Samsom, 1975), pp. 15-28, 44-67.

27. See R. Kroes, 'Nieuw Links in de PvdA', pp. 1-3, and J.Th.J. van den Berg and H.A.A. Molleman, *Crisis in de Nederlandse Politiek* (Alphen aan den Rijn, Samsom, 1974), pp. 113-15. The ideas and goals of New Left were set forth in a series of short books published from 1966 onwards. These include *Tien Over Rood* (Amsterdam, Polak & van Gennep, 1966); *De Meeste Mensen Willen Meer* (Amsterdam, Polak & van Gennep, 1967); and *De Macht van de rooie ruggen* (Amsterdam, Polak & van Gennep, 1967). As Kroes points out, the thrust of each book is different. The first stresses democratisation, social and economic policy, and foreign policy. The second deals with culture and 'cultural policy'. The third has tinges of Old Left: nationalisation is central. The themes discussed in the text come primarily from the first, *Tien Over Rood.* See Kroes, pp. 1-3.

28. Kroes, 'Nieuw Links in de PvdA', pp. 1, 5.

29. Ibid. pp. 1-3. Van den Berg and Molleman, pp. 110-13.

30. Van den Berg and Molleman, pp. 112-13.

31. The PvdA has strict rules governing the admission and exclusion of members. These reflect earlier fears of Communist infiltration. See Partij van de Arbeid, *Statuten en huishoudelijk reglement* (Amsterdam, PvdA, 1965), especially Articles 4, 7, 10 and 11 of the statutes and Articles 8 and 9 of the by-laws.

32. Kroes, 'Nieuw Links in de PvdA', pp. 5-7.

33. Van den Berg and Molleman, pp. 112-13, 120-1, Kroes, 'Nieuw Links in de PvdA', pp. 5-7. For a description of the New Left takeover in the city of Groningen, see Bert Middel, *De Nieuwe Elite van de PvdA: Een onderzoek naar de neiging tot oligarchie binnen de afdeling Groningen van de Partij van de*

Arbeid (Xeno, Groningen) 1976, pp. 30-7.

34. The immediate cause of the split was a dispute over a proposed election alliance for the 1971 election. A dispute over the inclusion of the Pacifist Socialists in the city of Eindhoven triggered splits elsewhere. Several well-known and prominent Socialists left the Party, including Willem Drees, jun., son of the post-war PvdA Prime Minister (1948-58). Drees sen. resigned from the PvdA in 1971.

35. The process of reconciliation began after the 1969 Congress. New Left was dissolved as part of an agreement between Vondeling (former parliamentary leader and Party Chairman from 1969-71) and van der Louw (Vice Chairman from 1967-71, and a member of New Left). Vondeling offered to support van der Louw for the Party Chairmanship provided that New Left would be dissolved. Vondeling would serve as Vice Chairman, and the transfer would not take place until after the 1971 elections. Van der Louw accepted on the condition that the PvdA would evolve into an 'action' party. See Kroes, 'Nieuw Links in de PvdA', p. 13.

36. Because New Left had no fixed membership, it is difficult to assess the exact degree of penetration. For example, Kroes claims that there were twelve members of New Left in the parliamentary fraction after 1972, while van den Berg and Molleman count ten. Similarly, if one counts sympathisers, it could be argued that there are two rather than one New Left ministers in the den Uyl cabinet. Getting an exact count is complicated by changes in the composition of the caucus. Membership in the cabinet is incompatible with membership in the parliament and the places vacated are filled by moving down the list of candidates submitted for the election. On the extent of New Left penetration, see van den Berg and Molleman pp. 112-13, and Kroes, 'Nieuw Links in de PvdA', p. 1.

37. The proportion of Catholics supporting the KVP had been declining throughout the post-war period. By 1967, this had dropped to 67 per cent. High birthrates enabled the KVP to maintain its electoral strength until the 1967 elections. See van den Berg and Molleman, pp. 64-5. On changes in the role of the church and changes in the Catholic subculture see van den Berg and Molleman, pp. 70-83. See also J.M.G. Thurlings, *De Wankele Zuil: Nederlandse Katholieken tussen assimilatie en pluralisme* (Nijmegen, Katholieke Documentatie Centrum, 1971), and Wolinetz, *Party Re-alignment in the Nederlands*, pp. 35-40, 73-7, 96-108.

38. Opinion polls and voting studies from the late 1960s showed D'66 winning from 10 to 20 per cent or more of the votes of younger age cohorts. See Wolinetz, *Party Re-alignment in the Netherlands*, pp. 92-6, 109. For a summary of the preferences of the younger age cohorts in surveys from 1961 to 1972, see Daalder, *Politisering en Lijdelijkheid*, p. 51.

39. Proportional representation was adopted in 1918 as part of the Pacification Settlements. Technically the country is divided up into eighteen districts, but by permitting the pooling of votes won by allied lists in different districts, the electoral law effectively creates one national constituency in which parties with or without geographic concentrations of votes can readily compete. To win a seat (after 1933), a party merely had to gain the electoral divisor (average number of votes per seat) or one-hundredth of the national vote. Parties had to put up a nominal deposit, to be forfeited if the party failed to win three-quarters of the divisor. Seats are allocated according to the d'Hondt (highest averages) formula. In 1956, the parliament was enlarged from 100 to 150 seats. This lowered the threshold to 0.67 per cent and the percentage required to avoid forfeiture to 0.50 per cent. Until 1970 the electoral law also included a requirement that voters appear at the polls. They could, however,

spoil their ballots. See Hans Daalder, 'De Kleine Partijen', pp. 173-81 and Lijphart, *The Politics of Accommodation,* pp. 162-9.

40. For further elaboration, see Wolinetz, *Party Re-alignment in the Netherlands,* pp. 154-62. The argument draws on Albert O. Hirschman, *Exit, Voice and Loyalty* (Cambridge, Harvard University Press, 1970).

41. Windmuller, pp. 225-30.

42. PvdA, *Statuten en huishoudelijk reglement.* See also I. Lipschitz, 'De organisatorische structuur der Nederlandse politieke partijen', *Acta Politica,* vol. 2, no. 4 (1966-7), pp. 265-96.

43. See van den Berg and Molleman, pp. 99-107, pp. 126-8.

44. Material for this and the subsequent paragraph has been distilled from 'Turning Point', the joint 1972 programme of the PvdA, Democrats '66 and the Radical Politcal party (PPR). Although the programme was jointly sponsored by the three parties, it received the approval of the PvdA Congress and is used as a reference point for evaluating the present cabinet. See PvdA, D'66, PPR, *Keerpunt 1972: Regeerakkoord van de progressieve drie* (Amsterdam, PvdA, 1972).

45. PvdA views on NATO and defence expenditures are drastically changed. In 1963 a resolution in favour of disarmament won the support of only 15 per cent of the Party Congress. In 1967, 25 per cent supported a resolution demanding withdrawal from NATO. At the October 1972 Congress, 40 per cent supported a strong anti-NATO resolution and 70 per cent supported a compromise resolution demanding that Dutch membership of NATO be predicated on the ability to use the alliance as a vehicle for the relaxation of East-West tensions. M. van Amerongen, *Vrij Nederland,* 14 Oct. 1972.

46. See *Keerpunt,* pp. 40-3.

47. Van den Berg and Molleman, pp. 120-2. It would be a mistake to view the PvdA as an organisation governed by all of its members. Participatory democracy rarely produces mass participation; instead it shifts power from one group or minority to another. For a discussion of oligarchical tendencies in the New Left dominated PvdA in the city of Groningen, see Bert Middel, *De Nieuwe Elite van de PvdA,* pp. 47-65. Middel regards the New Left takeover in Groningen (in which he participated) as an example of the rotation of élites, in the sense described by Michels. Van den Berg and Molleman, however, view the PvdA at the national level as the site of an ongoing struggle between competing élites. See van den Berg and Molleman, pp. 126-8.

48. PvdA, *Beschrijvingsbrief van het zevende Congres van de PvdA op 12-14 Nov. 1959 te Amsterdam,* and PvdA, *Beschrijvingsbrief van het dertiende Congres van de PvdA, 4-6 Februari, 1971 te Amsterdam.*

49. Van den Berg and Molleman, pp. 121-2.

50. Ibid. pp. 156-64.

51. Originally, electoral alliances were regarded as the first step in a major restructuring of the Dutch party system. After Democrats '66 sudden success in the 1967 election, the PvdA tried to enlist D'66 and the PPR in the formation of a broadly based progressive party. This was part of the PvdA's attempt to shed its establishment image. However, D'66, although organised with the explicit purpose of reforming the party system, was unwilling to tarnish its image by drawing too close to the PvdA. The Radical Party – formed by Catholic Radicals who bolted from the KVP in 1969 – was initially much more favourable. The election agreement in 1971 was concluded just prior to the elections. After 1972, Democrats '66 began to advocate a merger of the three parties (variously known as 'the progressive three' or 'the progressive alliance') into a single progressive party. The PvdA, however, was cool to the idea. The change reflects the election results: the PvdA gained votes and rose

to 27.4 per cent while D'66 dropped from 6.8 per cent in 1971 to 4.2 per cent in 1972. Since then, the prospects of a new fused party have become extremely remote. At the moment, Democrats '66 is acting independently. However, the PvdA and the PPR are proceeding with plans for an alliance and joint programme for the 1977 parliamentary elections. For a discussion of the reasons for the formation of alliances but the failure of mergers, see Wolinetz, *Party Re-alignment in the Netherlands*, pp. 144-68.

52. See Lijphart, *The Politics of Accommodation*, pp. 196-208 and van den Berg and Molleman, pp. 165-74.

53. H. Daudt, 'Constante kiezers, wisselaars en thuisblijvers', *Acta Politica*, vol. 7, no. 1 (Jan. 1972), p. 32.

54. The data utilised in this section were made available by the Inter-University Consortium for Political Research and the S.S.R.C. Survey Archive, University of Essex. The data for the Dutch Parliamentary Election Study, 1971 were originally collected by Robert J. Mokken and Frans M. Roschar. Neither the original collectors of the data nor the consortium bear any responsibility for the analyses or interpretations presented here.

55. Some 33.3 per cent of the 2,495 respondents failed to indicate a party preference. In order to simplify the analysis, they have been excluded from the discussion. When those without a party preference are included the proportion supporting the PvdA among those identifying as working or lower working class drops to 26.9 per cent.

56. Preliminary reports of a 1972 national election survey show similar results: 18 per cent of the PvdA's voters were Catholic and 13.7 per cent of those Catholics who voted supported the PvdA. See Werkgroep National Verkiezingsonderzoek, 1972, *De Nederlandse Kiezer '72* (Alphen aan den Rijn, Samsom, 1973), pp. 33-5.

57. Lijphart discovered similar relationships in the 1956 data. See Lijphart, 'The Netherlands: Continuity and Change in Voting Behaviour', pp. 243-50.

58. Socialists have historically been strong in agrarian areas in the north. See Dr Wiardi Beckman Stichting, *Verkiezingen in Nederland* (Wiardi Beckman Stichting, 1951), pp. 15-17ff.

59. *De Nederlandse Kiezer '72*, pp.23, 27, 35.

60. Van den Berg and Molleman, pp. 171-4.

61. Mistrust of the KVP stems from the fall of the Cals cabinet in 1966. It was the KVP and not the ARP which brought that cabinet down.

62. Otto Kirchheimer, 'The Transformation of Western European Party Systems', in Joseph La Palombara and Myron Weiner (eds.), *Political Parties and Political Development* (Princeton, Princeton University Press, 1966), pp. 184-200.

63. In 1972, only 38 per cent of all Catholics (53 per cent of regular church attenders and 25 per cent of irregular church attenders supported the KVP. Only 56 per cent of all Orthodox Reformed (61 per cent of regular church attenders and 36 per cent of irregular church attenders) supported the ARP. Only 18 per cent of all Dutch Reformed (42 per cent of regular church attenders and 8 per cent of irregular church attenders) supported the CHU. (*De Nederlandse Kiezer '72*, pp. 30-4.) On changing patterns of confessional attachment see Warren E. Miller and Philip Stouthard, 'Confessional Attachment and Electoral Behaviour in the Netherlands', *European Journal of Political Research*, vol. 3 (1975), pp. 219-58.

64. The voting age was lowered from twenty-one to eighteen before the 1972 election. On the behaviour of younger voters see, *De Nederlandse Kiezer '72*, pp. 26-8.

65. In areas where it competed separately and not as part of a progressive alliance,

Democrats '66 received only 1 per cent of the vote in the 1974 provincial elections and only 0.5 per cent in the 1974 municipal elections. Democratic Socialists '70 won 1.5 per cent in the provincial elections and 0.5 per cent in the municipal elections. Centraal Bureau voor de Statistiek, *Statistiek der Verkiezingen, 1974 Gemeenteraden* (The Hague, Centraal Bureau voor de Statistiek, 1975), pp. 18-19.

66. The confessional parties have been discussing possible mergers since 1968. In 1972, the three parties have tentatively agreed to form a Christian Democratic Party but were divided over two issues: whether the new party should be a religious party explicitly based on the gospel or a party open to all those who agree with its programmes, and whether the new party should be a Centre or a Left of Centre formation. The Anti-Revolutionaries favoured a party explictly based on the gospel and preferred a slightly Left of Centre party. The KVP preferred an open but centrist party. On the whole, the KVP has promoted fusion, while the Anti-Revolutionary Party has been a reluctant partner and the Christian Historical Union fell in between. In September 1976, the Anti-Revolutionaries finally agreed to go ahead with plans to submit a joint list in the 1977 parliamentary elections.

Table 5. Social class and party 1971:
self-identified social class by vote intention

a. The class composition of party support, 1971

Social class	PvdA	VVD	KVP	ARP	CHU	D'66	Other	Total
	%	%	%	%	%	%	%	%
Upper or upper-middle	7	42	7	16	13	15	15	13
Middle	27	50	47	53	48	44	46	42
Working or lower working	67	9	46	31	39	41	39	45
%	100	100	100	100	100	100	100	100
Total N	401	149	363	132	94	108	233	1,480

b. Social class and party preference, 1971

Social class	PvdA	VVD	KVP	ARP	CHU	D'66	Other	%	N
	%	%	%	%	%	%	%		
Upper or upper-middle	13	31	14	11	6	8	18	100	199
Middle	17	12	27	11	7	8	17	100	623
Working or lower working	41	2	25	6	6	7	14	100	658
Total	27	10	25	9	6	7	16	100	1,480

Source: Dutch Parliamentary Election Study, 1971.
NB: Percentages may not sum to 100 because of rounding.

Table 6. Income and party, 1971

a. The composition of party support, 1971

Annual income (guilders)	Vote intention, 1971							
	PvdA	VVD	KVP	ARP	CHU	D'66	Other	Total
	%	%	%	%	%	%	%	%
less than £6,500	9	2	10	8	8	4	4	7
£6,500 — 9,100	21	4	19	19	23	7	15	17
£9,100 — 11,700	22	7	17	20	18	20	18	18
£11,700 — 15,600	25	9	23	23	18	31	23	23
£15,600 — 26,000	19	41	23	18	23	30	30	25
more than £26,000	4	38	8	13	10	8	11	11
%	100	100	100	100	100	100	100	100
N	387	136	313	113	83	102	217	1,351

b. Income and party preference, 1971

Annual income (guilders)	Vote intention, 1971								
	PvdA	VVD	KVP	ARP	CHU	D'66	Other	%	N
	%	%	%	%	%	%	%	%	%
Less than £6,500	35	2	32	10	7	4	10	100	94
£6,500 — 9,100	36	3	26	9	8	3	14	100	225
£9,100 — 11,700	35	4	22	9	6	8	16	100	244
£11,700 — 15,600	32	4	24	8	5	11	16	100	306
£15,600 — 26,000	22	17	21	6	6	9	20	100	336
more than £26,000	20	35	18	10	10	6	16	100	146
Total	29	10	23	8	6	8	16	100	1,351

Source: Dutch Parliamentary Election Study, 1971.

N.B.: Percentages may not sum to 100 because of rounding.

Table 7. Religion and party, 1971

---

a. The religious composition of party support, 1971

Religion	Vote intention, 1971							
	PvdA	VVD	KVP	ARP	CHU	D'66	Other	Total
	%	%	%	%	%	%	%	%
Dutch Reformed	28	23	0	13	84	15	22	21
Orthodox Reformed	2	1	1	81	5	1	17	11
Roman Catholic	17	19	97	0	2	34	22	36
Other	4	9	0	4	6	6	5	4
No Religion	50	49	3	3	4	44	35	28
%	100	100	100	100	100	100	100	100
N	448	171	406	143	197	120	268	1,663

---

b. Religion and party preference, 1971

Religion	Vote intention, 1971								
	PvdA	VVD	KVP	ARP	CHU	D'66	Other	%	N
	%	%	%	%	%	%	%	%	%
Dutch Reformed	36	11	0	5	26	5	17	100	348
Orthodox Reformed	5	1	2	64	3	1	25	100	180
Roman Catholic	13	5	65	0	0	7	10	100	602
Other	25	25	0	8	10	11	21	100	63
No Religion	47	18	2	1	1	11	20	100	470
Total	27	20	24	9	6	7	16	100	1,663

Source: Dutch Parliamentary Election Study, 1971.

N.B.: Percentages may not sum to 100 because of rounding.

Table 8. Social class, church attendance, and party preference, 1971:
Percentages of regular and irregular church attenders and those with
no religion favouring the PvdA according to respondents' social class

| Social class | Church attendance | | |
	Once per week	Seldom or never	No religion
Upper or upper middle	3% (73)	12% (59)	25% (67)
Middle	4% (297)	23% (172)	37% (154)
Working or lower working	14% (278)	57% (187)	64% (193)

Source: Dutch Parliamentary Election Study, 1971.
N.B.: Figures in parenthesis are N's on which percentages are based.

Table 9. Religion, social class, and party preference, 1971: percentage
supporting the PvdA by religion and social class

| Social class | Religion | | | |
	Dutch Reformed	Orthodox Reformed	Catholics	No religion
Upper or upper middle	10% (42)	4% (26)	10% (50)	25% (67)
Middle	22% (129)	3% (78)	6% (235)	37% (154)
Working or lower working	58% (143)	10% (59)	21% (257)	64% (193)

Source: Dutch Parliamentary Election Study, 1971.
N.B.: Figures in parenthesis are N's on which percentages are based.

Table 10. Age and party, 1971

a. The composition of party support, 1971

Age	Vote intention, 1971							
	PvdA	VVD	KVP	ARP	CHU	D'66	Other	Total
	%	%	%	%	%	%	%	%
21 – 30	20	18	13	20	16	47	34	22
31 – 40	17	22	21	22	22	26	20	20
41 – 50	23	22	19	15	15	16	16	19
51 – 65	23	28	30	27	30	9	21	25
65 or older	18	10	17	18	18	2	9	14
%	100	100	100	100	100	100	100	100
N	448	171	405	143	107	120	268	1,662

b. Age and party preference, 1971

Age	Vote intention, 1971							%	N
	PvdA	VVD	KVP	ARP	CHU	D'66	Other	%	%
21 – 30	25	8	14	8	5	15	25	100	369
31 – 40	23	11	25	9	7	9	16	100	339
41 – 50	32	12	24	7	5	6	14	100	315
51 – 65	25	12	30	9	8	3	14	100	406
65 or older	34	7	29	11	8	1	10	100	233
Total	27	10	24	9	6	7	16	100	1,662

Source: Dutch Parliamentary Election Study, 1971.
N.B.: Percentages may not sum to 100 because of rounding.

Table 11. Support for secular and confessional parties by age, 1971

Age	Vote intention, 1971			
	Secular party*	Confessional party*	%	N
	%	%	%	
21 – 30	71	29	100	369
31 – 40	55	45	100	339
41 – 50	62	38	100	315
51 – 65	49	51	100	406
65 or older	48	52	100	233

* including minor parties

Source: Dutch Parliamentary Election Study, 1971.

Table 12. Parliamentary election results, 1971 and 1972

	1971		1972	
	% of vote	number of seats	% of vote	number of seats
PvdA	24.7	39	27.3	43
D'66	6.8	11	4.2	6
PPR	1.8	2	4.8	7
Total progressive bloc	33.3	52	36.4	56
KVP	21.9	35	17.7	27
ARP	8.6	13	8.8	14
CHU	6.3	10	4.8	7
Total confessional bloc	36.8	58	31.3	48
VVD	10.4	16	14.4	22
DS'70	5.3	8	4.1	6
CPN	3.9	6	4.5	7
PSP	1.4	2	1.5	2
SGP	2.3	3	2.2	3
GPV	1.6	2	1.8	2
BP	1.1	1	1.9	3
NMP	1.5	2	0.4	—
RKPN	—	—	0.9	1
Other parties	2.4	—	1.0	—
	100	150	100	150

Source: Centraal Bureau voor de Statistiek, *Statistiek der Verkiezingen, 1972*
(The Hague, Staatsuitgeverij, 1973), pp. 9, 23.

Table 13. Parliamentary elections in the Netherlands, 1971 and 1972

		% of vote 1971	number of seats 1971	% of vote 1972	number of seats 1972
Partij van de Arbeid	Labour Party (PvdA)	24.7	39	27.3	43
Katholieke Volkspartij	Catholic Peoples Party (KVP)	21.9	35	17.7	27
Anti-Revolutionaire Partij	Anti-Revolutionary Party (ARP)	8.6	13	8.8	14
Christelijk-Historische Unie	Christian Historical Union (CHU)	6.3	10	4.8	7
Volkspartij voor Vrijheid en Democratie	Peoples Party for Freedom and Democracy (Liberals) (VVD)	10.4	16	14.4	22
Democraten '66	Democrats '66 (D'66)	6.8	11	4.2	6
Politieke Partij Radikalen	Radical Party (PPR)	1.8	2	4.8	7
Democratisch Socialisten '70	Democratic Socialists '70 (DS'70)	5.3	8	4.1	6
Pacifistisch Socialistische Partij	Pacifist Socialist Party (PSP)	1.4	2	1.5	2
Communistische Partij van Nederland	Communist Party of the Netherlands (CPN)	3.9	6	4.5	7
Staatkundige Gereformeerde Partij	Political Reformed Party (SGP)	2.3	3	2.2	3
Gereformeerde Politiek Verbond	Reformed Political League (GPV)	1.6	2	1.8	2
Boeren-Partij	Farmers Party (BP)	1.1	1	1.9	3
Nederlandse Middenstands Partij	Dutch Middle-class Party (NMP)	1.5	2	0.4	0
Rooms Katholieke Partij Nederland	Roman Catholic Party of the Netherlands (RKPN)	–	–	0.9	1
Other		2.4	0	1.0	0
		100	150	100	150

Source: Centraal Bureau voor de Statistiek, *Statistiek der Verkiezingen, 1972* (The Hague, Staatsuitgeverij, 1973), pp. 9, 23.

Table 14. PvdA Membership (rounded off to nearest 100)

1947	117,700
1948	113,000
1949	113,400
1950-1	108,700
1951-2	111,600
1952-3	112,100
1953-4	116,200
1954-5	122,100
1955-6	133,400
1956-7	142,500
1957-8	140,300
1958-9	142,400
1959-60	144,800
1960-1	140,700
1961-2	139,100
1962-3	139,000
1963-4	140,500
1964-5	141,700
1965-6	136,700
1966-7	133,300
Oct. 1967	131,000
Oct. 1968	116,700
Oct. 1969	107,000
Oct. 1970	98,700
Oct. 1971	98,300
Oct. 1972	94,300
Oct. 1973	97,800
Oct. 1974	103,100
Oct. 1975	102,100
Apr. 1976	98,300

Source: Data supplied by the PvdA: figures to 1967 represent the average
membership on four dates within the specified period. Central membership
administration was established in 1970.

Further Reading

Daalder, Hans. 'The Netherlands: Opposition in a Segmented Society.' In Robert Dahl (ed.), *Political Oppositions in Western Democracies.* New Haven, Yale Press, 1966. Pp. 188-236.

Lijphart, Arend. 'The Netherlands: Continuity and Change in Voting Behaviour'. In Richard Rose (ed.), *Electoral Behaviour: a Comparative Handbook.* New York, The Free Press, 1974. Pp. 227-70.

Lijphart, Arend. *The Politics of Accommodation.* 2nd edition. Berkeley, University of California Press, 1975.

Wolinetz, Steven B. 'New Left and the Transformation of the Dutch Socialist Party.' (Paper presented to the Annual Convention of the American Political Science Association, San Francisco, 1975.)

Wolinetz, Steven B. *Party Re-alignment in the Netherlands.* PhD. dissertation, Yale University, 1973.

14 THE BELGIAN SOCIALIST PARTY

Xavier Mabille and Val R. Lorwin

The Belgian Socialists who formed their national party in 1885 called it the Workers' Party. The choice of name had its significance. In order not to frighten or to antagonise people by the word 'socialist', the founders used the name of the social class for whom they claimed to speak, rather than the programmatic name. It was not until sixty years later, when the Party reconstituted itself after the war, that it took its present name of the Socialist Party. We shall, however, use that name throughout this article, for the sake of simplicity.

The Party was indeed a workers' party in social recruitment, in electoral support, and in programmatic emphasis, although it had many intellectuals, some of international distinction, in its leadership. Under the party's aegis were grouped other organisations primarily of workers: consumer co-operatives, friendly societies, and trade unions, with collective membership in the Party. The Party also included political circles and individual members, but these were less important than the socio-economic organisations.

From its inception, the Party's appeal to the working class of the first industrialising nation on the Continent was limited by the religious cleavage which also divided members of the middle and upper classes. Catholic workers, following the Socialist lead, organised co-operatives, friendly societies, and unions of their own and, when male workers received the suffrage, tended to vote for the Catholic Party.

The Socialists thus came to take their place as one of three parties of a pluralist system in which most political and voluntary associational life, press and education were segemented along the lines of religious and ideological cleavage into a Catholic world, a Liberal world, and a Socialist world.[1] Socialist leaders, like those of the Catholic world, sought to encapsulate their members from the cradle to the grave, and to create a 'state within the (bourgeois) State'.[2] They joined the Liberals in support of lay public schools against the Catholic school system, in the *Kulturkampf* that was long (if intermittently) the sharpest conflict in Belgian public life.

Belgian Reformism

In all the societies in which workers were more or less free to organise,

Socialist parties soon moved from their initial revolutionary platforms to moderate political behaviour and parliamentary practices. It is therefore unnecessary to explain the Belgian Socialists' early turn to reformism by specific Belgian conditions or unique Belgian decisions.

'They are not even revisionists,' sneered Karl Kautsky, writing about the Belgian Socialists to Viktor Adler, 'for they have no theory to revise.'[3] The Belgians, it is true, had less use for theoretical debate than the parties which had the advantage of speaking the tongue of Karl Marx. But that meant that the contradictions between words and actions were for a long time less striking in Belgium than in Germany.

In addition to the general European reasons for the early 'domestication' of Socialism, some specifically Belgian circumstances, structures, and decisions were important. The consumer co-operatives had great influence on the outlook, ideology, and political style of the movement in its formative phase. For a time the most dynamic sector of the Socialist movement, they emphasised day-to-day issues of a (literally) bread-and-butter nature, as against either theoretical debate or revolutionary demands. (It is of course possible to be theoretical without being revolutionary, just as it is possible to be revolutionary without being theoretical.)

The Belgian Socialists early chose to emphasise, not class struggle, but the demand for universal suffrage — or at least what they and everyone else called 'universal' suffrage, although it was only male suffrage that they fought for. Frenchmen received full and equal voting rights early on, and many of the workers and their élites tended to deprecate it for its failure to lead to economic and social equality. Not so with the Belgians; deprived through the nineteenth century of the right to vote, they saw it as the key to social reform. To achieve it, they allied themselves with the progressive wing of the Liberal Party. For it, they went beyond their usual parliamentary methods, and engaged in a series of general strikes, the first of which won universal male voting rights in 1894, but only on a weighted, not an equal, basis. With the First World War, finally, came universal equal male suffrage, in 1919. (Female suffrage in national elections had to wait a full generation longer, until 1948 and the election of 1949.) The electoral alliance with the Liberals, which lasted until the First World War, was both a reformist strategy and tactic, and itself the cause of further reformism in Socialist political action.

As early as 1910, the Socialist Party declared itself willing to take part in a national government with the Liberals. This was a harbinger of later governmentalism, although the Socialists' chief coalition partners turned out to be the Catholics and not the Liberals. The Catholic Party was in sole control of national government for the three decades before 1914. The outbreak of war produced a coalition of the three parties, with the Socialists in a very junior role. But the nation's wartime experiences led to the acceptance by the two older parties of the Socialist Party as patriotic, legitimate, and coalition-worthy.

The war, which rent the Socialist movements of the major Continental belligerents, confirmed the moderate course of the Belgian party. This small country, neutral by decision of the great Powers since it had won independence in the 1830s, almost overwhelmed by the German war machine at the outbreak of the war, bravely defended its neutrality and its independence. Without dreams or capabilities of aggression, it had been 'cornered into heroism', as its king, Albert, modestly put it.

Resistance to Communism

In the light of that experience, Left-wing arguments against Socialist co-operation with the wartime government made no sense. The nascent Communist movement was denied the entering wedge it drove so deep into the French and German and Italian Socialist movements.

The closely articulated sections of the Belgian movement — unions, co-operatives and friendly societies in organic ties with the Party — resisted Communist penetration with a force which the less structured Socialist movements of France and Italy could not muster. Organisation was more important than doctrine in the largely successful opposition to Communism.

Reformism seemed to pay off, too. Socialist co-operation in the struggle for national survival and workers' sacrifices in the trenches, in occupied Belgium, and in prison camps and forced labour in Germany — along with the authorities' fear of revolution à la russe as the country was being liberated — resulted in a spate of immediate postwar reforms. These included universal equal male suffrage at last, the eight-hour day, the encouragement of collective bargaining, and full recognition of the right to strike. These reforms justified Socialist participation in the three-party coalition which ruled Belgium for several years after the war, in the decisive period when Communist movements either established or failed to establish themselves.

With universal equal male suffrage and proportional representation (the latter dating from 1898), no party would any longer have a majority in both houses of parliament, except for a Catholic majority in the 1950-4 legislature. With no taste for either minority cab:nets or cabinets of 'technicians' or 'experts', the Belgians went in for coalition government. The coalition of 1925 looked as if it might become a turning point, until history refused to turn. In the 1925 elections, the Socialists received the highest percentage of the national vote which they have ever received, which stimulated them to hope that continuing industrialisation would produce an increasingly Socialist working-class electorate. This was obviously a long-term aim, but there was another closer to hand. Could they not at once detach the Catholic working-class electorate, which was of decisive numbers in Flanders, from the bourgeois and aristocratic and generally conservative leadership of the Catholic Party? The Poullet-Vandervelde cabinet of 1925 was a coalition of the Socialists (under the leadership of the eminent Emile Vandervelde, the long-time head of the party) with the labour and pro-labour intellectual wing of the Catholic Party. But with the cabinet's demise in less than a year, in a financial crisis, or (as many saw it) a bankers' ramp, the Catholic labour groups returned to their uneasy role in the inter-class coalition which was the Catholic Party.

Continuing industrialisation did not produce in most of Flanders the 'dechristianisation' which earlier industrial development had produced in Wallonia, the southern half of the country; in the nation's capital, Brussels; and indeed in the working-classes of the largest Flemish cities, Antwerp and Ghent. Nor since then have industrial growth and urbanisation and *déracinement,* or the choices of Catholic labour, produced the Socialist majority which watered-down Marxist prediction and electoral hopes had for a moment made plausible.

The Socialist Party weathered the depression of the 1930s without significant long-term losses to the Communists. Communist Party weakness and parliamentary arithmetic meant that there was none of the Popular Front appeal which forced the hands of Socialist Party and trade union leaders in France in 1935-6. Instead, the Socialist Party joined with the other two traditional parties in a coalition government under the Catholic Paul Van Zeeland. Belgium made a better recovery from unemployment and economic stagnation than either the US of the New Deal or France of the Popular Front.

The reorganisation of the Party after the liberation brought changes in structure and in name but not in basic outlook, strategy, or style. Hoping to enlarge their constituency to include more people not of the working-classes, the Party dropped the name 'Workers' for that of Socialist.

The Party did not revive the collective affiliations of the prewar era.

Nor would the Socialist-led trade unions have countenanced such a revival. For the first time, they now took their places as equal partners with the Party. Moreover, the old collective affiliation would have given the Communists, who were important in the immediate post-liberation unions, a role in Party affairs which Socialist leaders of both Party and unions naturally wanted to prevent.

A few years later the Party, unions, co-operatives, and friendly societies of the Socialist world set up an organisation called Common Action, to co-ordinate their efforts at national and local levels. An immediate task was the mobilisation of all these groups against the return of Leopold III, and in the general strike of 1950 they were successful in preventing the return to the throne of the wartime monarch. Since then the chief activity of Common Action has been spreading the costs of party electoral campaigns among the socio-economic organisations, which, as in other European democracies, are richer than the Party. But more significant than formal Common Action decisions have been the informal personal ties, the interlocking directorates, and the mutuality of aims of Socialist organisations.

With the rapid reassertion of the traditional national parties after the war and the dimming of the momentary strength of the Communist Party (as in other northern European countries except Finland and Iceland), the political landscape reassumed pretty much its old configuration. That configuration was to change only when the new linguistic — regional parties became part of the political scene in the 1960s. The Socialist Party was to hold out better against the centrifugal forces of ethnicity, language, and regionalism in Flanders and Wallonia (though not in Brussels) than the other two national parties, as we shall see.

The PSB in the Party System

The PSB *(Parti Socialiste Belge,* Belgian Socialist Party) has long constituted the second largest political force in Belgium.[4] We are counting the Social Christians of Flemish and of French-speaking ('francophone') Belgium as a single political force, and hence the largest in Belgium, although the Flemish and the francophone wings are autonomous to all practical intents and purposes, with only tenuous organisational ties and programmes more and more distinct since 1968.

Ever since 1919, with the exception of the years 1950-4, the party system has functioned on the basis of interparty coalitions, not only at the national level but much of the time at the levels of local government (in the larger towns and cities) and provincial government. The electoral system of proportional representation at all these levels works against single party majorities, although in various local and provincial 'fiefs' one or another party has held a comfortable majority, as does the PSB in some Walloon bastions.

The concessions which coalition government demands of each partner often aggravate tensions already existing in each party. Since the rather well-contained split of the Communists from the PSB, the Party has lived with tensions which at times have been fruitful of change and at other times sterile.

Discontent with coalition policies is naturally greatest among those elements politically farthest from the Party's coalition partners. In the Socialist Party this means – on social and economic issues – its Left wing. On the old clerical-anti-clerical cleavage of Belgian politics, however, which still affects attitudes in all the parties, Socialists do not follow any Right-Left lines of division. Those lines reappear on the rare occasions when there is any real choice for Belgium in international affairs.

Other and larger sections of the Party than the Left may manifest discontent. For coalition means concessions, not only in doctrine and in policy, but in the practical advantages expected from that very coalition, for example in favours to economic regions or localities or enterprises, or in appointments to the bureaucracy of the state and the parastatal administrations so important in Belgium.

Return to the opposition may reaffirm the Party's cohesion, by making it easier to take positions supported by large majorities unburdened (for the moment) by power. Thus, soon after the PSB left the Government in 1966, a large majority manifested its discontent with the Government's NATO policies by opposing the implantation of SHAPE in Belgium. Had the Party remained in government, with or even without its pro-NATO leader, Paul-Henri Spaak, it would not have made the same gesture or at least would not have been nearly as unified in it.

Participation in national government – as well as in provincial and, more important, local government – has undeniable advantages for a party representing a large sector of society. This is especially true in a country in which appointments and promotions in the administration are highly politicised, and in which the Government plays an important role in recognising the legitimacy of organisations and in subsidising many of all kinds, including those of the political parties and of groups allied with them.

An Alternation of Participation and Opposition

The PSB's position in the party system may be seen in its alternating roles of participation and (more briefly) opposition in national politics in the fifteen years since 1961. The Christian Socials have been the chief partners of the Socialists at the national level, and in many cases at other levels as well. The coalition led by the Catholic Lefèvre and the Socialist Spaak lasted through the four years of the legislature elected in 1961. It was fertile in achievements, but each of its major achievements, notably in tax reform and in regional-linguistic legislation, displeased one section or another of public opinion, and that displeasure was manifested in the election results in 1965.

A new Catholic-Socialist coalition lasted only a few months, and in the next two years the Socialists took an 'opposition cure'. They clarified their aims on the issues of government decentralisation and economic planning, notably by separate Walloon and Flemish regional party conventions in 1967. The next phase of Socialist collaboration with the Christian Socials, from 1968 to 1972, saw a partial federalisation of the nation's once strongly unitary structures. A constitutional revision gave recognition to the cultural autonomy of the country's two major linguistic communities[5] and to the principle of three regions.

For a year in 1972-3 the Socialist Leburton headed an uneasy coalition with both Catholics and Liberals. That was the first and, as of the beginning of 1977, the only government headed by a Socialist since the Van Acker Socialist-Liberal government of the mid-1950s. The Leburton cabinet disintegrated on the issue of the creation by government initiative of an oil refining complex in the Liège region of Wallonia. That issue focused both regional rivalries (Walloon versus Flemish interests) and rivalries between advocates and opponents of public enterprise. Unlike most other Western European countries, Belgium has little public industrial enterprise (except of course the railways).

The Socialists marked their return to the opposition by a 'doctrinal convention' in 1974 which adopted workers' self-management ('autogestion') and regional autonomy as major party demands. Both had come primarily from the Walloon trade unionists of the FGTB (*Fédération Générale du Travail de Belgique*, General Federation of Labour of Belgium), and especially those of the militant region of Liège.

The phase of opposition also became one of internal party reorganisation. Reforms of the Party statutes set a compulsory retirement age for holders of elective office and a ban on the simultaneous holding of important elective public office at local and national levels, known as the *cumul,* which has been so important in all parties.[6] A new generation of regional and national leaders replaced the rather over-aged leadership which the party had acquired and retained by its stress on seniority and the mutual reinforcement of local and national power through the *cumul,* the weight of local party machines, and patronage in Party-controlled public institutions.

The Regional Bases of the Party

The PSB has long been the most national of Belgian parties in structure and support. The distribution of its membership and electoral following and of the membership of the Socialist unions comes much closer to a regional equilibrium than does that of its Catholic Party rivals and of the Catholic unions. That has made it possible for the PSB to present common positions in accordance with its national vocation in a period when neither the Christian Socials nor the Liberals have been able even to paper over their regional differences. The table below shows the regional balance of the PSB.

Relative Strength of Regions in Belgian Socialist Support

Region	Percentage of Party Membership (1972)	Percentage of National Vote for Party (1974)
Flanders	44	47
Wallonia	46	44
Brussels	9	9
	99	100

(First total does not reach 100 because of rounding off of components.)

The Flemish majority in the nation's population means, however, that the apparent equilibrium between Flanders and Wallonia in the Party does not correspond to the national balance. While in Wallonia the Party is easily the strongest, in Flanders it is a distant second to the CVP (*Christelijke Volkspartij*, Christian Social Party) with less than a fourth of the region's votes. It is rather isolated in Flanders, although there are exceptions to this isolation, notably the long-standing municipal coalition with the Catholics in Antwerp, which produced a local precedent for the national school truce negotiated in 1958. The municipal elections held in all Belgium in 1976 underlined the disparity in political forces among the three regions, confirming the lead of the PSB in Wallonia, of the CVP in Flanders, and in Brussels of one of the new 'community parties', the French-speakers' Democratic Front (*Front Démocratique des Francophones,* FDF).

The national political confrontations of the postwar era have shown different majorities from region to region, as in the 1950 referendum on the return of Leopold III to his prewar throne, when Flanders followed the CVP in voting 'yes', while Brussels and Wallonia voted 'no'. These differences were also evident in the most recent (and probably the last) episode in the 'school war', involving state subsidies for Catholic secondary schools, an issue solved by the compromise of the 1958 'school pact'. Obviously these differences are of the essence in language and regional issues, especially in their economic dimension, but they also show in debates over public enterprise, over the abortion law, and sometimes even over international relations.

It is not only the simple relationship between majority and minority which differs from region to region, but also the general configuration of Belgium's political sub-systems. The history, and especially the timing and the rhythms of social and economic change, of the regions help to explain why the political distance between opposing alignments — between Right and Left, to simplify — is greater in Wallonia than in Flanders. The Right is more to the right, and the Left more to the left, in the older industrial region than in Flanders, whose modern industrial spurt has come only since World War Two. The Flemish bourgeoisie seems to have learnt from the radicalisation of Wallonia, and the Catholic Church from Wallonia's dechristianisation: as a result, Flanders has resisted the penetration of Socialism and anti-clericalism with more success than did Wallonia during its industrial transformation in the nineteenth century and the beginning of the twentieth.

Brussels and its environs make up the third region, the zone of encounter, of competition, and of the sharpest conflict between the Flemish and the francophone communities. The latter is by far the stronger within Brussels, but the former is supported by the Flemish community as a whole. Socialist support in Brussels, especially among its francophone population, has been undermined by the language cleavage, in two related ways. Socialist participation in the Government which in 1962-3 rewrote the Belgian language laws, to right old wrongs to the Flemish population, alienated many Brussels francophone Socialists. Conflict between Flemish and francophone Socialists resulted in the coexistence and electoral competition of two Socialist federations in Brussels, one Flemish and the other nominally bilingual but overwhelmingly francophone. Doctrine and party loyalty, nationalism and internationalism, proved less potent than ethnic-linguistic identification in determining the political behaviour of the Socialists of the Brussels area.

Here we see the principal difficulty of the PSB in relation to what Belgians have come to call 'community problems'. The Party must maintain the bonds of solidarity between Socialists of the three regions. But it must also achieve something of the regionalism demanded by its Walloon federations.

The PSB is almost the mirror image of the Christian Social Party in its regional tensions. The Flemish CVP is the stronger wing, the more regionally self-sufficient, and the more demanding within the Christian Social ranks. The PSC (*Parti Social Chrétien,* Christian Social Party) of Wallonia[7] is more national in its outlook, as befits a minority within its own region. The CVP has to meet the competitive pressures of the federalist Flemish People's Union *(Volks-Unie).* The Walloon Socialists have had to meet the competition of the Walloon Party (*Rassemblement Wallon,* RW), which also appeals to some Socialist trade unionists and voters. In late 1976 the Walloon Party suffered a serious split, but its formation and the support it found in Socialist union circles help to explain the federalist evolution of the PSB.

The chief demands for what became the 1970 law on planning and decentralisation came from the Socialists, especially those of Wallonia. The first planning bureau in the national government, however, was a creation (in 1959) of a government without Socialist participation. The 1970 law shows the propensity of Belgian Socialists to think that they solve a problem when they create an official institution with a formal mandate to solve it. They often pay more attention to the institutional framework than to the action within it. But the institutions which they helped write into the 1970 law are not organs of decision; in the grammar of planning, their mood is only indicative. They consult a series of political and socio-economic bodies, but the final decisions and the tasks of execution remain with the general political authorities. The law's framework therefore tends merely to reproduce the political and economic debates which go on in other circles. It is far from the Socialists' initial project, and it cannot satisfy them. (Still it is enough to worry some of their opponents. Recently the Right went so far as to propose the suppression of the planning mechanism, under the pretext of simplifying an institutional framework which is indeed excessively complicated.)

Another major issue is that of regionalisation in general (or, some would say, federalism). The principle was consecrated by constitutional amendment, but only in the vaguest way, by an enabling provision specifying the number of regions and leaving it to parliament to specify — by special majorities — the composition and competence of the organs to be created. The government headed by Tindemans of the CVP, with the Socialists in the opposition, has put through parliament a so-called 'preparatory' partial regionalisation, which has satisfied no one.

In contrast, the PSB has offered a project of definitive and more thoroughgoing regionalisation, worked out, along the lines of the 1974 accord between the PSB and the FGTB, in negotiations among Walloon, Flemish, and (least happy with the results) Brussels Socialists. The project reaffirms the principle of the three regions, although some Flemish groups still insist upon only two regions so as not to have two regions of francophone majorities *vis-à-vis* a single region of the Flemish who are a majority of all Belgians. The PSB proposes to simplify the incredible complexity and overlapping of existing institutions, provisional and 'definitive', which only a few experts in such matters understand. The project would suppress the present senate (which duplicates the functions of the House of Representatives) and the nine provinces, fuse at least partially the bodies supposed to represent the cultural communities and those representing the regions, and give the regions directly elected legislatures and executives responsible to them. The PSB has declared itself willing to take part in discussion and implementation of the proposal even while remaining in opposition. But a more logical outcome of the PSB's project becoming the basis of discussion and action would be the Party's return to governmental participation.

The Future of the Party

In 1985 Belgian Socialists will celebrate the centenary of their party. A historical experience of so many generations inevitably submits an organisation to considerable wear and tear. Many among the younger generations are unaware of the role of the Party and of the whole Socialist movement in the social and political progress of the near-century of its work. That is why the benefits of Government participation also carry their electoral costs for the Party.

In no visible future can the PSB hope to attain a national majority on its own. It must pose in somewhat different terms than in the past the fundamental question of how it can take part in constituting a stable and coherent majority around a common programme consonant with its ideals and ideas, and acceptable to its social and its regional constituencies. That is the chief meaning of the appeals for a 'regrouping of progressives' which successive Walloon Party co-presidents have launched since 1969. These appeals were addressed to independent Leftists, to the Communists (in Belgium a tepid lot in programme and in political style, except for some intellectuals and some francophone FGTB members), and, most important, to the Christian Democrats. (This term has a significance in Belgium different from that of other countries. It refers only to the labour and pro-labour intellectual elements within Catholic political action, whereas in other countries it generally refers to the political action of all Catholics in a party of their own or that of Catholics and Protestants in a joint party.)

The obstacles to such a regrouping, especially with the Christian Democrats, are formidable. The pluralism of working-class action in Belgium is deeply rooted. History seemed to graft the internal religious cleavage of the nineteenth-century bourgeoisie onto the organisation of labour in the twentieth century. To be sure, the Catholic movement has shed most of the virulent anti-Socialism which characterised its earlier years, and the Socialist movement has shed a good deal of its virulent anti-Catholicism. But the Socialist Party remains the party of laicity, the only one since the Liberals in 1961 ostentatiously reorganised to shed their anti-clericalism and to welcome prominent Catholics as candidates of their new party.[8] Many of the Socialist leaders continue to harbour suspicions of Catholic motives and action which indicate they are still carrying on the good fight against Pius IX. Such attitudes naturally repel Christian Democrats, even those most pessimistic about the PSC-CVP or separate Catholic political action in general.

The trade unions of the two movements are strongly institutionalised, and show no signs — particularly on the Catholic side — of wishing to merge. They are far closer in almost all programmatic positions and even in style of action than they were a generation or two earlier. The FGTB and the CSC (*Confédération des Syndicats Chrétiens,* Confederation of Christian Trade Unions) have been co-operating for almost two decades in two powerful 'Common Fronts', one in the public sector and one in the private sector.[9] The vitality of these Common Fronts has the paradoxical effect, not of moving the two union federations to merge, but of making it less necessary to merge, since their joint bargaining and lobbying activities have been successful enough so that workers' interests have hardly suffered and in some ways gained — by pluralism and a mild amount of competition. The Common

Front activities have continued, for the most part, even when the Socialists have been in opposition. (The Catholics have been in the Government all through this period.) Incidentally the Common Front strategy sometimes costs the Socialists tactical advantages they might otherwise achieve when, the Party being in opposition, the FGTB on its own might be more militant and thereby increase workers' support for itself and the Party.

The ties of the Common Front require that Socialist Party candidates be members of the FGTB and of Socialist mutual aid societies and co-operatives, as well as subscribers to the Socialist press. This requirement effectively cuts off any legitimate (or careerist) aspirations which a Catholic militant might have in the Socialist Party if he does not wish to drop his activities within one or more of the Catholic socio-economic organisations. The Socialist requirement also feeds the suspicion of some Catholics that the invitation to a 'regrouping of progressives' is simply a disguised invitation to drop other affiliations and join an unrenovated Socialist Party.

It is difficult to bring together interlocutors of comparable levels of organisation in the two movements. The Catholic labour groups — unions, co-operatives, mutual aid societies, men's and women's study groups, the Young Catholic Workers — are affiliated to a co-ordinating organisation known as the Christian Labour Movement (*Mouvement Ouvrier Chrétien*, MOC) which represents their political concerns. This has far more structure and continuing activity than the Socialist Common Action. But its francophone organisation is independent of the political party of Catholicism, the PSC, although some of its members constitute an organised pressure group within the Party, under the name of 'Christian Democracy'. In Flanders the Christian Labour Movement is integrated with the CVP.

The weakness of the Socialist press hampers the Party's efforts at outreach to new constituencies. The crisis of the press is an element — both effect and cause — of the crisis of Social Democratic parties everywhere. Not even the largest parties are able to sustain a decent daily press: look, for example, at the British Labour Party. In a small country, and doubly so in a country divided into two language communities, the difficulties of sustaining daily newspapers are multiplied. Yet the sympathetic observer would think that the wealthy and powerful Belgian Socialist unions, and mutual aid societies, if not the somnolent consumer co-operatives and the poverty stricken party, might have the will and the means to support a better press than they now half-support. Socialist Party candidates themselves in francophone

Belgium, for example, reiterate the bitter jest: 'Under the rules, of course I have to subscribe to *Le Peuple*. But they do not say that I have to read it.'

The press, however, is only a minor reason in the failure of the Party to attract much support from what we may call the 'independent left'. That is the rather heterogeneous aggregate of women and men of a generally Leftish orientation in social and economic matters – as 'Left' is understood in the moderate political climate of Belgium – but independent of traditional political organisations, although in some cases members of trade unions. Many of these people are repelled by the bureaucratisation of the PSB, the caution of its 'governmental vocation', the lack of dynamism or spontaneity of Party life in most Party sections, and the negative image created by years of governmental participation and the even more visible attachment to the seats of municipal power. The PSB is not a pole of attraction – the Socialist press diminishes its credibility more than does the bourgeois press – for this independent left. For example, the PSB has not yet effectively articulated or pressed the most reasonable claims of Belgian feminists or the large population of immigrant workers.

The obstacle which may finally be the most serious in the efforts at a political regrouping such as the PSB seeks is the difference in political profiles of the several regions of the country. A formula of *rassemblement des progressistes* which might enable the Walloon PSB to move from its present plurality to lead a majority would almost certainly weaken the Flemish wing of the Party and further isolate it in its region. The Socialists reject the regional catch-all style of the CVP-PSC and the Liberals, who have diversified their appeals for the maximum of immediate support in each region, but lost national cohesion and credibility in the process. The Socialists can insist, with reason, that they are a national party, even though there is a partial *de facto* federalism of structure in both the PSB and the FGTB.

As with so many other problems in Belgium these days, the regrouping of progressives is posed in terms of region and language community. In Wallonia a regrouping looks possible. There the dramatic renovation of the French Socialist Party and the 'common programme' of the French Left exercise their greatest seduction. It is there that the Socialists have defined a regional industrial policy which may offer a common platform for the region's progressives. In Wallonia Christians and people of the independent Left find the PSB more attractive than they do in other regions.

In Flanders, in both the Party and the trade unions, Socialists are for the most part less radical in programme and in political style than in Wallonia. In line with their historic concerns as a minority within their region, they are inclined to a national, rather than a regional, strategy. That has led them to go along with their more demanding Walloon comrades on many issues. But it also makes them wary of the risks to them of some of the positions which those comrades have been taking in the national party.

Like many other political parties, the Belgian Socialists would like to have the best of both worlds. They would remain the most national of Belgian parties, yet press the claims of Walloon federalism. They would remain the chief party of the workers, but reach out to members of the middle classes. They open their arms to Catholic workers, but at heart many deny the legitimacy of their faith and their institutions. They claim to repudiate capitalism root and branch, but they and their unions remain integrated into the institutions of the capitalist state and the bargaining and regulatory mechanisms of the labour market. They enjoy the freedom of opposition, but should they not, for the sake of the workers they represent and for the national interest, say many, abandon that freedom for the fruits of Government participation? As one of the Party's leaders remarked a few years ago, when the Party is in opposition, it feels the nostalgia of government, and when it is in Government, it feels the nostalgia of opposition.

Notes

1. For an attempt to put this development in a comparative European perspective, see Val R. Lorwin, 'Segmented Pluralism: Ideological Cleavages and Political Cohesion in the Smaller European Democracies,' *Comparative Politics*, III:2 (1971), pp. 141-75.
2. Louis Bertrand, *Histoire de la démocratie et du socialisme en Belgique depuis 1830* (Brussels, Dechenne, 1906), p. 608.
3. Kautsky to Viktor Adler in Adler, *Briefwechsel mit August Bebel und Karl Kautsky*, ed. Friedrich Adler (Vienna, Wiener Volksbuchhandlung, 1954), p. 200.
4. Since English language readers are far more likely to know French than Dutch, we use the initials for the French names of national parties or national trade union organisations, e.g., PSB or FGTB. For a regional organisation or semi-autonomous regional wing of a nominally national party, one must use the language of the region and the initials derived therefrom, e.g. CVP (see glossary).
5. The German language community, in eastern Belgium, constitutes less than one per cent of the nation, so we shall not refer further to it. Moreover, Socialist strength there is negligible.
6. Another form of 'cumul' often debated is the simultaneous holding of offices in political party and trade unions or other socio-economic organisations.
7. The PSC operates among the francophones of Brussels as well as in Wallonia, but here we are concerned only with the latter.

8. The official name of the Party is Party of Liberty and Progress, but people still speak of the 'Liberals', since the PLP has found no other name for its members or voters. In Brussels the term 'Liberal Party' has been revived by several competing organisations within the quarreling 'Liberal family'. **9.** The small Liberal trade union centre also joins in these bargaining fronts.

Glossary and Initials Used in Text

Parties

Socialist Party — Parti Socialiste Belge/Belgische Socialistische Partij PSB/BSP (Until 1940, the Belgian Workers' Party)

Christian Social Party — Parti Social Chrétien/Christelijke Volkspartij PSC/CVP (Until 1940, Catholic Party of Belgium and variants of that name)

Party of Liberty and of Progress — Parti de la Liberté et du Progrès/Partij van de Vrijheid en Vooruitgang PLP/PVV (Until 1961, Liberal Party of Belgium)

Communist Party — Parti Communiste de Belgique/Communistische Partij van België

Flemish People's Party — Vlaamse Volksunie

Walloon Party — Rassemblement Wallon RW

Francophone Democratic Front — Front Démocratique des Francophones Bruxellois FDF

Labour Organisations

General Federation of Labour — Fédération Générale du Travail de Belgique/Algemeen Belgisch Vakverbond FGTB/ABVV

Confederation of Christian Unions — Confédération des Syndicats Chrétiens/Algemeen Christelijk Vakverbond CSC/ACV

Christian Workers' Movement — Mouvement Ouvrier Chrétien/Algemeen Christelijk Werkersverbond MOC/ACW

On use of French and Dutch (= Flemish) names and initials, see note 4. On terms for PLP members and voters, see note 8.

Appendix

Votes for House of Representatives, by Party, 1946-1974 (as percentages of total numbers of valid ballots)

	Chr.	Soc.	Lib.	Com.	Flem.	FDF	RW	Misc.
1946	42.5	32.6	9.5	12.7	–			2.7
1949	43.6	29.8	15.3	7.5	2.1			1.9
1950	47.7	35.6	12.0	4.7	–			–
1954	41.1	38.6	13.0	3.6	2.0			1.5
1958	46.5	37.1	11.8	1.9	2.0			0.7
1961	41.5	36.7	12.3	3.1	3.5			2.9
1965	34.5	28.3	21.6	4.6	6.8	1.3	(1.1)†	1.8
1968	31.8	28.0	20.9	3.3	9.8	2.8	3.2	2.2
1971	30.0	27.3	16.7	3.1	11.1	4.8	6.3	0.5
1974	32.3	26.7	15.2*	3.2	10.2	–10.9$^\infty$–		1.4

* Some Brussels Liberals in electoral cartel with FDF and RW.
† Miscellaneous Walloon lists.
$^\infty$ FDF – RW cartel with some Brussels Liberals.

Chr. Christian Social Party.
Soc. Socialist Party.
Lib. Liberal Party until and including 1961 election; from late 1961, Party of
      Liberty and Progress.
Com. Communist Party.
Flem. Flemish People's Party.
FDF Francophone Democratic Front (Brussels area).
RW Walloon Party.
Misc. Miscellaneous lists.

Source: 1946-71, Keith Hill, 'Belgium: Political Change in a Segmented Society',
       in R. Rose (ed.), *Political Behaviour;* 1974 results from *Courrier
       Hebdomadaire* of CRISP (see bibliography).

Belgium: Statistical Appendix

Membership of Socialist Trade Unions: members of the FGIB by region
(Fédération Générale du Travail de Belgique)

	Flanders	Wallonia	Brussels	Total
1970	386,674	336,483	113,806	836,963
1971	401,554	361,447	123,174	886,175
1973	412,780	405,760	150,049	968,590
1974	429,635	417,620	156,218	1,003,473
1975	450,261	443,414	168,929	1,062,604

Party Membership: members of the PSB (Parti Socialiste Belge) by
region (to nearest thousand)

	Flanders	Wallonia	Brussels	Total
1966				204,000
1967				199,000
1968				201,000
1969				216,000
1970	100,000	105,000	21,000	225,000
1971	102,000	112,000	21,000	235,000
1972	107,000	112,000	23,000	241,000
1973	112,000	115,000	23,000	250,000
1974	113,000	118,000	24,000	258,000
1975	111,000	120,000	25,000	255,000

Some totals slightly off because of rounding.

Distribution of electorate by linguistic region (elections for the Chamber
of Representatives): percentages

	Flemish cantons	Walloon cantons	Brussels cantons	Cantons of the East (German-speaking)
1968	54.8	31.6	12.9	0.7
1971	55.4	31.4	12.5	0.7
1974	56.2	31.0	12.1	0.7

Further Reading

There is no nearly adequate history of the Party or current description of the Party. For a reference work on political history, Theo Luykx, *Politieke Geschiedenis van België*, 2nd ed. (Brussels, Elzevier, 1969). For the Party between the wars, Mieke Claeys Van Haegendoren, *25 Jaar belgisch socialisme* (Antwerp, Standaard, 1967). For a general description of the present background, Robert Senelle, *Political, Economic, and Social Structures of Belgium* (Brussels, Ministry of Foreign Affairs, 1970). Jean Meynaud, Jean Ladrière, and François Perin (eds.), *La Décision politique en Belgique*, Cahiers de la Fondation Nationale des Sciences Politiques, no. 138 (Paris, 1965). Luc. Huyse, *Passiviteit, pacificatie en verzuiling in de Belgische politiek* (Antwerp, Standaard, 1970). Keith Hill, 'Belgium: Political Change in a Segmented Society', in Richard Rose (ed.), *Electoral Behaviour* (New York, Free Press, 1974), pp. 29-107. Derek W. Urwin, 'Social Cleavages and Political Parties in Belgium: Problems of Institutionalisation', *Political Studies*, XVIII, 3 (1970), pp. 320-40. A. Van den Brande, 'Mogelijkheden van een sociologie der belgische conflicten na de Tweede Wereldoorlog, 1944-1961', *Sociologische Gids*, X (1963), pp. 2-29.

The best current analyses of Belgian political and social forces and events appear in the *Courriers Hebdomadaires* of the Centre de Recherche et d'Information Socio-Politiques (CRISP) of Brussels. See also its 'Dossier' on *Les Partis Politiques*, 1975. Xavier Mabille, 'Adaptation ou éclatement du système de décision en Belgique', *Recherches Sociologiques* (Université Catholique de Louvain), VII (1976), pp. 111-49. Val R. Lorwin, 'Belgium: Religion, Class, and Language in National Politics', in Robert A. Dahl (ed.), *Political Oppositions in Western Democracies* (New Haven, Conn., and London, 1966), pp. 147-87, 409-16, and 444-5; and 'Labour Unions and Political Parties in Belgium', *Industrial and Labour Relations Review*, 28:2, 1975, pp.243-63.

CO-OPERATION BETWEEN SOCIALIST PARTIES

James May

Introduction

Several aspects of the attitudes manifested by Socialist parties towards their transnational interactions suggest that such activity is of importance to them. First, they have shown *lasting* interest in promoting and maintaining their transnational links. Second, parliamentarians of the European parties have displayed considerable enthusiasm for institutionalising their contacts in a number of European assemblies. Third, when faced with a common problem the parties involved have frequently formed links with each other for purposes of discussion and the formation, if possible, of common attitudes. Finally, most Socialists active in the transnational context allege — correctly, in the writer's opinion — that their comrades engage in unofficial or extra-party transnational contacts to a far greater degree than the adherents of any other ideology.

The lasting interest of Socialists in maintaining their transnational links is perhaps best exemplified by the history of transnational Socialism's most eminent institutional expression, the Socialist International. Of the personalities active in transnational politics few — including the International's own officers — claim that it has been an actor of particular importance on the international scene.[1] Its general unimportance and its more particular failures notwithstanding, however, the several interruptions in the life of the International have been followed consistently by demands for its resurrection.

The International Working Men's Association, or First International, was founded in 1864. It failed in two ways, closely related: first, to prescribe the manner by which its goals might be attained; and second, to retain sufficient unity amongst its leading personalities to maintain its existence as an institution. The Second International was founded in 1889. This time its lack of influence as an actor was underlined by the clarity with which its members articulated their perceptions of the world and the behaviour they prescribed and committed themselves to in the light of them. In the Stuttgart Resolution of 1907, the member parties of the Second International stated clearly the overriding importance of class divisions. National prejudices were seen as something 'systematically cultivated . . . in the interests of the ruling classes'. Wars were favoured by such prejudices and were 'therefore . . . part of the very nature of capitalism'. Accordingly, the parties committed themselves 'to combat the naval and military armaments with all their might . . . and to refuse the means for those armaments'. If war threatened to break out, the parties agreed that it was their duty, supported by the co-ordinating activity of the International Socialist Bureau, to exert every effort in order to prevent [it]'.[2] The spirit of the Resolution was clear, and, in some respects, its substance also. So, too, were the actions of its signatories in 1914. Announcing their fear of Tsarist reaction, the Socialists of Austria and Germany voted for war credits. Substituting Prussian militarism for Tsarist reaction, the parties of Belgium, Britain and France adopted a similar stance and,

> . . . the International . . . fell, the first victim of the world war. It had been conceived as a brotherhood, uniting the workers of all countries in a spirit of solidarity for the joint struggle against the ruling classes. Now . . . the spirit of international solidarity of the working classes had been superseded by a spirit of national solidarity between the proletariat and the ruling classes.[3]

In 1923, after lengthy negotiations between Socialist and Communist parties had failed to provide the basis for an International acceptable to both, a conference of Socialist parties at Hamburg re-created the International under the title of the Labour and Socialist International. The suppression of the German and Eastern European Socialist parties prior to 1939 meant that the stark choice faced by the International's members in 1914 could not be repeated. The gap between their declaratory commitment and their actual behaviour was again a wide one, however. Article 3 of the LSI's statute boldly declared that: 'The Labour and Socialist International can be a reality only in so far as its decisions are binding on all its members. Every decision of the International thus represents a voluntarily accepted limitation of the autonomy of the parties . . . ' In practice, Hugh Dalton's subsequent assessment of its influence — much less authority — may be taken as a fair one: 'In theory it had great power; in practice it had very little, and it had less and less as the years passed.'[4] If the Second International had ended with a bang, its successor expired with hardly a whimper. Again, however, and even before the war's end, voices were raised calling for the re-creation of the International.[5] And, its history between 1945 and 1951 was essentially that of an *ad hoc* body, the International Socialist Conference, steadily becoming stronger both constitutionally and in the resources at its disposal until in 1951 the Socialist International proper was formally re-constituted.[6]

The predisposition of Socialist parties to institutionalise their transnational activity has been underlined by their behaviour in a variety of European assemblies in the post-World War II period. Socialist groups were formed in the assemblies of the Brussels Treaty Organisation/WEU and in the Common Assembly of the Coal and Steel Community — the latter at its constitutive session and several months before the formation of groups by the other ideologies.[7] The heterogeneity of the member states of the Council of Europe was inimical to ideologically based group formation generally, and divisions amongst its Socialist members also inhibited the formation of a Socialist Group *within its Assembly* for many years. The latter included divisions over fundamental issues — such as the future development of Europe — and occasional bitter clashes between individual Socialists. Guy Mollet, for example, at first refused to sit in a common meeting with Carlo Schmid of the SPD because the latter had been accused of war crimes at Lille.[8] In spite of differences both lasting and episodic, however, the Consultative Assembly's Socialists held their first meeting on the first day of its constitutive session and continued to meet periodically at Strasbourg in a Socialist 'Inter-Group'. On the formation of the Common Assembly, Socialists who were members of both assemblies immediately formed a sub-group within the Inter-Group. Finally, in the 'European' context, six months before the signing of the Rome Treaties, but after their substance had been the subject of inter-Governmental negotiations for more than a year and with the transformation of the Common Assembly into a European Parliament on the horizon, the Socialist parties of the member states of the EEC conferred to discuss problems of a 'European' nature — including future co-operation between themselves and the Socialist Group in the Common Assembly. They resolved to establish a Liaison Bureau to maintain contacts between themselves and their group, and to hold a conference at two-yearly intervals. In practice, the Bureau came to be perceived by some member parties as insufficiently significant to induce them to continue attending its meetings, and by the late 1960s it was widely held to be unsatisfactory. In spite of their disappointing experiences with the Liaison Bureau, however, the enthusiasm of the parties for institutionalised transnational links was again an important factor in the creation of a new, constitutionally stronger, organisation; and at a meeting at The Hague on 1-2 November 1974, they accepted a constitution for a Confederation of Socialist Parties of the European

Community, replacing the Liaison Bureau and including rules of procedure whereby *binding* decisions *might* be taken.[9]

In addition to their links in various institutional contexts, Socialist parties have frequently formed bilateral or multilateral links with each other when faced with common or similar situations or problems. The enumeration of the various links which have been formed at different times between Socialist parties, and also of the unofficial transnational contacts between their members, is beyond the space available to the writer. But a useful illustration of the former is the links which have developed in the 1970s amongst the Socialist parties of Southern Europe. Here, in spite of many differences,[10] *some* of the circumstances of the French, Greek, Italian, Portuguese and Spanish parties have encouraged the evolution of a network of links sufficiently well-elaborated to give rise to a concept of Socialism 'north and south' in Europe.

To summarise, in spite of past disappointments Socialists have been determined to retain their International, *re*-creating it when necessary, and the same tendency seems to be manifesting itself in the history to date of the Liaison Bureau/Confederation of the parties of the EEC. In the European assemblies, Socialist members have shown a consistent predilection for organising themselves and for regulating their relationships in Socialist 'Groups'. The predisposition of Socialists for engaging in transnational interactions with each other has also extended beyond the parameters provided by membership of the same organisations. Parties sharing a common problem or situation have frequently established links with each other; and some of their members have shown enthusiasm for unofficial transnational contacts even without the impulse provided by particular problems. In brief, a strong *prima facie* case clearly exists that their transnational links are important to Socialist parties. It is the purpose of this chapter to consider a number of questions suggested by this importance.

At its most ambitious, political science may be said to concern itself with attempting to facilitate accurate prediction. And, perhaps foremost amongst the questions which the 'ambitious' political scientist might ask about co-operation between Socialist parties is: do the transnational activities of the parties have action-guiding significance for individual Socialist parties? That is to say, do they affect the policy formation or decision-taking processes of individual parties or, put another way, have significance for their political output? If so, what is the nature of the effect and under what circumstances is it operative? Should the answer be negative, then two other questions arise: first, if transnational

Socialist interactions do not *directly* affect the political output of individual parties do they nevertheless serve some functions in political process and, if so, do these functions in any way affect the political output of the parties? Second, what is the nature of the attractiveness of Socialist internationalism? Why do the parties retain such strong interest in their transnational links if they are of little consequence? Are they, in fact, goal-orientated or are they primarily a form of institutionalised ritualisation?

Transnational Socialist Interactions and Political Output

European integration, it may be suggested, provides a particularly meaningful context in which to test the extent to which the transnational interactions of socialist parties are of action guiding significance for individual parties.

Social Democracy, it may be argued, is basically a *European* political phenomenon. Historically, Socialism has its origins in Europe, and European parties have dominated the Socialist International since its inception. The parties which have been active in the affairs of the International have been almost solely European;[11] and European parties have been its major financial contributors.[12] The nationality of the International's functionaries, and the location of its secretariat and of its meetings also suggest the close affinity of Europe and Social Democracy.

The reverse side of the coin supports the allegation. In some important non-European countries parties professing a Socialist faith have had little electoral success, and the International has had only limited success in involving Socialist parties outside Europe in its activities. The outstanding example of the first point is the USA where, in spite of massive industrialisation, ethnicity and — more arguably — social mobility have been inimical to the development of class-based politics. In respect of the second point, attempts were made by the International in the 1950s to expand in the Far East and Latin America. An Asian Socialists' Conference was established, and a Latin American Liaison Bureau. The Latin American Bureau was vitiated by fundamental division amongst Latin American parties in the wake of Castro's victory in Cuba. The Asian Socialists' Conference faded as the influence of Socialist parties in countries such as Burma and Nepal declined. A memorandum written at the time by an interested actor suggested several reasons for the reluctance of Asian Socialists to become involved in any regional organisation of the International or, indeed, with the International at all. Proposals for an Asian regional group, it noted, had received a 'cool reception' from Asian comrades. Its regional nature implied 'inferior status to full membership of the Socialist International'. Also, there was a feeling amongst Asian Socialists that European Socialists supported one of the two blocs within the international system 'whereas the Asian parties hold a "Third Force" or "neutral" position . . . '. There was also a suspicion that European Socialists were tainted with colonialism: ' . . . the Socialist International is regarded as a Western Socialist organisation, and is therefore not only suspect but also politically dangerous to the Asian parties in their respective countries.'[13]

The International was no more successful in the largely post-colonial era, and the reason for its lack of success was perceived by its General Secretary to be similar to that suggested twenty years earlier. In the late 1960s a new attempt was made to establish an Asian regional organisation and an Asian secretariat was established in Singapore. Its viability, like that of its predecessor, was soon in question. The personnel involved failed to take initiatives in respect of salient issues such as Bangla Desh. A more fundamental reason, however, in the eyes of Hans Janitschek, was the European dimension associated with the memberships of Australia, Israel and New Zealand. Their membership 'gives an image which is not received favourably in many Asian countries . . . it is predominantly white'.[14]

In brief, European integration seems to provide an issue — or set of issues — of continuing relevance to the parties whose habits of transnational activity are substantially those of transnational Socialism *per se*. And, accordingly, should the transnational activities of the parties have action-guiding significance for individual Socialist parties, then European integration seems to provide a context in which it is likely to manifest itself. Questions may be asked about the relevance accorded by individual Socialist parties to the attitudes manifested by fraternal parties without any actual contacts taking place between them; also, about the consequences of specific contacts between the parties or their parliamentary representatives in a number of institutional contexts; and finally, adopting a different perspective, about what the parties themselves regard as successful output from their transnational contacts. The answers all tend to suggest the same conclusion.

The relevance accorded by individual parties to the attitudes manifested by their fraternal parties in respect of particular issues may be tested by reference to studies of the factors which have motivated them in the formation of their attitudes to integration generally. Both secondary sources and the writer's own research suggest the same answer in respect of, at least, the British, French and German parties. Attitudes are found to have developed in response to (often overlapping) programmatic and electoral considerations, with both firmly related to domestic political objectives.[15] Where an international element obtruded, it too is found to have been an expression of fundamentally national concern, an example here being French concern about Germany in the development of the SFIO's attitude to integration between 1945 and 1957. A comparative study of the three parties reveals that fraternal parties played very little role in their attitudes even at a declaratory level; and suggests that the party which has shown the greatest predisposition to employ language of an 'internationalist' nature — the SFIO/Parti Socialiste — has in its action-guiding attitudes been dominated as surely as the British or German parties by concerns arising in the domestic political context.

Actual contacts between Socialist parties in the 'European' context include those between the party organisations; those between their parliamentarians in the European assemblies; and those between the parties and the Socialist Groups in the assemblies. Contacts between the parties within the ambit of the Liaison Bureau/Confederation and the occasional *ad hoc* meetings of the late 1940s and early 1950s provide examples of the first type of contact. The unsatisfactory nature of the Liaison Bureau has been remarked upon above,[16] and the brief existence of the Confederation and its Bureau renders any judgement of its output premature. But, earlier *ad hoc* meetings between the parties in response to stimuli of a 'European' nature tended to produce statements and resolutions either anodyne in nature or which were subsequently treated as meaningless by at least some of their signatories. In the *Resolution Passed Unanimously by International Conference of Socialist Parties on European Unity* at Paris on 24-5 April 1948, for example, the parties declared that 'the social, economic, political and cultural purposes of the workers of their respective countries can best be achieved in peace within the framework of a United States of Europe',[17] and Hugh Dalton signed the resolution on behalf of the Labour Party although both he and the party he represented were not only unenthusiastic for any capitalised United States of Europe but positively hostile to anything other than inter-governmental co-operation.[18]

Of the European assemblies, the European Parliament is at least potentially the most important; and the writer has argued elsewhere that — in the latter half of the 1960s and early 1970s — its Socialist members tended to be largely undistinguished in their behaviour but of high relative coherence in respect of issues.[19] The uncertainty of the former and the declaratory nature of the latter still leave much unexplained about the significance to Socialists of their membership of a multinational ideologically based group in the Parliament. Specifically in the context of this chapter, is their declaratory posture also of significance for action-guiding purposes? Is their coherence at a declaratory level reflected in, for example, attempts to affect Community process? Judgement of the extent to which the Socialist Group attempts to affect the output of the Community is rendered difficult by the limited powers of the Parliament to date in respect of the allocation of resources — the 'real stuff' of politics. But, in one significant issue area at least, relevant actors feel that the Group has failed to utilise the opportunities available to it. In the declaratory posture of the Group, the social policy of the Community has been of lasting and ubiquitous concern. Functionaries of the directorate-general for social affairs of the Commission — the official initiator of policy in the Community process — feel, however, that the Group has made little effort to exert influence in this area, and note that it has even ignored personal appeals from a high level within the directorate-general to raise points in the Parliament to which the latter might respond.[20]

In spite of its lack of power, the European Parliament provides a forum in which members of Community parties come together on a regular basis. And, should the parties wish to agree common positions for action-guiding purposes, then the Parliament's Socialist Group merits attention as one useful context in which they might attempt to do so. Two members of the Group made mutually exclusive allegations to the writer about the significance to the parties of the Group's activity. The first member refuted the notion that the positions adopted by the Group had any affect on the policies adopted by the parties: Group activity was essentially something you 'did' at Luxembourg or Strasbourg. The second claimed that Group members argued the positions agreed at Luxembourg/Strasbourg in their national capitals and thus constituted an input to the policy-formation process of their national parties. Perhaps significantly, he was unable to give examples of particular issues, claiming — when queried — that Group members argued in their national capitals 'everything' they had agreed in the Group. More conclusively, a senior functionary of this member's party, when questioned about this allegation, advised the writer that he could think of no instance of positions agreed by the Group affecting the policy-formation process of his party.

Enquiries made in national capitals about the policy-formation processes of individual Socialist parties in respect of 'European' matters also suggest that membership of the multinational Socialist Group in the European Parliament is of no action-guiding significance to individual parties. In Bonn, SPD members of the Bundestag who are also members of the European Parliament meet approximately once a month to discuss their 'European' business. The meeting is open to all members of the SPD *Fraktion* (parliamentary party) and offers a useful opportunity for members of the parliamentary party to acquaint themselves with the current positions of the Group and perhaps also to participate indirectly in its policy-formation process. Attendance records for the meeting are not available, but the attendance of deputies who are not members of the Group seems to be the exception rather than the rule.[21] A similar attitude to the Group prevails also in Paris. Here, those in the ambit of Mitterrand were clear that, when faced with the need to speak on a 'European' issue, he made no effort to acquaint himself with the positions of the Group or to contact its Parti Socialiste members.[22]

The irrelevance of fraternal parties to the policy-formation processes of individual Socialist parties is further suggested by the parties' concept of successful output from their transnational activity. Functionaries of the parties' international departments are generally reluctant to argue any significance for their transnational interactions. When pressed on the topic, however, they tend to point to meetings which have taken place or declaratory positions agreed. In this latter context, a rare instance quoted as an example of an especially successful conclusion to negotiations between the parties about a particular issue is instructive. At their 9th Congress, the parties were divided over *Mitbestimmung* with both the French and the Italian parties insisting that the divergence of their respective positions from the majority of the Congress be recorded.[23] Fifteen months later, however, in the *Europaische Aktiengesellschaft* debate in the Parliament, the parties were able to speak as a Group in response to the Commission's proposals on worker participation. A functionary of a major party adduced their unity at this time as a good example of a successful conclusion to lengthy and difficult negotiations between the parties and suggested that the amount of time available had been a crucial factor in reaching agreement.[24] The Group's position, however, welcoming the Commission's proposals as a step in the right direction but stating that they did not go far enough, failed to specify what the parties would regard as acceptable. In spite of the time which had been spent in negotiations between the parties, it avoided the vexed question of 'participation' or 'supervision', and could in no way be interpreted as constraining any party's freedom to decide its own policy in the future.[25]

Briefly put, the response of the parties to questions about what they regard as successful output from their transnational interactions suggests that the continuance of their transnational activity and the maintenance of a facade of unity is regarded as successful output in itself.

To summarise, European integration has been an issue of continuing relevance to European Socialist parties, and they have been keen to institutionalise their links and to maintain declaratory unity in the European context. But, a consideration of several relevant questions fails to suggest that the parties have had any action-guiding significance for each other as they have formed their attitudes to integration or to particular aspects of it. In brief, the relevance of the issue and the mutual irrelevance in respect of it to parties whose habits of transnational activity are substantially those of transnational socialism *per se* suggest a conclusion that transnational Socialist interactions have no effect at all on the political output of individual Socialist parties.

However, although of value, these conclusions have been based on the application of a rather mechanistic logic and an implicit assumption that the political world can be sufficiently well understood by such an approach. Should a less pristine view of the nature of political activity prevail, in which the political world is characterised by the complex interactions of innumerable factors and political output is the result of constantly changing and frequently unquantifiable shades of influence, then the transnational activities of the parties are of probable significance for political process in a number of ways.

The Political Significance of Transnational Socialist Interactions

Although their influence is usually unquantifiable, the transnational interactions of Socialist parties probably serve at least three functions in political process. First is their possible influence on national public opinions or those of the rank and file of particular parties in respect of some issues. Second is the use which can be made of them for *domestic political purposes* by individual parties or personalities within them. And third is the use which can be made of them for *governmental purposes* by parties in office.

The dictatorships of Southern Europe provide an example of an issue area in respect of which some Socialists have felt that activity in the transnational context might have at least some minor influence on the climates of opinion within which individual Socialist parties develop their attitudes. On the whole, Socialists who have displayed a particular concern about the Southern European dictatorships tend to feel that expressions of opposition to them — whether from Socialist *or other* sources — have been useful in three ways: first, in maintaining pressure on Socialist parties in Government; second, in maintaining it on the dictatorships themselves in respect of their treatment of the persecuted under them; and third, in sustaining the morale of domestic opponents of such regimes. Also, although a less persuasive argument, some Socialists have felt that the expression of a common attitude of hostility towards the dictatorships could offer something to which those with a particular concern about the dictatorships in parties less eager to oppose them might reach out and utilise in intra-party debate. In this context, the Socialist International has perhaps attempted to play something of a catalytic role. For example, it was quick to act as a 'multiplier' of its members' declarations of opposition to the establishment of military dictatorship in Greece in 1967 by publishing together the condemnations of the coup made separately by individual parties, and it continued thereafter to draw attention to the nature of the regime and the condition of the oppressed under it.[26] Also, the participation of its member parties in its study groups on the dictatorships in Greece, Portugal and Spain — designed 'to maintain pressure for the restoration of democracy'[27] — might have served to inhibit parties more reluctant to oppose the dictatorships from 'slippage' from positions of hostility commonly agreed.

The influence of fraternal parties on individual parties' attitudes towards the dictatorships should not be exaggerated, however. Interviews with several of the (British) Labour parliamentarians who had shown the greatest concern about the Greek regime failed to evoke any *particular* claims about their influence, and some of those interviewed stressed the importance of some non-Socialist actors — American liberals, for example — more than that of a Socialist actor like the International. Also, a case study made by the writer of the change in attitude of the British Labour *Government* towards the Greek dictatorship suggested that it was due essentially to widespread revulsion in the parliamentary party and the cabinet following disclosures of the use of torture by the regime rather than to the activities of other actors, Socialist or otherwise.[28] In brief, although of some possible significance as one factor affecting the 'background conditions' of public and party opinion, the influence of the parties' transnational activities on the policy-formation process of individual Socialist parties remains uncertain. The political *use* which can be made of the parties' transnational relations may be argued more persuasively, however.

In domestic politics, transnational Socialist relations have been used in both *intra* and *inter*-party struggles. Examples of the former include the European Defence Community and British entry into the EEC. The positions of fraternal parties were frequently adduced in the arguments of both supporters and opponents of the EDC in the SFIO; and a commitment to consult with fraternal parties was a major feature of the Labour leadership's successful appeal to the party's annual conference in respect of its policy on German rearmament in 1954. The attitudes of fraternal parties towards the EEC and towards Britain's membership of it often featured in the arguments advanced by Labour supporters of British membership; and the leader of the SPD and Chancellor of the Federal Republic, Helmut Schmidt, flew to London during the referendum campaign to assist the pro-membership majority of the Labour leadership by underlining the wish of Labour's fraternal parties that it should join them in the Community. Neither issue provides an example in respect of which the influence of fraternal parties can be proven; but in both cases references to the positions of fraternal parties by political actors widely experienced in judging finely what shades of influence may be derived from particular factors suggests a perception on their part that the attitudes of fraternal parties were of significance to at least part of the audience to which they were addressing themselves.

In the *inter*-party context, the most important benefit derived by Socialist parties from their relations with fraternal parties is the electoral benefit which occasionally accrues to particular party leaders. In addition to its Bureau, Council and Congress meetings,[29] the Socialist International occasionally organises party leaders' conferences. Although an *ad hoc* development, the sponsoring of these conferences was by the early 1970s regarded as amongst the most important of the International's activities. In addition to their communications function, the eminence of the personalities at party leaders' conferences casts a lustre over the proceedings which can be beneficial to the domestic image of the participants, and the location and the timing of the conferences may magnify the effect for specific individuals: a Paris party leaders' conference, for example, enhanced Mitterrand's image at a time when he was striving to establish firmly his leadership of the French democratic Left; Kreisky enjoyed a similar conference in Vienna prior to Austrian elections; and Jørgensen was able to enhance his party leadership of a minority government in Denmark.

Participation in transnational Socialist activity can be an especially valuable resource to less well-established parties. A particular example of this is Mario Soares whose participation in the transnational activities of the parties prior to the overthrow of the Portuguese dictatorship brought him into contact with the leading Social Democratic personalities of Western Europe and underlined his claim to the Portuguese foreign ministry after the coup in two ways. First, the draping of the mantle of Social Democratic values over his shoulders could help facilitate acceptance within the international system of any government in which he participated; and second, his personal contacts with Europe's many Socialist ministers enhanced the likelihood in many cases that approaches in respect of the external business of such a government would be met with 'at least a propensity to listen'.[30]

Socialist parties in office also use their transnational party links for *governmental* purposes. In this context, their transnational relations offer two valuable means of enhancing the communications facilities at the disposal of their governments: first, through participation in transnational Socialist meetings and conferences; and second, through the ability to communicate through the appropriate sections of party bureaucracies in addition to inter-governmental channels. The first is perhaps most useful to parties in office for explaining and promoting policies relevant to lasting concerns; the second in respect also of problems and policies confined to more limited periods.

Party leaders' conferences are one type of Socialist conference which parties in office may use for governmental purposes. Their importance to governing parties is derived from the level of the parties' representation at them and from the circumstances under which communication takes place. In respect of the first point, for example, at the International's conference on the Middle East, 'Golda Meir could come and address ten prime ministers . . . No mean audience'.[31] In respect of the second, features which might distinguish them from inter-governmental conferences from the point of view of heads of government attending them may include: a looser agenda and the freedom to discuss a wide range of issues; greater privacy than is usual at *multilateral* inter-governmental conferences; and an absence of the inhibiting of the free exchange of opinions which may accompany the need to agree a communiqué at the end of discussions. Once again, the effect on the political output of individual parties cannot be traced. But, the decisions of party leaders — many of them heads of government whose time is of great value — to attend such conferences suggests strongly that they are perceived to be of some practical value.

The ability of parties in office to communicate with each other through the international sections of their party bureaucracies constitutes both an alternative means of communication when inter-governmental channels have become 'bogged down', and an additional means of communication which may be particularly helpful during complex and lengthy foreign policy initiatives. A particular example of the latter was the SPD's use of its party machinery as it developed its *Ostpolitik*. Involved SPD actors stress that the *timing* of the various stages of the *Ostpolitik* was of particular importance and — although usually laying strong emphasis upon the need for 'realism' in assessing the practical importance of the parties' transnational relations — state that in this case party-to-party channels were 'extremely useful . . . we advised sister parties how long phases would take and where they could help us . . . it was . . . very important with the GDR'.[32]

To summarise, a conclusion that transnational Socialist interactions are of *some* significance for political process is suggested by the behaviour and the opinions of involved actors in a number of contexts. However, the ways in which the parties' transnational activities are politically significant are seen to be basically of two kinds, and neither constitutes an adequate explanation of the degree of interest the parties show in maintaining their transnational links. First, the uses which can be made of the parties' transnational interactions are those of communications and derived prestige, and stem *from* the existence of such activity rather than providing a motive for it. And second, in those aspects of the parties' interactions where a *possible* influence on individual parties may be suggested, it does not seem to amount to more than a minor one. The influence on the political output of individual parties of their participation in transnational declaratory activity in respect of issues such as the dictatorships of Southern Europe must be regarded as a minor one at most; and on the infrequent occasions when the positions of fraternal parties have been adduced in intra-party debate, it is the opinion of involved actors that their influence has probably been very small indeed — some Labour admirers of Schmidt's skilful appeal to Conference, for example, feel that its greatest value lay in dulling the sharpness of the cleavage within the party rather than in inducing anybody to change their minds.

Conclusions

Socialists, it is worth repeating, have shown lasting interest in their transnational links. Yet their activity in this area seems to have no direct significance for the policy-formation or decision-taking processes of individual parties and only negligible indirect significance. Accordingly, the question remains: what is the nature of the attractiveness of 'Socialist internationalism'? Why are the parties so tenacious in maintaining and even promoting their transnational links if they are of so little consequence?

Socialists show little predisposition to articulate what they understand by 'Socialist internationalism'. Enquiries made of the Socialist International, for example, elicited only the response that: 'doctrinal introspection is not a feature of the transnational activities of the parties'. The reasons suggested by a wide spectrum of involved actors for Socialists' concern to retain their transnational links may be reduced to three arguments, however. They may be called the 'inertia' and the 'internal' and 'external' identity arguments.

Briefly, the 'inertia' argument is that 'Socialist internationalism' is an inheritance: that its origins lay in a period when Socialist parties had not experienced the constraints of Government. In the twentieth century, although its irrelevance for the action-guiding policies of individual parties has become increasingly apparent, the parties have continued to maintain at least a tacit allegiance to it due to the minimal demands it makes on their resources[33] and to 'reinforcers' like the uses which can be made of it and the many personal friendships which have been formed between prominent Socialists in the course of the parties' transnational interactions.[34]

The 'external identity' argument is that participation in the transnational activities of the parties serves a useful identitive function *vis à vis* electoral competitors. In Italy, for example, acceptability in the world of transnational Socialist politics was sufficiently important to both 'Nenni' and 'Saragat' Socialists that both were prepared to allow the International Socialist Conference to intervene in their domestic differences rather than risk expulsion from the Conference.[35] Since then, each Italian — and each of the two Japanese — parties have underlined the importance they attach to participation in transnational Socialist activity by insisting that if their domestic rival occupies a seat on the International's Bureau then they should do so also.

The 'internal identity' argument is, briefly, that support for 'Socialist internationalism' serves an internal party function: that party leaders responding pragmatically to extra-party pressures and constraints believe that tacit expressions of loyalty to 'Socialist internationalism' are helpful to them in reassuring value-conscious rank and files of their own allegiance to the values of Socialism.

All three arguments have some persuasiveness and, almost certainly, some validity. And, if none of them quite constitutes a satisfactory explanation, one of them suggests what is perhaps the most potent single motive for Socialists' interest in promoting their transnational links. The 'inertia' argument is insufficiently persuasive in respect of the parties' tendency to form links in *new* institutional contexts — in the European assemblies, for example — or in respect of new problems. And, although some empirical evidence may be adduced in respect of the 'external identity' argument, the function served here by the parties' transnational relations is a double-edged one. For example, the promotion of a distinctively Socialist identity — especially by association with foreign political parties — is no guarantee of, and may even be detrimental to, a party's electoral appeal. The persuasiveness of the 'internal identity', like that of the 'inertia', argument is diminished by the variety of contexts in which Socialist parties have shown interest in promoting their transnational links. Should manifestations of support for 'Socialist internationalism' by party leaders be motivated primarily by their desire to reassure their rank and files of their commitment to Socialist values then, it may be suggested, continued membership of the International and the employment of appropriate rhetoric might be sufficient. The tacit premise of the importance of affirmations of support for Socialist values in this last argument, however, suggests a concern of more fundamental importance than mere relationships between leaderships and rank and files.

A political ideology involves at least two kinds of beliefs: one about the desirability of a particular priority of values, the other about the possibility of attaining a society which would reflect them. The relationship between Socialism and internationalism, it may be suggested, has significance for both kinds of belief. A wide range of historians, political philosophers and political scientists have suggested an *inherent* relationship between Socialism and internationalism. Sometimes this has been implicit as in Beer's assessment of Socialism as 'the doctrine of fellowship'[36] and Tawney's emphasis upon its ethical base. Sometimes it has been made explicit as in the writings of G.D.H. Cole or in Saul Rose's allegation that 'Socialism has always been an international movement because its principles are universal'.[37] Briefly, Socialism is argued as internationalist in nature because of the universal relevance of its values and/or the universal applicability of its principles. Viewed thus, to reject 'Socialist internationalism' by declaring irrelevant the attitudes of parties committed to the same *universally* relevant values and principles would be to call into question both the relevance in the contemporary world of Socialism's value structure *and* the possibility of attaining a society which would reflect it. That is to say, to do other than continue to maintain at least tacit support for the proposition that the positions of fraternal parties — fellow repositories of the same values and beliefs — are of some significance to individual

Socialist parties would be to call into question the belief system which distinguishes Socialism as a political ideology.

Finally, two particular issues of current transnational Socialist activity offer opportunities for testing the conclusions suggested by this paper: attitudes towards the relations of individual European parties with their national Communist parties, and the development of a programme to which all the European parties might adhere. In respect of the first issue a development in keeping with the conclusions of this paper is already discernible. Parties perceiving the need for an electoral alliance or other accommodation with their national Communist parties have made clear their intentions of pursuing such arrangements. Parties opposed to such arrangements themselves have, by and large, accepted their positions. In some instances, however, they have been reluctant to do so and have made it clear to their own members that the acceptance of fraternal parties' positions must not be construed as any relaxation of their own attitudes towards their national Communist parties.[38] That is to say, the fundamentally *national* nature of the situations and the problems of individual parties is recognised by all, and the positions of fraternal parties are — as usual — of no significance for the action-guiding policies of individual parties. Equally, differences in attitudes towards relations with Communist parties have not seriously threatened the maintenance of relations between Socialist parties — a point underlined by the second issue.

In spite of continuing differences in respect of issues like relations with Communist parties, the Socialist parties of member states of the EEC committed themselves in 1974 to the development of a programme to which all of them might ultimately adhere and which was to be more than a mere lowest common denominator of their individual programmes. At the time of writing the outcome of the development of a common programme remains unclear; but, should the conclusions of this chapter be correct, three possible reactions to it by the parties may be predicted. First, they may fail to reach agreement, perhaps evading the articulation of their disagreement by calling for further study. Second, they may agree a 'lowest common denominator' or essentially anodyne programme. Third, they may agree a non-anodyne programme which individual parties will then ignore as its requirements clash with pressures arising in their domestic political systems.[39] That is to say, any declaratory commitment to such a programme which may be forthcoming will in no way incline individual parties to place greater emphasis upon adherence to the programme than to the satisfaction of demands arising in their national political systems. Once again, the parties' transnational relations will remain irrelevant for action-guiding purposes; but, should the nature of the importance attributed here to 'Socialist internationalism' be correct, the parties' enthusiasm for the maintenance and the promotion of their transnational relations will in no way be diminished.

Notes

1. *Interviews*, April-May 1974. Due to assurances of non-attribution given to many personalities interviewed, I have elected to stick to anonymity as a general rule. Occasional exceptions have been made where a direct and non-controversial quotation is involved. The interviews were conducted mostly during 1974 and 1975, and involved approximately forty parliamentarians and party functionaries.
2. See, The Socialist International, *The Socialist International, A Short History* (1969), p. 12.
3. J. Braunthal, *History of the International 1864-1914* (1966), p. 355.
4. *Labour Party Annual Conference Report 1947*, p. 106; see also, *LPCR 1945*, p. 84. Dalton attended three Bureau meetings of the International prior to the German invasion of the Low Countries in 1940.
5. See, for example, *LPCR 1943*, p. 209; *LPCR 1944*, p. 41; *LPCR 1945*, pp. 13, 84.
6. 'The Socialist International', p. 14.
7. Van Oudenhove posited that a grouping process 'had become manifest' by March 1953, and that the groups became 'an accomplished fact' during the session of May-June 1953 (*The Political Parties in the European Parliament* (Leyden, 1965), pp. 19-20). However, the Common Assembly first met on 10 September, 1952, and the report of Saul Rose, Labour's International Secretary, on the *Consultative* Assembly's session of 15-30 September 1952 noted that 'The Socialist Group of the European Coal and Steel Community was constituted at the first meeting of the Schuman Plan Assembly . . . ' (*Labour Party Archives*).
8. Schmid was speedily absolved of any guilt by a Socialist commission of inquiry. (Labour Party Archives, 1950.)
9. *Rules of Procedure* of the Confederation of Socialist Parties of the European Community, 27 September 1964, p.4.
10. See, for example, Xavier Marchetti, 'Socialismes du nord au sud', *Figaro*, 26 May 1975.
11. Singapore is a minor exception. The two Japanese parties have occupied seats on the International's Bureau, but have been less active.
12. The International does not publish its accounts; but the Austrian, British, German and Swedish parties are said to be the 'big payers'.
13. Morgan Phillips (Ex-Chairman of the Labour Party's International Sub-Committee), u.d. (but with material of 1952) memorandum in *Labour Party Archives*.
14. Interview, 17 May 1974.
15. See, for example, B. Criddle, *Socialists and European Integration* (1969); and W. Paterson, *The SPD and European Integration* (1974).
16. p.410.
17. Available in *Mackay Papers*, group 14, file 1.
18. See, for example, *Dalton Diaries*, 16-20 June 1950.
19. See, J.P. May, 'Is There a European Socialism?', *Journal of Common Market Studies*, vol. XIII, no. 4 (June 1975).
20. Interviews, Brussels, May 1975.

21. Interviews, Bonn, June 1975.
22. Interviews, Paris, July 1974.
23. 9th Congress of the Socialist Parties of the European Community, *Towards A Social Europe* (Bonn, 26-7 Apr. 1973), pp. 16-17.
24. Interview, June 1975.
25. *Verhandlungen des Europäischen Parlaments,* 10 July 1974, pp. 154-5.
26. See, for example, *Socialist International Information,* 27 May 1967.
27. R. Balcomb, Assistant General Secretary, The Socialist International, interview, 18 Apr. 1974.
28. The feeling of revulsion at all levels in the Parliamentary Labour Party as allegations of torture gained in credibility and became widespread is attested to by Labour members with a particular concern about Greece. An example of the feelings aroused in the Cabinet was an unusually undiplomatic reference in the House by the Prime Minister who spoke of 'the bestialities perpetrated' in Greece. (*HC Deb,* 767, 241, 25 June 1968.)
29. Congress conferences are held every third year; Council conferences in the intervening years. Only Congress is empowered to alter the International's statute and to admit or expel members. Bureau meetings are held several times a year. All member parties are entitled to attend Congress and Council meetings; but membership of the Bureau is restricted to eighteen.
30. Interview with a senior functionary of a major party, June 1974.
31. Ibid.
32. Interview, Bonn, June 1975.
33. Financially, for example, the budget of the International was said to be running during 1973-4 at the modest sum of £70,000 per annum. More importantly, the International's relative lack of an initiatory role means that its demands upon its members' *political* resources are minimal.
34. Harold Wilson, for example, is said to have met Bruno Kreisky at an international Socialist youth conference after World War Two; and the thirty-year friendship of Denis Healey and Helmut Schmidt also had its origins in the transnational context.
35. See, for example, D. Healey, 'The International Socialist Conference 1946-1950', *International Affairs,* July 1950, p. 370.
36. S.H. Beer, *Modern British Politics* (1965), p. 238.
37. S. Rose, *The Socialist International* (u.d.), p. 5.
38. See, for example, *Der Spiegel's* interview with Willy Brandt, 26 Jan. 1976.
39. Developments between the writing (May-June 1976) of this paper and its going to press (November) tend to suggest a variation of the first reaction suggested. The parties have apparently failed to agree a programme, and have established a number of study groups.

Bibliographical Note

Secondary sources on relations between Socialist parties are confined, substantially, to two aspects of the topic: the Socialist International, and the Socialist groups in the European assemblies. Useful histories of the first include: J. Braunthal, *History of the International 1864-1914* (1966), and *1914-1943* (1963); D. Healey, 'The International Socialist Conference', *International Affairs,* July 1950; S. Rose, *The Socialist International,* u.d. See also, the International's own *The*

Socialist International A Short History (1969) and, suggesting the post-war concerns of the International, *Declarations of the International* (1951).

The Socialist groups in the European assemblies tend to be dealt with in the context of the political groups generally in the assemblies. For the Council of Europe, see K. Lindsay, *European Assemblies* (1960), and A.H. Robertson, *The Council of Europe* (1961). For the Common Assembly of the Coal and Steel Community and the European Parliament, see J. Fitzmaurice, *The Party Groups in the European Parliament* (1975); J.P. May, 'Is There a European Socialism?', *Journal of Common Market Studies,* vol. XIII, no. 4 (June, 1975); Guy Van Oudenhove, *The Political Parties in the European Parliament* (Leyden, 1965); and G. Zellentin, 'Form and Function of the Opposition in the European Communities', *Government and Opposition,* vol. 2, no. 3 (Apr.-July 1967).

In primary sources, the *Socialist International Information* can be helpful. The International's archives are in the Institute for Social History at Amsterdam, and the writer understands that they may be made available on application to St John's Wood. The *Reports* of the Congress of the Socialist Parties of the European Community are an essential source for the development of the concerns of the parties in the 'European' context. See also, the *Report on the Reform of the Bureau of the Socialist Parties in the European Community,* PS/CE/13/74. 8 Mar. 1974, and the *Rules of Procedure* of the Confederation of Socialist Parties of the European Community, 27 Sept. 1974.

On the transnational relations of individual parties, there are no particular secondary sources, and primary material is not easy to obtain. The dedicated, however, will find (very) occasional references to fraternal parties in the reports of the annual or biennial conferences of individual parties; also, in internal party publications or party-associated newspapers — for example, *le Bulletin Intérieur* and *le Populaire* respectively. The accessibility — and even the existence — of party archives depends very much on the individual party. Cité Malesherbes, for example, has little in the way of records; whilst, at the other extreme, the Friedrich Ebert Stiftung's concern to preserve the SPD's archives for future scholars is such that it is disinclined to make them available to present ones. Apart from ten years' post-war correspondence with fraternal parties, which has been inadvertently thrown out, Transport House's archives are available in respect of all material that does not come under its 'fifteen year' rule. The Labour

Party is the only party to have *continuously* sent a party representative with its Council of Europe delegation, and the reports of these representatives provide an invaluable source for the Socialist groups in the Consultative Assembly *and* for developments in the Socialist group of the *Common* Assembly.

Of possible sources unresearched by the writer, the archives of the PvdA are perhaps the most promising.

Finally, in spite of occasional frustrations, the writer would like to take this opportunity to place on record his gratitude to the archivists and the functionaries of the British, French and German Socialist parties, the Socialist International and the Socialist Group in the European Parliament. In each case, assistance was willingly forthcoming in response to his — sometimes ill-framed — questions.

A NOTE ON SWITZERLAND

Alastair H. Thomas[1]

The present Social Democratic Party of Switzerland was formed in
1888 and won its first seat in the National Council (the popular house
of the Federal Assembly) in 1893. Until 1911 the Social Democrats
formed part of the Social Political Group in the Nationalrat, an alliance
of several small cantonal parties which later became the Democrats. But
by 1917 the Social Democrats had increased their share of the national
vote to over 20 per cent and since the introduction of proportional
representation in 1919 they have retained between 23 per cent and
29 per cent, and have thus been one of the four main parties.

Switzerland has a permanent collegial government, the Federal
Council, whose seven members form a coalition the composition of
which is in approximate relation to the strength of the parties in the
National Council. The Social Democrats have been (by a small margin)
the largest party in terms of their share of the votes since 1928 and as
such have claimed representation in the Federal Council. They gained
their first member there in 1943 and since 1959 have had two members.
The other members are the Radical Democrats (two seats), the
Christian Democrat People's Party (two seats) and the Swiss People's
Party (Peasants') with one seat. The Government acts as a corporate
body and its actions are now seldom related to a party-political
philosophy. Party strength in the proportionally elected National
Council has varied little since PR was adopted and an overall majority
at the Federal level is not within reach of any one party. Representation
of the SDP in the Council of States (the other House of the Federal
Assembly) has been fitful and never anything approaching proportional
to the Social Democratic Party's voting strength. The two Houses have
equal powers.

The Party's 1888 programme was preoccupied with the issue of
centralisation, which the Party asserted against cantonalisation, and its
federal organisation remains more important than its organisation at
local level, in contrast to the other parties. The 1904 and 1920
programmes gave progressively greater emphasis to Marxist ideology,
class conflict and the dictatorship of the proletariat, influenced by the
Russian revolution and the two-day general strike of 1918. The dangers
of Fascism in the 1930s seemed more pressing than those of Capitalism,

however, and the 1935 programme was designed to project the Party as a potential ally or coalition partner for the 'bourgeois' parties. The 1959 programme is diffuse and undoctrinal.

Within the permanent governing coalition, 'Swiss socialists have at times been allies of the Radicals, as being anti-clerical and interested in political rights, but more recently they have explored common ground with the Peasants and Catholics, as being interested in protectionism, *étatisme,* paternalism, and generally in the priority of social-moral principles over economic expediency: the 'red-green-black' alliance'.[2]

Trade unions are organised separately from the Party and it has not succeeded in attracting all the votes of union members. But there is also a natural partnership of shared ideals between the two organisations and they have many leaders in common. There are similar relationships of the Catholic unions to the Catholic Party and the Peasants' Union to the Peasants' Party. The interaction of linguistic, religious and class cleavages in Switzerland is highly complex: Kerr found,[3] for example, that 'in Vaud, Neuchâtel and Geneva class opposition organised through the trade union movement dominated partisan conflict, whereas in Fribourg and Valais the religious factor permeates party life. This overlapping of the religious dimension with the relation between class and party preference indicates that religiosity is at least as important in determining partisan choice as is occupation'. The first point can be illustrated by the following table:[4]

Party preference by occupation: Socialist and Communist parties (percentages)

Manual Workers	Civil Servants	Other	Employees	Liberal Professions	Farmers
53	10	6	22	8	1

Kerr illustrates the second point by showing that the Socialist and Communist parties gain nearly twice as much of their support (32 per cent) from Protestants as from Catholics (17 per cent) and that identification with these parties declines as church attendance rises, much more sharply among Catholics than among Protestants: of those who attend church every Sunday, only 5 per cent of Catholics identified with these parties while 28 per cent of Protestants did so.[5] It is clear from more detailed regional studies that the solid basis of the Socialist electorate is clearly the urban worker, but there is also strong support from the salaried middle economic class.[6]

The stability of support for the Social Democratic Party is shown by its share of the votes cast at elections, 1947-75:

1947	1951	1955	1959	1963	1967	1971	1975
26.2	26.0	27.0	26.4	26.6	23.5	22.9	25.4

Notes

1. I am most grateful to Professor C.J. Hughes of the University of Leicester for his hospitality and assistance with this Note.
2. C.J. Hughes, 'Switzerland', in Stanley Henig and John Pinder (eds.), *European Political Parties* (Allen and Unwin/P.E.P., 1969), p. 378.
3. Henry H. Kerr jun. *Switzerland: Social Cleavages and Partisan Conflict* (Sage Professional Paper in Contemporary Political Sociology, vol. 1, no. 06-002. Sage Publications, 1974), pp. 11, 27.
4. Ibid. figures calculated from Table 3, p. 11.
5. Ibid. p. 12.
6. Jürg Steiner, *Das politische system der Schweiz* (München, R. Piper & Co. Verlag, 1971), p. 98.

Further Reading

The leading modern academic study of the Social Democratic Party is by François Masnata, *Le parti socialiste et la tradition démocratique en Suisse* (Neuchâtel, 1963).

On parties in general, E. Gruner, *Die Parteien in der Schweiz* (Bern, 1969) is a full-length study of Swiss political parties and includes an extensive bibliography.

Further information on Swiss government and politics is available in Hughes, Christopher. *Switzerland*. Benn, Nations of the Modern World, 1975.

The Federal Constitution of Switzerland. Oxford, 1954.

The Parliament of Switzerland. London, 1962.

Codding, G.A. *The Federal Government of Switzerland*. Boston, 1961.

Politics in Swiss Local Government: Governing the Commune of Veyrier. Boulder, Colo., 1967.

Meynaud, Jean. *Les organisations Professionelles en Suisse*. Lausanne, Payot, 1963.

Schumann, Klaus. *Das Regierungssystem der Schweiz*. Köln, 1971.

Membership of European Socialist Parties, 1900-55

	Germany	Austria	Denmark	France	Great Britain Trade Union Members	Great Britain Individual Members	Total	Norway	Holland	Sweden	Switzerland
1900					353,070		375,931		3,200	44,100	9,155
1901					455,450		469,311		4,000	48,241	8,912
1902					847,315		861,150		6,500	49,190	19,840
1903			22,061		956,025		969,800	17,000	5,600	54,552	20,337
1904					885,270		900,000		6,000	64,835	20,000
1905	400,000			34,688	904,496		921,280		6,816	67,325	
1906	384,327		29,651	40,000	975,182		998,338	19,100	7,471	101,929	
1907	530,466			52,913	1,049,673		1,072,418		8,423	133,388	
1908	587,338		34,078	56,963	1,127,035		1,158,565	27,838	8,748	112,693	20,439
1909	633,309			57,977	1,450,648		1,486,308	27,789	9,504	60,813	21,132
1910	720,038			69,085	1,394,402		1,430,539		9,980	55,248	20,671
1911	836,562			69,578	1,501,783		1,539,092		12,582	57,721	21,508
1912	970,112			72,692	1,858,178		1,895,498	43,557	15,667	61,000	27,500
1913	982,850	89,628	48,985	75,192					25,708	75,444	29,730
1914	1,085,905		57,115	93,218	1,572,391		1,612,147	53,866	25,609	84,410	29,585
1915	585,898		60,072	25,393	2,053,735		2,093,365	62,952	25,642	85,937	27,485
1916	432,618		67,724	25,879	2,170,782		2,219,764		24,018	105,275	31,307
1917	243,061		78,320	28,224	2,415,383		2,465,131		24,893	114,450	
1918	249,411		91,791	15,827	2,960,409		3,013,129	94,165	27,093	129,432	39,765
1919	1,012,299	332,391	115,900	133,277	3,464,020		3,511,290		37,628	151,364	52,163
1920	1,180,208	335,863	126,603	179,787	4,317,537		4,359,807		47,870	143,090	51,250
1921	1,028,574	491,160	129,756	50,449	3,973,558		4,010,361	45,946	37,412	134,753	40,483
1922	1,464,868	553,022	124,549	49,174	3,279,276		3,311,036		41,472	133,042	36,552
1923	1,261,072	514,273	130,371	50,496	3,120,149		3,155,911		42,047	138,510	34,000

Membership of European Socialist Parties, 1900-55 (continued)

	Germany	Austria	Denmark	France	Great Britain Trade Union Members	Great Britain Individual Members	Total	Norway	Holland	Sweden	Switzerland
1924	940,078	566,124	143,203	72,659	3,158,102		3,194,399	40,394	41,230	153,187	31,306
1925	844,495	576,107	146,496	111,276	3,337,635		3,373,870		37,894	167,843	31,788
1926	823,526	592,346	144,680	111,368	3,352,347		3,388,286	68,016	41,221	189,122	33,339
1927	867,671	669,586	148,472	98,034	3,238,939		3,293,615		43,196	203,338	36,727
1928	937,381	713,834	149,120	109,892	2,025,139	214,970	2,292,169		46,169	221,419	41,621
1929	1,021,777	718,056	163,193	119,519	2,044,279	227,897	2,330,845	76,579	53,395	234,962	43,867
1930	1,037,384	698,181	171,407	125,563	2,011,484	277,211	2,346,908	80,177	61,162	277,017	47,444
1931	1,008,953	653,605	173,890	130,864	2,024,216	297,003	2,358,066	83,071	69,263	296,507	50,722
1932		648,497	179,579	137,684	1,960,269	371,607	2,371,787	87,315	78,920	312,934	55,186
1933			190,070	131,044	1,899,007	366,013	2,305,030	95,327	81,914	326,734	57,227
1934			191,995	110,000	1,857,524	381,259	2,278,490	104,517	87,212	330,350	55,571
1935			195,142	120,083	1,912,924	419,311	2,377,515	122,007	84,269	346,786	52,881
1936			191,424	202,000	1,968,538	430,694	2,441,357	142,719	87,826	368,158	50,599
1937			199,283	286,604	2,037,071	447,150	2,527,672	160,245	87,312	398,625	45,039
1938			198,836	275,373	2,158,076	428,826	2,630,286	170,889	88,897	437,239	42,860
1939			206,995		2,214,070	408,844	2,663,067		82,145	458,831	37,129
1940			188,825		2,226,575	304,124	2,571,163			487,257	33,842
1941			193,599		2,230,728	226,622	2,485,458			498,209	31,742
1942			206,565		2,206,209	217,783	2,453,932			519,322	32,995
1943			216,816		2,237,307	235,501	2,503,240			538,747	34,606
1944			232,215		2,373,381	265,763	2,672,845			553,724	37,453
1945		357,818	243,532	335,705	2,510,369	487,047	3,038,697	191,045		563,981	40,956
1946	701,448	500,181	267,876	354,878	2,635,346	645,345	3,322,358	197,638	114,588	558,584	47,662
1947	875,479	570,768	287,736	296,314	4,386,074	608,487	5,040,299	202,043	108,813	588,004	51,342

Membership of European Socialist Parties, 1900-55 (continued)

	Germany	Austria	Denmark	France	Great Britain			Norway	Holland	Sweden	Switzerland
					Trade Union Members	Individual Members	Total				
1948	844,653	616,232	296,175	223,495	4,751,030	629,025	5,422,437	203,094	117,244	635,658	52,697
1949	736,218	614,366	294,969	157,897	4,946,207	729,624	5,716,947	204,055	109,608	668,817	52,983
1950	684,698	607,283	283,907	140,190	4,971,911	908,161	5,920,172	203,094	105,609	722,073	53,697
1951	649,529	621,074		126,858	4,937,427	876,275	5,849,002		112,000	739,474	53,852
1952	627,827	627,435		116,327	3,071,935	1,014,524	6,107,859		110,000	746,004	53,911
1953	607,456	657,042		113,455			6,096,022	178,004	111,000	753,785	54,346
1954	585,479	666,373	283,221	115,494	5,056,912	1,004,685	6,498,027	174,575	112,000	757,426	54,111
1955		689,040						174,080	125,000		

Germany: 1. Figures prior to 1919 from J. Longuet, *Le mouvement socialiste international* (Encyclopédie socialiste, syndicale et co-opérative de l'Internationale ouvrière) (Paris, 1913), pp. 231-2. Cf. also: *Yearbook of the International Labour Movement, 1956-7* (London, 1956).

2. 1946-50 figures relate to West Germany only (in the corresponding area, in 1931, the Socialist Party numbered 610,212 members).

Belgium: The Belgian Socialist Party claimed 150,000 members in 1951 (individual members) against 650,000 in 1931 (affiliated members: the two figures are not comparable because of dual or triple affiliations which magnify the real figures). In 1911 it claimed 222,669 (again affiliated members. Cf. J. Longuet, op. cit. pp. 115-16).

Great Britain: The total includes not only trade union and individual members but also members affiliated through Co-operative, Friendly, and Socialist Societies.

Holland: Figures from 1946 onwards are for 31 December each year, except in 1950 when figures are for 30 September. The December figures are generally about 2,000 below those for September.

Except where otherwise indicated all statistics are taken from the official party handbooks.

Source: From Maurice Duverger, *Political Parties* (Methuen, University Paperbacks), 1954.

The following table sets out basic statistical information on the Social Democratic parties of Western Europe in 1976. For electoral statistics for each country since the first competitive national elections the reader is referred to Thomas T. Mackie and Richard Rose, *The International Almanac of Electoral History* (London, 1974).

		Party's share of votes — per cent	Party's share of Assembly seats (%)	SD party membership		
				Total	Membership ratio (%) to voters	Percentage of electorate
AUSTRIA Sozialistische Partei Österreichs (SPÖ)	1975	50.4	50.8	687,650	29.6	13.7
BELGIUM Belgische Socialistische Partij (BSP) Parti Socialiste Belge (PSB)	1974	26.7	27.8	(1973) 246,000	17.1	3.9
DENMARK Socialdemokratiet (SD)	1975	29.9	30.3	(1974) 120,474	15.4	3.6
FINLAND Suomen Sosialdemokraattinen Puolue	1975	24.9	27.0	101,657	14.6	2.7
FRANCE Parti Socialiste (PS)	1973	19.0	20.8	150,000	3.3	0.5
GERMAN FEDERAL REPUBLIC Sozialdemokratische Partei Deutschlands (SPD)	1976	42.6	46.4	over 1,000,000	8.8	2.4
ICELAND Althýduflokkur	1974	9.1	8.3			
IRELAND Labour Party	1973	13.8	13.4			
ITALY Partito Socialista Italiano (PSI)	1976	9.7	9.1	(1973) 463,000	13.0	1.3
Partito Socialista Democratico Italiano (PSDI)		3.4	2.4	about 300,000	24.2	0.8
LUXEMBOURG Parti Ouvrier Socialiste Luxembourgeois	1974	29.1	28.8			
MALTA Labour Party	1976	51.2	52.3			
NETHERLANDS Partij van der Arbeid (PvdA)	1972	27.3	28.7	(1976) 98,300	4.86	1.1

	Party's share of votes — per cent	Party's share of Assembly seats (%)	SD party membership		
			Total Membership ratio (%) to voters	Percentage of electorate	
NORWAY Norske Arbeiderparti (DNA)	1973 35.3	40.0	(1974) 130,489	13.4	4.7
PORTUGAL Socialists	1976 35.1	41.0			
SWEDEN Sveriges Socialdemokratiska Arbetarparti	1976 42.7	43.6	(1974) 1,001,406	44.6	17.7
SWITZERLAND Sozialdemokratische Partei der Schweiz	1975 24.9	27.5			
UNITED KINGDOM Labour Party Oct. 1974	39.3	50.2	(1975) 6,468,874 (Total members)	56.5	21.5
			674,905 (Individual members)	5.9	2.2

INDEX